AN EXPLORER'S GUIDE

Southern California

AN EXPLORER'S GUIDE

Southern California

Debbie K. Hardin

with photographs by the author

FIRST EDITION

The Countryman Press ✷ Woodstock, Vermont

All photographs by the author unless otherwise specified
Maps by Erin Greb Cartography, © The Countryman Press
Book design by Bodenweber Design
Composition by PerfecType, Nashville, TN

Published by The Countryman Press, P.O. Box 748, Woodstock, VT 05091

Distributed by W. W. Norton & Company, Inc., 500 Fifth Avenue, New York, NY 10110

Printed in the United States of America

10 9 8 7 6 5 4 3 2 1

For Jon and Juliane, without whom writing this book
wouldn't have been nearly as much fun

EXPLORE WITH US!

Welcome to the first edition of the most comprehensive guide to Southern California. The geography in Southern California is vast, and thus to fit it all in, I've been discriminating in coverage, but at the same time touched on a broad spectrum of lodging, dining, and attraction options. My opinions are informed from my experiences of living and vacationing in Southern California for more than 35 years. All entries are chosen on the basis of personal experience and are not paid advertising.

I hope that the organization of the book makes it easy to read and use. The layout has been kept simple; the following pointers will help you get started.

WHAT'S WHERE

In the beginning of the book, I've included an alphabetical listing of special highlights and important information, arranged for quick reference. You'll find advice on everything from the best sites for birding to finding upscale yurt camping along the Central Coast.

LODGING

Please don't hold us or the respective innkeepers responsible for the rates listed as of press time. Changes are inevitable and vary widely from season to season.

RESTAURANTS

Throughout the book, note the distinction between *Dining Out* and *Eating Out.* Restaurants listed under *Eating Out* are generally inexpensive and more casual; reservations are often recommended for restaurants in *Dining Out.*

A NOTE ON PRICES

The accommodations and restaurants in this book represent a wide variety of price points. I use dollar-sign categories based on a range of prices. This range is based on the nightly weekend room rate for standard rooms within hotels and per unit for cottages or other rental units. For meals, the range reflects the typical price of a dinner entrée, not including appetizer, dessert, drinks, tax, or tip.

Lodgings

$	$100 or less
$$	$101–150
$$$	$151–250
$$$$	$251 and up

Restaurants

$	$10 and under
$$	$11–20
$$$	$21–30
$$$$	$31 and up

KEY TO SYMBOLS

- ✪ The star icon appears next to accommodations, restaurants, bars, and sights that are must-sees.
- The special value icon appears next to accommodations, restaurants, and activities that combine exceptional quality with moderate prices.
- The dog-paw icon appears next to accommodations where pets are welcome.
- The crayon icon appears next to accommodations, restaurants, and activities of special appeal to children and families.
- Y The martini glass icon appears next to restaurants and entertainment venues with good bars.
- The wedding-ring icon appears next to accommodations, restaurants, and gardens that are especially attractive for weddings and civil unions.
- ▼ The triangle icon appears next to accommodations, restaurants, and bars that cater to gay clientele.
- The leaf icon appears next to accommodations, restaurants, and bars that are especially ecofriendly.

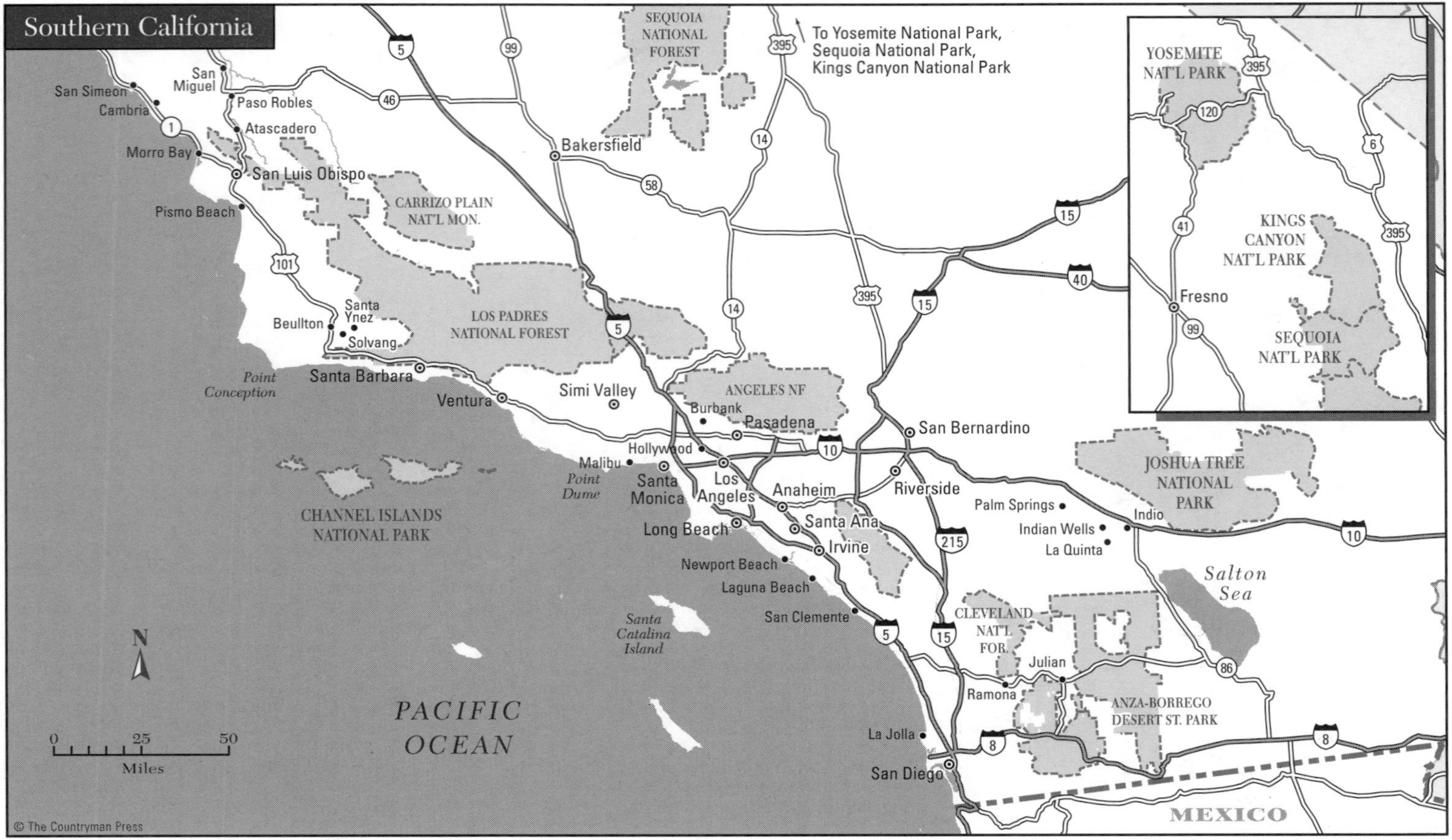
Southern California
To Yosemite National Park, Sequoia National Park, Kings Canyon National Park
SEQUOIA NATIONAL FOREST
CARRIZO PLAIN NAT'L MON.
LOS PADRES NATIONAL FOREST
ANGELES NF
JOSHUA TREE NATIONAL PARK
CLEVELAND NAT'L FOR.
ANZA-BORREGO DESERT ST. PARK
CHANNEL ISLANDS NATIONAL PARK
YOSEMITE NAT'L PARK
KINGS CANYON NAT'L PARK
SEQUOIA NAT'L PARK
Fresno
San Simeon
Cambria
San Miguel
Paso Robles
Atascadero
Morro Bay
San Luis Obispo
Pismo Beach
Bakersfield
Santa Ynez
Beullton
Solvang
Santa Barbara
Point Conception
Ventura
Simi Valley
Burbank
Pasadena
San Bernardino
Hollywood
Malibu
Point Dume
Santa Monica
Los Angeles
Anaheim
Riverside
Long Beach
Santa Ana
Irvine
Newport Beach
Laguna Beach
San Clemente
Santa Catalina Island
Palm Springs
Indian Wells
La Quinta
Indio
Salton Sea
Julian
Ramona
La Jolla
San Diego
PACIFIC OCEAN
MEXICO
0 25 50
Miles
N
© The Countryman Press

CONTENTS

LIST OF MAPS

ACKNOWLEDGMENTS

In writing this book, I relied on friends and family to share insider secrets and their own favorites throughout Southern California. For their generosity in providing suggestions I thank Bruce Block, Karen Carriere, Matt Cynaumon, Megan Cynaumon, Cate DaPron, Alyson Earnest, Linda Frandsen, Ron Frandsen, Eleanor Garner, Pat Gonzalez, Sharon Griggs, Donna Johnson, Emilee Legg, Kevin Legg, Larry Legg, Debi Leonard, Julie Leposky, Andrew Preimesberger, Becky Preimesberger, Joe Preimesberger, Jon Preimesberger, Juliane Preimesberger, Mel Preimesberger, David Pugh, Stacey Richards, Margie Rogers, Frank Safranek, Carol Simpson, Christina Simpson, Cindy Simpson, and Caty Van Housen. In addition, a number of public relations and marketing folks throughout the area made life a little bit easier for me by providing information, photographs, and answering questions in a pinch. These include Margaret Adamic, Erica Avila, Lauren Burdon, Kate Buska, Marguarite Clark, Carol Martinez, Kim Okeson, Wendy Schnee, Christina Simmons, and Janet Zaldua. Finally, I am grateful to the ace staff at Countryman Press for helping me bring this book to fruition: Kermit Hummel, editorial director; Kim Grant, acquisitions editor; Lisa Sacks, managing editor; Doug Yeager, production editor; Justine Rathbun, copy editor; and Tom Haushalter, promotions and marketing manager.

SUGGESTED ITINERARIES

Thanks for buying this book; I hope it will serve you well. It contains more information than you'll ever be able to use, because the scope of Southern California is vast, and visitors can easily spend a month and barely have time to see the expanse of attractions in one city. With that in mind, a couple of sample itineraries follow. Know in advance that because of the geographical sprawl between some of these destinations, you'll have to be efficient with your time: get an early start and keep a steady pace. Keep in mind the travel time between locations, which can vary greatly, depending on traffic.

IF YOU HAVE THREE DAYS

Start by spending a day in San Diego checking out the beaches in La Jolla, the renowned San Diego Zoo, and the popular Gaslamp Quarter downtown. Move on to Los Angeles for two days, concentrating first on Hollywood and Beverly Hills (check out a studio tour, visit the expansive Hollywood and Highland Center, or attend a live television taping; dine at a restaurant headed by a celebrity chef like Wolfgang Puck or Gordon Ramsey; shop on Rodeo Drive), and then Malibu, to spend the morning at the Getty Center and the afternoon at Zuma Beach.

IF YOU HAVE FIVE DAYS

Expand your visit to San Diego to include an additional day in North County: check out Legoland in Carlsbad, Swami's Beach in Encinitas, and the Del Mar Race Track (in season). Then squeeze in a day at Laguna Beach, exploring the quaint shops and restaurants downtown, visiting pristine beaches like Crescent Bay, and checking out one of the many fabulous art festivals in the city.

IF YOU HAVE SEVEN DAYS

Two more days allows for a visit to The Disneyland® Resort in Anaheim; purchase a Park Hopper Pass for both Disneyland and Disney's California Adventure, and be sure to stay until dark to see the fireworks shows. Spend the seventh day in downtown LA to gawk at the high-rises, enjoy Chinatown or Olvera Street, and see a live performance at one of the many world-class theaters.

IF YOU HAVE 10 DAYS

Ten days will allow time to get a little farther afield. Head north to Santa Barbara for a day exploring Stearns Wharf, the beautiful Santa Barbara Mission, the Botanical Garden, and the nighttime delights on State Street in downtown. From Santa Barbara city, head northeast to the Santa Ynez Valley to explore the wine country for a day: Pick up a wine trail map at the visitors center, check out a half dozen or so wineries, and then head to a wine country restaurant in Los Olivos or Santa Ynez to enjoy farm-to-table produce paired with the finest products of local vintners. Then spend a final day in sunny Palm Springs, to experience the desert culture of Southern California. Check out one of the many world-class golf courses in La Quinta or Indian Wells, shop for antiques on Palm Canyon Drive in downtown Palm Springs, and take the Palm Springs Aerial Tramway to the top of Mount San Jacinto for panoramic views.

IF YOU HAVE TWO WEEKS

Two weeks will allow time to add on one of two options: (1) Head farther northward and explore laid-back San Luis Obispo County, first stopping for a day at the beaches—Pismo Beach to check out the Oceana Dunes Vehicular State Park (the only place it's possible to drive on the beach in Southern California) and then up to Cambria or San Simeon to see scenic coves and observe sea lions on the shore; next spend a day in San Luis Obispo to tour the mission, check out the wacky Madonna Inn, explore the pedestrian-friendly downtown, and dine on organic local cuisine; and finally head to the Paso Robles wine country, to tour the wineries and experience the bucolic hillsides. *Or* (2) Head northeast to Yosemite, Kings Canyon, and Sequoia national parks, with a day spent in Yosemite Valley, a day in Tuolumne Meadows (also in Yosemite), and then a final day to see the big trees in both Kings Canyon and Sequoia.

IF YOU LIVE IN SOUTHERN CALIFORNIA

Thank your lucky stars. Those of us who live in Southern California are blessed with near perfect weather year-round; more than our fair share of natural beauty in the form of stunning beaches, rocky mountains, untouched deserts, and even a handful of exclusive islands off the coast; and limitless recreational activities that include boating, fishing, golfing, surfing, bicycling, and hiking. Make the most of the area and *explore*. There's a seemingly endless supply of new wonders to discover in Southern California, and for those of us who endure the high cost of living in this paradise, it makes good sense to get out there and take advantage of everything this beautiful region has to offer.

TOP 10 DAY LISTS

The town-by-town day tours I provide in each chapter will get you started on how best to explore a given location. Beware: Although it *is* possible to do everything in one day on my Top 10 Day lists, doing so could leave you feeling like you need a vacation to recover from your vacation. Take it easy, and use these lists only as a guide.

WHAT'S WHERE IN SOUTHERN CALIFORNIA

ACCESSIBILITY California is progressive by most standards, and visitors with physical challenges will find that the vast majority of hotels, restaurants, theme parks, and nighttime venues will offer accessibility. The major exceptions are beaches and parks, which are not often equipped for full access.

ALCOHOL In California, alcohol (beer and wine, along with hard liquor) can be purchased in grocery stores and specialty stores every day of the week, with no curfew. Note that alcohol is prohibited on the beaches of Southern California, and violators are very likely to be fined.

AREA CODES There are dozens of area codes in the Southern California area—with many different codes even within the same city for large areas like Los Angeles and San Diego.

ATTIRE Southern California is casual, and it's not uncommon for locals to live in shorts and flip-flops. With that said, a jacket for men and smart casual dress for women is more appropriate for upscale restaurants, and dressier attire is required to gain entry into the trendy nightclubs of Los Angeles, Orange County, Palm Springs, and San Diego. Formal wear is best for major cultural events, such as operas, symphonies, movie premieres, and international award ceremonies (e.g., the Oscars,' the Emmys, etc.).

AUTOMOBILES We Californians love our automobiles—in large part because cities like San Diego and Los Angeles are so spread out that they are often perceived as a necessity. This addiction to car travel results in serious traffic problems throughout the area, as well as air pollution concerns, especially in Los Angeles. Public transportation is always an option: LA has a relatively new subway system, and all cities covered in the book offer a public bus system and oftentimes a trolley or rail system as well. But the truth is, these can be challenging to use in many of Southern California's sprawling cities, and it is generally easier to navigate the expanses with a car.

🍸 **BARS** Look for this symbol next to restaurants and nightspots as an indicator of great places to sip cocktails or enjoy a glass of wine.

BICYCLING Bicycling is a popular sport throughout California, so much so that bike lanes in some neighborhoods can be congested on weekend mornings. Throughout the book I've summarized the biking scene in the given coverage area, as well as included good places to rent bikes. Note that helmets are required for bicycling on city roads and are encouraged for off-road biking as well. For great off-road bike route maps, check out www.trails.com/trails.

BIRDING There are a number of excellent birding sites in Southern California, particularly along the coastline. Among the best are the **San Elijo Lagoon,** between Encinitas and Carlsbad in North County San Diego; the **Bolsa Chica Ecological Preserve** in Orange County; the **Andree Clark Bird Refuge** in Santa Barbara; the **Channel Islands National Park,** off the coast of Santa Barbara; **Morro Rock,** near Pismo Beach; the **Monterey Bay National Sanctuary** in Cambria; **San Simeon State Park,** near Hearst Castle; **Carrizo Plain National Monument,** near San Luis Obispo; and the forests of **Yosemite** and **Sequoia national parks.**

CAMPING Camping is possible along select state beaches and throughout the state park system. Online reservations can be made through ReserveAmerica (800-444-7275; www.reserveamerica.com) seven months in advance on the first day of the month, beginning at 8 AM. Note that beachside campsites are highly coveted, especially in the summer, during spring break, and over the winter holidays. It is imperative to reserve on the earliest day possible for these busy periods. I've had more luck getting the reservations I want by using the online service; phone lines can be busy for hours at a time. Note that Yosemite, Sequoia, and Kings Canyon national parks have their own camping reservation systems, and reservations for these parks should be made months in advance to ensure availability.

CASINOS Native American gaming casinos have sprung up throughout Southern California and offer Las Vegas–style gambling, glitzy live entertainment, and full-blown resorts, many with fine dining, golf, and spas. Among the largest are **Pechanga Resort and Casino** (888-PECHANGA) in Temecula (in Riverside County, northeast of San Diego); in east county San Diego, **Viejas Casino** (800-847-6537) in Alpine, **Barona Casino** (888-722-7662) in Lakeside, and **Sycuan Casino** (619-445-6002) in El Cajon; **Chumash Casino and Resort** (800-CHUMASH) in Santa Ynez; and **Morongo Casino** (800-252-4499) near Palm Springs.

CELL PHONES California law requires a hands-free device when using a cell phone while driving. Texting is not allowed while driving.

🍼 **CHILDREN** Look for this symbol to indicate activities, lodging, and restaurants that are particularly well suited for those traveling with children. Note that Southern California is family friendly in general, and there are very few restaurants, hotels, and attractions that do *not* welcome children (especially well-behaved ones). The obvious exceptions, of course, are bars and nightspots.

COVERAGE Defining what constitutes "Southern California" is trickier than it might sound. Some locals claim that nothing north of Los Angeles truly "counts" as Southern California—and in fact, Santa Barbara and San Luis Obispo are distinct in terms of geography, climate, and indigenous flora, falling within what is generally referred to as the Central Coast. For the purposes of this book, I simply divided the state in half. I start in the south with San Diego (part 1) and work my way upward through Orange County (parts 2 and 3), Los Angeles (part 4), Palm Springs (part 5), Santa Barbara (part 6), and San Luis Obispo (part 7)—with a slightly northward detour for Yosemite, Kings Canyon, and Sequoia national parks (part 8).

CRUISES Major cruise lines depart from San Diego and Los Angeles for three- and seven-day Mexican Riviera tours (generally stopping in Cabo San Lucas, Mazatlan, and Puerto Vallarta, with some longer cruises continuing to Acapulco). Some lines also sail to Hawaii and Alaska. At certain times of the year, several ships based in Southern California will make a 14-day trip through the Panama Canal, through the Caribbean, and moor in Florida. The cruise ship terminal in San Diego is centrally located in the downtown harbor front, within easy walking distance to **Seaport Village,** a quaint shopping and tourist zone, and a quick taxi ride to the popular **Gaslamp Quarter** downtown. The terminal in Los Angeles is actually to the south of the city, in the port of San Pedro, an industrial area that isn't close to any major LA attractions. When cruising from Los Angeles, it is wise to spend a few days in the city before beginning a cruise in more isolated San Pedro.

CULTURE Local culture has been defined and refined over the years by myriad racial and ethnic influences, beginning with the Native Americans who lived and worked on the land when the Spanish missionaries arrived hundreds of years ago, to the European colonists who came with the missionaries, to the Hispanic influence from immigrating Mexican and Central American nationals, to the growing importance of Asian culture. To be a "local" thus means many different things. There's a small percentage of those of us who were actually born and raised in Southern California, and even fewer in number are those who can say their parents or grandparents were born in the area. We are largely a collection of immigrants and migrants who are generally quite friendly to newcomers and eager to share our hometowns with visitors.

DESERTS Southern California is an arid region, and just east of many of the irrigated and artificially green cities are true deserts, many of which are protected as state and national parks. These include **Anza-Borrego Desert,** which falls east of San Diego and adjacent to the Salton Sea; **Joshua Tree National Park,** which is east of Palm Springs—itself falling in a desert valley at the feet of the San Jacinto Mountains;

Mojave National Preserve, east of Los Angeles; and the expansive **Death Valley National Park,** which falls east of the Sierra Nevadas. The best time to visit any Southern California desert is between the months of October and April. By May, the heat is already unbearable (reaching as high as 120 degrees). The late fall and spring months are also the best times to see wildflowers (February and March) and the wildly colorful, waxy blossoms of cacti (March and April).

DINING You'll notice that *Dining Out* and *Eating Out* are listed separately in this guide. Entries in the first category are sit-down, formal establishments and are usually more expensive than *Eating Out* restaurants. Entries in the second category are either take-out or casual eat-in joints, and these are the places that offer the best bargains—as well as some of the most authentic regional food. The line between the two sometimes blurs; for example, when upscale food is offered in a dive or more casual cuisine is presented in a fancier venue.

DISCOUNTS Whenever possible, I've included tips throughout the book to help visitors save money. As a general rule, purchasing attraction tickets online can save as much as 25 percent. Hotels also often run Web specials that are available only to those who book online. It's also worth calling the hotel to ask about any specials it may be offering.

DROUGHT As noted, Southern California is an arid place. We've suffered through decades of lower-than-average precipitation and have lived with a burgeoning population that uses much more water than is sustainable. Conserving water is thus a way of life in the area, and most locals are careful to take shorter showers, avoid letting the water run while we brush our teeth, and landscape with native (drought-tolerant) plants whenever possible. Many municipalities have even instituted mandatory water-conservation efforts: my own hometown of San Diego, for example, limits watering lawns and washing cars to every other day (with constant threats of cutting the privilege to once weekly). Visitors will notice that many restaurants will not automatically bring water to the table; this must often be ordered (tap water is always free, of course). In addition, hotels throughout Southern California use low-flow water fixtures and ask guests to hang up towels they are willing to reuse, to save the immense water needed to launder linens daily.

EARTHQUAKES Although major earthquakes are relatively uncommon in Southern California, there are a number of faults that threaten "the big one"—most notably the San Andreas fault, which runs from Brawley (east of San Diego) through Palm Springs, Parkfield (northeast of San Luis Obispo), San Francisco, and all the way to Eureka in the far northern part of the state. There are dozens of smaller faults throughout all of the cities in Southern California. Small quakes from these faults are more prevalent, usually lasting only a minute or so and generally doing little more than rattling the windows. If a major seismic event does occur, the U.S. Federal Emergency Management Agency (FEMA) recommends individuals "drop, cover, and hold on"—in other words, drop to the ground, take cover under a sturdy table or desk, and hold on to it until the earthquake subsides. Note that if your accommodation remains safe, you are better off remaining indoors after an earthquake. If you're inside, check for gas leaks, watch out for loose and broken plaster that could fall, and avoid broken windows and mirrors. If you're outside, stay away from fallen power lines, which can be deadly, and avoid spilled chemicals. Use telephones (both land lines and cells) only in emergencies; as other recent natural disasters have demonstrated, the communications infrastructure can become overloaded quickly, and tying up lines unnecessarily may prevent emergency and rescue workers from doing their jobs. Use a portable radio to tune in to safety advisories and to get more information. And expect aftershocks from major quakes. These can be almost as strong as the original earthquakes and can cause already compromised structures to fail completely.

ECOFRIENDLY Look for this symbol to indicate establishments that are particularly ecofriendly.

EMERGENCIES Call 911 anywhere in Southern California for immediate response to health-related, fire, and crime emergencies.

FAMILIES See *Children.*

FIRE SEASON Drought conditions that have prevailed for decades have greatly increased the hazard of wildfires throughout Southern California, and in recent years, the area has seen devastating fires that have burned for weeks, destroying precious wilderness and causing billions in damage to private property. Exercise extreme caution: never toss away a burning cigarette, and do not barbecue or create a bonfire unless in designated areas (and during permissible low-risk periods). Historically, September and October have seen the worst fires, which are often exacerbated by the seasonal Santa Ana winds—hot, dry, high-speed winds that play havoc with firefighters' efforts to contain conflagrations.

FISHING Individuals 16 and older are required to obtain a California fishing license to fish in lakes, rivers, and the ocean—with the exception of piers. Anglers can cast a line off most Southern California piers without a license.

FOUR-WHEELING Off-roading and four-wheeling are extremely popular in some Southern California desert areas, especially in the **Anza-Borrego Desert,** east of San Diego, which includes nearly a dozen areas open to dune buggies, four-wheel-drive vehicles, motorbikes, and ATVs. Another popular spot for ATVs is the **Oceana Dunes Vehicular Recreation Area** in Pismo Beach.

▼ **GAY AND LESBIAN** Look for this symbol to indicate those establishments that cater to gay clientele.

GOLF Tiger Woods learned to play golf in Southern California (spending thousands of hours at the lovely Torrey Pines Course in North County San Diego), and Phil Mickelson grew up in San Diego playing the local courses. North Coastal and east county San Diego, Palm Springs, and Orange County offer hundreds of world-class golfing options, and I've included both the finest courses and the best values in the region. Note the green fees given are for nonresidents; if it's possible to book a tee time with a local friend, significant discounts will apply at many of the pricier courses.

GREEN SPACE In each chapter, I've included information on green spaces, which I've divided among beaches, gardens, and nature preserves.

HISTORICAL SITES Aside from the Spanish missions that date to nearly 250 years ago, Southern California historical sites generally don't go back much further than the late 19th and early 20th centuries. I've included in this category as much true history as possible; I've also included some sites that aren't really historic but *do* act as local icons—like **Bubblegum Alley** in San Luis Obispo or the relatively new **Cathedral of Our Lady of the Angels** in downtown Los Angeles.

INSIDER TIPS Throughout the book, I've included Insider Tips, which are designed to help visitors save money and time, get the most out of regional attractions, and in general live like the locals.

ITINERARY SUGGESTIONS Look for the **Top 10 Day** features scattered throughout the book, which offer a sample day's itinerary for each city or region I discuss. These offer suggestions for attractions, recreation, lodging, and meals, and represent both the best the area has to offer and my personal favorites.

KAYAKING Ocean paddling is increasingly popular in Southern California, especially in San Diego and Orange County, which offer dozens of interesting caves and outcroppings to explore via kayak. I cover guided kayak tours and offer suggestions for equipment rentals along with general boating in my discussion of water sports in most chapters (inland locales excluded).

LODGING In most cities throughout Southern California, there are dozens—if not hundreds—of lodging options. I've included here those properties that stand out either because of their location, their service, their décor, their amenities, or any combination thereof. I've also tried to cover a variety of price points when recommending lodging, but a word of caution is in order: Southern California is an expensive place to live and thus a relatively expensive place to visit. Nightly rates here tend to be higher on weekends and depend on the view—with ocean view rooms fetching top dollar. In some cities (like pricey Newport Beach or Beverly Hills), there really are no independent "bargain" accommodations to be had.

MAPS Look for regional maps at the beginning of each chapter, and a general map of Southern California at the front of the book. For those planning to drive in Southern California, it is vital to invest in comprehensive road maps—or a good GPS system.

MEXICO Just south of San Diego, Tijuana, Mexico, is the largest border crossing into the United States and the second-largest city on the West Coast (only Los Angeles is bigger). For years it was possible for vacationers and locals from Southern California to walk across the border to enjoy the restaurants, shopping, and nightlife of this Mexican border town. Sadly, the horrific crime associated with the drug cartel in Mexico has made visiting Tijuana (and nearby cities like Rosarito and Ensenada, to the south) foolhardy. Hundreds of innocent bystanders have been killed in recent years in Tijuana alone, and it simply isn't safe to visit the city during this turmoil. Indeed, even cruising visitors to what have long been primarily tourist destinations in Mexico (Cabo San Lucas, Puerta Vallarta, Acapulco) have cause to be wary—although these cities are more vigilant about posting armed police and soldiers along the tourist thoroughfares (especially on those days when cruise ships are in town).

MUSEUMS Southern California offers a number of world-class art, history, and science exhibitions, which will be welcome to those who naturally seek out museums. The area also boasts attractions that fall into this category that are likely to appeal to even those who think they don't enjoy museums—for example, the **Museum of Making Music** in Carlsbad, the **International Surfing Museum** in Huntington Beach, or the **Hollywood Museum** in Los Angeles. Note that city- and state-operated museums are facing serious budgetary crises, and thus museum hours for many institutions are expected to decrease in the coming months and years, so be sure to check Web sites or phone for the most up-to-date schedules.

✪ **MUST SEE** Look for this symbol, which indicates must-see attractions and establishments, marking them as some of the best of the best in the region.

NEWSPAPERS Major newspapers in the Southern California area include the *Los Angeles Times*, the *Orange County Register*, the *San Diego Union Tribune*, the *San Luis Obispo Tribune*, and the *Santa Barbara News-Press*.

NIGHTLIFE Near the end of each geographical region, I've included a discussion on nightlife and evening entertainment. Note that clubs and bars tend to come and go quickly, especially in trendy Los Angeles, and so I've included those establishments that have demonstrated staying power. I've also included a wide variety of nightlife, from those places that offer quiet places to chat and sip wine, to

Courtesy of Jon Preimesberger

artisanal breweries, to exclusive music and dance clubs, to billiards joints and cozy pubs.

OCEAN The Pacific Ocean is arguably the biggest tourist draw of Southern California, and the shoreline really is breathtaking. In the south, from San Diego to Malibu, long stretches of white sandy beaches nestle against sun-bleached cliffs. Along the Central Coast, from Santa Barbara through Pismo Beach, Cambria, and San Simeon, the shoreline is more rugged, with rocky or pebbly beaches; there are more submerged rocks just off the waterline; and the beaches are generally smaller in length and in width. Ocean temperatures range from the mid-50s in winter to the low 70s in late August and into September.

PACIFIC COAST HIGHWAY (PCH) Be aware: some locals call coastal Highway 1 and Highway 101 the Pacific Coast Highway—or just PCH. Street signs use the names interchangeably, but note that many maps *only* cite the highway designations. (To complicate matters even more, Highway 1 sometimes runs concurrently with Highway 101!)

PARKING Free street parking is increasingly hard to come by in major cities (especially downtown in San Diego, Laguna Beach, and Santa Barbara and anywhere in Los Angeles). Most of these municipalities have adequate parking lots or parking structures, and every city offers parking meters. Expect to pay between $3 to $10 per hour or as much as $30 for a full day. Most downtown hotels also offer valet parking at a rate of $30–40 per day.

PETS Look for this symbol, which indicates a pet-friendly establishment.

QUESTIONS There are dozens of convention and visitors bureaus throughout the region, staffed with knowledgeable, helpful folks. When in doubt, call or e-mail them; they are listed at the beginning of each chapter.

RECOMMENDED READING Fiction and nonfiction works well worth reading (before or during a trip to Southern California) include Vincent Bugliosi, *Helter Skelter;* Aline Coquelle, *Palm Springs Style;* Raymond Chandler, *The Big Sleep;* Richard Henry Dana, *Two Years Before the Mast;* Joan Didion, *Play It as It Lays;* Bret Easton Ellis, *Less than Zero;* F. Scott Fitzgerald, *The Love of the Last Tycoon;* Thomas S. Hines, *Irving Gill and the Architecture of Reform: A Study in the Modernist Architectural Culture;* Richard Matheson, *Somewhere in Time;* Walter Mosley, *White Butterfly;* John Muir, *The Yosemite;* Kem Nunn, *Tapping the Source;* Scott O'Dell, *Island of the Blue Dolphins;* Abigail Padgett, *Moonbird Boy;* John Steinbeck, *The Grapes of Wrath;* Bob Thomas, *Walt Disney: An American Original;* Jeanne Wakatsuki and James D. Houston, *Farewell to Manzanar: A True Story of Japanese American Experience During and After the World War II Internment;* and Tom Wolfe, *The Pump House Gang.*

SAN DIEGO FREEWAY Be aware: The so-called San Diego Freeway is actually I-405, and it doesn't even run through San Diego, it runs north from Irvine. Many locals use the name "San Diego Freeway" (and it is so designated on some freeway signs), but most road maps use I-405.

SKYSCRAPERS Although San Diego and Los Angeles are major cities, don't expect to find the concentration of skyscrapers in the downtown zones as one would see in cities in other regions, like New York or Chicago. Because of the immense expanse of real estate in Southern California, cities tend to grow *out* rather than *up*.

SMOG Sadly, smog is omnipresent in some parts of Southern California—most notably Los Angeles, which is ranked as having among the worst air qualities in the country; this is also a problem for San Diego and Orange County, to much lesser degrees. Smog is more prevalent inland, because coastal winds tend to blow the bad air near the shoreline out to sea—whereas valleys tend to hold it in place. Air quality is usually worse in the summertime, because of natural climatic conditions and because of increased traffic on the roadways caused by greater numbers of seasonal residents and visitors.

SMOKING Smoking is not allowed indoors throughout California, and this includes nightclubs, bars, and restaurants. Indeed, prohibitions state that smoking is forbidden within 50 feet of the entries of such establishments. Most beaches are also nonsmoking.

SNAKES Rattlesnakes are native to Southern California and are abundant, especially in wilderness areas. Exercise caution when hiking through undeveloped areas, especially in late spring through early fall, when the warm weather encourages them to be out and about.

SNORKELING Southern California waters are chilly, and low visibility and often choppy waters aren't ideal for snorkeling. The best snorkeling can be found in **La Jolla Cove** in San Diego, **Crescent Beach** in Laguna, and throughout **Santa Catalina Island.** Expect to see kelp beds and a handful of uncolorful fish, with the noted exception of the Garibaldi, a bright orange species, sometimes with neon blue markings, that is indigenous to the area.

SPECIAL EVENTS I've included a list of special events at the end of the final chapter of each section, broken down by month. Beware that lodging is apt to be more expensive (with vacancies harder to find) in the days immediately surrounding large-scale events, such as in Pasadena close to the Rose Bowl and Rose Parade, and in LA during the massive city marathon.

STARGAZING The population explosion—and subsequent light pollution—in Southern California has all but nixed the possibility of stargazing in major cities. Notable exceptions are Palm Springs, Santa Catalina Island, and the Central Coast beaches (e.g., Pismo, Shell Beach, Cambria). Anza-Borrego Desert, Joshua Tree National Park, Yosemite, Sequoia, and Kings Canyon parks are also good places to drag along a telescope.

SUNSCREEN Use sunscreen when outdoors. Really. Southern California sun is stronger than in most regions of the country, and overexposure happens faster than most people expect.

Courtesy of Jon Preimesberger

SURFING Surfing is hugely popular, especially from San Diego to Santa Barbara, where just about every beach with waves is dominated by surfers in the early morning hours (when the best waves roll in). It is unsafe to swim near surfers, and thus there are usually designated areas on most beaches where surfers aren't allowed. I've noted throughout the book the best places for surfing, as well as included a number of surfing schools that will help novices get up and at it in no time.

TAXES The combined city and state sales tax in Southern California ranges from 8.25 percent (San Luis Obispo), to 8.75 percent (San Diego, Santa Barbara, Orange County, Palm Springs, and Mariposa County/Yosemite), to 9.75 percent throughout much of Los Angeles. Visitors should also beware of the Transient Occupancy Tax levied on top of all temporary accommodations (hotels, bed & breakfasts, motels). The top tax hits visitors to Anaheim (home of Disneyland), at 15 percent; Los Angeles averages to 14 percent; San Diego to 13 percent; Santa Barbara to 12 percent; Palm Springs to 11 percent; San Luis Obispo and Orange County to 10 percent.

THEME PARKS There are a number of theme parks and zoos throughout the region, and most are huge. Plan to spend a full day at the larger parks (like The Disney® Resort, Knott's Berry Farm, SeaWorld, and Six Flags Magic Mountain). Wear comfortable shoes and set an easy pace: remember, you're on vacation!

TIDES There are two high tides and two low tides every day, and the timing varies. During low tide, the shoreline is at its most expansive, and it is in this period when tidepooling along low-lying reefs and shoreline rocks is possible. Watch out for high tide along beaches that front steep cliffs (which is the majority of SoCal beaches). Rising water levels can strand folks on isolated beaches that don't have immediate access or, worse, obliterate most of the sandy shore altogether.

TIME ZONE Southern California is in the Pacific time zone and observes daylight saving time.

TO DO Throughout the book, I have included active pursuits under the rubric of "To Do." These include bicycling, golf, spas, theme parks and zoos, and water sports (including boating, diving and snorkeling, fishing, and surfing).

TO SEE In each chapter, I have included worthy sites under the category of "To See." These include historic sites, museums, and parks.

TOP 10 DAY For nearly every locale, I've included a Top 10 Day box that outlines my picks for the best the area has to offer, including lodging, dining, recreational activities, museums, gardens, beaches, shopping, and entertainment. I've tried to group activities by neighborhood, to minimize the amount of travel necessary to get from one point to the next. Although it would be tight to do some of these suggested itineraries in one day, it *is* possible—although some might make for very long days!

TRAFFIC Expect traffic throughout Southern California, with the possible exception of San Luis Obispo and the rest of the Central Coast, which is much less dense than Los Angeles southward.

UNDERWATER PRESERVES Look for signs along beaches and on piers to indicate the existence of an underwater preserve. There are several in Southern California, and they extend from the shoreline to several miles off the coast. In these protected zones, fishing is not allowed. Likewise, collecting seashells and stones is also prohibited on these beaches.

VALUE This symbol indicates an establishment that offers a particularly good value. This doesn't necessarily mean a place is "cheap"—just that it is a good bet for the money, especially compared with similar establishments in the same neighborhood. For example, a "value" lodging option in Beverly Hills might very well be quite a bit more expensive than a luxury hotel in, say, less-pricey San Luis Obispo.

WATER QUALITY The vast majority of the time, water quality at Southern California beaches is good. However, there are times when sewage spills (or rarely, oil spills) cause beach closures. Local health officials are responsible for issuing advisories, which are usually posted as signs at the beach and often along access points to the shore.

WEATHER Most of Southern California is semiarid, with low rainfall levels and an excess of 300 sunny days a year. Temperatures vary by locale, based on latitude and proximity to the ocean. Coastal communities range from an average low of 50 degrees to highs in the low 80s. Note that even in summer, nighttime temperatures can get chilly in Southern California, especially along the coast. Inland valleys are often much hotter, generally 10 to 15 degrees warmer than communities adjacent to the ocean. Far inland deserts are the most extreme environments in the state, with the possibility of below-freezing temperatures at night and scorching daytime temperatures of more than 120 degrees. High-elevation locales like Yosemite and the San Bernardino Mountains get snow in the winter, but low-lying areas almost never do. Southern California rarely experiences high humidity levels, and thunder and lightning storms are rare. Hot, dry wind storms, called Santa Anas, typically rage through the southernmost portion of the state for a few days at a time in late summer and throughout fall—dangerously coinciding with the fire season.

WEDDINGS This symbol indicates a hotel, park, or restaurant that is especially suited to host weddings and civil unions.

WHALE WATCHING Gray whales pass by the Southern California coastline every year during their 10,000-mile round-trip migration from the frigid Arctic Sea to the warm and shallow lagoons of Baja Mexico to mate and have their babies, starting in late December through the end of March. About 200 whales pass by any given point in a day during the peak migration period (late January and through February). To get a closer look, check out chartered whale-watching tours or observe the action from seaside cliffs.

WHEN TO VISIT Thanks to mild weather, anytime is a good time to visit Southern California. In winter, cooler temperatures preclude most water sports, but it's still possible to enjoy beaches from the shoreline; fuchsia bougainvillea and deep purple statis are in full bloom; and lodging rates are at their lowest. In spring, the otherwise dry hillsides of Southern California come alive with wildflowers and bright green foliage, making this the most colorful season, and a favorite of mine because of the nearly constant sunshine and blue sky. In summertime, temperatures are all but perfect—usually not too hot and almost never humid; theme parks like The Disneyland® Resort and SeaWorld stay open longer and offer even more entertainment and attractions; and restaurants and cafés throw open their doors to breezy outside patios. In fall, the crowds go back to school and the beaches are left mostly to locals, who know that September and early October are the best oceangoing months because of the warmest water temperatures and vastly less shoreline congestion.

WILDFLOWERS Depending on rainfall, wildflower shows in the Southern California deserts of **Anza-Borrego** and **Joshua Tree** offer amazing diversity: on the best blooming years, there are literally thousands of species, which generally bloom at low altitudes from late February through March. Other good places to find wildflower displays include the **Channel Islands National Park,** off the Santa Barbara coast; **Carrizo Plain National Monument,** near San Luis Obispo; and **Yosemite, Kings Canyon, and Sequoia** national parks.

WINERIES Southern California, including the Central Coast, has several famous winemaking regions, including Temecula in Riverside County, Santa Ynez in Santa Barbara County, and Paso Robles in San Luis Obispo County. The warmer temperatures and granitic soils lend themselves to big, bold red wines; the area is famous for

Syrahs and cabs, and a pocket in the Santa Rita Hills near Santa Ynez offers lovely pinot noirs.

YURTS Try upscale camping in a yurt at Cachuma Lake, near Santa Barbara. Yurts are wooden-framed canvas structures, and they are available lakeside and come complete with redwood decks. Expect to pay about $70 per night. Call 805-686-5050 for more information.

ZOOS The **San Diego Zoo,** and its sister park in nearby Escondido, the **San Diego Zoo Safari Park,** are world-famous attractions, not only because of their vast collections of animals but because of their extensive efforts to rescue endangered species. Although the **Los Angeles Zoo and Botanical Gardens** is smaller, it is designed at a scale that makes for a pleasant afternoon of strolling. The **Santa Barbara Zoo** is also well worth a visit.

San Diego 1

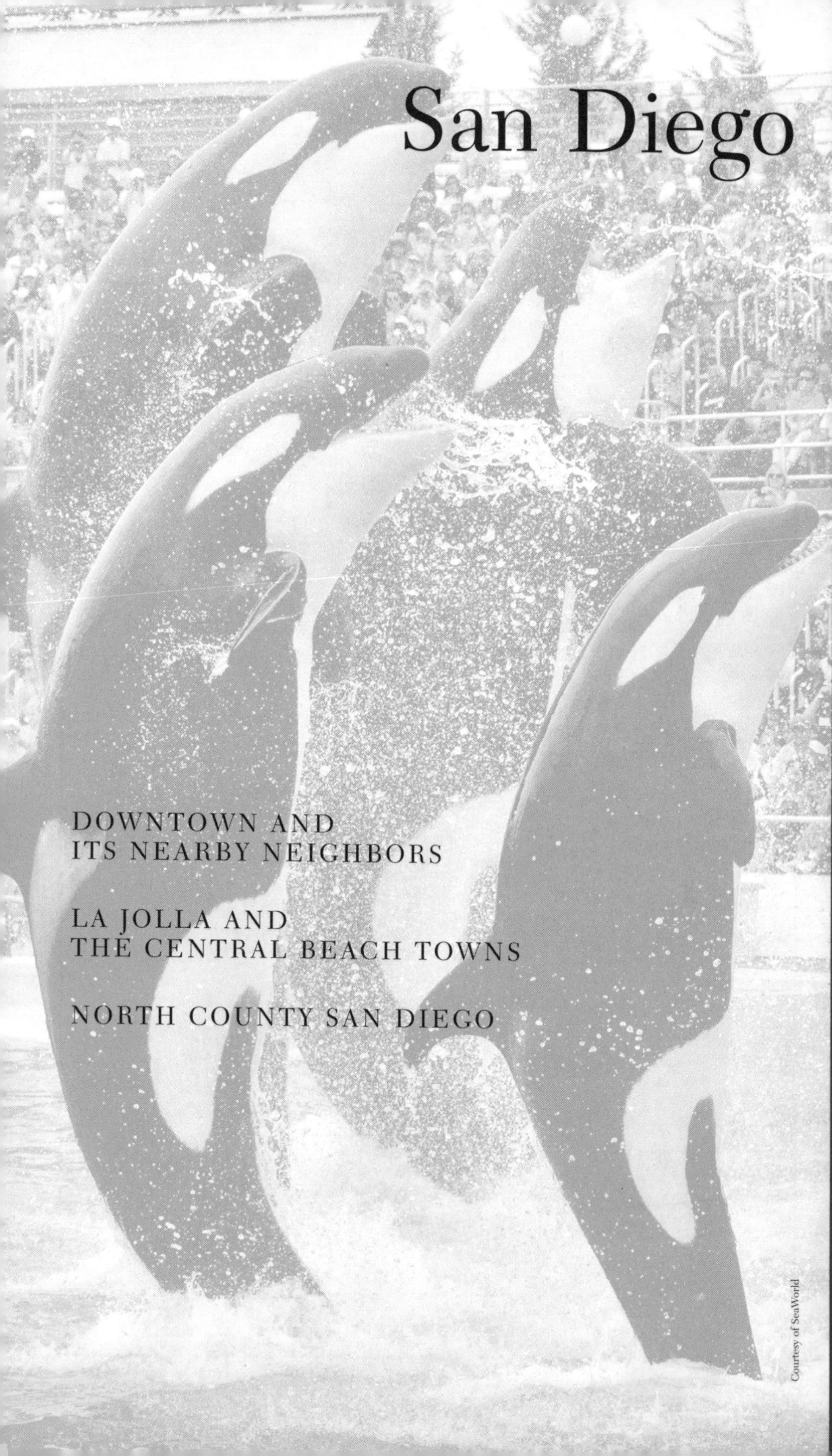

Courtesy of SeaWorld

DOWNTOWN AND
ITS NEARBY NEIGHBORS

LA JOLLA AND
THE CENTRAL BEACH TOWNS

NORTH COUNTY SAN DIEGO

San Diego County
CAMP PENDLETON
MARINE CORPS
BASE
CLEVELAND
NATIONAL
FOREST
15
5
Oceanside
Carlsbad
78
Escondido
78
ANZA-BORREGO
DESERT
STATE PARK
78
Julian
Ramona
15
67
Encinitas
Solana Beach
Del Mar
56
79
805
La Jolla
52
5
15
8
CLEVELAND
NATIONAL
FOREST
PACIFIC
OCEAN
San Diego
125
8
94
54
75
Chula Vista
N
5
805
0 5 10
Miles
Tijuana
MEXICO

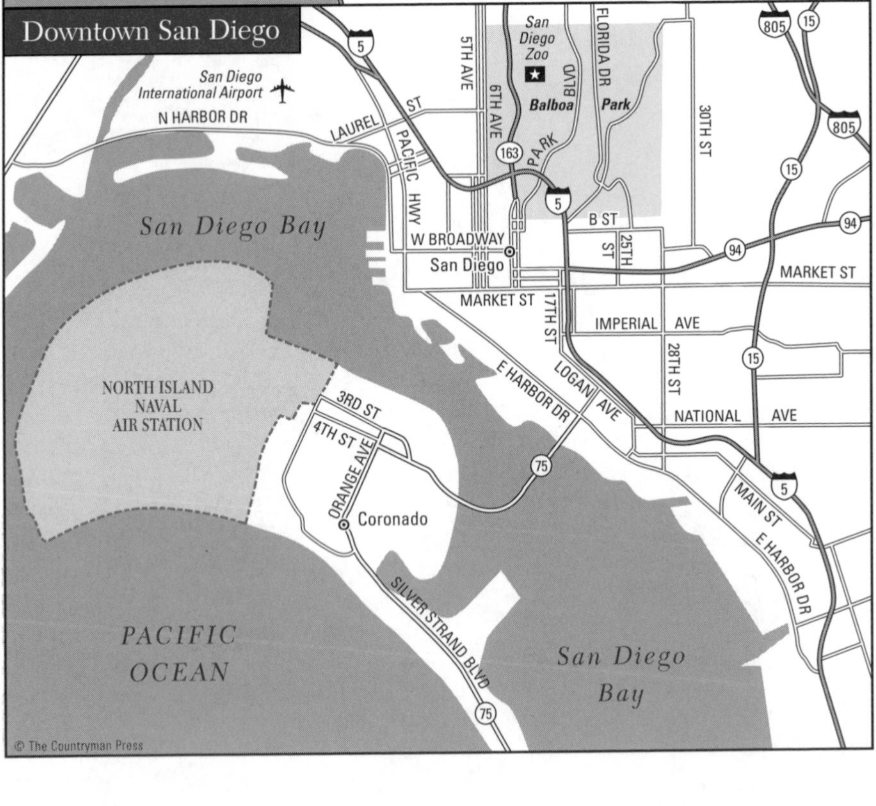
Downtown San Diego
5
5TH AVE
San Diego Zoo
FLORIDA DR
805
15
San Diego International Airport
6TH AVE
BLVD
Balboa
Park
N HARBOR DR
LAUREL
ST
PACIFIC
HWY
163
PARK
30TH ST
805
15
5
San Diego Bay
B ST
94
W BROADWAY
25TH
ST
94
San Diego
MARKET ST
MARKET ST
17TH ST
IMPERIAL AVE
28TH ST
15
E HARBOR DR
LOGAN AVE
NORTH ISLAND
NAVAL
AIR STATION
3RD ST
NATIONAL AVE
4TH ST
ORANGE AVE
75
5
MAIN ST
Coronado
E HARBOR DR
SILVER STRAND BLVD
PACIFIC
OCEAN
San Diego
Bay
75
© The Countryman Press

INTRODUCTION

People who've never been to San Diego have an idea of the place, thanks to years of billing as "America's Finest City." Most imagine perfect weather, miles of beaches, and a resort lifestyle. This is all true: the 70-some miles of coastline, bathed in more than 325 days of sunshine a year, make San Diego an ideal warm-weather getaway. Luxurious spas, seemingly limitless sports and recreational opportunities, and a liberal share of some of the best amusement parks and zoological preserves in the country make San Diego the kind of vacation destination that appeals to everyone in the family. But there's more to San Diego than the stereotype of an idyllic town on the water: San Diego is a cosmopolitan city—the eighth largest in the country. Guests will find world-class theater, hundreds of opportunities for extraordinary dining, and a rich multicultural heritage.

The 4,269 square miles of San Diego County hug the coastline from Tijuana, the largest border crossing with Mexico, in the south, to the huge Camp Pendleton Marine base in Oceanside, to the north. The county stretches east to the bucolic Cuyamaca Mountains and the Anza-Borrego Desert beyond. Connecting the huge expanse of real estate is a web of freeways and highways, and clustered between are more than a hundred neighborhoods and incorporated townships, each with their own distinct personalities and attractions.

Downtown San Diego is the new heart of the city, and for those of us who've called the area home for most of our lives, this couldn't be more surprising. The formerly rough and tumble city center has undergone remarkable revitalization that would have been nearly unimaginable 20 years ago. Today, this vibrant, stunningly beautiful downtown is home to several extremely popular micro neighborhoods, such as the lively historic Gaslamp Quarter, which comprises 16 blocks of carefully preserved Victorian storefronts housing some of the finest dining options in the city, as well as some of the most popular nightclubs, fun boutique shopping, and dozens of galleries. Nearby is the trendy, artsy East Village, home to the San Diego Padre's Petco Park baseball stadium and site of burgeoning mid-rise condo developments and an explosion of new bistros and wine bars. The Harbor District runs adjacent to the beautiful San Diego Bay and is home to resort hotels, the quaint Seaport Village Shopping Center, and the San Diego Convention Center, one of the largest facilities of its kind in the country. On the north end of downtown is another revitalized area: Little Italy, a historic district where locals flock for some of the best Italian food in the city.

To the south of the city center, tucked onto a peninsula that is the westernmost point of the city, is historic Point Loma, the site that was first discovered by Spanish conquistadors in the 16th century and is now home to a large fishing and boating community, the remnants of an old naval training center (which has been spruced up as the new Liberty Station shopping center), and several elegant and exclusive residential areas.

Just across the San Diego Bay, and accessed via the iconic blue bridge, is Coronado—often called an "island," but in fact it's a peninsula (connected to the mainland by a sliver of land to the south). This upscale beach community is a throwback to simpler times, with mom-and-pop diners, coffee shops, quaint boutiques, miles of gorgeous sand, and one of the most famous, historic beach resorts on the West Coast: the venerable Hotel del Coronado.

Hugging the coastline, just northwest of downtown, you'll find a string of beach communities, starting with Ocean Beach, an iconoclastic neighborhood that is immensely popular with surfers; Mission Beach—and the huge aquatic park just to the east, Mission Bay (home of SeaWorld); party-central Pacific Beach; and elegant La Jolla, San Diego's answer to Beverly Hills. San Diego's North County extends beyond to Del Mar, also upscale and fabulous, with thoroughbred racing and polo fields; Encinitas, a haven for surfers and artists that is increasingly attracting fine restaurants and shopping; Carlsbad, a quaint suburb patterned on a Danish village and home to Legoland and the posh La Costa Resort; and Oceanside, a military town with deep surfing roots and the longest wooden pier on the West Coast.

Although many natives will tell you "there is no life east of I-5" (the major north–south freeway that runs near the coastline), don't believe it: there are vibrant inland communities that have much to offer, too, including Mission Valley, home to the San Diego mission as well as enormous shopping opportunities, thanks to two major malls and hundreds of independent stores; exclusive Rancho Santa Fe, named by *Fortune* as the wealthiest zip code in America; Escondido, home to the San Diego Zoo Safari Park and a favorite area for equestrians; and Julian, a delightful small town in the nearby mountains.

GUIDANCE **San Diego Convention and Visitors Bureau** (619-232-3101; www.sandiego.org/nav/Visitors), 2215 India St., San Diego. The San Diego CVB operates two visitors' information centers, one in downtown San Diego, at the corner of W. Broadway and Harbor Dr., near the cruise ship terminal; and one in La Jolla, at the corner of Hershel and Prospect.

MORE HELPFUL WEB SITES

East county: www.visitsandiegoeast.com

Gaslamp Quarter: www.gaslamp.org

La Jolla: www.lajollabythesea.com

San Diego: www.sandiego.com

San Diego North Convention and Visitors Bureau: www.sandiegonorth.com

MEDICAL EMERGENCIES The only number to remember in a medical emergency is 911. Operators are available immediately and will dispatch ambulances and rescue personnel. Throughout town there are a number of hospitals with 24-hour emergency-room care:

Coronado Hospital (619-435-6251), 250 Prospect Pl., Coronado.

Scripps Memorial Hospital Encinitas (760-633-6501), 354 Santa Fe Dr., Encinitas.

Scripps Memorial Hospital La Jolla (858-626-4123), 9888 Genesee Ave., La Jolla.

Sharp Memorial Hospital San Diego (858-939-3400), 7901 Frost St., San Diego.

UCSD Medical Center Hillcrest (619-543-6400), 200 W. Arbor Dr., San Diego.

GETTING THERE *By air:* San Diego is served by **Lindbergh Field** (619-400-2400), 3225 N. Harbor Drive, San Diego. There are three terminals and free transportation between them via a bus shuttle service that loops between Terminals 1 and 2 and the Commuter Terminal. Additional airports in nearby cities include the **John Wayne Airport** (949-252-5200), 18601 Airport Way, in Santa Ana; and the **Long Beach Airport** (562-570-2600), 4100 Donald Douglas Drive, in Long Beach.

By bus: Arrive in downtown San Diego by bus at the **Greyhound Bus Terminal** (619-239-3266), 120 W. Broadway, San Diego. The terminal is within easy walking distance of the popular Gaslamp Quarter and its many hotels and restaurants, across the street from a trolley stop, and about five minutes by taxi to the harbor and the cruise ship terminal.

By car: Visitors arriving to San Diego by car will find well-marked freeways—and lots of them. Major corridors include I-5, I-15, I-163, and I-805, which run south to north; and I-8, I-52, I-56, and I-78, which run east to west.

By cruise ship: The number of visitors arriving in San Diego via cruise ships that dock at the B Street Pier **Cruise Ship Terminal** has tripled since 2001, and in 2010, approximately 700,000 guests made their way to the city via cruise ship. In addition, major carriers such as Carnival and Holland America initiate cruises to the Mexican Riviera (aka Cabo San Lucas, Puerto Vallarta, and Mazatlan), the Sea of Cortez, and Hawaii from the Port of San Diego. Cruise ship guests at the port are ideally situated to explore the Harbor District downtown, including the shopping mecca of Seaport Village, and are within easy walking distance of the lively downtown Gaslamp Quarter as well.

By train: **AMTRAK** trains arrive in San Diego downtown at the **Santa Fe Depot** (800-872-7245), 1050 Kettner Boulevard, San Diego. Visitors traveling through Southern California can take advantage of the *Pacific Surfliner* service, which runs from San Luis Obispo to San Diego along a coastline route aboard bi-level cars with panoramic windows.

GETTING AROUND *By car:* Overwhelmingly congested freeways are not just a Southern California stereotype: traffic can be a nightmare in San Diego (although it's not nearly as bad as in Los Angeles), and those driving through the city will be well advised to avoid traditional commute times. These include weekday mornings 7–9, especially on roads running north to south and east to west; and weekday afternoons 3–6, especially on roads running south to north and west to east. Friday rush hour generally begins as early as 2 PM, especially during summer months. That said, San Diego is a city that relies on automobiles, and visitors interested in really exploring the area are well advised to bring their own cars or plan to rent one.

By public transportation: The Metropolitan Transit Service (MTS) is the local institution that runs most of the public transportation throughout the city, including bus lines; the *Coaster* train service that runs along the coastline from downtown San Diego to Oceanside; and the San Diego Trolley, which serves downtown, Old Town, and parts of east county. For specific routes, schedules, and fares, visit the MTS Web site at www.sdcommute.com.

By alternative means: In the past several years, independent pedicabs have become plentiful in downtown (indeed, so plentiful that the city limited their numbers recently) and can be hailed readily for short trips in the Gaslamp Quarter and along the Embarcadero that runs adjacent to the San Diego Bay. Another new option for tooling around town is via **GoCar Tours** (www.gocartours.com), a fleet of tiny three-wheeled vehicles that come equipped with a GPS-guided audio tour that highlights one hundred San Diego sites. Or if you want to access your inner princess, check out **Cinderella Carriage Co.** (www.cinderella-carriage.com), which offers fairy-tale perfect horse-drawn carriage rides along the waterfront Embarcadero and through the romantic Gaslamp Quarter downtown.

DOWNTOWN AND ITS NEARBY NEIGHBORS

If you arrive in San Diego by airplane, you'll fly right over the mid-rises of downtown—and if you know where to look, you'll probably see the Coronado Bridge and the pretty little community it connects to as well. If you're looking for culture and nightlife, you'll want to stay in the city center, near the heart of the action. **Downtown** is clean, gorgeous, and easy to navigate, even for folks who don't know the area. It is compact enough to be accessible by foot and has reliable (and fun) public transportation via the bright-red San Diego Trolley system. It is possible to spend several weeks downtown and never run out of activities. And although the city can't quite boast being one that never sleeps, downtown San Diego is generally crawling with people every night of the week until midnight—and on the weekends, sidewalks are bustling until 2 or 3.

If you're looking for *less* action—but still want to be close in—look to **Coronado,** which is relatively sleepy after dark. You'll still find lots of quality restaurants, shops, and entertainment options, but the pace is slower.

BAY-FRONT DOWNTOWN AND CORONADO BEYOND

✷ To See

HISTORICAL SITES ✐ **Cabrillo National Monument and Old Point Loma Lighthouse** (619-557-5450; www.nps.gov/cabr/index.htm), 1800 Cabrillo Memorial Dr., San Diego. Open daily 9–5. Juan Rodriguez Cabrillo, said to be the first European to set foot on the west coast of what is now the United States, sailed into the San Diego harbor on September 28, 1542, on his way to search for a shortcut from Central America to Asia. En route he claimed San Diego for Spain. The scenic Cabrillo National Monument at

OLD POINT LOMA LIGHTHOUSE

the very tip of the Point Loma peninsula memorializes his accomplishments with a sculpture of the famous conquistador. On-site is a tiny museum that displays Cabrillo artifacts, and a bookstore that sells prints and posters. Also on the property is the picturesque Old Point Loma Lighthouse, which dates to 1854. Visitors can peek into re-created rooms that show how the original light keeper and his family lived for 30-plus years. $10 per vehicle.

Marston House (619-298-3142; www.marstonhouse.org), 3525 Seventh Ave., San Diego. Open Fri.–Sun. 10–5. On the outskirts of **Balboa Park,** the Marston House was once home to a wealthy businessman and remains an excellent example of the Arts and Crafts style. The structure was designed by noted architects Irving Gill and William S. Hebbard, students of Frank Lloyd Wright. Adults $8, seniors and active military $6, children $4.

✪ ✐ **Mission Basilica San Diego de Alcala** (619-281-8449; www.missionsandiego.com), 10818 San Diego Mission Rd., San Diego. Open daily 9–4:45. Padre Junípero Serra arrived in San Diego in 1769 to establish this first of 21 Spanish missions in California (although the original mission was moved to the current location a few years after Serra arrived). The mission has been rebuilt many times after it was destroyed by fires, and what is displayed today dates to 1931, when the mission was redone to look like the church in 1813. Self-guided tours take visitors through Father Serra's apartment, a small chapel, and through a lovely garden that offers pretty views of the 50-foot bell tower. Also on-site is the Padre Luis Jayme

SAN DIEGO MISSION

Mission Museum (Jayme was Serra's successor, who was murdered in a Native raid of the mission). Adults $3, seniors and students $2, children $1.

Old Town San Diego State Historic Park (619-220-5422), 4002 Wallace St., San Diego. Open daily 10–5. Site of one of the first European settlements on the West Coast, and in the shadows of the original mission (since relocated) and the presidio built to protect it, the restored and reconstructed buildings in Old Town San Diego offer a glimpse into the early pueblo era of 1821–1872, with dozens of themed buildings (some museums and some shops) and docents dressed in period costumes. Museum exhibits highlight the commercial and personal lives of the missionaries, Spanish colonists, wealthy Mexican families, and the native Kumeyaay Indians who lived in early San Diego. Also on-site is the **Fiesta de Reyes** (www.fiestadereyes.com), formerly known as the Plaza del Posada (and not too long before that, the famous Bazaar del Mundo, which has since been relocated), a shopping and restaurant center that offers a taste of the Old West, and the tiny **Cosmopolitan Hotel.** Admission is free.

Villa Montezuma (619-239-2211; www.villamontezuma.org), 1925 K St., San Diego. A storybook Victorian house designed in 1887, the Villa Montezuma is the best example of Queen Anne architecture in San Diego. Built for a prominent early San Diego citizen, this old home offers lush Spanish cedar and redwood details, extensive stained-glass windows, and fanciful gargoyles. The villa has been undergoing renovation for many years, with no firm schedule for reopening. Call ahead for information on the availability and hours of public tours.

Whaley House (619-297-7511; www.whaleyhouse.org), 2476 San Diego Ave., San Diego. Hours are seasonal. Built in 1885, the Greek Revival–style Whaley House is famous because of its longtime occupants: many people consider this to be one of the most haunted structures in America, no doubt because the Whaley House was the site of many tragedies throughout the years. For example, in 1885, after a scandalous divorce from her first cousin and a prolonged battle with depression, a young woman who lived in the home committed suicide by shooting herself through the heart. Visitors and curators swear they have seen spooky apparitions and heard unexplainable noises. Adults $6, seniors $5, children $4.

William Heath Davis House (619-233-4692; www.gaslampquarter.org/history/thehouse.php), 410 Island Ave., San Diego. Open Tues.–Sat. 10–6 and Sun. 9–3. Headquarters of the Gaslamp Quarter Historical Foundation, this museum is housed in the oldest remaining wooden structure in San Diego, dating to 1850 (it was relocated to its present site in 1984). Davis was an early developer of downtown, and he built the home for himself. Several years after Davis moved on, Alonzo E. Horton—another important developer in early San Diego—lived in the house with his family. Adults $5, seniors $4, children free.

MUSEUMS **Mingei International Museum** (619-239-0003; www.mingei.org), 1439 El Prado, San Diego. Open Tues.–Sun. 10–4. A giant green mosaic serpent covered in marbles, river stones, and mirrors stands watch outside the entrance to this museum. Inside, rotating exhibits feature international art and cultural artifacts. Adults $7, seniors $5, students and active military $4.

Museum of Contemporary Art San Diego—Downtown (858-454-3541; www.mcasd.org), 1100 Kettner Blvd., San Diego. Open Thurs.–Tues. 11–5. This center-city venue of MCASD (its sister museum is in La Jolla; see the "La Jolla

WYATT EARP AND THE STINGAREE DISTRICT

During a population boom in the late 19th century, downtown San Diego was a wild and dangerous place. By the late 1880s, there were more than one hundred bordellos downtown and an estimated 350 prostitutes working in them. In addition, there were 70 saloons, dance halls, and gambling parlors, many of which were open 24–7. The Gaslamp Quarter at the time was called the Stingaree District, because it was said that people could get stung as badly there as they could by the ubiquitous stingrays in the San Diego Bay. During this period, the infamous gunslinger Wyatt Earp rolled into town with his third wife, Josie. It was 1885—a few years after Earp's gunfight at the OK Corral in Tombstone, Arizona—and Earp was looking to make some fast cash. Earp bought or leased several saloons in the Stingaree—and dropped even more cash gambling in establishments owned by others. But in 1888, the boom in population that San Diego had enjoyed went bust, and Earp and his wife moved on as quickly as they came. Soon after, the San Diego police cleared out the Stingaree, eventually making way for the law-abiding, upscale businesses that now call the Gaslamp Quarter home.

and Central Beach Towns" chapter) explores national and regional trends in contemporary art, with an emphasis on works by artists from San Diego and Tijuana. On the first Thurs. of every month, the museum hosts TNT, a popular cocktail hour at the museum. Adults $10, seniors and active military $5, 25 years and younger free.

Museum of Photographic Arts (619-238-7559; www.mopa.org), 1649 El Prado, San Diego. Open Tues.–Sun. 10–5, with sporadic early closing at 4. Focusing on the photographic, film, and video arts, MOPA, in Balboa Park, offers rotating exhibits that highlight past and current photographers. Adults $8, seniors and students $5.

✐ **New Children's Museum** (619-233-8792; www.thinkplaycreate.org), 200 W. Island Ave., San Diego. Open Mon., Tues., Thurs.–Sat. 10–4, Sun. noon–4. Opened in May 2008, the New Children's Museum is a light-filled, three-story glass and concrete space with soaring ceilings, open steel beams, and floating staircases. The museum is filled with interactive experiences, giving kids the opportunity to play with, create, and experience art. Adults and children $10, seniors and active military $5.

✐ **Reuben H. Fleet Science Center** (619-238-1233; www.rhfleet.org), 1875 El Prado, San Diego. Open daily at 10; closing times vary. The Reuben H. Fleet, in Balboa Park, offers more than one hundred fun and interactive experiments demonstrating the principles of science. The museum is also home to San Diego's only IMAX Dome Theater, which plays several regular features throughout the week (the offerings change every few months) as well as a wide variety of special after-hours shows on Fri. nights. Adults $10, seniors and children $8.75. IMAX films additional.

San Diego Maritime Museum (619-234-9153; www.sdmaritime.com), 1492 N. Harbor Dr., San Diego. Open daily 9–8. The sailing vessels that make up this museum have defined the San Diego harbor front for decades and include the magnificent *Star of India,* built in 1863 and currently the oldest active sailing ship in the world; the *Berkeley,* an 1898 steam ferry; the HMS *Surprise,* a replica of an 18th-century Royal Navy frigate; the *Medea,* a 1914 steam yacht; and a B-39 Russian attack submarine. Adults $12, seniors and active military $10, children $7.

San Diego Model Railroad Museum (619-696-0199; www.sdmodelrailroadm.com), 1649 El Prado, San Diego. Open Tues.–Fri. 11–4, Sat. and Sun. 11–5. Visitors to this charming museum can enjoy more than 28,000 square feet of scale model railroad layouts, which boast amazing attention to detail. Adults $7; children under 15 free with a paying adult.

San Diego Museum of Art (619-232-7931; www.sdmart.org), 1450 El Prado, San Diego. Open Tues.–Sat. 10–5, Sun. noon–5. The SDMA, in Balboa Park, attracts world-class touring exhibits. The small permanent collection includes a few memorable pieces by William Bouguereau, Renoir, and El Greco. Adults $12, seniors and active military $9, children $4.50.

San Diego Natural History Museum (619-232-3821; www.sdnhm.org), 1788 El Prado, San Diego. Open Sun.–Thurs. 10–7, Fri.–Sat. 10–9:30. Look for exhibits highlighting the natural history of Southern California and Baja Mexico. Downstairs, the museum shows big-screen science movies, free with admission. Adults $17, seniors $15, students and active military $12, children $11.

USS *Midway* Aircraft Carrier Museum (619-544-9600; www.midway.org), 910 N. Harbor Dr., San Diego. Open daily 10–5. The decommissioned USS *Midway,* the longest-serving aircraft carrier in U.S. Navy history, now permanently docked at the Navy Pier on the San Diego harbor, provides a unique experience for civilian visitors. It is 1,001 feet long, 258 feet wide, and has more than 4 acres of flight deck up top, so guests can lose themselves wandering onboard in what remain surprisingly authentic surroundings. Visit the cavernous hangar, sit in the cockpit of a Phantom fighter jet, and engage in a virtual dogfight with friends and family with networked video simulators. The museum entrance fee includes an audio tour. Adults $18, seniors $15, children over five $10.

PARKS **Balboa Park** (619-239-0512; www.balboapark.org), off Park Blvd., San Diego. Balboa Park was the site of the 1915–1916 Panama–California Exposition, and today the El Prado pedestrian thoroughfare at its center appears much as it did then, with elaborate Spanish Renaissance architecture in rosy hues; expansive gardens that overflow with Eucalyptus, palms, and purple-blooming jacaranda; and a handful of major theatrical venues—several of which are outdoors. The park complex—often referred to as the Smithsonian of the West—is home to the **San Diego Zoo;** more than a dozen museums; several cultural venues, including the **Centro Cultural de la Raza** (619-235-6135), which is dedicated to educating the public about Chicano, Mexican, and Native American art and culture; the **House of Pacific Relations** (619-234-0739), nearly two dozen cottages representing the culture and history of as many different nations; the **WorldBeat Center** (619-230-1190), which offers eclectic music and dance lessons from around the world; and expansive park grounds spread out over 1,200 acres. The iconic blue-domed Balboa Tower that anchors the park houses a one-hundred-bell

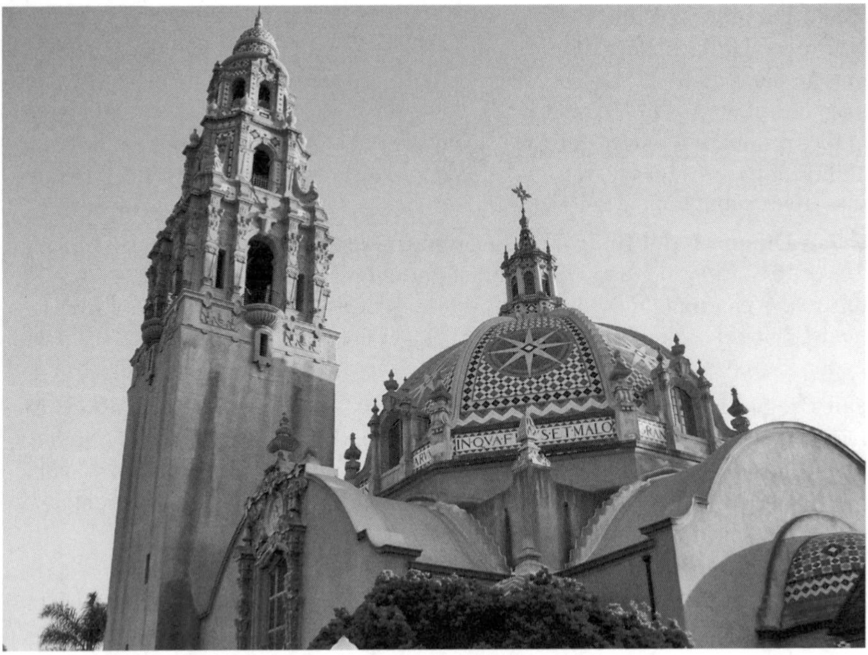

BALBOA PARK

carillon, which chimes every 15 minutes. Children will not want to miss the 1922 carousel on the northeast end of the park, near the zoo. Another kid pleaser is the **Balboa Park Miniature Railroad** (www.balboapark.org/in-the-park/detail.php?OrgID=33). The **Balboa Park Visitors Center** (www.balboapark.org) offers one-hour audio tours, which highlight the park's history, botanical features, and architecture. Note that most museums are free one Tues. a month, on a rotating schedule; check the Web site for up-to-date schedules. There is a free shuttle bus for all visitors that runs every 15 minutes, with stops throughout the park.

INSIDER TIP: Purchase a Balboa Park "Passport" at the visitors center, located in the Hospitality House on El Prado, and save as much as 50 percent off full-price admission to the park's museums and attractions.

🐾 **Embarcadero Park** (North and South), off Harbor Dr., downtown San Diego. These twin parks surround **Seaport Village** and the San Diego Convention Center, and offer walking paths that rim the bay and plenty of grassy lawn. In the summertime, the Embarcadero is home to the **Summer Pops** concerts.

🐾 ✐ **Presidio Park** (www.sandiego.gov/park-and-recreation/parks/presidio), 2727 Presidio Dr., San Diego. This park near Old Town is anchored by the **Junípero Serra Museum,** which features archaeological finds from early San Diego and on a clear day boasts a far-off view of the harbor. The park can be sketchy at night, so head out before sunset.

✷ To Do

BICYCLING Bicycling is hugely popular throughout Southern California, and in San Diego there are bike lanes on nearly every major roadway (aside from freeways, of course!). To explore the pathways on your own, rent bicycles at **Holland's Bicycles** (619-435-3153), at the corner of 10th and Orange in Coronado; and **Bike and Kayak Rentals** (858-454-1010), near La Jolla Shores—this rental agency will even deliver a bike right to your hotel room anywhere in the city. Detailed route information and trail maps are available at MapMyRide.com (www.mapmyride.com/find-ride/united-states/ca/san-diego). There are a number of organized bike tours in town as well, including **Bike Revolution** (619-564-4843; www.bike-tours.com/index.html), **San Diego Bike and Kayak Tours** (858-454-1010; www.sandiegobikeandkayaktours.com), and **Where You Want to Be Tours** (619-917-6037; www.wheretours.com).

GOLF San Diego County is home to almost one hundred golf courses, many of which are located in the northern- and easternmost quadrants of San Diego. (See also the "North County San Diego" chapter.)

✪ **Barona Creek Golf Club** (619-443-2300; www.barona.com), 1932 Wildcat Canyon Rd., Lakeside. Located in Lakeside, 30 miles east of downtown San Diego, Barona was voted by *Golfweek* as the fourth-best course in the state and *the* best in San Diego County. The championship course offers five tees to accommodate golfers of all skill levels and is surrounded by the natural beauty of east county. Note: This course is owned and operated as part of the Barona Resort and Casino. Green fee: $120–160.

✪ **Coronado Municipal Golf Course** (619-435-3121; www.golfcoronado.com), 2000 Visalia Row, San Diego. One of the loveliest municipal parks in the state is within minutes of downtown: locals adore this course, but it remains a relatively undiscovered gem for visitors. The course boasts some of the best views of San Diego Bay and the Coronado Bridge you'll find in the city, is well maintained and challenging, and has inexpensive rates. Reserve a tee time 8 to 14 days in advance or participate in a lottery, conducted between 6:30 and 9 every morning. Green fee: $15–35.

SPAS San Diegans know how to pamper ourselves, which means there are world-class spas throughout the city; many of the best are part of luxury hotels, but there are an increasing number of high-quality day spas springing up throughout the city.

✪ **KIN Spa** (619-232-1234; http://manchestergrandhyatt.com/hyatt/pure/spas), 1 Market Pl., San Diego. This quiet spa that belongs to the **Manchester Grand Hyatt,** on the downtown waterfront, offers massages, facial treatments, and full-body treatments. Try the decadent 90-minute

BARONA CREEK GOLF CLUB

Courtesy of Barona Casino

PETCO PARK: TAKE ME DOWNTOWN FOR A BALLGAME

Petco Park (619-795-5011; www.padres.com), 100 Park Boulevard, San Diego, is the pride of downtown and home to San Diego's major league baseball team, the Padres. The parklike surroundings draw loyal fans by the droves, and there are plenty of seating options, beyond the typical seats in the stands. For less than $10, visitors can gain admission to the extremely popular "Park in the Park" behind center field, a pretty grassy area elevated enough to see into the ballpark or to watch the game on a giant video screen. Guests will find another small ballpark here, where kids can run the bases while parents picnic and watch the professionals play. Or for a few dollars more, fans can sit at "The Beach," a series of benches set in a sand pit. Baseball fans can arrange for a behind-the-scenes tour of Petco any time of the year, and the Park in the Park is open to the public for free when there are no games.

lemongrass and sea enzyme body wrap, which starts with a full-body mandarin orange scrub, followed up with a body wrap with lemongrass, and finally moisturizing with lemongrass lotion. After enjoying treatments, guests can sip cucumber water beside the peaceful spa-guests-only rooftop pool.

✪ **Spa at the Del** (800-468-3533; www.hoteldel.com/spa.aspx), 1500 Orange Ave., Coronado. Although located in one of the most beautiful 19th-century beach resorts in the world (the **Hotel del Coronado**), the Spa at the Del offers 21st-century luxury, including state-of-the-art facilities and fine bioengineered products. Try the Islands Body Polish, a full-body scrub with desert mineral salts and citrus gel; or if you've spent too much time enjoying the sun on the beautiful Coronado Beach, treat yourself to the Sunburn Relief treatment, a cooling aloe vera and Hawaiian Noni wrap that will help ease the immediate pain as well as help to prevent future peeling.

Spa Sè (619-515-3000; www.sesandiego.com/experience.php), 1047 Fifth Ave., San Diego. Located in the **Sè Hotel** downtown, Spa Sè is a luxurious, tranquil Asian-inspired oasis. Start out with a cup of blooming-flower tea in the spa's Relaxation Room, and then indulge in the Tala, a four-hands synchronized massage, or an Indian Head Massage that concentrates on the scalp, ears, and face and finishes with shirodhara, a ritualistic form of healing that involves pouring liquids over the forehead.

Spa Velia (619-235-0000; www.spavelia.com), 401 W. A St., San Diego. Near the Little Italy neighborhood of downtown, Spa Velia is a day spa that is part of the Green Spa Network, an elite group of spas around the country that use environmentally friendly, fair-trade products. Don't miss the relaxing Mediterranean Clay Wrap, featuring a warm mud wrap enriched with avocado oils. Afterward, check out the complimentary Aromatic Steam Room and cold plunge showers.

THEME PARKS AND ZOOS ✪ **San Diego Zoo** (619-234-3153; www.sandiegozoo.org), 2920 Zoo Dr., San Diego. Open daily; hours vary by season. The

Courtesy of the San Diego Zoo

SAN DIEGO ZOO

100-acre San Diego Zoo in Balboa Park (just north of downtown) is world renowned as one of the largest and most innovative zoological parks in existence. Guests will enjoy more than 3,500 rare and endangered animals representing more than four hundred species, as well as nearly 700,000 exotic plants. Popular exhibits include the Conrad Prebys Polar Bear Plunge, an aquatic enclosure that allows visitors to get up close to the playful animals; a naturalistic gorilla exhibit; a sprawling monkey exhibit that meanders through a tropical forest; and the ever-popular (and ever-crowded) panda research station. To date, the San Diego Zoo is the only U.S. park to successfully breed and rear healthy panda cubs. Guests can hop aboard a double-decker bus for a guided tour of the zoo, which runs past giraffes, rare deer and antelope, meerkats, and spectacled bears, among others. The bus is a good way to save a little shoe leather, and because the zoo is a big place, with uneven and hilly terrain in spots, this is sometimes a welcome alternative to hoofing it. The popular Skyfari Aerial Tram is another must-see: a gondola car glides directly over the gorilla enclosure, for premier viewing access, as well as a handful of other animal exhibits that span the expanse of the zoo. The view of the nearby San Diego skyline alone is worth the extra price of the ticket. Adults $37, children 3 to 11 $27. During the entire month of Oct., the zoo is free to children.

INSIDER TIP: The east Skyfari terminal, near the zoo entrance, is usually overcrowded. Walk to the west end of the park, near the polar bear exhibit, and you'll find much shorter waits to board.

✱ Water Sports

It's almost hard to find someone in San Diego who doesn't regularly participate in at least one water sport. Visitors can live like the locals and get out on the water in any number of ways—some of which require nothing more than a credit card and willingness to climb aboard a staffed vessel, and some of which require a true adventurous nature.

BOATING Dennis Conner's America's Cup Experience (800-644-3454; www.stars-stripes.com), next to the USS *Midway* on the harbor. This unique company offers two-hour harbor cruises, charters, and sailing lessons aboard 80-foot International America's Cup Class yachts, the fastest mono-hull sailing vessels in the world. The thrilling excursions are limited—and popular—so book well in advance.

SAILBOATS OFF POINT LOMA

🍸 **Hornblower Cruises** (888-551-4855; www.hornblower.com), 1066 N. Harbor Dr., San Diego. One of the best ways to see the San Diego skyline is by boat. Hornblower offers nightly dinner cruises in the harbor, leaving just in time to catch the sunset and then watch the city lights start to glow. They also have champagne brunches on weekends and private charters, as well as daily one- and two-hour tours throughout the bay. Call ahead for reservations.

San Diego Harbor Excursions (619-234-4111; www.sdhe.com), 1050 N. Harbor Dr., San Diego. San Diego Harbor Excursions offers a wide variety of services, including day cruises on the harbor, nightly dinner dance cruises, guided whale-watching tours, and holiday (Fourth of July and Christmas) cruises.

✷ Green Space

BEACHES ✪ Coronado Beach, off Orange Ave., Coronado. With the luxurious **Hotel del Coronado** as the romantic backdrop, this exclusive and exceptionally wide expanse of shoreline is a favorite with locals and visitors. Waves are generally gentle, making this a good choice for children (and usually not so good for surfers), and public facilities are among the best kept in the city.

🐾 **Ocean Beach,** south of the channel entrance to Mission Bay, off Abbott St., Ocean Beach. This beach is popular with surfers (and street people, especially on the south end of the pier). You'll also find the popular **Dog Beach** at the north end. Parking is limited, and swimmers should beware: the rip currents can be uncommonly strong.

Silver Strand State Beach, off Orange Ave., south of Coronado. This is the best bet in the area for finding seashells—but arrive early, because local beachcombers scour the area at first light. Silver Strand is also a gentle swimming beach for children, because the water gets deep very gradually.

Sunset Cliffs, west off Sunset Cliffs Blvd., Point Loma. Staircases lead to beach access. A relatively remote beach that is popular with locals and surfers, Sunset Cliffs has more seclusion than most other beaches in town. Go toward the south near Cabrillo Point (also accessible from the **Cabrillo Monument**) and find great tidepooling; there are bigger waves and more surfers on the north end.

GARDENS ✪ **Botanical Building and Lily Pond,** off El Prado, in Balboa Park, San Diego. Open Fri.–Wed. 10–4. This beautiful wooden structure in the center of Balboa Park houses more than two thousand orchids and exotic palms in a serene enclosure. The Botanical Building is the backdrop of the much-photographed reflecting Lily Pond, which blooms in summer and is home to koi year-round. Admission is free.

Desert Garden, over the footbridge that crosses Park Blvd. at the end of El Prado in Balboa Park, San Diego. This oasis is home to more than 1,200 plants on 2.5 acres, including succulents and drought-resistant cacti. The peak blooming period is Jan.–Mar. Admission is free.

Inez Grant Parker Memorial Rose Garden, over the footbridge that crosses Park Blvd. at the end of El Prado in Balboa Park (south of the Desert Garden),

ANZA-BORREGO DESERT

About 60 miles east of downtown San Diego, the rolling hills and seemingly desolate flatlands of the Anza-Borrego Desert State Park are teeming with life. In addition to rattlesnakes, scorpions, and jackrabbits, more than 268 species of birds have been recorded in this park. The endangered Peninsular bighorn sheep calls Anza-Borrego home as well. In spring (which can come as early as February), the area transforms with wildflowers that include primrose, verbena, purple nightshade, and apricot mallow. The extensiveness of the wildflowers varies widely from year to year, depending on the amount of rainfall and the ferocity of the winds. Check the wildflower hotline beforehand for tips on when and where to find the best displays (760-767-4684 or www.anzaborrego.statepark.org). Hikers will find more than 100 miles of trails winding through the lowlands, canyons, and rock formations. For those looking for a little more excitement in the desert, **Ocotillo Wells,** in the eastern portion of the park, is the place: this 80,000-acre recreational area is set aside for dune buggies, motorcycles, and other noisy desert toys. The interesting rock formations and the rolling dunes make for exciting and challenging off-roading. It's possible to pitch a tent and camp anywhere in the park without a campsite (although check with the rangers about building fires in such open areas). Cushier accommodations include the moderately priced **Palm Canyon Resort** (760-767-5341; 221 Palm Canyon Drive, Borrego Springs), a large property with a hotel and an RV park; and the pricier **Palms at Indian Head** (760-767-7788 or 800-519-2624; 2220 Hoberg Road, Borrego Springs), a smaller Southwestern-themed property. Be sure to stay on the paths, to preserve the ecological balance of the park and to avoid any unfriendly creatures (e.g., rattlesnakes and scorpions). And come prepared—the desert is an unforgiving environment, with scorching temperatures in summer and canyons subject to flash floods year-round. Carry plenty of water, wear sunscreen and a hat, and always check weather forecasts.

San Diego. More than two hundred varieties of roses bloom in this often overlooked garden, which is at its most spectacular Mar.–Dec. Admission is free.

✪ **Japanese Friendship Garden,** near the Spreckels Organ Pavilion in Balboa Park, San Diego. Open Tues.–Sun. 10–4. This small, serene garden is a relative newcomer to the park and offers a lovely bonsai exhibit and a well-stocked koi pond. (Check out the teahouse at the entrance for lunch or a light snack.) Adults $3, seniors $2.50, children and active military $2.

✸ Lodging

PRICE KEY FOR A STANDARD ROOM:	
$	$100 or less
$$	$101–150
$$$	$151–250
$$$$	$251 and up

Coronado

⚤ **Glorietta Bay Inn** (619-435-3101; www.gloriettabayinn.com), 1630 Glorietta Blvd. This beautiful historic property was built in 1906 for a wealthy San Diego businessman on Glorietta Bay in Coronado, which today has jaw-dropping views of the downtown San Diego skyline. A few decades back the Italianesque mansion was lovingly restored to its original grandeur. There are 11 suites in the original mansion, as well as 89 contemporary rooms available next door. Guests will be treated to milk and cookies at bedtime, a continental breakfast, and an afternoon snack. $$$

✪ ⚤ **Hotel del Coronado** (619-435-6611; www.hoteldel.com), 1500 Orange Ave. Built in 1888, this beautiful old resort hotel is a National Historic Landmark and considered by many to be one of the top destination hotels in the country. The sprawling complex sits on a sugary white-sand beach that is exceptionally wide by San Diego standards. Public rooms are rich in carved mahogany wood details, plush rugs, and extravagant Victorian furnishings. Guest accommodations are sited in three distinct locations: the original and historic Victorian Building; the 1970s-era Towers and Cabana; and the brand new, sumptuous Beach Village, featuring condo properties. This full-service resort also offers a large sparkling pool and new state-of-the-art spa; numerous boutiques, including upscale clothing stores and fine jewelry stores; kids' and teens' activities in the summer; and several on-site bars and restaurants. Visit **Babcock and Story** for cocktails with a view of the ocean in a setting that is straight out of the 19th century. **1500 Ocean** (see *Where to Eat*) offers contemporary California coastal cuisine with impeccable views. And the historic **Crown Room** (619-435-6611) has long been voted the best Sunday brunch in San Diego by local newspapers and magazines. You can also indulge in a Victorian high tea on Sun. afternoons (or every day during

HOTEL DEL CORONADO

the month of Dec., when the Del is decked out to the nines in holiday decorations). $$$$

Downtown San Diego

🍸 **Hard Rock Hotel** (866-751-7625; www.hardrockhotelsd.com), 207 Fifth Ave. The new Hard Rock Hotel is at the pulse point of the Gaslamp Quarter and right across the street from the convention center downtown. The lobby offers pounding music, an oversized screen behind the reception desk that plays a stream of psychedelic videos, a lighting system built directly into the floors, and a cadre of roadie look-alikes ready to help with bags. Explore the hallways of the public spaces, because this property also serves as a rock and roll museum, displaying scribbled cartoons by John Lennon, a bustier that once belonged to Madonna, and a top hat worn onstage by guitarist Slash. Standard guest rooms are stylish and modern, but if you really want to party like a rock star, splurge on one of the individually decorated suites, each of which offers an expansive space that includes several televisions, a spa-worthy bathroom with soaking tub built for two, and room enough to invite your whole posse. Be sure to check out **Float** (619-277-7721), a rooftop bar with fire pit seating and private VIP cabanas overlooking the sleek pool. $$$$

▼ **Horton Grand Hotel** (619-544-1886; www.hortongrand.com), 311 Island Ave. When the gentrification of the Gaslamp Quarter kicked off in the 1980s with the construction of the Horton Plaza shopping mall, two historic buildings that were in the way—the Horton Grand Hotel and Kable Saddlery—faced the wrecking ball. Enterprising preservationists bought each building for $1 and moved them to a new, now premium location off Fourth Ave., combining them into a gingerbread-trimmed Victorian beauty that's within easy walking distance of the best restaurants and bars downtown has to offer, and just blocks from the convention center. Guest rooms are individually decorated in cheerful period fabrics; count on period reproductions, a working gas fireplace in each room, and small bathrooms with classic water closets. $$$

Hotel Indigo (619-727-4000; www.ichotelsgroup.com/h/d/in/1/en/hotel/sanis), 509 Ninth Ave. One of the newest lodging options downtown, the hip Hotel Indigo offers 100 percent smoke-free accommodations and a youthful vibe. The chic hotel is located in the up-and-coming East Village neighborhood of downtown, easy walking distance from the Padres' Petco ballpark. Guest rooms feature hardwood floors, plush bedding, wall murals, and spacious spalike bathrooms. The rooftop **Phi Terrace** bar and lounge is small but welcoming, thanks to inviting fire pits and nice skyline views. Frequent visitors will notice that the hotel undergoes seasonal transformations, so that music, artwork, murals, and even scents correlate with the time of year. $$$

HOTEL INDIGO

✪ ⇐ **Hotel Solamar** (877-230-0300; www.hotelsolamar.com), 435 Sixth Ave. A midsized hotel in downtown's East Village that is part of the eclectic Kimpton chain, the stylish Hotel Solamar offers 235 rooms, with ergonomic desks and work chairs and complimentary yoga accessories. Rooms are decorated with bold, simple patterns and oversized furniture. At the water's edge of a fourth-floor rooftop pool, the trendy **Jbar Lounge** (619-531-8744) attracts a stylish crowd of locals and visitors on the weekends. Downstairs is the surprising **JSix Restaurant,** a treat for the eyes and the taste buds. $$$

Y **Keating Hotel** (619-814-5700; www.thekeating.com), 432 F St. The clean lines and upscale amenities of this small boutique property are reminiscent of what's available in Milan and Rome, and for good reason—the hotel was designed by the famed Italian firm Pininfarina, responsible for masterminding the Maserati and Ferrari lines. Each guest accommodation has high ceilings, the latest in audio equipment, plasma TVs that carry 150 channels, and gleaming espresso machines. In the baths, the stainless-steel vanities, rain-shower fixtures, and frosted glass panels are sleek and modern—although they offer very little privacy (there are no solid walls to separate the bathing area from the sleeping area). The location is noisy—the historic building is surrounded by nightclubs that offer live music until the wee hours—but the hotel management wisely provides earplugs and white-noise machines to drown out the worst of the din. On-site is the hip **MerK Bistro Italiano,** which offers rustic Italian fare in a sophisticated, sleek environment. The members-only club **Sway,** which is the site of some of the best exclusive parties in town, is open to hotel guests. $$$$

INSIDER TIP: The Keating Hotel is in the heart of the Gaslamp Quarter, where parking is precious. Valet parking is an exorbitant $60. Save a few bucks and park at the Horton Plaza Shopping Center across the street for a fraction of the cost.

✪ ✐ **Manchester Grand Hyatt** (619-232-1234; http://manchestergrand.hyatt.com/hyatt/hotels/index.jsp), 1 Market Pl. At 40 stories tall, the Manchester Grand Hyatt is the tallest waterfront hotel on the West Coast, and guest rooms boast breathtaking views of the San Diego Bay, the vibrant harbor front, and the sparkling downtown skyline. The myriad amenities include a 24-hour gym with state-of-the-art equipment; a full-service spa that specializes in reflexology and Swedish massage; a 25,000-foot fourth-floor deck that offers a huge pool, whirlpools nestled beneath curving pergolas, a festive outdoor bar, ample lounge space, and a fire pit—all with lovely water views; tennis, volleyball,

MANCHESTER GRAND HYATT

and basketball courts; seasonal children's programs, including popular "dive-in" movies; several in-house boutiques; and a handful of exceptional restaurants and bars. Grab a cocktail at the **Top of the Hyatt** on the 40th floor at sunset and enjoy possibly the best views in San Diego. $$$–$$$$

Sé San Diego (619-515-3000; www.sesandiego.com), 1047 Fifth Ave. Formerly known as the Setai San Diego, this property has a Zen-chic aesthetic with sultry Asian design. Public spaces are bold and textural, and private spaces are serene. Accommodations range from a small basic guest room to the most exclusive three-story penthouse on the West Coast. There are also residential condominiums on the property. Service is top-shelf, and amenities are wide-ranging, including the impeccable **Sé Spa,** state-of-the-art workout facilities, an exclusive movie-screening room, and a rooftop pool and nightclub. On-site dining is at **Suite and Tender,** a fine-dining establishment that includes a "create your own" raw bar and features exotic specialties like Wagyu beef sliders and duck confit gratin. $$$

✪ **U.S. Grant Hotel** (619-232-3121; www.usgrant.net), 326 Broadway. Remodeled guest rooms in this grand 19th-century hotel in the middle of downtown are sumptuous, and bathrooms are spalike. Indulgent suites have comfortable living rooms and feature a "shower experience" in the bathrooms—a large walk-in affair with six shower heads. This 270-room hotel is just across the street from the slightly gritty Horton Plaza shopping mall, and a few blocks from the trendy Gaslamp Quarter. On-site you'll find the clubby **Grant Grill** (619-239-6806), as well as a lobby bar. $$$$

Westgate Hotel (619-238-1818; www.westgatehotel.com), 1055 Second Ave. Public spaces in this French palatial hotel are dressed to impress, with museum-quality antiques, original oil paintings and tapestries, luxurious silk fabrics, and enormous crystal chandeliers. Guest rooms are commodious and well appointed, with marble and brass bathrooms. On-site is the luxe **Westgate Room** (619-557-3650)—don't miss the freshly made fruit smoothies and hot churros (Mexican donuts covered in cinnamon and sugar) for breakfast. Exceptional hospitality ensures that all this opulence doesn't feel stuffy. $$$

✷ Where to Eat

DINING OUT

Coronado

Coronado Boathouse (619-435-0155; www.coronado-boathouse.com), 1701 Strand Way. Open daily for dinner. This eye-catching restaurant built on a pier overhanging the water in Glorietta Bay in Coronado, just across the street from the **Hotel del Coronado,** specializes in steak and seafood, and has premier views of nearby downtown San Diego. The stuffed prawns with Dungeness crab and smoked bacon served with a cream sauce is a perennial favorite, as is the authentic Key lime pie for dessert. $$$

✪ **1500 Ocean** (619-522-8490; www.dine1500ocean.com), 1500 Orange Ave. Open daily for dinner. Don't dismiss this as just another hotel restaurant. True, it is the new anchor

PRICE KEY FOR A TYPICAL ENTRÉE:

$	$10 and under
$$	$11–20
$$$	$21–30
$$$$	$31 and up

restaurant at the **Hotel del Coronado,** with premium views of the ocean that alone would be worth the visit, but beyond location, it offers some of the finest cuisine in the city. Seafood is a specialty, of course, but steak is done equally well. Try the delicate northern halibut served with baby artichokes and a saffron emulsion, along with sides like French green beans with walnuts and the oh-so-creamy baked macaroni and cheese. $$$

Downtown San Diego

✪ 🍸 **Café Chloe** (619-232-3242; www.cafechloe.com), 721 Ninth St. Open daily for breakfast, lunch, and dinner. The secret is out, and this little bit of Paris in the East Village has gained huge popularity, especially among the locals who have recently moved into this gentrified neighborhood. This adorable bistro, wine bar, and sidewalk café offers Francophile comfort food. I especially love the breakfast bread pudding served alongside a glass of freshly squeezed orange juice. Whatever meal you choose, do not miss the *affogato* for dessert—a scoop of Chloe's buttery homemade vanilla ice cream topped with a shot of espresso. $$

✪ 🍸 **Lou and Mickey's** (619-237-4900; www.louandmickeys.com), 224 Fifth Ave. Open daily for dinner, sporadically for lunch. Conveniently located across the train tracks from the convention center and in the heart of the Gaslamp, Lou and Mickey's is a romantic homage to East Coast steak and martini houses from the midcentury. Dark woods, manly furniture, moody lighting, and World War II–era tunes combine to provide a clubby atmosphere indoors. Or enjoy the extensive outdoor patio, festooned with palm trees and plentiful heat lamps for cool evenings. Entrées arrive alone on the plate, so order up family-style sides like garlic mashed potatoes or creamed spinach to round out the meal. Service is elegant and friendly. $$$

Monsoon (619-234-5555; www.monsoonrestaurant.com), 729 Fourth Ave. Open Mon.–Sat. for lunch and dinner. Featuring finely prepared Northern Indian cuisine, this swanky restaurant is an oasis on bustling Fourth Ave. A vertical wall of rain running through the middle of the dining room—a clever allegory—drowns out the considerable noise outside, while the exotic murals, jewel-encrusted chandeliers, and comfortable high-backed chairs create intimacy. Start with *papadum* (seasoned wafers toasted in a tandoori oven) and assorted *pakoras* (vegetable fritters served with yogurt and mint dipping sauces). Main courses offer curries in lamb, chicken, fish, and tofu; *biriyani,* rice and vegetables sautéed with your choice of protein; juicy, flavorful tandoori grilled meats; and plentiful vegetarian choices. Finish with a steaming cup of chai. $$

🍸 **Nobu** (866-751-7625; www.hardrockhotelsd.com/dining-&-nightlife/nobu), 207 Fifth Ave. Open daily for dinner. The signature restaurant at the **Hard Rock Hotel,** this gleaming restaurant is part of the empire created by world-famous chef Nobu Matsuhisu and

NOBU

Courtesy of Hard Rock Hotel

> **INSIDER TIP:** Celebrity-watchers would do well to come to Nobu for a late dinner during Comic-Con in mid-July, when the city is crawling with Hollywood actors participating in the hugely popular comic-book and sci-fi convention at the convention center across the street.

offers classical sushi and modern Japanese cuisine. Expect creative dishes you won't see anywhere else in the city, like octopus carpaccio served with a jalapeño dressing, sashimi tacos with yellowfin tuna and crab, and live local uni in the shell. Desserts are whimsical and luxurious, like the Bento Box, a warm Valrhona chocolate cake with shiso syrup and green tea ice cream, and the Gingered Kabocha, a pumpkin cream layered with gingersnaps and served with mandarin granita. The bar offers an extensive selection of wine and saki. Beware: This is a *popular* restaurant, and advanced reservations are an absolute must. $$$$

🍸 **Osetra: The Fish House** (619-239-1800; www.osetrafishhouse.com), 904 Fifth Ave. Open daily for dinner. Dominating the space of a chic two-tiered dining room is a glowing glass tower housing an extensive wine collection, including an impressive list of California reds. "Wine angels"—attractive young women—retrieve the appropriate bottle via a lift system that hoists them dramatically into the air. The bar packs in a crowd, especially on weekend nights, but first and foremost, this is a dining destination. Start with the lobster three-way, with creamy lobster bisque, subtle lobster salad with avocado, and Lobster Dynamite, a spicy and tangy custard that is bursting with lobster meat. For dinner, consider the stuffed shrimp, grilled and presented with a stuffing of lobster, scallops, and crabmeat, drizzled with a beurre blanc sauce and served with creamy asparagus risotto. Hint: This is a great date-night destination. $$$

EATING OUT

Coronado

Beach Diner (619-437-6087; www.nadolife.com), 1015 Orange Ave. Open daily for breakfast, lunch, and dinner. Breakfasts are especially good at this retro diner, and portions are large: check out the pile of homemade waffles or any entrée that comes with the fresh hash browns. For lunch and dinner, consider the chili cheese fries piled high with melting cheddar or a plate of three sliders, served with grilled onions and pickles. Soda fountain selections include traditional New York egg creams, purple cows (vanilla ice cream and grape soda), and root beer floats. Word of warning: Service can be (and usually is) slow. $

✪ **Lil' Piggy's Barbeque** (619-522-0217), 1201 First St. Open daily for lunch and dinner. In the Coronado Ferry Landing shopping center, Lil' Piggy's packs them in for authentic Southern barbecue that includes pulled pork, beef brisket, and sticky baby back ribs. The restaurant also offers a huge selection of beers. Dine inside or out, and don't miss the fried pickles. $$

Miguel's Cocina (619-437-4237; www.brigantine.com/locations_miguels.html), 1351 Orange Ave. Open daily for lunch and dinner. Across the street from the Hotel del Coronado, this Miguel's (there are two others—one in Point Loma and another in Chula Vista) is a sit-down restaurant that offers authentic carne asada burritos and tacos, along with interesting entrées like calamari rellenos and

MIGUEL'S COCINA

jalapeño shrimp. Snag a table on the outside patio for a festive atmosphere. $$

Stretch's Café (619-435-8886), 943 Orange Ave. Open daily for breakfast and lunch. This casual eatery offers wholesome, tasty dishes, with many vegetarian options. Check out the Spinach Fandango, a casserole of spinach, mushrooms, brown rice, and cheese; homemade soups served with corn bread or banana bread; and the healthy smoothies. $

Downtown

🍸 **BASIC** (619-531-8869; www.barbasic.com), 410 10th Ave. Open daily for dinner (until 2 AM) and sporadically for lunch. In the East Village of downtown, near Petco Park, this favorite with the before- and after-Padres baseball crowd serves thin-crust Connecticut-style pizzas and top-shelf cocktails. The chic space is industrial—it was converted from a 1912 warehouse—with exposed bricks, high ceilings, and garage doors. Locals have voted this the best pizza in the city for several years, thanks to simple, high-quality ingredients. BASIC takes on a second life as an über-cool hangout when the cocktail crowd moves in after midnight. $$

✪ 🏵 ▼ **Café 222** (619-236-9902; www.cafe222.com), 222 Island St. Open daily for breakfast and lunch. Take your time reading the entertaining breakfast menu; it's clear the owner has a keen sense of humor. The café is famous for its pumpkin waffles, which are light and delicately flavored, and the amusing green eggs and Spam, a scramble served with spinach and jack cheese. Because of its diminutive interior, Café 222 is usually packed on weekend mornings. $

🏵 ✐ **Filippi's Pizza Grotto** (619-232-5094), 1747 India St. Open daily for lunch and dinner. A longtime staple of the charming Little Italy neighborhood, Filippi's has been a San Diego institution since 1950. In addition to extra-cheesy meatball and pepperoni pizzas, Filippi's serves an awesome veggie special, with black olives, mushrooms, bell pepper, and onions. The red-and-white vinyl tablecloths and inexpensive bottles of Chianti remind visitors that this restaurant was a mainstay even before the neighborhood underwent a dramatic revitalization in the late 1990s. $

🏵 **Greek Islands Café** (619-234-2407), 879 W. Harbor Dr. Open daily for lunch and dinner. This little take-out Greek restaurant is the best dining value in Seaport Village (on the harbor downtown, and within easy walking distance of the cruise ship terminal), serving classic Greek appetizers like hummus and *tzatziki* (yogurt with cucumber), and especially good spanakopita (spinach pie). Eat on the patio outside and enjoy million-dollar views of the harbor. $

🏵 🍸 **Kansas City Barbeque** (619-231-9680; www.kcbbq.net), 610 W. Market St. Open daily for lunch and dinner. Made famous in the 1986 Tom

Cruise movie *Top Gun*, Kansas City Barbeque has been in the same harbor-front location for years, and the downtown gentrification has grown up around it without in any way touching it. It's just as greasy and rough around the edges as it was when Maverick and Goose bellied up to the bar. Try the meaty baby back ribs (ask for extra sauce). $$

Old Town

El Indio (619-299-0333; www.el-indio.com/), 3695 India St. Open daily for lunch and dinner. When much else has changed in the city, El Indio, near Old Town, remains remarkably similar to its 1940s roots. Soft grilled chicken tacos and carnitas are among the best in town. Homemade guacamole and chips are for sale to go, which is a perfect way to start a fiesta at home (or in your hotel room). Parking is tight, but it's worth the effort. $

Y **Old Town Mexican Café** (619-297-4330; www.oldtownmexcafe.com), 2489 San Diego Ave. Open daily for lunch and dinner. Old Town Mexican Café is a longtime favorite with locals, not the least because of their monster margaritas. (Try the Purple Cadillac.) Combinations featuring typical Mexican fare (tacos, enchiladas, burritos, fajitas) are all good choices. Look for the "tortilla ladies" cranking out handmade tortillas by the thousands. $$

Uptown

▼ **Hash House A Go Go** (619-298-4646; www.hashhouseagogo.com/breakfast.html), 3628 Fifth Ave. Open Tues.–Sun. for breakfast and lunch. This extremely popular uptown café in Hillcrest (an artsy neighborhood just north of downtown) merits the standing-room-only crowd that lines up every weekend. Portions are massive and reasonably priced. Although the hash for which the place is named is extraordinary (especially the unusual meat loaf hash with spinach and mozzarella), I'm a big fan of the pizza-sized flapjacks. $

▼ **Urban Mo's** (619-491-0400; www.urbanmos.com), 308 University Ave. Open daily for breakfast, lunch, and dinner. Describing itself as a "hetero-friendly gay restaurant," this upscale comfort-food haven in Hillcrest offers daily specials like tequila shrimp and fajitas. Try the stuffed burgers for a gourmet treat, or build your own burger with their long list of fixings. $$

> **INSIDER TIP:** To stretch your dining dollar, check out Urban Mo's $5 weekday breakfast special, which includes scrumptious French toast and hearty breakfast burritos.

✱ Entertainment

San Diego rivals Los Angeles for live music venues and rivals New York for quality theater. Clubs come and go quickly, so those listed have proven staying power. To locate the newest underground clubs and to get listings for live music, check the local *Reader* newspaper (available throughout downtown and at most hotels) or online at www.lo-cal.com/venues/sandiego.

CLUBS Y **Altitude Sky Lounge** (619-696-0234; www.altitudeskylounge.com), 660 K. St., San Diego. Located on the 22nd floor of the San Diego Marriott Gaslamp Quarter, Altitude has my vote as the best rooftop bar in the city. Imagine a beach party in the middle of the city, with a casual urban vibe and plenty of beautiful people. Guests can snuggle up in lounge beds next to fire pits, nibble on appetizers like truffle French fries, or enjoy the truly inspiring views of the skyline, the harbor, and Petco Park. (On game days you can even watch a game from the lounge.)

✪ 🍸 **East Village Tavern and Bowl** (619-677-2695; www.bowlet.com), 930 Market St., San Diego. This downtown newcomer in East Village is part sports bar, part bowling alley, part pool hall, part gastropub—and 100 percent fun. Food selections are typical but tasty (burgers, tacos, and even some salads), and the bar is extensive.

🍸 **The Fleetwood** (619-702-7700), 639 J St., San Diego. This Gaslamp restaurant and bar is casual and hip, and for these reasons is the very essence of San Diego nightlife. In addition to a $4 cocktail "Power Hour" and a well-loved Sun. champagne brunch, The Fleetwood offers karaoke every Sun. at 9 PM, dancing and DJs every Thurs.–Sat., and 50 percent off all bottles of wine every Wed. The signature cocktail is the La Parma, fashioned from vodka, pear puree, and Parmesean cheese. (Trust me: it's better than it sounds.)

🍸 **4th and B** (619-231-4343; www.4thandb.com), 345 B St., San Diego. One of the premier live music venues in town, this 20,000-square-foot, one-thousand-seat Gaslamp Quarter facility (housed in a former bank) features live music from just about every genre.

🍸 **Jimmy Love's** (619-595-0123), 672 Fifth Ave., San Diego. Housed in the beautiful old City Hall building (and onetime city library), dating to 1887, this large Gaslamp restaurant and bar features contemporary American cuisine and live music nightly, including jazz, blues, and 1980s dance music.

THEATERS ✪ **Old Globe Theater** (619-234-5623; www.theoldglobe.org), 1363 Old Globe Way, San Diego. The Tony Award–winning Old Globe is the oldest professional theater in California, located at the center of Balboa Park. It is home to more than five hundred performances a year on its three stages, and an astonishing number of original shows have gone on to Broadway. The outdoor Lowell Davies Festival Stage hosts the Summer Shakespeare Festival from mid-June through the end of Sept.

San Diego Repertory Theater (619-544-1000; www.sdrep.org), 79 Horton Plaza, San Diego. The nationally acclaimed San Diego Repertory Theater started out in 1976 as a street theater company in which one time San Diegan Whoopi Goldberg was involved. A decade later, the Rep partnered with the City of San Diego when it moved into the downtown Lyceum Theater at Horton Plaza Shopping Center and became steward to the Lyceum complex.

Spreckels Organ Pavilion (619-702-8138), south of El Prado in Balboa Park. The pavilion in Balboa Park, which seats 2,400 and is also the site of community dance and music groups, houses the Spreckels Organ, the largest outdoor musical instrument in the world. There are free concerts year-round every Sun. 2–3.

Starlight Theater (619-544-7827; www.starlighttheatre.org), 2005 Pan American Plaza, San Diego. The Starlight Bowl in Balboa Park hosts

> **INSIDER TIP:** For half-price discounts on day-of-performance tickets, check out the ARTS TIX booth at the front of Horton Plaza downtown (www.sandiegoperforms.com).

outdoor musical productions in a venue that just happens to be right in the (noisy) flight path of the jets landing at Lindbergh Field. Actors often pause midsentence to allow a plane to pass.

✷ Selective Shopping

There are a number of eclectic, entertaining shopping areas in and around downtown San Diego, including **Horton Plaza** (619-239-8180), a mainstream outdoor mall with dazzling multilevel architecture. Just off the harbor, **Seaport Village** (619-235-4014) is a 14-acre waterfront shopping district that is designed to look like a well-manicured fishing village at the turn of the 20th century. Be sure to let little ones ride the relocated 1895 carousel. Just north of town, check out the **Kettner Art and Design District,** along Kettner Boulevard in Little Italy, which comprises more than 20 unique home-décor boutiques. In Old Town, look for the relocated **Bazaar del Mundo** (619-296-3161), just a few blocks from its old site in the Old Town State Historic Park. **Fiesta de Reyes** (619-297-3100), in the heart of Old Town, is a pseudo-period retail and dining complex; the Old West/Old Mexico–themed area offers live music and entertainment on the weekends on an open-air stage; small shops scattered throughout sell period souvenirs, toys, crafts, and books. To the south, check out Point Loma's old Naval Training Center, which is now an expansive retail, entertainment, and dining complex called **Liberty Station** (www.libertystation.com), at Rosecrans Street and Womble Road.

TOP 10 DAY IN DOWNTOWN SAN DIEGO

1. Indulge in a breakfast bread pudding at Café Chloe (see p. 48)
2. Stroll along El Prado in Balboa Park (see pp. 37–38)
3. Make a morning visit to the pandas at the San Diego Zoo (see pp. 40–41)
4. Lunch on vegetarian pie at Filippi's Pizza Grotto (see p. 50)
5. Shop at Seaport Village (see p. 53)
6. Visit the USS *Midway* Aircraft Carrier Museum (see p. 37)
7. Dig in to filet mignon at Lou and Mickey's in the Gaslamp (see p. 48)
8. Attend a live performance at the Old Globe Theater (see p. 52)
9. Relax with a nightcap at Jbar on the roof of Hotel Solamar (see p. 46)
10. Overnight at the Manchester Grand Hyatt (see pp. 46–47)

LA JOLLA AND THE CENTRAL BEACH TOWNS

Hardly a person arrives in San Diego without visiting at least one of the popular beaches that stretch north of downtown. Just beyond Lindbergh Field Airport and the mid-rises of the city center is Mission Beach, a youthful neighborhood that is dominated by a lovely white-sand beach, an old-fashioned boardwalk, and a vintage roller coaster. This is a major party scene, especially on weekends and holidays, and it is *the* place to experience the exuberant carnivalesque atmosphere that is inherent in a handful of beaches in Southern California. Just east of the coastline of Mission Beach, across a small expanse of pricey real estate, is Mission Bay, a human-made aquatic park that serves as every San Diegan's backyard. Here guests will find miles of flat bike paths (popular with runners and in-line skaters), dozens of children's playgrounds, acres of tropically landscaped lawn for picnics and flying kites, and the lovely bay itself, which is ideal for waterskiing, Jet Skiing, and fishing. Northward along the coastline is Pacific Beach, dominated by the old pier and home to thousands of surfers who claim these waters starting at sunrise. Travel a few miles northward to upscale La Jolla, quite literally "the jewel" of Southern California. In addition to stunning natural beauty, which rivals the Amalfi Coast for pristine blue waters and sculptural cliff formations, La Jolla offers some of the best luxury shopping, galleries, and fine restaurants in the city.

PLEASURE POINT (2006), BY NANCY RUBINS, AT THE MUSEUM OF CONTEMPORARY ART SAN DIEGO

Photo by Pablo Mason. Used with permission.

TORREY PINES STATE BEACH

✷ To See

MUSEUMS ✪ **Museum of Contemporary Art San Diego** (858-454-3541; www.mcasd.org), 700 Prospect St., La Jolla. Open Tues.–Thurs. 11–5. This internationally known museum has a permanent collection of more than three thousand works representing myriad art genres from the past half century and includes paintings, sculpture, photography, video, and multimedia works. The beautiful building, which was designed by famous architect Irving Gill in 1916, is spectacularly located on the La Jolla Cliffs overlooking the ocean. General admission $10, students and seniors $5, individuals 25 and younger free. There is also a downtown venue (see the "Downtown and Its Nearby Neighbors" chapter).

PARKS **Kate Sessions Memorial Park,** in Pacific Beach; take Lamont St. north. Named after the legendary landscape designer of Balboa Park, this hilltop green space has a sweeping view of the ocean and bay and beautiful city lights after dark, as well as a large expanse of lawn with mature trees and miles of dirt hiking trails.

Mission Bay Park, off Mission Bay Dr. Mission Bay offers numerous recreational activities, especially for families and fitness buffs. Visitors will find a paved and nearly flat bike path that runs from De Anza Cove on the northeast side of the park (accessed off the Mission Bay Dr. exit from I-5) through a 2.5-mile arc that passes several children's playgrounds, acres of lush grass lawn, and follows the waterline to the Mission Bay Parkway bridge. It's possible to rent sailboats, Jet Skis, powerboats, and aquatic bicycles at several junctions or launch your own watercraft via one of several public boat launches. The area has fire rings, picnic tables, and large covered pavilions (most of the latter

INSIDER TIP: Although there are usually a few children splashing in the calm waters of Mission Bay, the pollution levels, thanks to the powerboats and runoff from local drains, makes this a fairly bad idea.

require a permit to reserve them). **Fiesta Island,** little more than a dirt mound in the middle of the eastern portion of the bay, is the site of the raunchy, softball-like Over-the-Line Tournament every summer; the rest of the year it reigns as party central. **SeaWorld** is sited along the southern perimeter.

Mount Soledad Park, north of Mount Soledad Rd., La Jolla. The 43-foot cross on the top of Mount Soledad in La Jolla that is part of a monument to war veterans has been a source of controversy over the years, but recent Supreme Court rulings have determined that the religious symbol is a local institution and thus will stay put—at least for now. The park provides panoramic views of La Jolla and, on really clear days, south to Mexico and north to Santa Catalina Island.

Sunny Jim Cave (858-459-0746; www.cavestore.com), 1325 Cave St., La Jolla. Open daily 9–5. Kayakers in La Jolla Cove can explore six different ocean caves, carved through the years by the relentless waves. The most interesting of these is probably the Sunny Jim Cave, named by L. Frank Baum (author of *The Wizard of Oz*) after a 1920s cartoon character the opening of the cave is said to resemble. The cave is also accessible via a human-made tunnel and network of 145 steps (which can be slippery) through the **Cave Store.** Adults $4, children $3.

✱ To Do

BICYCLING Independent bikers will find miles of beautiful coastline to explore in this area. Some of the easiest routes can be found on the flat bike paths that crisscross Mission Bay (see *Parks*). Those seeking some guidance are well advised to book an organized trip, which usually includes bike rentals. Check out the following organizations: **Hike Bike Kayak Surf** (858-551-9510; www.hikebikekayak.com/Biking_San_Diego.php) and **La Jolla Kayak** (858-459-1114; www.lajollakayak.com).

GOLF **Mission Bay Golf Course** (858-581-7880; www.sandiego.gov/park-and-recreation/golf/mbgolf.shtml), 2702 N. Mission Bay Dr., San Diego. Guests to this small establishment will find a par 58 executive course with 18 holes near Mission Bay. The course is lighted at night until 10 PM. Green fee: $23–29.

✪ **Torrey Pines Golf Course** (800-985-4653; www.torreypinesgolfcourse.com), 11480 N. Torrey Pines Rd., La Jolla. One of the nation's premier municipal golf facilities and home of the 2008 U.S. Open, with 36 holes, a driving range, and equipment rentals, this PGA-sanctioned course is extremely popular with serious local golfers and is a must-play for visiting duffers. Deep canyons and dense vegetation make the course feel farther away from civilization than it really is. Almost every hole has a view of the ocean. Green fee: $250.

SPAS ✪ **The Spa at Estancia** (858-550-1000; www.estancialajolla.com/la-jolla-california-spa), 9700 N. Torrey Pines Rd., La Jolla. Part of the **Estancia Resort** (www.estancialajolla.com), near the University of California, San Diego, this lovely spa offers serene surroundings amid native gardens. Specialties include the hot stone massage, which features heated basalt stones soaked in aromatic oils, and a Gentleman's Cleanse, a manly facial.

The Spa at Torrey Pines (858-453-4420; http://spatorreypines.com), 11480 N. Torrey Pines Rd., La Jolla. Offering day-spa services as well as exclusive amenities for guests of **The Lodge at Torrey Pines,** this elegant spa offers detoxifying seaweed and mud wraps, soothing milk baths, and a panoply of massage treatments.

SpaTerre at Paradise Point (858-274-4630; www.paradisepoint.com/paradise_spaterre.aspx), 1404 Vacation Rd., San Diego. On Mission Bay, at the secluded **Paradise Point Resort and Spa,** this tropical sanctuary specializes in a blissful all-day Thai herbal therapy that blends aromatherapy, full-body massage, and a decadent facial. Also popular is the Balinese massage, which combines acupressure with rolling motions to ease sore muscles.

THEME PARKS AND ZOOS ✐ **Belmont Park** (858-488-1549; www.belmontpark.com), 3190 Mission Blvd., San Diego. Hours vary by season. Drive into Mission Beach, and you can't miss the white-washed wooden roller coaster called the Giant Dipper, which has been rattling riders for eight decades. You'll also find the newer Beach Blaster, a giant "arm ride," and the FlowRider, a simulated wave maker. The iconic coaster closes down for several weeks in the winter for routine repairs, and then reopens Thurs.–Sun. until late May. Park admission is calculated by height (because young children and petite adults are not allowed on many of the rides): over 50 inches, $23; under 50 inches, $16. Or purchase individual ride tickets for $2–6.

✐ **Birch Aquarium at Scripps** (858-534-3474; www.aquarium.ucsd.edu), 2300 Expedition Way, La Jolla. Open daily 9–5. A compact aquarium that is part of the Scripps Institution of Oceanography at the University of California, San Diego, the Birch sits atop a cliff overlooking one of the most spectacular ocean views in the city. Enjoy these vistas at the extensive outdoor tide pool exhibit, where visitors can touch creatures such as starfish and sea cucumbers and watch local Garibaldi fish swim through human-made ponds. More exotic specimens are available inside the aquarium, including ethereal jellyfish, leafy sea dragons that look like something out of a Dr. Seuss book, and various varieties of small sharks. Adults $12, seniors $9, children $8.

> **INSIDER TIP:** The Birch Aquarium hosts a summertime concert series and is one of the best vantage points from which to watch the Fourth of July fireworks in La Jolla.

✪ ✐ **SeaWorld** (800-257-4268; www.seaworld.com), 500 Sea World Dr., San Diego. Open daily; hours vary by season. Part aquarium, part amusement park, and part botanical garden, SeaWorld is deservedly world famous, and its feature killer whale Shamu has been San Diego's unofficial mascot for decades. Animal shows are the heart of this 189-acre aquatic park, so be sure to get a map and show schedule at the front entrance and plan the day accordingly. During off-peak season, there are only two Shamu shows a day. On busy days plan to arrive about 30 to 45 minutes prior to showtime to get a good seat. Another highlight of the park for little ones is the Sesame Street Bay of Play, a 2-acre Sesame Street–themed interactive fun zone with rides, movies, and character meet-and-greets. If you visited SeaWorld a decade or so ago and haven't been back lately, you'll be surprised to find several water-themed thrill rides on the property, including the newest, Journey to Atlantis, a fast-paced water roller coaster ride that plunges 60 feet while riders listen to a soundtrack of dolphin calls; Shipwreck Rapids, a white-water raft adventure through waterfalls and spouting water jets that is guaranteed to leave you drenched; and Wild Arctic, a convincing simulator ride onboard a faux helicopter. The real fun of SeaWorld is getting personally involved with the attractions. Pet a California bat ray at Forbidden Reef, watch the antics of the tuxedoed cuties at the indoor Penguin Encounter, stroll through a 57-foot acrylic tube as sand tiger and bonnethead sharks swim overhead at the 280,000-gallon Shark Encounter, or visit the classic Tide Pool exhibit to pet starfish and sea cucumbers. For a considerable investment, guests 13 years and older can also climb into a pool with beluga whales for a chance to be an animal trainer for the day at the Wild Arctic Interaction attraction. Adults and children 10 and older $69, children two to nine $59.

INSIDER TIP: Watch out for the marked bleachers in the first dozen or so rows in SeaWorld arenas, which indicate the "soak zone." It's a near certainty that occupants of these seats will get drenched with 50-degree salt water that smells of fish.

✷ Water Sports

BOATING ✪ ❀ ***Bahia Belle*** (858-488-0551; www.catamaranresort.com/dining3.html), 998 W. Mission Bay Dr., San Diego. For only $10, you can board this Mississippi riverboat stern-wheeler and cruise Mission Bay, all the while dancing and enjoying cocktails (for an additional charge). Purchase boarding tickets at the Bahia and Catamaran resorts (the *Bahia Bell* sails between the two). Early cruises are family friendly, and children can board for only $3. Note that cruises are seasonal, so call ahead for precise operating days and hours.

✐ **La Jolla Kayak** (858-459-1114; www.lajollakayak.com), 2199 Avenida de la Playa, La Jolla. La Jolla Kayak rents kayaks to experienced paddlers, and for novices offers one-and-a-half-hour guided tours through the La Jolla caves, including a special sunset tour. Be sure to make an advance reservation for both tours and rentals.

Mission Bay Aquatic Center (858-488-1000; www.missionbayaquaticcenter.com), 1001 Santa Clara Pt., San Diego. The Mission Bay Aquatic Center claims to be the largest waterfront instructional facility in the world, offering classes in sailing, kayaking, rowing, windsurfing, and wakeboarding.

Seaforth Boat Rental (619-223-1681; www.seaforthboatrental.com), 1641 Quivira Rd., San Diego. Located on Mission Bay (as well as Coronado and the harbor downtown), this company rents out sailboats, Jet Skis, and speedboats. They also provide crewed sunset sail cruises and charter fishing expeditions.

DIVING AND SNORKELING Two favorite dive spots in this area are the La Jolla kelp forests and **Wreck Alley,** an artificial reef made up of sunken vessels. Dive shops and charter boats will ferry guests out to the wrecks, which are thriving with marine life. The **San Diego–La Jolla Underwater Park Ecological Preserve,** just off the coast of La Jolla Cove and running north to Torrey Pines State Preserve, is a 6,000-acre marine habitat. The visibility is generally good and the waters are relatively calm, which makes for some of the best diving on the coast (although waters are cold year-round; bring a wet suit!). The **La Jolla Submarine**

Canyon off La Jolla Shores is one of the deepest places in the world and offers divers a dramatic series of clifflike ledges to explore. The San Diego City Lifeguard Service provides updated recorded diving information (619-231-8824). Note that spearfishing requires a license (available at most dive stores), although it is illegal year-round to take any sea life from the San Diego–La Jolla Underwater Park Ecological Preserve. Local dive shops include **Diving Locker** (858-272-1120; www.divinglocker.com), 6167 Balboa Avenue, San Diego, and **Scuba San Diego** (619-260-1880; www.scubasandiego.com), 1775 E. Mission Bay Drive, San Diego.

FISHING Mission Bay has several launch points for deep-sea fishing, including **Mission Bay Sportfishing** (619-222-1164; http://missionbaysportfishing.com), 1551 W. Mission Bay Drive, San Diego, and **Seaforth Landing** (619-224-3383; www.seaforthboatrental.com), 1717 Quivira Road, San Diego, which offer day trips to the Point Loma kelp beds and multiple-day trips aboard the long-range fleet of fishing boats. Anglers can expect to reel in bonito, yellowtail tuna, and—seasonally—giant squid (which makes for very good eating).

SURFING Some of the best surfing in San Diego County can be found in this region, including the shores at Mission Beach, especially near the jetty off Mission Boulevard; Pacific Beach; Tourmaline Surfing Park; La Jolla Shores; Scripps Pier; and Black's Beach (see the detailed list of beaches in *Green Space*). Beware: The waves are crowded, and the natives are territorial, especially at the beaches in La Jolla. Surf lessons will get beginners up on a board in less time than you might expect, although it takes years of practice and innate athletic ability to really be good. Reliable surf schools include **Menehune Surf** (858-663-7299; www.menehunesurf.com), 8070 La Jolla Shores Drive, #478, La Jolla, **Mission Bay Aquatic Center** (858-488-1000; www.missionbayaquaticcenter.com), 1001 Santa Clara Point, San Diego, and **Surf Diva** (858-454-8273; www.surfdiva.com), 2160 Avenida de la Playa, La Jolla, the latter of which offers girls- and women-only classes in addition to coeducational lessons and camps. If the waves are flat at the beach, check out the **Wave House Athletic Club** (858-228-9300; www.wavehouseathleticclub.com), 3115 Ocean Front Walk, San Diego, in Mission Beach, where patrons ride a wave-generating device that promises the perfect swell every time.

✷ Green Space

BEACHES **Black's Beach.** From Torrey Pines Rd., follow the signs to the Glider Port; park in the dirt lot and hike down the cliff pathways (or during low tide, walk north past the Scripps Pier from La Jolla Shores). Between 1974 and 1977, Black's Beach, just north of La Jolla Shores, was officially designated as a swimsuit-optional beach. Because nudity was (and still is) banned at all other San Diego–area beaches, uninhibited people were attracted in droves to Black's. Although Black's lost its official designation as a nude beach decades ago, the tradition continues at the northern end. This is also a popular beach with surfers.

Children's Pool, off Coast Blvd., south of La Jolla Cove. Despite its name, this crescent-shaped beach just south of La Jolla Cove is not overrun with children but rather with sea lions. The city has made recent attempts to take back the beach for the children for whom it was intended, but environmentalists have balked—and

SEA LIONS AT CHILDREN'S POOL

federally protected sea lions are likely to rule the shore for years to come. It is illegal to approach the wildlife, and thus the beach itself usually isn't accessible, but it is fun to watch the entertaining (albeit smelly) creatures bask on the sand from the elevated walkway above. Also look for **Seal Rock** just offshore, another favorite spot for sea lions.

✪ **La Jolla Cove,** off Coast Blvd., west of Prospect St., La Jolla. This gorgeous small beach is protected on three sides by the *C*-shaped cliffs, and water here is generally clear emerald green. The waters are calm enough for snorkeling (and thanks to the San Diego–La Jolla Underwater Ecological Reserve just off the coast, there's a decent chance of spotting sea life, especially the bright orange Garibaldi that call Southern California home). You might even find yourself swimming alongside a sea lion. The adjacent **Ellen Browning Scripps Park** is an expansive grassy lawn at the top of the Cove stairs, ringed by a sidewalk that follows the lines of the Cove and heads south to Children's Pool.

LA JOLLA COVE

✪ **La Jolla Shores,** off Vallecitos St., La Jolla. Crystal blue waters, white-sand beaches, and countless oiled bodies baking in the sun define La Jolla Shores, which has some of the loveliest views, calmest waves, and widest strips of sand in the city. This is a great place to kayak, thanks to the gentle waves, and it's a popular place to take surf lessons as well. Hike from the parking lot north past the Scripps Pier to get away from the crowds—although be careful not to get stranded during high tide (and too far north ventures into the clothing-optional zone of Black's Beach).

Mission Beach, south off Mission Blvd., Mission Beach. There are 2 miles of sand from the north entrance of Mission Beach to Pacific Beach, and these 2 miles are packed body to body on weekends and all through the summer, making this one of the most popular—and crowded—beaches in the city. The wide boardwalk is immensely popular with in-line skaters, runners, and bikers.

Pacific Beach, north off Mission Blvd., Pacific Beach. Pacific Beach officially runs from the north end of Mission Beach, where the boardwalk terminates and becomes a sidewalk, north to the Crystal Pier. This can be a raucous scene and not necessarily the best for families. This beach is popular with surfers as well. Restroom facilities, showers, and fire rings are plentiful, although parking is not.

✪ ✐ **Torrey Pines State Beach and Reserve** (858-755-2063), off Hwy. 101, north of La Jolla. This is a quiet, relatively uncrowded beach on all but the hottest summer weekends. Access the shores via the many trails coming down off the cliffs (although be careful, because these can be unstable) or park in the adjacent lot and walk southward. This is one of the best family beaches in the city and very popular with longtime locals.

Windansea, off Nautilus St., La Jolla. An offshore reef makes for huge waves (when the conditions are right), making this a world-class surfing destination—made famous by Tom Wolfe in his novel *The Pump House Gang*. This is a popular beach for sunbathing as well, even though the shoreline is rocky; the extra effort to hike in keeps the beach secluded.

NATURE PRESERVES ✪ **Torrey Pines State Reserve** (858-755-2063; www.torreypine.org), off Hwy. 101, north of La Jolla. Well-worn trails wind through the native scrub brush and indigenous (and rare) Torrey pines and along cliffs that lead to pristine ocean vistas. These trails are heavily trafficked, especially on weekends. Enter via the ranger station entrance near the beach and drive up the steep

LA JOLLA SHORES

roadway to the top of the cliff to access the trails. Or for a serious workout, park at the beach and hike up (but watch out for cars—there are no sidewalks). Parking $12.

✷ Lodging

La Jolla

PRICE KEY FOR A STANDARD ROOM:	
$	$100 or less
$$	$101–150
$$$	$151–250
$$$$	$251 and up

✪ **The Grande Colonial** (858-454-2181; www.thegrandecolonial.com), 910 Prospect St. The immaculately preserved Grande Colonial is the oldest hotel in La Jolla, dating to 1913. Idyllic guest rooms are decorated in a romantic cottage style featuring sunny citrus fabrics and vintage details. Bathrooms are somewhat small but make up for their size with sleek finishes and thick robes. The small round pool is heated to a comfortable 82 degrees year-round. The Grande Colonial allows nearly instant access to La Jolla Cove, upscale shopping, and fine dining, but guests needn't stray off property to experience exquisite California cuisine: **Nine-Ten** on-site is one of the most highly regarded restaurants in the city. In addition to the main hotel, the property also owns and manages the eight-room **Little Hotel by the Sea** next door and the adjacent 10-room **Garden Terraces,** each of which offer small kitchens and more room to spread out. Both of these accommodations are quite pricey but offer the chance to feel like a resident, thanks to homey touches like wooden floors, deep whirlpool tubs, and plenty of seating for friends. $$$$

Hotel La Jolla (800-237-5211; www.sealodge.com), 8110 Camino del Oro. Formerly known as the Sea Lodge, the Hotel La Jolla is directly on the sands of La Jolla Shores, one of the most swimmable and family-friendly beaches in San Diego. The resort offers a small heated pool and a tiny spa, as well as a spacious courtyard. Oceanside accommodations have balconies or patios looking toward the sea, just a few dozen yards from the water's edge. The interiors are decorated with lustrous Italian wood furniture and warm fabrics. The bathrooms aren't as luxurious as one might expect for these prices, and the architectural design screams 1970s, but the overall vibe is understated elegance. $$$–$$$$

⚤ **La Jolla Beach and Tennis Club** (800-624-2582; www.ljbtc.com), 2000 Spindrift Dr. An elite gathering place for locals who come for the 12 championship tennis courts and the landmark **Marine Room** restaurant, the distinctly upscale La Jolla Beach and Tennis Club, directly on La Jolla Shores, is an exclusive enclave for the well-heeled. The property offers guest rooms and suites, including one- to three-bedroom beachfront accommodations that are big enough for families. Public spaces show off gleaming wood and clubby accents, and private interiors are decorated with beach-inspired motifs. $$$$

La Jolla Cove Suites (888-525-6552; www.lajollacove.com), 1155 Coast Blvd. I highly recommend this hotel to anyone on a tight budget. It isn't luxurious or trendy, but the location can't be beat: it is just across the street from La Jolla Cove and within easy walking distance of some of the finest restaurants in San Diego. The suites feature commodious seating areas, full kitchens, and expansive balconies—and those that face the ocean have incomparable views across the water. There's a small pool and spa in the back, and the views from the rooftop deck are breathtaking. $$–$$$

La Valencia (858-454-0771; www.lavalencia.com), 1132 Prospect St. Since 1926, the much-lauded Spanish Colonial "pink lady"—just steps from the beloved La Jolla Cove beach—has lured the rich and famous with its impeccable service and considerable snob appeal. While on property, enjoy the clubby on-site **Whaling Bar** and rub elbows with gentrified locals; this is also a good place for a power lunch. There are three restaurants on-site, including the **Mediterranean Room** (858-551-3765) and the **Sky Room** (858-551-3765), the fine-dining venue. Thanks to an impressive reputation, the La Valencia commands blisteringly expensive rates, but note that the standard guest rooms (which can be priced at close to $400 in season without an ocean view) are tiny, as are the bathrooms. $$$$

The Lodge at Torrey Pines (858-453-4420; www.lodgetorreypines.com), 11480 N. Torrey Pines Rd. This immaculate Craftsman-style property sits on the 18th green of the famous **Torrey Pines Golf Course** and is considered one of the finest resort destinations in the state. Although the lodge isn't directly on the beach, many rooms offer distant views of the water, as well as some equally spectacular views of the golf course. Due to the premier on-site **Spa at Torrey Pines** and world-class dining at **A.R. Valentien,** many guests find it hard to leave the property. The posh lodging is surprisingly family friendly, too, with

Courtesy of The Lodge at Torrey Pines

THE LODGE AT TORREY PINES

organized activities for kids like water-balloon fights, scavenger hunts, and Lincoln Log building contests. $$$$

Mission Bay

Bahia Resort (800-576-4229; www.bahiahotel.com), 998 W. Mission Bay Dr. A Mission Bay fixture for half a century, the Bahia is evocative of the tropics, with meandering water features and palm trees. The resort is family friendly, with an active kids' club throughout the year and a "Mad Science" camp for the 5- to 12-year-old set in the summer. Children will also enjoy the seal pond, where the Bahia has license to keep seals on the property. $$$

Paradise Point Resort and Spa (858-274-4630; www.paradisepoint.com), 1404 Vacation Rd. The self-contained island in Mission Bay on which this resort sits has more than a mile of sandy beaches; expansive, lush gardens; an 18-hole putting course; five pools, one of them with a spectacular tropical waterfall; championship tennis courts; a full-service marina to rent a wide variety of boats and water toys; two on-site restaurants; and an exotic spa. There's almost no reason to leave this property—but the resort is centrally located, which means no more than a 10- to 15-minute drive to downtown or to nearby La Jolla. The property has been recently renovated. $$$.

Pacific Beach

Crystal Pier Hotel (800-748-5894; www.crystalpier.com), 4500 Ocean Blvd. You can't get any closer to sleeping on the water without a boat: this collection of tidy white and blue cottages is built right on the Crystal Pier in Pacific Beach, directly above crashing waves. Cottages are equipped with hardwood floors, simple furniture, and kitchenettes. Book at least six months in advance for summer and holiday stays. $$$

▼ **Tower 23** (858-270-2323; www.t23hotel.com), 723 Felspar St. Named after the nearby lifeguard tower of the same number, this ultrahip hotel sports minimalist design fashioned from glass, concrete, and steel. Guest rooms have spare interior design and feature walk-in rain showers and aromatherapy baths. The hotel is within easy walking distance to the Crystal Pier, numerous restaurants, and the rowdy nightlife that makes Pacific Beach a perennial favorite with twentysomethings. Guests don't have to go off-site for a great cocktail lounge. The chic on-site restaurant, **Jrdn** (858-270-5736), boasts a sleek interior and a large outdoor patio just off the boardwalk, with a sushi bar, a fireside patio, and a casual fire pit. $$$

PARADISE POINT RESORT

Courtesy of Paradise Point Resort

INSIDER TIP: Check the Web site for good values on hotel and spa packages at the Paradise Point Resort. Online rates can be dramatically lower than those quoted over the telephone.

✷ Where to Eat

DINING OUT

La Jolla

A.R. Valentien (858-453-4420; www.arvalentien.com), 11480 N. Torrey Pines Rd. Open daily for lunch and dinner. At the **Lodge at Torrey Pines,** A.R. Valentien was voted by *Condé Nast Traveler* magazine as one of the top 10 farm-to-table restaurants in the country. Chef Jeff Jackson is committed to buying only locally raised produce and meat and seafood that has been harvested in a sustainable fashion, and he and his accomplished staff prepare these ingredients with a light hand. The food is clean, bright, and

PRICE KEY FOR A TYPICAL ENTRÉE:

$	$10 and under
$$	$11–20
$$$	$21–30
$$$$	$31 and up

surprising. The seasonal menu can include braised pork belly with blue-cheese-stuffed dates, roasted chicken with fennel, and divine *tres leches* cake with roasted apple cream. Every Thurs. the restaurant features a communal Artisan Table, with a four-course menu served family style and paired with wines selected by the chef ($75). Between courses guests have the opportunity to meet the chefs and discuss the evening's menu. $$$$

✪ **Cody's** (858-459-0040; www.codys .com), 8030 Girard Ave. Open daily for breakfast, lunch, and dinner. Housed in a charming yellow cottage surrounded by a white picket fence, Cody's is a comfortable place to enjoy a casual meal on the patio while looking out over La Jolla Cove. For breakfast, the classic eggs Benedict is served over your choice of a crispy bed of oniony home fries or a mound of grits. Or for an intimate dinner, dine inside in the bistro-style dining room on the likes of duck confit quesadilla with jalapeños and red onions, or the crostini with Brie, pear-jalapeño jam, and fig compote. For an unusual entrée, try the pumpkin-seed- and coriander-crusted tuna served rare with white bean and garlic puree. Desserts are comfortingly homey and include apple pie à la mode, Southern red velvet cake, and a decadent flourless chocolate cake. $$

Y **George's at the Cove** (858-454-4244; www.georgesatthecove.com), 1250 Prospect St. Open daily; times vary by venue. For decades, George's in La Jolla (sitting just above the La Jolla Cove) has been *the* place to celebrate a special occasion, thanks to impeccable cuisine and spectacular oceanfront views. The recently renovated George's is actually a collection of three venues: **George's Modern,** a fine-dining option with an ever-changing seasonal menu of California dishes, featuring Nieman Ranch beef and sustainable seafood; the **Ocean Terrace,** which offers a more casual atmosphere and rooftop dining; and **George's Bar,** a gastropub that offers entrées like steak frites and spaghetti with clams. (Foodies will want to check out the restaurant's Web site, which often shares recipes.) $$–$$$$

✪ **The Marine Room** (858-459-7222; www.marineroom.com), 2000 Spindrift Dr. Open daily for dinner. This La Jolla landmark is considered by many locals to be the most romantic place to dine in San Diego. The restaurant juts out over the sand, and during high tide the waves sometimes crash against the expansive windows. As lovely as the seaside setting is, the real attraction is Chef Bernard Guillas's exquisite French cuisine: exotic ingredients arrayed in inventive recipes are brought to the table with formality and panache. When available, don't miss the fennel-pollen scented Maine lobster tail served with a perfumy fruit polenta and Lemoncello butter. Or for red-meat lovers, try the game trilogy (elk, antelope, and venison) served with a trio of chutneys and white asparagus. $$$$.

✪ **Nine-Ten** (858-964-5400; www .nine-ten.com), 910 Prospect St. Open daily for breakfast, lunch, and dinner. This intimate restaurant in the **Grande Colonial Hotel** offers a bevy of cutting-edge, high-style California choices. Menus change seasonally, but look for first courses like the baby beet salad served with roasted carrots, toasted walnuts, baby fennel, and arugula, and the marinated black mission figs with white truffle oil, both exquisitely plated. Nine-Ten serves my all-time favorite interpretation of wine-braised short ribs, tender, meaty, and succulent. (These are so popular the restaurant even offers a version for breakfast:

tasty short-ribs hash.) For $120, guests can put themselves at the "Mercy of the Chef" for an unforgettable five-course meal paired with wines (or $90 without wines). $$$

🍸 **Roppongi** (858-551-5252; www.roppongiusa.com), 875 Prospect St. Open daily for lunch and dinner. This popular weekday happy hour destination has a lively sidewalk patio, as well as a Zen-like indoor dining room, a full bar, and a small sushi bar. Try the signature starter, the Polynesian crab stack, a gorgeously engineered tower of crabmeat, avocado, mango, red onions, and pea shoots served with an oil-free ginger sauce. Main courses are generously proportioned and are perfect for sharing: Favorites include the crispy striped whole bass, pan-seared mahimahi, and the luscious pineapple fried rice. $$–$$$

Trattoria Acqua (858-454-0709; www.trattoriaacqua.com), 1298 Prospect St. Open daily for dinner, weekends for brunch. It is hard to imagine a prettier venue: outdoor terraces brimming with flowers, cozy patios with killer views of the La Jolla Cove, and a festive gazebo room for large parties create an inviting ambiance. The extensive Mediterranean menu offers luxurious jumbo shrimp wrapped in phyllo pastry with creamy avocado and a tangerine and orange vin cotto, and paper-thin ahi served with shaved fennel, arugula, watermelon, and lemon-horseradish vinaigrette. On weekends brunch is served, including creamy eggs Benedict paired with crabcakes, washed down with a generous glass of mimosa. $$$

Whisknladle (858-551-7575; www.whisknladle.com), 1044 Wall St. Open daily for dinner. Tucked into a quiet section off the main drag of La Jolla, this pretty patio bistro has created a

Courtesy of Amy Fellows

FARE FROM WHISKNLADLE

buzz in the culinary world. In 2008, Condé Nast picked this locavore eatery as among the top 125 tables in the world. Chef Ryan Johnston controls everything he serves by making it all in-house: Whisknladle bakes its own breads, smokes its own meats, pickles its own pickles, and churns its own ice creams and sorbets. The management is committed to securing everything else locally, from the best organic farms in Southern California. The result is a menu that changes constantly with the seasons. $$$

EATING OUT

Mission Bay

✪ 🏵 **Rubio's** (858-272-2801; www.rubios.com), 4504 E. Mission Bay Dr. Open daily for lunch and dinner. The original site of a beloved local chain of Mexican grills that can now be found throughout Southern California, this walk-up taco stand is the brainchild of local boy Ralph Rubio, who during his college years fell in love with authentic

INSIDER TIP: Look for $1.25 fish or shrimp tacos at Rubio's every Tuesday.

street tacos in the surfing town of Ensenada, Mexico. Ralph started this first small taco shop in the early 1980s, and it was here that locals were first introduced to the Baja-style fish taco, now unofficially recognized as the signature dish of San Diego, consisting of fried whitefish in a corn tortilla, a creamy white sauce and another spicy sauce made from smoky chiles, topped with a mound of shredded cabbage. The tacos are served with limes to squeeze on top, and there is a salsa bar on the premises. $

Pacific Beach

Kono's Café (858-483-1669), 704 Garnet Ave. Open daily for breakfast, lunch, and dinner. Just west of the famous Crystal Pier in party-hearty Pacific Beach, this Hawaiian-themed diner is a longtime local favorite, serving up huge portions of good food at an exceptional value. Expect long lines stretching around the corner on weekends (although the line usually moves fast). Order one of the famous hamburgers, or consider the breakfast items, which are served all day long. $

RUBIO'S FISH TACOS

Los Panchos Taco Shop (858-272-0567), 1775 Garnett Ave. Open daily for lunch and dinner. Pacific Beach has no shortage of inexpensive Mexican joints, but the authenticity of Los Panchos makes it stand out from the crowd: here you'll get more Mex and less Cal. Try the crispy carnitas tacos and burritos. $

Rocky's Crown Pub (858-273-9140; www.rockyburgers.com/Rockys), 3786 Ingraham St. Open daily for lunch and dinner. This unassuming joint in Pacific Beach claims to be the home of the best burger in San Diego—and who are we to argue? Mix one-third-pounder juicy burgers with raw or grilled onions, a side of salty fries, and beer on tap, and you have the recipe for a heavenly afternoon. Don't bring the kids along, however. No one under 21 is admitted. $

La Jolla

Elijah's Delicatessen (858-455-1461), 8861 Villa La Jolla Dr. Open daily for breakfast, lunch, and dinner. Located near the University of California, San Diego, and tucked into a nondescript strip mall, Elijah's has been a local favorite for decades, thanks to exceptional quality, huge portions, and inexpensive prices. I favor the mile-high Reuben, but you can't go wrong with any sandwich featuring pastrami. Hot specials include stuffed cabbage rolls, beef brisket, and a hearty chicken noodle soup. Breakfasts come with some of the best bagels in the city, and there is also an on-site bakery with authentic New York cheesecake and raspberry rugelach. $–$$

Girard Gourmet (858-454-3325; www.girardgourmet.com), 7837 Girard Ave. Open daily for breakfast and lunch. This gourmet deli and Belgian bakery specializes in flaky breakfast croissants, delectable cookies, and gourmet items sold by the pound. There are a handful of tables to eat on-site, but most folks take their food to go; this is a great place to gather supplies for a picnic at the nearby Ellen Scripps Park that overlooks lovely La Jolla Cove. $$

Y **La Jolla Brewhouse** (858-456-6279; www.lajollabrewhouse.com), 7536 Fay Ave. Open daily for dinner. This brewhouse isn't what you'd expect in hoity-toity La Jolla: the slightly rough-around-the-edges bar decorated with surfboards and fishing trophies attracts a mostly locals crowd, from longtime neighborhood devotees to college students. Guests can pick from a seasonal menu of beers brewed on-site, as well as a selection of casual food. $–$$

Y **The Spot** (858-459-0800; www.thespotonline.com), 1005 Prospect St. Open daily for dinner. This establishment holds a special place in my heart, because it is one of the few I could afford on luxe Prospect St. when I was a college student living nearby. Although there are a handful of pricey surf-and-turf options on the menu, the Build-Your-Own Burger is a bargain—and a treat. Choose everything to your liking, from the patty (beef, bean, chicken, turkey), to the bun (wheat, sourdough, jalapeño, etc.), to the sauce (wasabi cucumber, Thai peanut, garlic aioli, etc.). The Spot also offers great thin-crust pizzas. The place still draws college students and gets a little rowdy after 9 PM on weekends. $–$$

✱ Entertainment

CLUBS Y **Comedy Store La Jolla** (858-454-9176; www.comedystorelajolla.com), 916 Pearl St., La Jolla. Some of the best comedy acts in the country have made their way to the stage at the famous Comedy Store. In its heyday in the 1980s, Robin Williams used to show up unannounced and unbilled, and Whoopi Goldberg got her start here.

Y **Whaling Bar** (858-531-3764; www.lavalencia.com/dining/whaling-bar-grill.php), 1132 Prospect St., La Jolla. Within the hallowed halls of the exclusive **La Valencia Hotel,** the Whaling Bar is a clubby, old-fashioned lounge with mahogany tables, retro décor, and scrimshaw collections. Come for a subdued evening of cocktails and quiet discussions.

THEATERS **La Jolla Playhouse** (858-550-1070; www.lajollaplayhouse.org), campus of the University of California, San Diego, La Jolla. Considered one of the finest regional theaters in the country, the La Jolla Playhouse has premiered more than 30 productions that have gone on to Broadway. The theater was founded in 1947 by La Jolla native Gregory Peck. The venue includes four stages, allowing for a variety of experiences and wildly imaginative staging.

✱ Selective Shopping

Serious shoppers will gravitate to two of the largest malls in the city: **Fashion Valley Mall** (619-688-9113), 7007 Friars Road, just off I-163; and just a few miles east, **Mission Valley Mall** (619-296-6375), 1640 Camino del Rio N. For more intimate shopping, fashionistas from around the world flock to **La Jolla's Prospect Street,** in downtown La Jolla, and its almost-as-fabulous sister Girard Street (which runs perpendicular to Prospect). Shop at high-end clothing and home décor boutiques, browse abundant art galleries, and rub elbows with the beautiful people. While in the area,

ARTISANAL BEER IN SAN DIEGO

San Diego is increasingly known as a destination for brew connoisseurs, thanks to a growing collection of microbreweries around town, which include the following.

- **Ballast Point Brewing Company** (858-695-2739; www.ballastpoint.com), in the tiny community of Linda Vista, just north of Mission Valley, offers scotch ales and German Klosch-style beers.
- **Karl Strauss Brewing Company** (858-273-2739; www.karlstrauss.com) calls Southern California home, with locations in downtown, La Jolla, and Carlsbad. Check out seasonal beers like the Fullsuit Belgian-style Brown Ale.
- **Port Brewing** (800-918-6816; www.portbrewing.com), an offshoot of the popular **Pizza Port** (858-481-7332) restaurant in Solana Beach (with additional locations in Carlsbad and San Clemente in Orange County), offers up their own label, known as The Lost Abbey (www.lostabbey.com), for which the company follows monastic and artistic Belgian brewing traditions.
- **San Diego Brewing Company** (619-284-2739; www.sandiegobrewing.com), near the Qualcomm Stadium in Mission Valley, offers one of the largest draft selections in the county, with more than 50 beers on tap daily, seven of which are brewed on-site. Note that there is also a restaurant on-site that serves exceptionally tasty burgers.
- **Stone Brewing Company** (760-471-4999; www.stonebrew.com) in Escondido (eastern North County) is considered to be one of the best breweries in the United States by Ratebeer.com and Beer Advocate.com. The company brews more than 50,000 barrels a year. The site offers public brewery tours twice daily on weekdays and every hour on the hour during regular weekend hours. Private tours can also be arranged.

If you're serious about checking out several breweries in one day, consider tours like the **Brew Hop** (858-361-8457; www.brewhop.com), a two-and-a-half-hour tour through three breweries that includes samples; or the **Brewery Tours of San Diego** (619-961-7999; www.brewerytoursofsandiego.com), which includes transportation, tours, and tastings Friday through Sunday.

don't miss the opportunity to peruse the books at the fine independent bookstore and stationer **Warwicks** (858-454-0347), 7812 Girard Street, and check out stunning photographs at **Images of Nature** (858-551-9553), 7916 Girard Ave. In Pacific Beach, look for the **Pangaea Outpost** (858-581-0555), 909 Garnet Avenue, which offers more than 70 merchants under one roof selling clothing and home décor from around the world.

TOP 10 DAY IN LA JOLLA

1. Wake up with crab Benedict and home fries on Cody's patio (see p. 65)
2. Window-shop along Prospect Street (see p. 68)
3. Peruse the latest exhibit at the Museum of Contemporary Art San Diego (see p. 55)
4. Picnic at La Jolla Cove on chicken curry and almond salad from Girard Gourmet (see p. 67–68)
5. Snorkel and swim at La Jolla Cove (see p. 60)
6. Watch the sunset over Children's Pool and a beach full of sea lions (see p. 59)
7. Sip an aperitif in the lobby at La Valencia (see p. 63)
8. Dine on braised short ribs at Nine-Ten (see pp. 65–66)
9. Finish the day with late-night cocktails at the Whaling Bar (see p. 68)
10. Overnight at the elegant Grande Colonial (see p. 62)

NORTH COUNTY SAN DIEGO

North County San Diego officially begins just beyond La Jolla and runs along the coastline through Del Mar (which incorporates Solana Beach), Encinitas (which incorporates Cardiff-by-the-Sea), and Carlsbad (which incorporates Leucadia). To the east is Escondido, and beyond the lovely mountain town of Julian. A few decades ago, coastal North County was little more than a collection of strawberry fields (in Carlsbad) and poinsettia farms (in Encinitas)—two of the largest agricultural businesses in the area, sprinkled amid sleepy surf towns. Although small farms can still be found today, rural areas are isolated pockets that are now overwhelmed by the sprawling, upscale suburbs and increasingly popular beach towns. The vibe is definitively more laid-back here than in San Diego City proper, thanks to less congestion (although you'll doubt my word if you travel the horrendous I-5 freeway during rush hour through Del Mar and Carlsbad). Visitors will find the major attractions of San Diego a little far flung from North County, but if you appreciate the greater serenity—or if you want to concentrate on the attractions here (Legoland, the San Diego Zoo Safari Park, and fabulous beaches, to name a few), the rewards include slightly less expensive lodging and fine dining, the best selection in the area of spas and golf resorts, and friendly natives who couldn't be happier with their hometowns.

✷ To See

HISTORICAL SITES ✐ ⚥ **Mission San Luis Rey de Francia** (760-757-3651; www.sanluisrey.org), 4050 Mission Ave., Oceanside. Open daily 9:30–4:30. Often called the "King of the Missions" (because it is the largest), the Mission San Luis Rey is the 18th in a line of 21 Spanish missions established in California. Visitors can stroll through re-creations of mission living quarters and explore a small garden courtyard before stepping into the large church, which has hand-painted ceilings and walls, a bright cupola highlighted with skylights, and carved and painted wooden religious statues. An audio tour narrates continually during visiting hours. Adults $6, students $4, children under seven free.

Oceanside Pier, located off Third St., Oceanside. This historic structure is the longest wooden pier on the West Coast, spanning nearly 2,000 feet in length. The pier was originally built in the late 19th century and was subsequently destroyed by storms several times over. The current pier was rebuilt in 1987 and is a popular spot for fishing.

MUSEUMS **California Surf Museum** (760-721-6876; www.surfmuseum.org), 312 Pier View Way, Oceanside. Open daily 10–4. Surfing is a way of life for many who live in San Diego, and this fun museum (recently relocated) is dedicated to all things that pertain to board sports. Check out the hundred-year time line of surfing culture in Southern California, vintage boards, photographs, and interactive exhibits. Adults $3, children $1.

✐ **Lux Art Institute** (760-436-6611; www.luxartinstitute.org), 1550 S. El Camino Real, Encinitas. Open Thurs. and Fri. 1–5, Sat. 11–5. The Lux Art Institute is an exhibit venue that highlights the work of contemporary artists—and it is also a place where visitors can go to watch art-making in progress. The artist-in-residence program allows guests to observe artists painting, sculpting, and so forth, and at the same time experience their finished works in a vibrant museum setting. Adults $10, visitors under 21 free.

✐ **Museum of Making Music** (760-438-5996; www.museumofmakingmusic.org), 5790 Armada Dr., Carlsbad. Open 10–5; closed Mon. and holidays. You'll find more than five hundred instruments on display, as well as traveling exhibits, at this small museum near Legoland. There are also hands-on exhibits that allow patrons the chance to make their own music. The museum hosts a Local Flavor concert series featuring musicians from Southern California. Adults $7; seniors, active military, and students $5.

PARKS ✐ **Leo Carrillo Park** (760-476-1042), 6200 Flying LC Lane, Carlsbad. Open 10–5; closed Mon. This rambling ranch and restored original adobe buildings gives visitors a taste of old California. Leo Carrillo, a prominent San Diegan in the mid-20th century and an actor (best known for his role as Pancho in the 1950s *Cisco Kid* series), bought the ranch in 1937 and restored the 1800s-era buildings himself. Today visitors can stroll the trails, take a guided tour through the buildings, and observe native vegetation in the extensive gardens. Throughout are cacti specimens that are more than one hundred years old, and pathways are lined with citrus trees and aloe vera plants. Look for the wild peacocks, descended from a

PONTO BEACH IN CARLSBAD

TOP 10 DAY IN NORTH COUNTY SAN DIEGO

1. Enjoy a "black egg" breakfast burrito at Swami's Café (see p. 85)
2. Stroll the San Diego Botanic Gardens (see p. 79)
3. Visit Minitown at Legoland (see p. 75)
4. Stage a photo op at the Flower Fields of Carlsbad (see p. 79)
5. Lunch on a pulled pork sandwich at Smokin' Joeys Barbeque (see p. 84)
6. Indulge in a Lomi Lomi massage at the nearby Spa at La Costa (see p. 74)
7. Check out happy hour at the BlueFire Grill at La Costa (see p. 80)
8. Dine on lobster and blue crab potpie at Twenty/20 Grill and Bar (see p. 82)
9. Dance the night away to live bands at the Belly Up Tavern (see p. 85)
10. Overnight at the Grand Del Mar Hotel and Resort (see p. 81)

flock Carrillo kept, that roam the grounds. The park periodically sponsors a night-time film festival, with screenings in the old stable. Admission is free.

✷ To Do

GOLF **Arrowood Golf Course** (760-967-8400; www.jcgolf.com/courses-arrowood.php), 5201A Village Dr., Oceanside. Located next to a protected wildlife refuge at the far reaches of North County, in Oceanside, this serene course was designed by Ted Robinson Jr. Green fee: $100.

Crossings at Carlsbad (760-444-1800; www.thecrossingsatcarlsbad.com), 5800 The Crossings Dr., Carlsbad. This new municipal course in south Carlsbad takes its design inspiration from the canyons and surrounding wetlands. Note that this course is directly in the flight path of the small Palomar Airport, which is just down the road, and the air traffic—and noise—from small commercial jets and recreational planes is especially heavy on weekends. Green fee: $85–120.

Encinitas Ranch Golf Course (760-944-1936; www.jcgolf.com/courses-encinitas.php), 1275 Quail Gardens Dr., Encinitas. With 18 championship holes carved into the bluffs of Encinitas, overlooking the ocean, Encinitas Ranch provides a scenic golfing experience on a par 72 course. Green fee: $75.

✪ **Grand Golf Course** (858-314-2000; www.thegranddelmar.com/golf), 5300 Grand Del Mar Ct., Del Mar. Located on the property of the exquisite **Grand Del Mar Resort,** this par 71 course designed by Tom Fazio offers more than 7,000 yards of greens and deceptive bunkers, making this one of the most challenging courses in the city. Green fee: $195–215.

> **INSIDER TIP:** Significant discounts apply at the posh Grand Golf Course for twilight tee-offs.

✪ **Park Hyatt Aviara Golf Club** (760-603-6900; www.jcgolf.com/courses-encinitas.php), 7447 Batiquitos Dr., Carlsbad. Formerly known as the

Four Seasons Aviara, this pricey, 18-hole course in the suburbs of south Carlsbad was picked by *Condé Nast Traveler* as the number one golf resort in Southern California. Designed by Arnold Palmer to take advantage of the lovely views of the adjacent Batiquitos Lagoon, the course has great variety and some especially difficult holes. Green fee: $215–235.

SPAS **Golden Door** (760-744-5777; www.goldendoor.com), near Escondido (mailing address: P.O. Box 463077, Escondido, CA 92046). This legendary spa has spawned a handful of upscale offshoots throughout the country, but the tranquil, lush site in eastern North County San Diego is the original. The Golden Door is one of the most exclusive spas in the world and offers weeklong stays in plush accommodations, surrounded by Zen-like Japanese gardens. Facilities include three guest lounges, a dining room, indoor-outdoor exercise facilities, two swimming pools, and a bathhouse with steam room, sauna, showers, and a therapy pool. Traditional spa treatments like massage and facials are offered, as well as fitness classes, yoga and meditation, and nutritional services.

L'Auberge Del Mar Spa (800-245-9757; www.laubergedelmar.com/california-spas), 1540 Camino Del Mar, Del Mar. Located at the resort of the same name, this spa was completely renovated and newly reopened in 2009. Indulge in the Polynesian Journey, a nearly two-hour treatment that begins with a luxurious coconut pulp and sea salt scrub exfoliation that finishes with a warm coconut wrap.

Ocean Pearl Spa (760-827-2702; www.oceanpearlspa.com), 5480 Grand Pacific Dr., Carlsbad. At the **Sheraton Carlsbad Resort,** the Ocean Pearl Spa offers a sophisticated, serene setting and myriad indulgent treatments. Try the signature Coastal Waters Body Mask, which includes an organic ocean-mud wrap and a full-body sea salt exfoliation (which smells a tiny bit fishy, but it washes away easily and leaves the skin glowing). Many packages include a light spa luncheon as well, provided by the impeccable **Twenty/20 Grill.**

✪ **Spa at La Costa** (800-854-5000; www.lacosta.com), 2100 Costa Del Mar, Carlsbad. This grand dame of spas has been a mecca for decades for the well-heeled looking to rejuvenate and relax. On-site guests will find luxury accommodations, a championship golf course, and this expansive spa—home of the Chopra Center for Well Being, founded by Deepak Chopra. The white Spanish-style architecture, manicured gardens, and the ever-present sound of flowing water are enough to put guests in a relaxed state of mind, but don't miss the opportunity to indulge in at least one treatment before giving over a day to relaxing at the delightful spa pool. The one-hundred-minute Passport Indulgence starts with a brown sugar and Dead Sea salt scrub, moves on to a luxurious Egyptian milk bath, then a massage

SPA AT LA COSTA

Courtesy of La Costa Spa & Resort

with aromatic oils, and finally a lotus body wrap.

THEME PARKS AND ZOOS

Legoland (760-918-5346; www.lego.com/legoland), 1 Legoland Dr., Carlsbad. Open Thurs.–Mon. (Sept.–May) and daily June–Aug. Opens 10 AM; closing is seasonal. Legoland California is a theme park unlike any other, because in addition to the usual rides and attractions, this 100-plus-acre park is largely made up of the tiny, colorful namesake bricks, which are used in enormous quantity and to staggering effect. More than 20 million Legos were used just to design Minitown—a small portion of the park that features scale models of famous cities. The rest of the park is divided into several zones, including Dino Island, Fun Town, Explore Village, Knights Kingdom, and Imagination Zone, together offering more than 50 rides and attractions, many of which are kid powered via rope pulling, pedal pushing, and water squirting. Children past 10 or so will probably not be excited by the park, unless they are huge Lego fans. Beware of strict height restrictions for the little ones, however, which range from 34 to 48 inches for even the tamest rides. Adults $67, children under 13 $57.

Courtesy of San Diego CVB

LEGOLAND

Legoland Water Park (760-918-5346; www.legoland.com), 1 Legoland Dr., Carlsbad. Open Thurs.–Mon. (Sept.–May) and daily June–Aug. Opens 10 AM; closing is seasonal. Opened in the summer of 2010, the more than 5-acre Legoland Water Park extends the appeal of the adjacent **Legoland** by including attractions that will amuse a wider range of ages. Offerings include six-person raft slides, single-person tube slides, and extensive water play areas for toddlers and young children. The Lego branding is never out of sight, as the new park is adorned with Lego statues and decked out in Lego colors. This is unlike other water parks in Southern California in that families can interact with hands-on projects, like a build-your-own raft, which once completed serves as a rideable vehicle for the lazy river attraction. A separate entry fee is required, but significant discounts apply when purchased as a package with either Legoland or **Sea Life Aquarium,** or both. Adults $77, children under 13 $67 (includes admission to Legoland).

✪ **San Diego Zoo Safari Park** (760-747-8702; www.sandiegozoo.org/wap), 15500 San Pasqual Valley Rd., Escondido. Opens 9 AM daily. Part of the San Diego Zoological Society (which also operates the **San Diego Zoo**), the Safari Park (formerly known as the Wild Animal Park) is a 2,200-acre wildlife preserve located 30 miles northeast of San Diego where visitors have a chance to see animals in huge enclosures that mimic their natural habitats. More than three thousand animals

Courtesy of San Diego CVB

SAN DIEGO ZOO SAFARI PARK

call the park home, including almost 50 species that are endangered. There are miles of trails winding through the beautifully landscaped grounds—which include approximately 4,000 species of plants, more than 250 of which are also endangered—and dozens of exhibits and guided hikes. The highlight of a park visit is the Journey into Africa Tour, which takes visitors into the wide-open enclosures for a close-up look at the animals. Guests will see giraffes, elephants, gazelles, zebras, rhinoceros, and dozens of other rare and endangered animals. Other not-to-be-missed exhibits include the Lion Camp, where visitors view lions through a glass wall at exhibits designed to allow the animals to come closer than they otherwise could in a traditional enclosure; Condor Ridge, a scenic trail through a habitat created for animals indigenous to North America; and a children's petting zoo. For an additional fee, guests can take part in such adventures as the Photo Caravan Safaris and the extremely popular overnight Roar and Snore camping adventure, where guests overnight in tents set up adjacent to the elephants and the African savanna. Adults $37, children $27.

INSIDER TIP: Considerable savings are available with multiday and multipark passes that allow visits to the San Diego Zoo, the San Diego Zoo Safari Park, and SeaWorld. Three-park passes are available at each location.

Sea Life Aquarium (760-918-LEGO; www.sealifeus.com), 1 Legoland Dr., Carlsbad. Open daily; hours vary by season. In 2008, this aquarium and ocean-themed park opened right next door to Legoland. (Sea Life Aquarium has a secondary entrance that allows guests to walk in directly from Legoland.) Although there are tanks of sea life to observe and sea life exhibits and attractions, guests never get far from the Lego brand here: expect to see Lego buildings underwater, too! The highlight is the Lost City of Atlantis exhibit, which offers up enormous fish tanks and whimsical faux Lego reefs. There are also a handful of small-scale rides, a petting pool, and gift shops. The Legoland parent company has plans to expand this park, but for now it is very small, and even for the most curious children can be seen in fewer than two hours. Note, also, that this is themed to very young children. Anyone older than seven or eight is likely to be bored. Adults $19, children $12. (Combination Legoland/Sea Life Aquarium tickets offer substantial discounts.)

✷ Water Sports

FISHING Catch deep-sea fishing trips from Oceanside Harbor via **Helgren's Oceanside Sportfishing** (760-722-2133; www.helgrensportfishing.com), 315 Harbor Dr. S., Oceanside, which offers day trips to local kelp beds up to 3 miles out and multiple-day trips (up to six days) to Guadalupe and islands off the coast of Mexico, depending on where the fish are running. (This is also a good bet for whale-watching tours out of North County in the winter.)

SURFING

Don't let the increasingly sophisticated restaurants, wine bars, and upscale shopping fool you: North County San Diego is still a surfer's paradise. **Swami's** is a world-famous surfing beach in Encinitas, chosen by *Surfing* magazine as one of the 10 best surfing cities in the country—only one of four in California and the only one chosen in San Diego County. Wave riders should also check out **15th Street Beach** in Del Mar and **Cardiff Reef,** and farther north **Leucadia State Beach, Ponto Beach** (aka Carlsbad State Beach), and **Tamarack Surf Beach** in Carlsbad. **Oceanside Beach** at the Strand and Sixth Street are also popular. Good surf schools include **Kahuna Bob's Surf School** (760-721-7700; www.kahunabob.com), 2526 Woodland Way, Oceanside, and **Surfin' Fire** (760-473-2281; www.surfinfire.com/oceanside.html), which has lessons at Ponto Beach in Carlsbad, near the pier in Oceanside, and Moonlight Beach in Encinitas.

WHALE WATCHING

From December through March, it's possible to observe the southerly migration of California gray whales from Alaska to the warm-water lagoons of Baja California, where they give birth and raise their young. The massive creatures come within a few miles of the San Diego coastline during their 5,000-mile migration, so it's easy to spot them from the shoreline—and several organized boat tours offer a money-back guarantee if you do *not* see a whale while aboard one of their excursions. Good options include tours originating from **H&M Landing** (www.hmlanding.com), **Hornblower Cruises** (www.hornblower.com), and **OEX Dive and Kayak Centers** (www.oexcalifornia.com), which offers a guided kayak tour. Landlubbers will get their best views from the **Birch Aquarium at Scripps** in La Jolla, the **Cabrillo National Monument,** or the pier in Oceanside. Peak migration is mid-January, when as many as two hundred whales a day have been spotted off the coastline.

✷ Green Space

BEACHES **Carlsbad State Beach,** off Hwy. 101, north of La Costa Blvd. South Carlsbad Beach, known to locals as Ponto Beach, has a paid parking lot ($12 for a weekend day, with seasonal passes available), and a long expanse of free street parking to the north of La Costa Blvd. (although this can be next to impossible to find, especially in the early morning hours, when surfers arrive before dawn). The crowds are generally manageable, and the beach is popular with families and local surfers.

Del Mar City Beach, 15th St. and Coast Blvd. Except during high tides, visitors can walk all the way down the coast from the northernmost stretch of beautiful Del Mar City Beach to Torrey Pines State Beach to the south. Several reefs off the coast make for good surf breaks, especially at 15th St. and 11th St. From Oct. through May, dogs are allowed to run at Rivermouth, the northernmost section of the beach.

Moonlight State Beach, off Encinitas Blvd., Encinitas. Waves at this romantically named beach can be massive, which translates to heavy surfer traffic. There are fire rings and volleyball courts just beneath the elevated parking lot.

Oceanside City Beach, off N. Coast Hwy. Just north of the Oceanside Pier, near the Oceanside Harbor, Oceanside City Beach has a nice covered picnic area. The beach is wide and long, and waves are good—this is the site of several surfing championships throughout the year.

✪ **Swami's Beach,** off Hwy. 101, south of the Self-Realization and Fellowship Center, Encinitas. Made famous by the Beach Boys' unofficial California anthem, *Surfin' USA*, the breaks off Swami's are world renowned. The secluded beach has a tiny off-street parking lot that fills up quickly, but roadside parking is generally available. Take the steep staircase from the parking lot at the top of the cliffs down

SWAMI'S BEACH

to the shores to a peaceful, relatively uncrowded stretch of sand. In early winter (at low tide), the beach offers good tidepooling, with anemones, starfish, sea cucumbers, and even the occasional tiny octopus.

GARDENS ✐ **Flower Fields of Carlsbad** (760-431-0352), corner of Palomar Airport Rd. and Paseo del Norte, Carlsbad. In the spring these 50 acres transform into a dazzling mosaic of brilliantly colored flowers, planted in rainbow ribbons. Growers harvest more than 8 million ranunculus here every year. For a (somewhat hefty) price, starting in Mar. and through early May, visitors can stroll through the fields, take photographs, and enjoy other garden-related attractions, including a sweet pea maze and activities for children. The fields overlook the ocean and a decorative windmill, which give the feeling of being someplace altogether different than North County San Diego. Call ahead for prices and hours, as these change every season.

✐ **San Diego Botanic Gardens** (760-436-3036; www.sdbgarden.org), 230 Quail Gardens Dr., Encinitas. Open daily 9–5. Formerly known as Quail Botanical Gardens, the 35 acres of exhibits at this oasis include a bamboo orchard, a Mediterranean landscapes garden, and a subtropical fruit garden. The miles of trails that crisscross the property wind by a gingerbread-style gazebo that is a child magnet. You'll also find a lily pond (that blooms most prodigiously in Aug.) and a peaceful, secluded waterfall. Don't miss the Garden of Lights (5–9 PM) during Dec., when the park strings up more than 100,000 lights to celebrate the holidays. Adults $12, seniors and active military $8, children 12 and younger $6. Parking $2.

Self-Realization Fellowship Temple and Ashram Center (760-753-2888), 215 K St., Encinitas. Open Tues.–Sat. 9–5 and Sun. 11–5. You can't miss the temple driving along the Coast Hwy. in Encinitas; the large cream-colored structure is topped with several gold-leafed onion domes, and the temple itself is surrounded by a high stucco wall. Along the side entrance on K St., access the small meditation gardens, which are open to the public during daytime hours. Stroll through a well-manicured shade garden and enjoy a koi pond and small waterfall. At the summit of the garden there is a panoramic view of the ocean and several benches to contemplate the beauty of the surroundings. Admission is free.

"WHERE THE SURF MEETS THE TURF"

The **Del Mar Race Track and Fairgrounds** (858-755-1161), 2260 Jimmy Durante Boulevard, Del Mar, has been billed as the place "Where the Turf Meets the Surf" for the past half century. This glamorous seaside thoroughbred racing track is one of the best racing venues in the world and in the summer one of the biggest parties on the West Coast. Del Mar consistently posts record-breaking pari-mutuel exchanges, and track attendance has grown consistently over the past several decades. Races run six days a week (the track is closed on Tuesday) in August through early September, with post times generally at 2 PM. Del Mar is home to the Pacific Classic, a Grade I event that draws the nation's top thoroughbreds and the season's largest crowds.

✷ Lodging

Carlsbad

✐ ▼ **La Costa Resort and Spa** (760-438-9111; www.lacosta.com), 2100 Costa Del Mar Rd. This longtime North County resort is internationally known as a premier spa and the site of several important golfing and tennis events throughout the year. Guests can enjoy seven sparkling pools (one with a water slide worthy of a theme park, alongside an extensive water-play area designed for young children), world-class golf on two PGA 18-hole courses, and boutique shopping. Guests enjoy premier access to the exceptional spa, which includes a thunderous Roman waterfall and 15,000-square-foot outdoor patio. On-site dining includes **Legends Bistro** (800-854-5000) and the **BlueFire Grill** (800-854-5000). Children will love the new Kid's Club at La Costa, with a 7-foot tree house, a 600-gallon saltwater aquarium, computer and video games, and a teen lounge that offers music and dancing, billiards, and a gaming lounge. $$$$

✪ ⚥ **Park Hyatt Aviara Resort** (760-603-6800; www.parkaviara.hyatt.com), 7100 Four Seasons Pt. Formerly the Four Seasons Aviara, this gorgeous property perched on a hill in south Carlsbad overlooks its own golf course, the Batiquitos Lagoon (a protected wildlife sanctuary), and the Pacific Ocean in the distance. On-site is an incomparable spa that offers more than 20 kinds of massages, facials, and body scrubs; an Arnold Palmer–designed golf course; a tennis center with lighted clay and hard courts; outstanding on-site restaurants; and a complimentary children's program. The Lobby Lounge offers a luxurious afternoon high tea for a moderate price. The main north–south freeway (I-5) is only miles away, and the restaurants and shops of downtown Carlsbad and Encinitas are also nearby. $$$$

PRICE KEY FOR A STANDARD ROOM:

$	$100 or less
$$	$101–150
$$$	$151–250
$$$$	$251 and up

✐ **Sheraton Carlsbad** (800-325-3535; www.sheratoncarlsbad.com), 5480 Grand Pacific Dr. This Mediterranean beauty perched on a cliff overlooking Legoland is one of the newest luxury resorts in North County and offers something for everyone. The expansive, tropical pool is pre-equipped with floating toys for young children. There is also a Ping-Pong table, a bean-bag toss area, and a huge play lawn in front, perfect for a breakfast picnic or just letting the kids run off some energy. The biggest draw for families is the proximity to **Legoland;** this property offers discount tickets for the park, as well as a private entrance. For adult indulgences, try the **Ocean Pearl Spa** on-site.The hotel also boasts one of the finest restaurants in Carlsbad: the **Twenty/20 Grill and Bar.** $$$

SHERATON CARLSBAD

Del Mar

⚭ **Grand Del Mar** (858-350-7600; www.thegranddelmar.com), 5200 Grand Del Mar Way. This landmark property in North County debuted its five-star accommodations in late 2007. Although it offers club membership and has 39 exclusive "ownership" suites, the Grand Del Mar also offers 249 guest rooms and 19 suites available for rent. The luxurious resort combines Spanish, Portuguese, Moroccan, and Venetian design elements, all of which reflect the indigenous architecture of San Diego. Guest rooms are spacious, elegant, and intended to pamper. The resort offers a kids' club and a fun teen lounge, so that busy parents can indulge their offspring while they visit the spa or get in a round of golf at the on-site, 18-hole Tom Fazio–designed course. The hotel restaurant **Addison** is making serious waves in the culinary world, thanks to renowned chef William Bradley's Mediterranean interpretation of fresh, local ingredients. $$$$

L'Auberge del Mar Resort and Spa (858-259-1515; www.laubergedelmar.com), 1540 Camino Del Mar. Across the street from the beach and in the heart of downtown Del Mar, this full-service resort pampers guests with superior service and immaculate attention to detail. Recently remodeled guest rooms are bright and light, decorated with cottage-style furnishings in sunny colors, and some include fireplaces. The hotel has lighted tennis courts and a professional on staff for private or group instruction; there is also a pool, an outdoor hot tub, and a lap pool. On-site dining is at the **Kitchen 1540,** which offers sustainable seafood and hormone-free meats. $$$$

✷ Where to Eat

DINING OUT

Carlsbad

Fish House Vera Cruz (760-434-6777), 417 Carlsbad Village Dr. Open daily for dinner. This restaurant–fish house combo constantly changes its menu, based on the catch of the day, but count on mahimahi, salmon, and halibut straight off the boat. All fish is mesquite grilled, which gives it a smoky, light flavor. Start out with the oysters Rockefeller or a bowl of the Boston clam chowder. Each meal comes with a crisp salad and two generously proportioned sides (the cheddar mashed potatoes alone are worth the trip). The portions are really too big to allow for dessert, but if you're game, the pecan apple cheesecake or the rocky road cake are among the many options. Because of the crowds (especially on weekends), don't be surprised if you are rushed a bit through dinner. $$–$$$

Norte (760-729-0903), 3003 Carlsbad Blvd. Open daily for lunch and dinner. Located in the accessible tourist destination of Carlsbad Village, Norte (known for 30 years previously as Fidel's) is a family-run restaurant that is beloved by locals and tourists alike. Try the spicy *albondigas* soup, or for the more adventurous, menudo, a tripe and hominy soup (an acquired taste, for sure). Entrées include carne asada, a buttery, thinly sliced flank steak

PRICE KEY FOR A TYPICAL ENTRÉE:

$	$10 and under
$$	$11–20
$$$	$21–30
$$$$	$31 and up

served with onions and peppers; *pescado ranchero,* grilled mahimahi smothered in a mild red sauce; or nopales, cactus cooked in a spicy tomato and serrano chile sauce and topped with cheese. If the weather permits, request seating in the large outdoor patio beneath colorful umbrellas. $$

✪ 🍸 **Twenty/20 Grill and Bar** (760-827-2400; www.twenty20grill.com), 5480 Grand Pacific Dr. Open daily for breakfast, lunch, and dinner. Suburban hotels like this one don't always offer exceptional restaurants, but Twenty/20 at the **Sheraton Carlsbad** delivers. Step inside to three-sided booths, rough-hewn stone walls, an outdoor patio with distant views of the ocean and an inviting open-air fireplace, and an expansive wine collection. Inventive dishes offer their own whimsical delights—like deep-fried lemon slices mixed amid the exceptional fried calamari, creamy tempura avocado heady with lime juice, and day-boat bisque that can feature either catch of the day or locally grown produce. Specialties include shrimp panzanella, local growers' risotto with squash, and classic steak au poivre. $$$

Del Mar

✪ **Addison** (858-314-1900; www.addisondelmar.com), 5200 Grand Del Mar Way. Open daily for dinner. The signature restaurant of the **Grand Del Mar** resort, this impressive fine-dining venue has been racking up the awards since its debut: *Mobile Travel Guide* awarded the restaurant five stars, and AAA bestowed five diamonds. Culinary superstar chef William Bradley routinely creates masterful dishes, plated artistically and prepared with the freshest, finest ingredients available. Guests can enjoy a three-course meal for $80 or a four-course meal for $98. The seasonal menu changes frequently, but expect gems like risotto with preserved lemon and butternut squash, butter-baked salmon, and black-fig brûlée. $$$$

Arterra (858-369-6032; www.arterrarestaurant.com), 11966 El Camino Real. Open daily for dinner. Arterra, which translates to "art of the earth," specializes in contemporary cuisine that highlights regional products, and the menu changes according to the availability of produce and meats. Look for starters that feature Chino Farms produce, a local grower that consistently provides the best the county has to offer. In season, heirloom tomatoes are served with a cucumber sorbet and a light balsamic vinaigrette, and pepper soup is accented with shrimp and curry croutons. Main courses include Kobe beef and locally caught seafood along with the best imported fish. There is also an extensive sushi menu. $$$

🍸 **Jake's Del Mar** (858-755-2002; www.hulapie.com), 1660 Coast Blvd. Open daily for dinner and for lunch on weekends. Jake's is right on the beach in Del Mar, and the views are no less than breathtaking. The relaxed atmosphere and friendly service attract crowds of all ages, and the food manages to live up to the beautiful surroundings. Fresh fish is always featured on the daily specials, and Jake's will prepare it however you like. For a special treat, order the two oven-roasted Maine lobster tails served with cognac butter. Jake's bar packs them in at sunset, so even if you don't have an appetite, grab a cocktail and enjoy the ocean view. $$

Encinitas

🍸 **El Callejon** (760-758-5651; www.el-callejon.com), 345 S. Coast Hwy. 101. Open daily for lunch and dinner. This colorful patio restaurant tucked in front of the train tracks and near Moonlight Beach has an added bonus:

the bar boasts a selection of more than 75 kinds of tequila, and the bartenders make a mean margarita. The guacamole is mixed fresh daily, and the cream of black bean soup served with bacon and tortillas is a good bet to start. The restaurant offers the usual combination plates, but consider instead the *medallones al cilantro,* filet mignon medallions served with melted cheese and topped with a piquant cilantro sauce. This is a popular choice for young families and tends to be noisy in the early evenings. $$

Trattoria I Trulli (760-943-6800; www.itrulli.signonsandiego.com), 830 S. Coast Hwy. Open daily for lunch and dinner. In the heart of downtown Encinitas, this picturesque Italian bistro has a rustic dining room and well-stocked wine bar, as well as a tiny, romantic sidewalk patio that is perfect for people watching on warm summer evenings. To start, try the simple caprese salad with beefsteak tomatoes and fresh mozzarella, which is as beautiful as it is tasty. Other specialties include *Orecchiette alla Barese*, pasta with broccoli rabe and Italian sausage; juicy roasted chicken stuffed with cheese, spinach, and artichokes; and exquisite homemade ravioli. The wine list is extensive and the offerings are well-priced. The intimate atmosphere and twinkling lights make this restaurant especially appealing for couples in the evenings. $$

Vigilucci's Trattoria Italiano (760-942-7332; www.vigiluccis.com), 505 S. Coast Hwy. Open daily for lunch and dinner. The Vigilucci family has more than a half dozen restaurants throughout the county, and this small trattoria in downtown Encinitas is particularly popular thanks to a cozy candlelit interior and a lively sidewalk dining patio. The salads at Vigilucci's are gorgeous: don't miss their interpretation of a Caesar salad, with hearts of romaine, a creamy house dressing, and fresh shaved Parmesan, which is even better when topped off with fried calamari. Pastas are fresh and substantial; especially good is the *Penne alla Vodka con Porcini,* with mushrooms, fresh tomatoes, and basil in a creamy vodka sauce. And don't miss the *Torta della Nonna,* a sublime dessert pastry filled with lemon cream and dusted with pine nuts. $$

EATING OUT

Carlsbad

Allen's New York Pizza (760-918-9999), 6943 El Camino Real. Open daily for dinner. Allen's is my go-to delivery pizza: thin, crunchy crust;

JULIAN: THE APPLE PIE OF EVERY SAN DIEGAN'S EYE

Say "Julian," and most locals will think of apple pie: this quaint, turn-of-the-20th-century mining town in the Cuyamaca Mountains northeast of San Diego has a half-dozen bakeries on its tiny Main Street that churn out thousands of fragrant pies a weekend, many of them made from fruit harvested from local orchards. Check out the apple crumb at **Mom's Pies** (www.momspiesjulian.com), 2119 Main Street, Julian, for what I think is the best of the bunch. From mid-September through mid-November guests to the area can enjoy the Annual Julian Fall Apple Harvest, which is celebrated with music, art shows, cider pressings, apple picking, and—of course—more apple pies.

good-quality mozzarella; and generous toppings. The restaurant is tucked into a strip mall in Carlsbad, just north of the Spa at La Costa. $

Roberto's (760-634-2909), 1900 Coast Hwy. 101. Open daily for lunch and dinner. Every day Roberto's, in the Leucadia neighborhood of south Carlsbad, cranks out hundreds of inexpensive, authentic tacos, made with thick, crispy corn tortillas and stuffed generously with shredded beef or chicken. This ubiquitous local chain has been serving addictive, slightly greasy food at an extremely good value for years. The lines can be long during mealtime rush, but for about $5 a pop, it's worth the wait. $

Smokin' Joey's Barbeque (760-929-1396; www.joeyssmokinbbq.com), 6955 El Camino Real. Open daily for lunch and dinner. Tucked into a barely noticeable corner of a suburban strip mall and all but hidden from everyone except locals and those in the know, this original outpost of Smokin' Joey's (a small San Diego chain) offers up reliably good barbecue, with the right amount of smoke and a delicious homemade sauce with a little spice and a little sweet. Specialties include spoon-tender baby back ribs, served wet or dry; moist pulled pork and chicken; and—according to my Texan relatives—the best brisket outside the Lone Star State. $

Del Mar

Champagne French Bakery and Café (858-792-2222), 12955 El Camino Real. Open daily for breakfast, lunch, and dinner. This Parisian-style bakery east of Del Mar serves fragrant pastries like chocolate croissants, cinnamon elephant ears, and deep, dark chocolate tortes. $

Taste of Thai (858-793-9695; www.tasteofthaidelmar.com), 15770 San Andreas Dr. Open daily for lunch and dinner. At the east end of Flower Hill Mall, just off I-5 and near the Del Mar Race Track, the popular Taste of Thai serves creamy Thai curries perfumed with coconut milk and a wide selection of noodle dishes, including the popular pad thai—rice noodles with dried shrimp, bean sprouts, scallions, eggs, and ground nuts. There is a second location in Hillcrest in Uptown (619-291-7525; 527 University Ave., San Diego). $$

Tony's Jacal (858-755-2274), 621 Valley Ave. Open Wed.–Mon. for dinner, Mon. and Wed.–Sat. for lunch. This San Diego institution, located in a residential neighborhood of Solana Beach, in northern Del Mar, has been serving home-style Mexican food to locals since 1947. On warm days, grab a table on the pretty patio, which features a water pond surrounded by arching trees and blooming flowers. The menu is extensive, so if you can't decide, look to the combos, which let you try a little bit of just about everything—but take note: the chiles rellenos are top-notch. A trip to Tony's is not complete without an order of sopapillas for dessert: these delicate pillows of fried pastry are hollow inside, which allows them to be filled to the brim with honey. $$

Encinitas

Los Olas (760-942-1860), 2655 S. Coast Hwy. 101, Cardiff-by-the-Sea. Open daily for dinner. Just south of Chestfield Ave., overlooking the San Elijo Lagoon, Los Olas is a funky, always crowded, and usually noisy Mexican joint that serves up great fish tacos. They also feature Puerto Nuevo–style lobster (boiled in oil and highly seasoned with garlic and oregano). The otherwise moderately priced food and full bar attract a young happy-hour crowd. Parking is in a dirt lot next door. $$

Swami's Café (760-944-0612), 1163 S. Coast Hwy. 101. Open daily for breakfast, lunch, and dinner. Across the street from **Swami's Beach** (a world-famous surfing destination), this hipster café offers fresh whole foods and vegan specialties. Weekend mornings are insanely busy, and the outdoor seating is a little noisy, thanks to the proximity to Hwy. 101 just steps away. $

Oceanside

Longboarder Café (760-721-6776), corner of Tremont and Mission. Open daily for breakfast, lunch, and dinner. On the main drag of downtown Oceanside, a pretty, nostalgic area full of vintage movie theaters and midcentury-modern architecture, the café itself is unpretentious, with a casual interior decorated with surf memorabilia. Food is basic as well—hamburgers, grilled sandwiches, salads—but the portions are huge, and as the name implies, this eatery is a favorite with the local surf community. $

101 Café (760-722-5220), 631 S. Coast Hwy. Open daily for breakfast, lunch, and dinner. The oldest restaurant in Oceanside (and perhaps one of the oldest in the county—it opened in 1928), the relaxed 101 Café is a comfort-food diner that has a devoted local following. Burgers are a good bet, as are familiar dinner specials like meat loaf and gravy, fried chicken, and even liver and onions. Don't miss the butterscotch malt. $

✱ Entertainment

CLUBS ✪ **The Belly Up Tavern** (858-481-8140; www.bellyup.com), 143 S. Cedros Ave., Solana Beach. Closed Mon. Locals have been rocking at the Belly Up since 1974, and it is still the premier live-music nightclub in North County San Diego. The warehouse space in Solana Beach has enough room for a huge bar, a handful of billiards tables, and a cavernous dance floor. The Belly Up features eclectic live music from local bands as well as nationally recognized artists. Cover charge varies.

Gaffney's Wine Bar (760-633-1011; www.gaffneyswinebar.com), 166B El Camino Real, Encinitas. Open Mon.–Sat. 5–10 or 11. Newly relocated in the midst of strip malls and medical buildings in inland Encinitas, this mom-and-pop establishment likes to bill itself as "like home, but with a better wine collection." The friendly place specializes in small-production wines from around the world, and the list changes daily.

Hensley's Flying Elephant Pub and Grill (760-434-2660), 850 Tamarack, Carlsbad. Owned by a local skating celebrity (Matthew Hensley), the Flying Elephant Pub is a large, lively bar in quiet Carlsbad, with billiards, live music, food, and plenty of space. Look for two-for-one pizza night on Thurs., and expect weekend crowds.

Jimmy O's Sports Bar (858-350-3735; www.jimmyosdelmar.com), 225 W. 15th St., Del Mar. A sports bar and restaurant in the heart of Del Mar with a lively nightlife, Jimmy O's is lined with TVs, so you won't miss a minute of the action. The kitchen is open until midnight and has a nice variety of salads, pastas, and respectable steaks. Happy hour specials include discounted drinks (4–6 and then again 10–midnight) and an abbreviated appetizer and sandwich menu for only $6.

✱ Selective Shopping

In addition to **Carlsbad Mall,** 2525 El Camino Real, a fairly generic retail center in north Carlsbad, there are some fun alternative shopping options in the coastal North County. **Cedros Design Center** in Solana Beach (www.cedrosdesigndistrict.net/directions_page.htm), along S. Cedros Avenue, just south of Lomas Santa Fe Drive, has become *the* place for designers and decorating divas to find unusual furniture and accessories. **The Carlsbad Company Stores,** 5600 Paseo del Norte, Carlsbad, is an upscale outlet mall in south Carlsbad featuring bargains on such name brands as Waterford, Coach, and Wedgwood. And the small, European-style **Del Mar Plaza,** 1555 Camino del Mar, Del Mar, has eclectic boutiques in a storybook outdoor setting.

✷ Special Events

(in Greater San Diego County)
January: **San Diego Restaurant Week** (www.sandiegorestaurantweek.com) offers stellar bargains from some of the best restaurants in the city. The **Annual Martin Luther King Jr. Day Parade** starts at the County Administration Building in downtown San Diego and rolls through to Seaport Village along Harbor Dr. **San Diego Marathon in Carlsbad** starts at the Westfield Mall on Plaza Camino Real on the first Saturday of January.

February: **Buick Invitational,** an annual PGA Tour men's golf tournament, is played at Torrey Pines Golf Course.

March: Running through mid-May, **Flower Fields at Carlsbad Ranch** (760-431-0352) is open for tours of the 50-acre rananculas fields. **Saint Patrick's Day Parade** (858-268-9111), downtown, on Fifth and Sixth Avenues. alongside Balboa Park, has bands, floats, dancers, and the Smilin' Irishman contest. **Annual San Diego Indie Music Fest,** in the North Park

DOWNTOWN SAN DIEGO

Courtesy of San Diego CVB

neighborhood near downtown, celebrates contemporary independent music with more than 75 acts across a half dozen venues.

April: The **San Diego Crew Classic** (619-225-0300), at Crown Point Shores Park in Mission Bay, is an annual regatta featuring more than three thousand collegiate, masters, and high school rowers.

May: **Old Town Fiesta Cinco de Mayo** (619-220-5422), on May 5, is consistently one of the best parties in town, with plenty of food, drinks, and mariachi music.

June: Starting in mid-June and stretching through the Fourth of July, the **San Diego County Fair** (858-755-4111), held on the Del Mar Fairgrounds and Racetrack, features animal displays, cooking contests, arts and crafts displays, and a midway with more than 50 thrill rides and nearly one hundred games. **Summer Organ Festival** (619-702-8138), a Monday-night free concert series (running through August), is held at Balboa Park's outdoor Spreckels Organ Pavilion.

July: **Del Mar Racing** (www.dmtc.com) has thoroughbred racing though early September. The **San Diego LGBT Pride Parade, Rally, and Festival** (www.sdpride.org) includes a parade and a two-day festival held in Hillcrest and Balboa Park. **ComicCon** (www.comic-con.org), a huge comic book and sci-fi convention, is held at the downtown convention center. **San Diego Symphony Summer Pops** (619-235-0804) offers outdoor nighttime musical entertainment in a festive atmosphere on the Embarcadero downtown, running through September.

August: The **World Body Surfing Championships** (www.worldbodysurfing.org) are in Oceanside. La Jolla Music Society's **SummerFest** (858-459-3724) features more than a dozen performances of classical and new compositions performed by ensembles and world-class artists in venues throughout the city.

September: **Thunderboat Regatta** (619-225-9160) is a hydroplane show in Mission Bay.

October: **Underwater Pumpkin Carving Contest** (858-565-6054) is held off La Jolla Shores, where scuba divers compete to carve the best jack-o'-lanterns while submerged in the ocean.

December: At **Holiday Lights at Del Mar** (www.holidayoflights.com), the public is allowed to drive around the infield racetrack of the Del Mar Fairgrounds to view more than 350 holiday lights displays. The **Pacific Life Holiday Bowl** (www.pacificlifeholidaybowl.com), a PAC 10, Big 12 college bowl game, is played at Qualcomm Stadium in Mission Valley.

Orange County 2

COASTAL ORANGE COUNTY

INLAND ORANGE COUNTY

SANTA CATALINA ISLAND

Courtesy of Visit Newport Beach Inc.

INTRODUCTION

Don't expect to see the citrus groves that gave Orange County its name. Today, this is one of the most expensive, elegant counties in the state, with seemingly endless pristine coastline; myriad shopping and dining opportunities; and numerous upscale resorts, golf courses, and spas—and nary an agricultural zone to be found (at least not on the tony coastline). The county is dense, especially along the Pacific—although not nearly as congested as its big sister to the north, Los Angeles. The area is blessed with mostly smog-free skies and a scandalous number of perfect sunny days, and the many beach cities offer a charming, village atmosphere that is quaint, cultured, and friendly.

Orange County runs along the coast north of Camp Pendleton—the huge marine base that is the northernmost border of western San Diego County—to Seal Beach and beyond to the border of Los Angeles County, encompassing along the way a string of stunning beach cities that include San Clemente, San Juan Capistrano, Dana Point, Laguna Beach, Newport Beach, and Huntington Beach. The OC stretches eastward to Riverside County and includes Santa Ana, Buena Park, Irvine, Tustin, Yorba Linda, and the infamous Cota de Caza (a small, high-end suburb that has received national attention because of the television show *The Real Housewives of Orange County*). A little more than 20 miles off the coast of Dana Point (and easily accessible by ferry or helicopter) is Santa Catalina, a small island that offers great expanses of untouched wilderness, along with a tiny resort town in the main harbor city of Avalon. Also within Orange County, to the northeast of Seal Beach, is Anaheim, which is home to The Disneyland® Resort, covered in depth in part 3.

GUIDANCE **Catalina Island Visitor's Bureau** (310-510-7606; www.catalina.com).

Laguna Beach Convention and Visitors Bureau (www.lagunabeachinfo.com).

Huntington Beach Convention and Visitors Bureau (www.surfcityusa.com).

Irvine Convention and Visitors Bureau (www.irvinecvb.org).

Newport Beach Convention and Visitors Bureau (www.visitnewportbeach.com).

OTHER HELPFUL SITES **San Clemente Chamber of Commerce** (949-492-1131; www.scchamber.com).

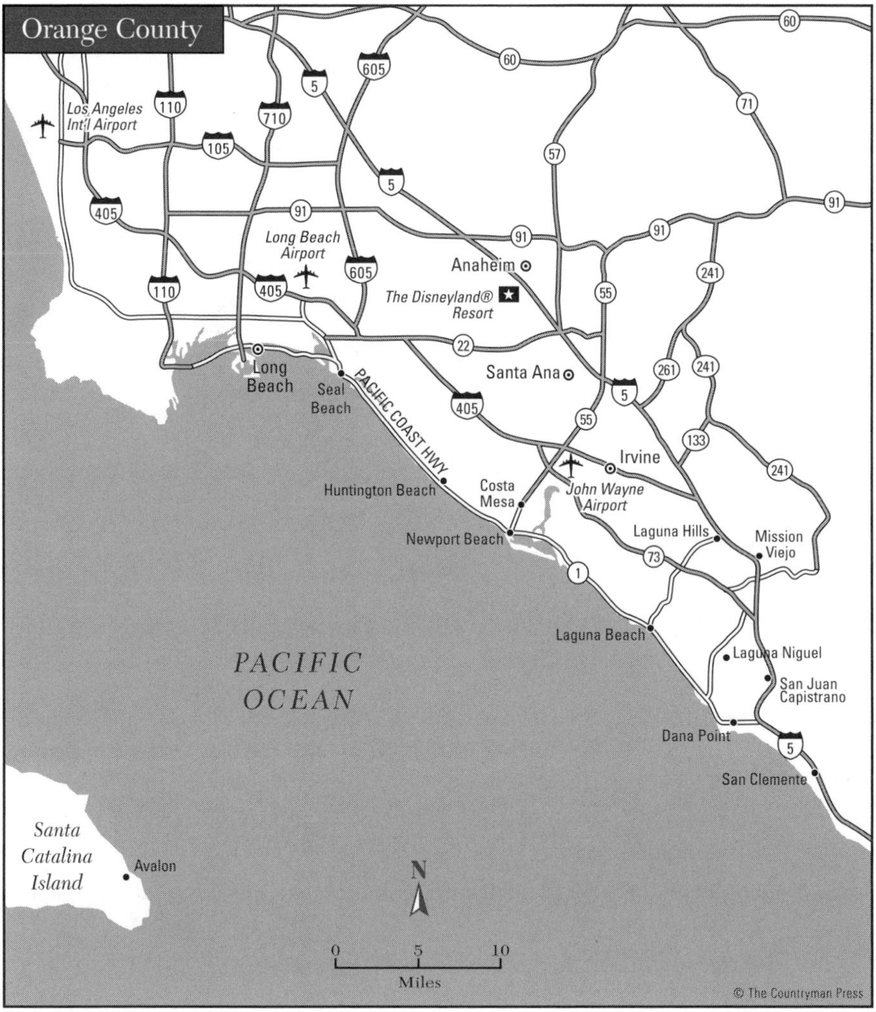

San Juan Capistrano Civic Center (949-493-1171; www.sanjuancapistrano.net/community/index.html).

San Juan Capistrano Community and Visitors Guide (www.sanjuancapistrano.net).

Santa Catalina Island Company (800-414-2754; www.visitcatalinaisland.com).

MEDICAL EMERGENCIES As with all locations in Southern California, dial 911 for immediate response to medical emergencies. The following are hospitals in the area that offer emergency services, divided by region.

Coastal Orange County

Hoag Memorial Hospital Presbyterian (949-645-8600), 1 Hoag Dr., Newport Beach.

Huntington Beach Hospital (714-842-1473), 17772 Beach Blvd., Huntington Beach.

Saddleback Memorial Medical Center (949-837-4500; www.memorialcare.org/saddleback), 24451 Health Center Dr., Laguna Hills.

Saddleback Memorial San Clemente Campus (949-496-1122; www.memorialcare.org/saddleback/about.cfm), 654 Camino de los Mares, San Clemente.

South Coast Medical Center (949-499-1311), 31872 Coast Hwy., Laguna Beach.

Inland Orange County

Anaheim General Hospital (714-827-6700), 3350 W. Ball Rd., Anaheim.

Anaheim Memorial Medical Center (714-774-1450), 1111 W. La Palma Ave., Anaheim.

Irvine Regional Hospital and Medical Center (949-753-2000), 16200 Sand Canyon Ave., Irvine.

Orange Coast Memorial Medical Center (714-378-7000; www.memorialcare.org/orange_coast), 9920 Talbert Ave., Fountain Valley.

St. Jude Medical Center (714-871-3280), 101 E. Valencia Mesa Dr., Fullerton.

Santa Catalina

Catalina Island Medical Center (310-510-0700; www.cimedicalcenter.org), 100 Falls Canyon Rd., Avalon.

GETTING THERE *By air:* There are three primary airports in the Orange County area, but note that the OC is easily accessible from both the San Diego and Los Angeles international airports as well.

John Wayne Orange County Airport (949-252-5200; www.ocair.com), 18601 Airport Way, Santa Ana.

Long Beach Airport (562-570-2600; www.longbeach.gov/airport), 4100 Donald Douglas Dr., Long Beach.

Ontario International Airport (909-937-2700; www.lawa.org), 1923 E. Avion St., Ontario.

By bus: Orange County light rail and bus services are served by the **Orange County Transportation Service** (714-636-7433; www.octa.net), which offers routes into San Clemente, San Juan Capistrano, Irvine, Santa Ana, Anaheim, Costa Mesa, and Laguna Beach.

By ferry: To reach tiny Balboa Island, the quaint heart of Newport Beach, visitors can either approach from the north via the Pacific Coast Highway, drive over the Balboa Bridge (off Jamboree), or take the **Newport Beach Ferry** (410 S. Bayfront Street, Newport Beach) next to the Balboa Pavilion. This tiny ferry connects the mainland peninsula of Newport Beach to Balboa Island. Pedestrians and bikers can walk on for a quick trip across; the ferry can also accommodate up to two cars at one time. (Expect a 20- to 30-minute wait on weekends.)

By train: **AMTRAK**'s *Pacific Surfliner* route connects San Diego, Los Angeles, Santa Barbara, and San Luis Obispo, with stations in San Clemente, San Juan Capistrano, Irvine, Santa Ana, Anaheim, and Fullerton. Most stops in Orange County are also served by regional light rail services. There are Anaheim Resort Transit (ART; www.rideart.org) shuttles from the Anaheim AMTRAK station to

Courtesy of Visit Newport Beach Inc.

NEWPORT BEACH FERRY

The Disneyland® Resort and a number of local hotels, which meet all northbound and southbound *Pacific Surfliner* trains. Tickets are $3 for adults and $1 for children.

GETTING AROUND *By bus:* Within Orange County, light rail and bus services are served by the **Orange County Transportation Service** (714-636-7433). Laguna Beach is also served by the **Mainline Bus** (www.laguna-beachinfo.com /visitors), which operates along three routes Monday–Friday 6:30–6:30 and Saturday 9:30–6:30.

By car: As with most other counties in Southern California, it is all but imperative to have a car to get around the full expanse of Orange County. The area is large, sprawling, interconnected by freeways (and the appealing Pacific Coast Highway, also known as Highway 1), and somewhat underserved by public transportation. The good news is that navigating through the beach cities of Orange County and the inland areas is fairly straightforward, with well-marked freeways and fairly well-maintained roads. The bad news is that drivers are sure to encounter traffic in the OC—especially in downtown Laguna and through any beach city in summertime months—but most of the time it isn't oppressive.

By trolley: During the summer art festival season in Laguna Beach, there is a free trolley service that runs through three routes in Laguna Beach. (Check with the visitors center at 381 Forest Avenue for route maps.)

AMTRAK'S *PACIFIC SURFLINER*

Courtesy of Anaheim Convention and Visitors Bureau

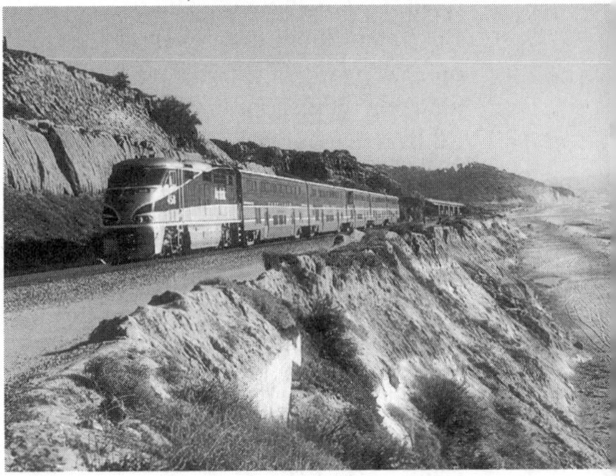

COASTAL ORANGE COUNTY

San Clemente and tiny San Juan Capistrano are tucked between the Pacific and a ridge of small mountains, which are nearly paved over with the infamous California "stilt" houses—pricey hillside homes built on steep slopes that overlook ocean views. The historic San Juan Capistrano has excellent surfing beaches and a quaint downtown, which centers on the San Juan mission, one of the prettiest remnants of colonial Spain in Southern California. San Clemente is well remembered as President Richard Nixon's "Western White House," so named because his home in this city was the president's favored vacation option; San Clemente is also a favorite surfing destination and home to many surfboard manufacturers.

Up the Pacific Coast Highway is Laguna Beach, which is stunning in just about every way—with natural beauty from pristine beaches, rolling hills that rise up just east of the shoreline, and cultural opportunities that are disproportionate to the size of the city. Laguna Beach was founded at the turn of the 20th century as an artists' colony and today comprises hundreds of art galleries, quaint clothing boutiques, seafood and ethnic restaurants, and a handful of idyllic beaches with some of the whitest sand and clearest aquamarine water in California. Every year the city hosts several well-attended arts festivals, including the Pageant of the Masters and the Sawdust Festival. The city also includes world-class resorts and a seemingly endless supply of outdoor sporting options.

Up the coast a few miles is Newport Beach, a *very* wealthy area situated along a natural harbor that is chock-full of yachts and sailboats. Newport Beach city comprises two main areas: The first is the mainland strip adjacent to the large Newport Beach and the historic pier, which overflows with casual eateries and fine dining options (many of which have been Newport staples for decades), whimsical bars, and a boardwalk that is ideal for exploring via bike or skates. The second area of Newport is charming Balboa Island, a pleasing combination of Venice, Italy, and Mayberry USA, which is accessible from the south by a two-car ferry (expect long waits) or from the north via the Balboa Bridge, off Jamboree.

INSIDER TIP: Save on the Laguna Beach art festivals by buying a summer-long pass for $19 at www.lagunabeachpassport.com, which will grant admission to the Festival of Arts, Art-a-Fair, and the Sawdust Art Festival.

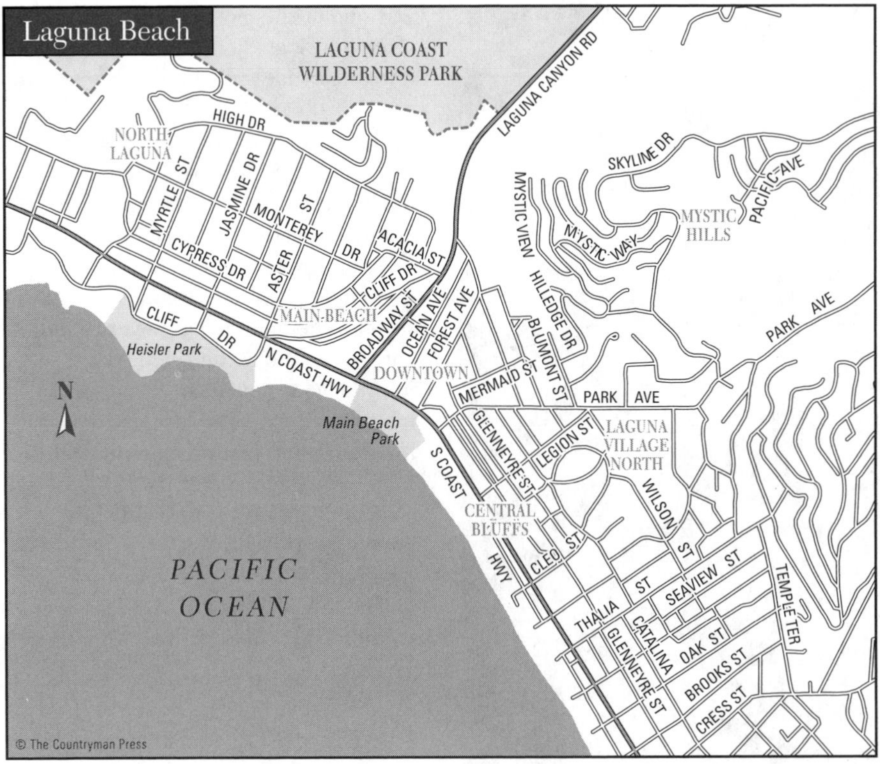

Farther to the north is Huntington Beach, another deep-pockets zip code, this one obsessed with surf culture. In fact, the city bills itself as "Surf City USA"—thanks to Huntington Beach native Dean Torrence, one half of the Jan and Dean duo that recorded the surf anthem (with the help of the Beach Boys) back in 1963—and hosts some of the most prestigious surf competitions in the world. Huntington Beach also has two main focal points: Main Street Huntington Beach and the Huntington Beach Pier area, both overflowing with restaurants, boutiques, and fun and funky bars.

✷ To See

HISTORICAL SITES ✐ **Huntington Pier,** Huntington Beach. A pier in some form has been on this site since 1904, although many have been built and then destroyed by storms over the years. The current 1,800-foot version was refurbished in 1990, and it remains the focal point of Huntington Beach. Check out the nostalgic burger joint chain, **Ruby's** (714-969-7829; www.rubys.com), at the end of the pier, which offers stellar water views.

✪ **Mission San Juan Capistrano** (949-234-1300; www.missionsjc.com), Camino Capistrano and Ortega Hwy., San Juan Capistrano. Open daily 8:30–5. This mission

MISSION SAN JUAN CAPISTRANO

was one of the most successful in the string of 21 missions founded throughout California, and at one time it boasted an 1806-era stone building that was to be the largest church in the state. In December 1812, however, an earthquake destroyed the grand church, killing 40 Native Americans, including two young boys who were ringing the mission bells at the instant the quake struck. The church was never rebuilt, and guests today can see the still-impressive remnants of this once majestic chapel. The lush gardens, fountains, and picturesque ruins of this mission make it one of the loveliest in California—but it is probably best known for the cliff swallows (natives of Argentina) that routinely and promptly make their way back to the area every spring. Adults $9, children $5.

Murphy-Smith House, 278 Ocean Ave., Laguna Beach. Open Fri.–Sun. 1–4. This 1920 Builder Bungalow is an early Laguna Beach cottage, the current home of the Laguna Beach Historical Society.

St. Francis by the Sea Cathedral, 430 Park Ave., Laguna Beach. This *tiny* church is listed on the National Register of Historic Places and holds the honor of being one of the smallest cathedrals in the world, at 17 feet by 16 feet. It is also quite beautiful, inside and out.

Surfers' Hall of Fame (714-841-4000), 300 Pacific Coast Hwy., Huntington Beach. Much like **Grauman's Chinese Theater** in Hollywood immortalizes stars of the big screen, the Surfers' Hall of Fame in Huntington Beach honors legends of surfing by preserving their footprints, handprints, and signatures.

MUSEUMS Huntington Beach Art Center (714-374-1650), 538 Main St., Huntington Beach. Open Wed.–Sat. noon–6, Sun. noon–4. This small museum and gallery space showcases artists working in all media from around the world. This is a great place to see the work of up-and-coming local artists as well. Admission is free.

✪ **International Surfing Museum** (714-960-3483; www.surfingmuseum.org), 411 Olive Ave., Huntington Beach, just up the street from the Huntington Pier. Open daily noon–5. Paying homage to all things boards-sports related, the International Surfing Museum is befittingly located in the city that is nicknamed "Surf City USA." Admission is free.

Laguna Art Museum (949-494-8971; www.lagunaartmuseum.org), 307 Cliff Dr.,

Laguna Beach. Open daily 11–5. The permanent collection of this small museum includes more than 3,500 pieces of American art, from the 19th century to the 21st century, focusing particularly on California-centric themes. Adults $12; students, seniors, and active military $10; children under 12 free.

Newport Harbor Nautical Museum/ExplorOcean (949-675-8915; www.nhnm.org), 600 E. Bay Ave., Newport Beach. Open 10–6; closed Tues. Originally known as the Newport Harbor Nautical Museum, this organization, dedicated to preserving the maritime history of the region, is in the process of expanding into what will be called ExplorOcean, which aims to serve also as an architectural icon and a gathering place for locals and visitors. Admission is free.

Orange County Museum of Art (949-759-1122; www.ocma.net), 850 San Clemente Dr., Newport Beach. Open Wed.–Sun. 11–5, Thurs. 11–8. The leading visual arts institution in Orange County, this museum is known for world-class touring exhibits as well as a permanent collection of more than two thousand pieces, with a focus on California art from the early 20th century to contemporary pieces. Adults $12, students and seniors $10.

PARKS **Aliso and Wood Canyons Wilderness Park** (949-923-2200; www.ocparks.com/alisoandwoodcanyons), 28373 Alicia Pkwy., Laguna Nigel. This 3,900-acre park south of Laguna Beach has more than 30 miles of multiuse trails that are well worn by hikers, bikers, and equestrians. It is also home to several endangered or protected species.

✪ ✐ **Crystal Cove State Park** (949-497-7647; www.crystalcovestatepark.com), off Los Trancos. This surprisingly pristine bit of wilderness falls just north of Laguna Beach. The 2,400 acres include open grassland and more than 3 miles of scenic coastline. The offshore waters are designated as an underwater park—which means no fishing and absolutely no specimen collecting. Parking $15.

Huntington Central Park (714-842-4772), 17851 Goldenwest St., Huntington Beach. This expansive city park is the largest in Orange County and includes more than 350 acres. Within the park, guests will find the **Shipley Nature Center,** an 18-acre zone that features well-manicured trails and an interpretive center with exhibits on native wildlife.

NEWPORT BEACH

✐ **Laguna Coast Wilderness Park** (949-923-2235; www.ocparks.com/laguna coast), 18751 Laguna Canyon Rd., Laguna Beach. Open daily 7–sunset. This coastal canyon reserve is on 6,400 acres in the San Joachin Hills and comprises the **Big Bend Staging Area,** reserved for equestrians; **James Dilley Preserve,** home to Barbara's Lake and Bubbles Pond; and **Willow and Laurel Canyons.** The park offers hiking and riding trails, oak woodlands, and vast expanses of coastal sage scrub. Look for the **Nix Nature Center,** which offers information on hiking trails and sponsors Junior Ranger programs and other ranger-led activities. Admission is free; parking is $3.

✪ **Marine Park,** above Goff Island Cove, Laguna Beach. This perfectly manicured park has curving walkways that showcase breathtaking views of the ocean, overflowing native flower gardens, lush lawn, and intimate benches overlooking the cliffs and the Pacific Ocean beyond. This lovely area is best accessed from the **Montage Laguna Beach** resort.

Norma Gibbs Park, 16641 Graham St., Huntington Beach. Come to this pretty public garden and park to see the expansive Monarch Butterfly Grove, which is most active from late fall through spring.

✷ To Do

BICYCLING Most parks and nature reserves in the area (see *Parks*) offer fine biking, generally with ocean views. The **Newport Beach Boardwalk** is a favorite with locals, who share the pathway with walkers and in-line skaters. **Laguna Coast Wilderness Park** (949-923-2235; www.lagunacanyon.org) offers mountain biking trails that rim the coastline. Throughout the beach neighborhoods, bikers will find dedicated bike lanes, most of which are congested on the weekends. For mountain biking, check out **Big Bend** and **Willow Canyon,** off Laguna Canyon Road, in Laguna Beach.

GOFF ISLAND COVE

Courtesy of Jon Preimesberger

NEWPORT BEACH BOARDWALK

Bike rentals in the region include **Balboa Main St. Bike Rental** (949-723-1320), in Newport Beach; **Boardwalk Sports** (949-673-1767), in Newport Beach; **Dwight's Beach Concession** (714-536-8083), in Huntington Beach; **Easy Ride Tricycle Rentals** (949-723-1516), in Newport Beach; and **Wheel Fun Rentals,** in Dana Point (949-496-7433) and in Huntington Beach (714-861-4408).

GOLF **Aliso Creek Inn Golf Course** (949-499-2271; www.alisocreekinn.com), 31106 S. Coast Hwy., Laguna Beach. This nine-hole course, situated close to the beach, offers a beautiful, natural setting that is nestled in a canyon boasting extensive wildlife (including a family of deer). Green fee: $27–36.

Monarch Beach Golf Course (949-240-8247; www.monarchbeachgolf.com), 50 Monarch Beach Dr., Dana Point. Emerald greens and jaw-dropping ocean views make this one of the most beautiful courses in Orange County. A well-manicured course and challenging holes make it one of the locals' favorite courses as well. Green fee: $115–175.

Pelican Hill Golf Club (949-760-0707; www.pelicanhill.com), 22651 Pelican Hill S., Newport Beach. Along the coastline, the two courses at this upscale club (at the **Resort at Pelican Hill**) offer pristine views and well-manicured greens. Green fee: $250.

San Juan Hills Golf Club (949-493-1167; www.sanjuanhillsgolf.com), 32120 San Juan Creek, San Juan Capistrano. This par 71 course is considered to be among the best golf values in Orange County. The layout snuggles into the rolling hills of San Juan Capistrano, making for a scenic and serene day on the links. Green fee: $43–63.

Shorecliffs Golf Course (949-494-1177; www.shorecliffsgolfcouse.com), 501 Avenida Vaquero, San Clemente. A regulation 18-hole course, Shorecliffs is challenging for beginners and intermediates. Green fee: $38–52.

Talega Golf Club (949-369-6226; www.talegagolfclub), 990 Avenida Talega, San Clemente. Talega offers an 18-hole, par 72 championship golf course, which has been ranked as one of "America's Top Golf Courses" by *Golf Digest.* Green fee: $80–100.

SPAS Aquaterra Spa (949-376-2772; www.aquaterraspa.com), 1555 S. Coast Hwy., Laguna Beach. At the **Surf and Sand Resort,** Aquaterra Spa offers individualized treatments using natural botanicals and organic products harvested from the sea. Try the South Pacific Hot Shell Massage, a 75-minute treatment using warm polished sea shells, or the Sand Scrub Foot Therapy, an exfoliating treatment that requires less energy than a walk along the beach.

Pura Vida (949-582-3551; www.puravidadayspa.com), 27601 Forbes Rd., Laguna Nigel. This full-service day spa offers traditional spa treatments like Swedish massage and hot-stone therapy, sugar scrubs, and detoxifying facials, as well as waxing and tanning treatments.

Pure Blu (949-720-7900; www.purebluspa.com), 900 Newport Center Dr., Newport Beach. Part of the **Newport Beach Marriott Hotel and Spa,** Pure Blu is a tranquil, stylish new spa that offers innovative treatments like aloe vera gel wraps (great for soothing sunburns), oxygen-infused facials, and cinnamon-extract facial peels.

✪ ⇴ **Spa Montage** (949-715-6010; www.spamontage.com), 30801 S. Coast Hwy., Laguna Beach. Part of the beautiful **Montage Laguna Beach,** this oceanfront spa offers fitness classes that include Pilates and beach yoga, as well as sea-inspired treatments like the Marine Wrap, which uses exfoliating and detoxifying seaweed and aromatic sea salt scrubs.

INSIDER TIP: The upscale Spa Montage offers a Day of Indulgence package that is a true bargain: for about $200, patrons can enjoy a 60-minute massage, a scenic poolside lunch at the Mosaic Bar and Grille, and a sunset yoga class overlooking the ocean.

SPA MONTAGE

Courtesy of Montage Laguna Beach

THEME PARKS AND ZOOS ✐ **Pacific Marine Mammal Center** (949-494-3050; www.pacificmmc.org), 20612 Laguna Canyon Rd., Laguna Beach. Open daily 10–4. This marine mammal rescue center is a nonprofit organization largely operated by volunteers and is open to visitors. Admission is free, but donations are encouraged.

✷ Water Sports

BOATING ✐ **Balboa and Newport Beach Whale Watching at Newport Landing** (949-675-0551; www.newportwhales.com), 309 Palm St., Newport Beach. Unlike many whale-watching outfits in Southern California that operate only in the winter, during gray whale migration season, this organization offers year-round tours and claims a 96 percent success rate at either spotting a whale or dolphin.

✪ ✐ **Captain Dave's Dolphin Safari** (949-488-2828; www.dolphinsafari.com), 24440 Dana Point Harbor Dr., Dana Point. Hop aboard a 35-foot catamaran for the chance to see dolphins and migrating whales (in season). Reservations are required.

Davey's Locker (949-673-1434; www.daveyslocker.com), 400 Main St., Newport Beach, at the Balboa Pavilion. Davey's organizes sportfishing trips, whale-watching tours, and operates a full tackle shop.

North Laguna Float Company (949-494-5910), operating throughout Laguna. This company offers two-hour guided kayak tours aboard inflatables. Paddle the gorgeous Crescent Bay and Diver's Cove regions, which generally offer calm waters and thus are perfect for beginners.

DIVING AND SNORKELING Laguna Beach is the ideal place in Orange County to snorkel and dive, because the entire expanse of the beach (and some distance offshore) is a marine preserve and thus closed to fishing, and because the waves in many of the smaller pocket beaches are calm, increasing visibility. The marine preserve also means plentiful ocean life that is often more curious than frightened of divers. The best locations include **Diver's Cove Beach,** part of Heisler Park, and **Shaw's Cove,** at Fairview Street. This quiet cove offers a long, straight reef that is ideal for divers, especially on the west side.

FISHING As noted earlier, the coastline and adjacent waters of Laguna Beach are part of a protected marine ecological reserve, and thus fishing is permitted only northward, in Newport Beach, or south, from Dana Point. The best bet for beginners to hook "the big one" is with the help of a chartered sportfishing boat, from either of these organizations:

Dana Wharf Sportfishing and Whale Watching (949-496-5794; www.danawharf.com), at the Dana Point Harbor. In addition to whale-watching trips, this group offers year-round sportfishing trips. Be sure to call ahead for reservations.

✪ **Newport Landing Sportsfishing** (949-675-0550), 309 Palm St., #A, Newport Beach. Considered by many to be one of the best sportfishing operations in Southern California, Newport Landing offers private fishing excursions along Newport Beach as well as longer trips to Santa Catalina.

NEWPORT BEACH PIER

SURFING For surfers, it doesn't get much better than the OC coastline. Great surfing beaches in Laguna include **Agate Street Beach** (at the end of Agate Street, near Main Beach); **Rockpile Beach** (at the south end of Heisler Park); and **Thousand Steps Beach** (see *Green Space*). South of San Clemente, check out **San Onofre** (also called San O), where—locals joke—the water is a little bit warmer than the rest of the SoCal beaches, thanks to the nearby nuclear power plant. Also at the southern end of San Clemente is **Trestles,** a beach that is revered by locals for consistent surf. In Newport Beach, the surf zones are identified by numbered streets that run adjacent; one of the favorites for quick breaks is between **54th and 56th streets.** Also popular is the **Wedge** (see *Green Space*). To the south of Dana Point is the famous **Doheny Beach,** which offers rolling south swells. North of Dana Point is **Salt Creek,** a sandy beach that has reliably impressive waves. In Huntington Beach, a favorite surfing spot is off the **Huntington Beach Pier,** although surfing here is recommended only for experts, as this can be dangerous, especially during the strongest winter swells.

Surfing is a tough sport, and there is no better way to learn than to take an organized class, which will get even (most) beginners up for at least a few seconds. Good educational programs are available through **Corky Carroll's Surf School** (714-969-3959; www.surfschool.net), throughout Orange County, and **La Vida Laguna** (949-275-7544; www.lavidalaguna.com), throughout Laguna. In addition to offering kayak rentals, tours, and lessons, La Vida Laguna has responded to the latest board craze and now offers surf paddleboard lessons and rentals.

✷ Green Space

BEACHES ✪ ✐ **Aliso Beach Park,** 31131 S. Coast Hwy., South Laguna. A large, family-friendly beach, Aliso offers wide sandy beaches, picnic areas, fire pits, tot lots, and extensive facilities. This is a favorite with surfers and tidepoolers.

✐ **Bolsa Chica State Beach,** across from the **Bolsa Chica Ecological Reserve** in Huntington Beach. This beach is known for gentle surf, which makes it ideal for

TOP 10 DAY IN THE OC

1. Nosh on a fresh croissant and café au lait at C'est la Vie in Laguna Beach (see p. 112)
2. Stroll along Goff Island Cove in Laguna (see p. 98)
3. Tour Mission San Juan Capistrano (see pp. 95–96)
4. Order up the President's Special for lunch at El Adobe de Capistrano (see p. 111)
5. Head north to the International Surfing Museum in Huntington Beach (see p. 96)
6. Enjoy an afternoon whale-watching trip in Newport Beach (see p. 101)
7. Window-shop on Marine Ave. on Balboa Island (see p. 116)
8. Dine Continental style on steak au poivre and a glass of red wine at Basilic (see p. 110)
9. Shoot pool at the Beach Ball Bar (see p. 115)
10. Overnight in an oceanfront room at the Montage Laguna Beach (see p. 107)

swimming and beginning surfers, especially children. The facilities include fire pits, basketball courts, and plentiful picnic areas.

✪ **Crescent Bay Beach,** off Viejo and N. Coast Hwy. The northernmost beach in Laguna, the small Crescent Bay is postcard perfect, with white sand, crystalline waters, and a gently curving shoreline. Because of the generally calm waters and the reefs offshore, the beach is popular with scuba divers and snorkelers. There's also good tidepooling on the south end.

✪ **Goff Island Cove,** south Laguna Beach, below **Montage Laguna Beach.** This cove beach is part of a protected marine park, which means absolutely no seashell collecting is permitted. There's great tidepooling here, and the water is the color of bottle glass. Look for the pretty Keyhole Rock.

Huntington City Beach, off Pacific Coast Hwy. Anchored by the Surf City Pier, this 3-mile stretch of sand is in the heart of Huntington Beach and a favorite with board and body surfers. The fire pits are popular with locals, who claim them early in the mornings on most weekends.

INSIDER TIP: When tidepooling at protected Goff Island Cove—or any other beach in Southern California—remember to look but don't touch. In preserved marine parks, it is illegal to handle or move animals and plants. To get the best view of tide pool life without handling organisms, fashion a viewing apparatus from a waterproof tube (like a length of PVC pipe) covered over on one end with plastic wrap and secured with a rubber band. Place the tube (plastic side down) into the water, a few inches above an object of interest, and it will serve as a magnifying glass.

LAGUNA BEACH

✪ **Main Beach,** at Pacific Coast Hwy. and Ocean, Laguna Beach. This downtown beach is at the heart of the action and offers numerous beach volleyball courts, a small boardwalk, and an idyllic stretch of shoreline. The small, grassy park adjacent to the shoreline is the site of numerous art shows throughout the year.

✪ **San Clemente State Beach,** off Califia, San Clemente. Relatively uncrowded, the mile-long stretch of sand falls at the foot of a steep bluff and offers blue-green water and gently curling waves.

Thalia Street Beach, located below the Thalia Street Surf Shop (915 S. Coast Hwy.), Laguna Beach. Extremely popular with surfers, Thalia Street offers seclusion and reliable swells. This is not recommended for families or those out for a swim, because the rip tides can be fierce.

MAIN BEACH

Thousand Steps Beach, off S. Coast Hwy. at Ninth St. in Laguna Beach. There aren't really that many steps, but it is a hike to get to this surfers' favorite.

The Wedge, at the south end of the peninsula in Newport Beach, is one of the best body surfing locales on the West Coast—but this is only for experienced surfers and strong swimmers. The currents can be fierce, and the waves break close to the shore.

GARDENS Hortense Miller Garden (949-497-3311; www.hortensemiller

garden.org), Laguna Beach. Open for tours Wed., Sat., and alternating Tues. and Thurs., 10–4. Reservations are required several weeks in advance to tour this garden, which is only accessible via these preplanned docent-led programs.

NATURE PRESERVES **Bolsa Chica Ecological Reserve** (714-846-1114; www.bolsachica.org), off Pacific Coast Hwy., opposite Bolsa Chica State Beach, Huntington Beach. Open daily dawn–dusk. This exquisite natural reserve is one of the best birding locations in the United States and remains a pristine, unadulterated space—despite the active oil derricks just offshore. Admission is free.

✷ Lodging

PRICE KEY FOR A STANDARD ROOM:

$	$100 or less
$$	$101–150
$$$	$151–250
$$$$	$251 and up

Dana Point

⚥ **Ritz-Carlton, Laguna Nigel** (949-240-2000; www.ritzcarlton.com), 1 Ritz-Carlton Dr. Between Dana Point and Laguna Beach, the Ritz-Carlton, Laguna Nigel offers the luxury, exclusivity, and pomp and circumstance for which this brand is known. The resort is perched above a 150-foot cliff overlooking the Pacific, with unparalleled views from private balconies and patios. Guest rooms are sophisticated and spacious (the smallest is 400 square feet), with comfortable seating areas and luxurious bathrooms. On-site dining is at **Raya, Eno,** and a handful of poolside, ocean-view lounges. The large on-site spa offers traditional treatments as well as daily yoga and Pilates classes. $$$$

Huntington Beach

Hyatt Regency Huntington Beach Resort and Spa (714-698-1234; http://huntingtonbeach.hyatt.com/hyatt/hotels/index.jsp), 21500 Pacific Coast Hwy. Access the beach via an elevated pedestrian bridge from the Hyatt Regency, which offers great views and superior service. The hotel is a standout because of the extraordinary pools—a large lagoon-style pool with views of the Pacific, and three pool grottos, large jetted spas secluded within lush landscaping and rock outcroppings. There are also tennis courts on-site, a full-service spa with dry sauna and steam rooms, an expansive fitness center, and a salon. $$$

Shorebreak Hotel (714-861-4475; www.shorebreakhotel.com), 500 Pacific Coast Hwy. A new boutique hotel on The Strand promenade in downtown Huntington Beach, this property offers easy access to dining, nightlife, shopping, and the beach. The original décor is sporty and offers nods to the seaside location, including a lobby gallery that often features surfing photography and paintings. The hotel's "beach butler" will take care of everything a guest might need for a day at the shore, including bicycles, surf lessons, kites, and beach toys. This upscale hotel is also home to **Zimzala,** one of the most highly regarded new restaurants in the city. $$–$$$

Laguna Beach

⚥ **Hotel Laguna** (949-494-1151; www.hotellaguna.com), 425 S. Coast Hwy. The "Grand Old Lady" has been in Laguna for more than one hundred years, has hosted countless dignitaries and celebrities (it is said to have been a favorite with Humphrey Bogart and

Lauren Bacall), and remains one of the most recognizable landmarks in Laguna Beach. The secret to its success? Location, location, location: Hotel Laguna is smack downtown, within steps of dozens of the best restaurants and boutiques in Laguna, and it also fronts the wildly popular Main Beach, which is the site of many arts festivals throughout the year. Many of the 65 comfortable guest rooms boast premier views of the shoreline. On-site dining includes **Claes,** an elegant and pricey seafood restaurant with incomparable views of the Pacific, and **The Terrace,** an open-air patio restaurant that is perched above the beach, with equally stunning views—making this an ideal place for a sundowner cocktail. Also on-site is the lovely **Rose Garden,** a private Victorian garden that is the site of many weddings throughout the year. Don't miss the main hallway photo gallery that depicts Laguna Beach in its earliest days. $$$

Inn at Laguna Beach (949-497-9972; www.innatlagunabeach.com), 211 N. Coast Hwy. Just north of Main Beach, perched at the top of a small bluff that overlooks the ocean and the hillsides beyond, the intimate Inn at Laguna Beach is close to everything but ever slightly above it all, away from the crowds. Most guest rooms have lovely views of the ocean, most from small balconies, although there are a handful of bargain-priced rooms that offer views of the shops and restaurants along Pacific Coast Hwy. and the rising hills just beyond. Rooms are light, bright, and commodious, with luxurious linens and comfortable beds. Included in the rate is a complimentary continental breakfast brought to the room. $$–$$$$

INN AT LAGUNA BEACH

HOTEL LAGUNA

Courtesy of Jon Preimesberger

⚤ **La Casa del Camino** (949-497-2446; www.lacasadelcamino.com), 1289 S. Coast Hwy. A historic boutique property originally built in 1929 as a retreat for Hollywood movie stars, this eclectic hotel has personality to spare—and despite La Casa's long history, accommodations are surprisingly modern and youthful. Especially popular are the "Casa Surf Project" suites, all of which were individually designed to be part accommodation/part art gallery, and all of which offer unique touches like faux grass and vintage lawn chairs *inside* the guest room, a skateboard minibar, and wall-sized surfing murals. **The Rooftop Lounge,** on top of the hotel, has panoramic views of the Pacific, and the hip **K'ya Bistro Bar** offers a real bargain (all dishes are priced at $10 or less). $$$

✪ ⚤ **Montage Laguna Beach** (949-715-6000; www.montagelagunabeach.com), 30801 S. Coast Hwy. I can't think of a more impressive space in all of Southern California than the lobby of the Montage. The expansive reception area has rich appointments, omnipresent piano music, and floor-to-ceiling windows with nonstop stunning water views. This oasis of calm elegance is the epitome of Southern California chic and manages to be welcoming and comfortable at the same time that it is also opulent and exclusive. The Craftsman-style property sits on a cliff overlooking **Goff Island Cove,** surely one of the prettiest small beaches in Orange County, and many guest rooms also overlook the enormous mosaic pool. Service is impeccable, and the check-in process is painless: after pulling up to valet parking, guests are immediately escorted to their rooms, where they register in comfort. Accommodations offer breezy beach luxury: plush furnishings, top-quality linens, huge windows, and marble baths with every amenity. There is a kids' club and scheduled activities, and world-class dining on-site at **The Loft.** $$$$

Pacific Edge Hotel (949-494-8566; www.pacificedgehotel.com), 647 S. Coast Hwy. Two miles from downtown Laguna, and less swanky than many of the other options in the city, the comfortable and (relatively) affordable Pacific Edge nevertheless delivers on location: the hotel is right on the sand, and views from the guest room balconies are stellar. The property offers two heated swimming pools, a game room, and complimentary beach chairs and umbrellas. The basic décor includes seaside-themed accessories. There is a 4,000-square-foot stand-alone villa on the property that is available to rent for special events. $$–$$$

Surf and Sand Resort and Spa (877-349-0352; www.surfandsandresort.com), 1555 S. Coast Hwy. It's hard to stay closer to the water in Laguna than the Surf and Sand, which is situated right on the shore. The ocean views from the guest room balconies are second to none—in fact, the experience of

MONTAGE LAGUNA BEACH

staying at this resort is very much like being on a boat, such is the immediacy of the Pacific. The property is south of downtown Laguna, which means the resort is quiet, private, and peaceful. This four-diamond property is home to **Splashes Restaurant,** the delightful **Aquaterra Spa,** and an expansive, recently revamped pool overlooking the waterfront. Guest rooms are understated and elegant, with muted colors and clean lines. $$$$

Newport Beach

Balboa Bay Club and Resort (888-445-7153; www.balboabayclub.com), 1221 W. Coast Hwy. This ultraluxe resort is one of the finest in Newport Beach: the public spaces exude wealth, importance, and privilege, with nautical touches throughout and views of the Newport Harbor, which is perpetually littered with sailboats and yachts. Guest rooms offer large patios overlooking either the Newport Harbor or the well-landscaped courtyard and are furnished with comfy chaise lounges—perfect for curling up with a glass of wine to watch the sunset. The large pool also overlooks the harbor. The hotel is adjacent to the tony, private Balboa Bay Club, a favorite with the likes of Nancy Reagan and Jerry Seinfeld. The on-site **Newport Beach Day Spa** is available exclusively to club members and hotel guests. $$$$

❀ **Balboa Inn** (949-675-3412; www.balboainn.com), 105 Main St. On the boardwalk and across from the Balboa Pier, this Mediterranean-style hotel is just steps from the sand and close to dining and myriad seaside recreational activities. The guest rooms offer high-style décor with Italian marble bathrooms and plenty of space. The small private ocean sundeck includes a small "spool"—a cross between a spa and a pool. Although prices soar for suites and premier ocean views, this is one of the best bargains in what is otherwise an extremely pricey zip code. $$–$$$

Crystal Cove Cottages (949-497-0992; www.crystalcovebeachcottages.com), 35 Crystal Cove, Newport Coast. South of Newport Beach, this collection of historic, rustic cottages was built between the 1920s and 1950s, some as movie sets. The small buildings managed to survive over the years and collectively served as a thriving seaside colony for decades. Today the charming cottages have been restored to reflect the 1930s to 1950s eras, complete with original textiles, fashions, and furnishings, and have been converted to daily and weekly rentals, in either stand-alone cottages or in dorm-style cottages (with private rooms and community spaces). Cottages are located directly on the sand or overlooking the shoreline from the top of a small bluff. Each individual unit includes a very small kitchen with refrigerator and microwave, and some include an electric cook top. There is no housekeeping service, but towels are replaced every four days. Because of the prime location on the sand and the nostalgic appeal, reservations are hard to come by and thus are suggested well in advance. Note: The area is undergoing long-term reconstruction, so it is possible there will be noise, dust, and increased traffic for the next few years. $$–$$$

The Island Hotel (949-759-0808; www.theislandhotel.com), 690 Newport Center Dr. This high-rise property, close to the Newport Harbor and overlooking nearby Balboa Island, is an elegant, tropically themed full-service resort, featuring two lighted tennis courts, a serene pool area with a fireplace, a fitness center, a full-service spa, and **Palm Terrace,** the on-site restaurant. Water-view rooms are well worth the extra cost, especially from higher floors. The hotel offers a complimentary free limo pickup and drop-off to the nearby airports. $$$

✪ **Newport Beach Inn** (949-673-7030; www.newportbeachwalkhotel.com), 2306 W. Oceanfront Blvd. There is no hotel accommodation closer to the action of Newport Beach than the Newport Beach Inn, immediately across from the sand, near the pier, and within easy walking distance of dozens of lively restaurants and bars. The newly renovated hotel is decorated in clean style and minimalist colors, with luxurious bathrooms—many of which offer jetted tubs. Complimentary continental breakfast is included, as is the free use of the hotel's collection of beach-cruiser bicycles, perfect for plying the Newport Boardwalk that runs parallel to the beach right outside the hotel door. Note: This property is the heart of a youth-centric neighborhood, so expect noisy late nights, especially on weekends. $$$

⚤ **The Resort at Pelican Hill** (949-467-6800; www.pelicanhill.com), 22701 Pelican Hill Rd. S., Newport Coast. This luxurious new resort overlooking the Pacific Ocean looks more like a small Italian village perched above the sea than the full-service resort (with residential condos) that it is. The property sprawls across 500 coastal acres, with lush landscaping and a well-thought-out layout. Guest accommodations are in cozy individual bungalows and opulent villas, both of which offer enormous space and solitude. On-site is a 36-hole Tom Fazio–designed golf course (see *To Do*), an expansive spa, and a palatial-sized pool with tiered decks and private cabanas. Dining is at **Andrea,** which appropriately offers northern Italian cuisine. This resort offers a serene experience that certainly isn't affordable for many—but is nevertheless a unique indulgence for those with deep enough pockets. $$$$

✷ Where to Eat

DINING OUT

Huntington Beach

Zimzala (714-960-5050; www.restaurantzimzala.com), 500 Pacific Coast Hwy. Open daily for lunch and dinner. Part of the **Shorebreak Hotel,** this vaguely bohemian restaurant offers Mediterranean fusion cuisine that includes influences from North Africa, Spain, and Turkey, among others. Don't miss the Turkish cigar: baked phyllo dough tubes filled with herbed cheese. Small menu items allow for greater sampling. $$$

Laguna Beach

🍸 **Brussels Bistro** (949-376-7955; www.brusselsbistro.com), 222 Forest Ave. Open Sat. and Sun. for lunch and dinner, Mon.–Fri. for dinner. This European brasserie serves authentic Belgian fare like true *pommes frite* with a duo of dipping sauces, Flemish asparagus, ham and cheese crêpes, and mussels *marinière,* as well as European versions of American favorites like hamburgers with melted Gruyère, veal meat loaf with mustard sauce, and beef stew made with Stella Artois. The restaurant also serves a good variety of Belgian beers, including hard-to-find fruit ales. Expect live jazz concerts Tues.–Thurs., starting at 7 PM. $$

✪ **Five Feet** (949-497-4955; www.fivefeetrestaurants.com), 328 Glenneyre St.

PRICE KEY FOR A TYPICAL ENTRÉE:

$	$10 and under
$$	$11–20
$$$	$21–30
$$$$	$31 and up

Open daily for dinner. The brightly colored artwork against rough-hewn walls inside this entertaining, eclectic warehouse space gives a hint of the contrast in textures and flavors echoed in its Chinese cuisine served with a decidedly French accent. Playful appetizers like goat cheese wontons with raspberry coulis and vanilla-whiskey-apricot pork belly show off the chef's sense of fun. Don't miss the signature dish: a crispy farm-raised catfish served with a spicy ginger tomato sauce. $$$

✪ **The Loft** (949-715-6010; www.spamontage.com), 30801 S. Coast Hwy. Open daily for dinner. Part of the fabulous **Montage Laguna Beach,** The Loft draws locals throughout Southern California to enjoy inventive cuisine in an elegant atmosphere. The young, talented chef regularly plays with the menu, which features an organic farm-to-table approach. When available, don't miss the bouillabaisse—which my husband claims is the best he's eaten outside France. I love the garlicky fries with malt vinegar—which are served in such abundance that they could serve as a meal rather than as the appetizer that they were intended to be. The restaurant also boasts an in-house *fromagier,* who features more than 150 cheeses and one hundred different honeys every night. Request a table by the window and watch the sunset for dramatic, romantic views. $$$$

THE LOFT

Courtesy of the Montage Laguna Beach

Watermarc (949-376-6272; www.watermarcrestaurant.com), 448 S. Coast Hwy. Open daily for dinner. In the heart of downtown Laguna, this restaurant offers distinct dining spaces, including a European-style sidewalk café downstairs and a more sophisticated upstairs loft space. The menu is bewilderingly extensive, and for lighter appetites includes two-for-$10 grazing plates (served after 9 PM). Hungrier folks shouldn't miss the trio of filet mignon, with small portions of beef prepared with Oscar sauce, peppercorn sauce, or as a deconstructed beef Wellington. Order wine by the half glass, glass, half carafe, or bottle. $–$$$

Newport Beach

✪ **Basilic** (949-673-0570; www.basilicrestaurant.com), 217 Marine Ave., Balboa Island. Open Tues.–Sat. for dinner. This elegant, charming bistro offers Swiss French cuisine, which is both sophisticated and hearty. Start with traditional Swiss raclette cheese served with cornichons, fingerling potatoes, and pickled onions, or the cheesy French onion soup. Follow up with authentic coq au vin or steak au poivre. No French meal is complete without dessert, and Basilic offers a fine tarte tatin. A five-course prix fixe menu (plus a champagne sorbet refresher) is also available for $60. $$$–$$$$

The Cannery (949-566-0060; www.cannerynewport.com), 3010 Lafayette Rd. Open daily for lunch and dinner, brunch on Sun. On the harbor, The Cannery is an ideal fine-dining option for folks who can't make up their minds: there are several separate seating options, including the upstairs

Asian dining room, the water-level Grill Room, the water-view Jellyfish Bar, or the outdoor patio on the Rhine Channel. Menu options are equally eclectic, with sushi and sashimi, Maryland blue-crab cakes, Mexican chicken-lime *albondigas* soup, Australian rack of lamb, and herb-crusted Chilean sea bass. $$$

⇜ **Sol Cocina** (949-675-9800; www.solcocina.com), 251 E. Pacific Coast Hwy. Open daily for lunch and dinner, brunch on Sun. Sol offers nouveau Baja cuisine, with bright flavors and inventive presentation—in other words, upscale Cal-Mex. The restaurant features an open kitchen with counter seating, to allow guests to watch the chef in action, and a colorful dining room with traditional table seating. Grilled chicken tacos are superior, as is the guacamole. The bar offers more than 60 artisanal tequilas and a fun fire pit. Note that the owners are committed to sustainable products and purchase beef from a ranch that has been recognized by the Humane Society for ethical treatment of their animals; they are also passionate about recycling. $$$

21 Oceanfront (949-673-2100; www.21oceanfront.com), 2100 W. Oceanfront. Open daily for dinner. Across from Main Beach, with views to the pier, this elegant restaurant reminds me vaguely of the dining room in a vintage ocean liner. Befitting its beachside location, the restaurant specializes in seafood, including oysters on the half shell, crab claw cocktails, lobster, jumbo prawns, calamari, and the house specialty, pistachio-crusted halibut. In addition, 21 Oceanfront is one of the few restaurants in the area to offer Baja abalone steaks—my absolute favorite, but at $130 a pop, not an everyday indulgence. The restaurant is famous for its dessert soufflés: either chocolate or Grand Marnier. There is live entertainment every evening. $$$$

San Juan Capistrano

🍸 **El Adobe de Capistrano** (949-493-1163; www.eladobedecapistrano.com), 31891 Camino Capistrano. Open daily for lunch and dinner. This longtime SoCal favorite is housed in a historic building in downtown San Juan Capistrano that dates to 1778, and the rustic wood interior and leather furniture are evocative of colonial Mexico. Specialties include lobster tacos with habañera and former local President Richard Nixon's favorite combo: chiles rellenos, chicken enchilada, and a taco. The bar at the front of the establishment is an elegant place to unwind after a long day at the beach. $$

L'Hirondelle (949-661-0425; www.lhirondellesjc.com), 31631 Camino Capistrano. Open daily for dinner, Sun. for brunch. Across the street from the Capistrano mission, this French restaurant is charmingly inviting. Inside is reminiscent of an elegant home, complete with cozy fireplace and a comfy lounge; outside is a pretty, bougainvillea-shaded patio with colorful umbrellas. Try the crispy garlic fries and the trout with lemon and caper, or the Francophile favorite: steak with green peppercorn sauce. Entrées come with an authentic onion soup and delicious bread. $$$

✪ **The Ramos House Café** (949-443-1342), 31752 Los Rios St. Open Tues.–Sun. for breakfast and lunch; brunch on the weekend. Near the railroad tracks in the Los Rios Historic District in a building that dates to 1881, the Ramos House offers contemporary American cuisine, which in this instance means that everything on the menu is made from scratch. Herbs are grown in the garden, breads are baked fresh daily, and the ice cream is hand churned. The menu changes seasonally, and note that the weekend brunch has vastly more choice—and is more expensive. When you can find them, don't miss the apple cinnamon beignets and the spicy crabcake salad. On warm days, dine outdoors on the patio beneath a hundreds-year-old mulberry tree. $$$

Sun Dried Tomato Café (949-661-1167; www.sundriedtomatocafe.com), 31781 Camino Capistrano. Open daily for breakfast, lunch, and dinner; brunch on Sun. This bistro housed in an adobe in the heart of Old Town Capistrano has a tiny outdoor patio, an upstairs bar, and a casually elegant dining room. Try the lamb burger with Gorgonzola or the golden beet salad with goat cheese and cranberries. For breakfast, don't miss the fried egg sandwich with bacon and Anaheim chiles. $$

EATING OUT

Huntington Beach

Bukhara (714-842-3171), 7594 Edinger Ave. Open daily for lunch and dinner. It's hard for me to resist an Indian restaurant, especially a relatively undiscovered one like Bukhara, which is tucked away into the obscurity of a strip mall—keeping prices low and crowds manageable. Curries are a specialty, as is the spinach *saag*. Be sure to order garlic naan, and try the mint chutney as an accompaniment to just about anything on the menu. $$

Slowfish (714-846-6951; www.slowfishusa.com), 16051 Bolsa Chica St. Open Mon.–Fri. for lunch and dinner, Sat. for lunch. Secreted away in an unassuming mall, this fun diner serves Korean cuisine with a California flair: the braised short ribs over black rice are tender, flavorful, and comforting. The restaurant also offers a small sushi bar. $$$

Y **25 Degrees** (714-960-2525; www.25degreesrestaurant.com/25-Degrees-Huntington-Beach.aspx), 412 Walnut Ave. Open Mon. for dinner; Tues.–Fri. for lunch and dinner; Sat. for breakfast and lunch; Sun. for breakfast, lunch, and dinner. The imaginative name refers to the temperature difference between a medium rare and well-done hamburger—the first clue that this is no ordinary burger joint. On offer are beef, veggie, tuna, and turkey burgers, which can be topped with any of 14 cheeses, a dozen house-made sauces, and unusual toppings like fried eggs or prosciutto. The place also offers an extensive wine list and a selection of beers on draft. $$

Laguna Beach

✪ Y **C'est la Vie** (949-497-5100; www.cestlavierestaurant.com), 373 S. Coast Hwy. Open daily for breakfast, lunch, and dinner. This very cute bistro, with a pastry and coffee bar up front, offers romantic indoor dining and an expansive ocean-view dining patio in the back. But it's not all about *looking* authentic: C'est la Vie offers impressively authentic bistro fare, with dinner favorites like Dover sole filet with white asparagus, roasted duck with orange sauce, and rack of lamb with rosemary. Pastries are de rigueur and include raspberry tarts, chocolate croissants, and divine Napoleons. $$–$$$

Crab Zone (949-376-7035; www.crab-zone.com), 217 Broadway. Open daily for dinner. This casual eatery a block off Main Beach is an intriguing blend of Vietnamese, Chinese, and French, and specializes in jumbo crab legs, crabcakes, and Dungeness crab. Don't miss the chance to try the Vietnamese coffee. (The interior wood siding is signed by thousands of happy patrons.) $$$

Greeter's Corner Restaurant (949-494-0361), 329 S. Coast Hwy.

Open daily for breakfast, lunch, and dinner. Just off Main Beach, in the heart of downtown Laguna, Greeter's Corner has a pleasant indoor dining room and an even more inviting large outdoor patio. Breakfast omelets are large and flavorful—make sure to order the fried potatoes, which are perfectly crispy. Also on offer are hamburgers, sandwiches, and salads. Given the location and the views, the prices are bargain-basement. $–$$

Y **House of Big Fish and Ice Cold Beer** (949-715-4500; www.houseofbigfish.com), 540 S. Coast Hwy., #200. Open daily for lunch and dinner. This unassuming neighborhood favorite overlooks the ocean and offers casual dining in an elegant atmosphere. Expect simply prepared fish, either grilled or fried, as well as soups, sandwiches, and tacos. $$

Nick's Laguna Beach (949-376-8595; www.nickslaguna.com), 440 S. Coast Hwy. Open daily for breakfast, lunch, and dinner. In the heart of downtown, tiny Nick's is cozy and intimate, with a colorful outdoor dining patio. Appetizers are especially fun and inventive, like the short rib sliders served with horseradish, asparagus fries with a Parmesan crust, and fried deviled eggs. $$

The Stand (949-494-8101), 238 Thalia St. Open daily for breakfast, lunch, and dinner. This vegan snack bar offers up healthy food to a loyal clientele. Standouts include the hummus, veggie burgers, hearty barley soup, and an exceptional avocado sandwich. Seating is extremely limited and outdoors only. $

Newport Beach

✪ **Beachcomber Café** (949-376-6900; www.thebeachcombercafe.com), 15 Crystal Cove, Newport Coast. Open daily for breakfast, lunch, and dinner. This *extremely* popular beachside diner is located in the Crystal Cove Historic District, near the **Crystal Cove Cottages,** and is just about every local's favorite for upscale cuisine in a casual atmosphere. Try the mac and cheese with wild mushrooms and truffles, or if you come for breakfast, don't miss the famous corned beef hash and eggs. $$

Charlie's Chili (949-675-7991), 102 McFadden Pl. Open daily for breakfast, lunch, and dinner. Located just off the Newport Beach pier, and a local institution in Newport since the early 1970s, Charlie's offers a casual atmosphere, loyal fan base, and friendly servers. The chili is good—especially in the breakfast chili omelets; for those who love it, there is an all-you-can-eat option. The ambiance is the main draw. Inside seating is tight, but the large outdoor patio overlooking the beach is a fun way to spend a few hours people watching. The place has had some famous fans, too: legend has it that John Wayne used to buy chili by the 5-gallon bucket at Charlie's for his annual boat parade party. $

✪ **Ciao** (949-675-6193), 223 Marine Ave., Balboa Island. Open daily for lunch and dinner. This small Italian restaurant on quaint Balboa Island has

> **INSIDER TIP:** The Beachcomber Café is extremely popular, and waits for a table, especially on sunny weekends, can be hours. The restaurant maintains 70 percent of the seating on a first-come, first-served basis and will not accept reservations over the phone or in person at the café. However, it is possible to secure a reservation well in advance via www.opentable.com.

CHARLIE'S CHILI

the feel of being inside a dark, cool wine cave—a happy circumstance for me, but there are also a couple of prime tables fronting windows onto bustling Marine Ave. Pasta and pizza are homemade tasting and reasonably priced, but don't miss the exceptional calzones, especially the prosciutto and ricotta. (Hint: These are big enough to share.) $$

Crab Cooker (949-673-0100; www.crabcooker.com), 2200 Newport Blvd. Open daily for lunch and dinner. It's impossible to miss this bright red building festooned with neon, located across from the Newport Pier: subtle, it is not. The Crab Cooker is, however, another local institution, which has been feeding locals fresh seafood in a fun and festive atmosphere since 1951. Alaskan king crabs are a specialty and come with potatoes or pilaf and coleslaw. When in season, don't miss the soft-shell crab. $$

Dad's, 318 Marine Ave., Balboa Island. Open daily 5:30–10 PM. This donut shop/frozen banana stand sells a Newport Beach food staple: the Balboa Bar, an ice cream bar hand-dipped in chocolate and then rolled in toppings like peanuts, crushed Oreos, or butterbrickle candy. $

Wilma's Patio (949-675-5542; www.wilmaspatio.com), 203 Marine Ave., Balboa Island. Open daily for breakfast, lunch, and dinner. This old-style diner, with a tiny sidewalk patio, is a family-run business since 1975 and offers comfort food to a regularly packed house. For *big* appetites, don't miss the famous Balboa Belly Bombers, a round French bread hollowed out and stuffed to overflowing with eggs, ham, and cheese or eggs and Italian sausage. $$

San Juan Capistrano

Pedro's Tacos (949-489-7752), 31721 Camino Capistrano. Open daily for lunch and dinner. Across the street from the San Juan mission, this local favorite taco shack serves *amazing* carne asada tacos, with authentic salsa, at very inexpensive prices. Expect a long line at the walk-up order window, and plan to eat at the picnic tables out front. $

DAD'S

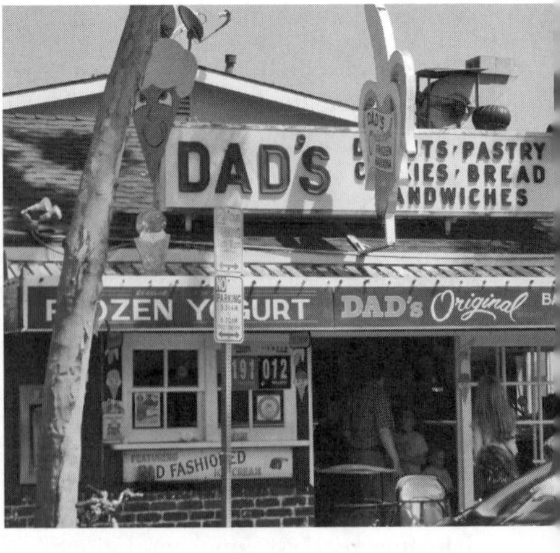

✷ Entertainment

CLUBS 🍸 **Beach Ball Bar** (949-675-8041), 2116 W. Oceanfront, Newport Beach. Just a few feet from the sand and the Newport Beach Pier, the landmark Beach Ball offers pool tables, a juke box, and inexpensive drinks—all in a casual, beachy atmosphere that makes it easy to meet people and have a good time. It's open pretty much constantly (6–2 AM), so no need to wait for happy hour here.

🍸 **Malarkey's Irish Pub** (949-675-2340), 3011 Newport Blvd., Newport Beach. Near the beach, this large Irish bar is casual and friendly, offering draft beer, cocktails, and decent pub grub. Needless to say, this is *the* place to be for St. Patrick's Day in Newport Beach.

🍸 **Ocean Brewing Company** (949-497-3381; www.oceanbrewing.com), 237 Ocean Ave., Laguna Beach. This inviting microbrewery and restaurant serves breakfast and lunch daily, and offers handcrafted beers and an inventive martini bar. The casual environment makes this a great place for date night or an evening out with friends.

🍸 **Royal Hawaiian** (949-494-8001; www.royalhawaiianlaguna.com), 331 N. Coast Hwy., Laguna Beach. Befitting Laguna's many idyllic beaches, the Royal Hawaiian offers an authentic tiki bar, a favorite since 1947. Enjoy happy hour and nightly live entertainment, and catch sports action at the enormous bar.

✪ 🍸 **The White House** (949-494-8088; www.whitehouserestaurant.com), 340 S. Coast Hwy., Laguna Beach. In downtown, this restaurant and nightclub has been a Laguna landmark since 1918. In addition to daily breakfast, lunch, and dinner, the White House offers live entertainment and dancing every evening.

THEATERS The Laguna Playhouse (949-497-2787; www.lagunaplayhouse.com), 606 Laguna Canyon Rd., Laguna Beach. Since the 1920s, the Laguna Playhouse has been an active community theater that has earned critical acclaim for professional excellence. The main stage hosts seven productions a year. Here's a little trivia: Harrison Ford got his start at the Laguna Playhouse, in a play titled *John Brown's Body*.

✷ Selective Shopping

Shopping is Orange County's favorite sport, and there are seemingly endless opportunities for visitors to find fashion, artwork, jewelry, home fashions, and antiques. In Laguna Niguel, **Plaza de La Paz** (27241 La Paz Road) offers more than 40 restaurants, home furnishing stores, and specialty shops. The **Laguna Hills Mall** (949-586-8283), 24155 Laguna Hills Mall Drive, in nearby Laguna, is a traditional mall anchored by Macy's and features more than one hundred specialty stores. In Newport Beach, check out **Fashion Island** (949-721-2000), 401 Newport Center Drive, an outdoor retail and

PEDRO'S TACOS

entertainment center overlooking the ocean featuring lush landscaping, a koi pond, and a carousel. For those looking for a more intimate shopping experience, tiny **Balboa Island** in Newport Beach offers bikini boutiques, children's clothing, and home and garden furnishings on Marine Avenue. (Serious shoppers will want to head inland for the *really* big shopping opportunities; see *Shopping* in the "Inland Orange County" chapter.)

INSIDER TIP: The first Thursday of every month in Laguna Beach is Art Walk. From 6 to 9 pm patrons can explore more than 50 galleries for a fun, free evening of culture. A free shuttle service runs from the Laguna Art Museum at Bluebird Center (at Bluebird and Pacific Coast Highway) to the participating galleries.

INLAND ORANGE COUNTY

Inland Orange County is famous for upscale suburbs, high-tech industries (especially in the brain-trust region around the University of California, Irvine), and theme parks. Buena Park is home to **Knott's Berry Farm** and its sister water park, **Soak City,** and Anaheim is home to The Disneyland® Resort, which comprises **Disneyland, Disney's California Adventure,** and **Downtown Disney.** Note that because of the huge popularity of The Disneyland® Resort, I discuss the latter three parks and adjacent restaurants and lodging options in an extended, separate section (part 3).

Visitors will find inland OC more spread out than the coastal region, which means more driving to and from and more congestion getting to destinations. Nevertheless, this region offers myriad recreational opportunities, including some of the best golf in the area, and a surprising number of world-class museums.

✱ To See

HISTORICAL SITES Crystal Cathedral (714-971-4000), 12141 Lewis St., Garden Grove (southwest of Anaheim). Home to the weekly *Hour of Power* broadcast, this stunning architectural achievement is worth touring, regardless of one's faith. Every year, the cathedral stages two large pageants: *The Glory of Christmas* and *The Glory of Easter.*

Old Town Irvine, Sand Canyon Ave. and Burt Rd., Irvine. Dating to 1887, this area started out as a distribution and storage center of the 100,000-acre Irvine Ranch. It developed and grew over the years to include a granary, a storage warehouse, a blacksmith's shop, a hotel, a general store, and bungalows for employees. Today these structures have been restored for commercial purposes, but the exteriors remain authentic.

KNOTT'S BERRY FARM

© Knott's

Courtesy of the Anaheim Convention and Visitors Bureau

THE BOWERS MUSEUM OF CULTURAL ART

MUSEUMS ✪ ✐ **Bowers Museum of Cultural Art** (714-567-3600; www.bowers.org), 2002 N. Main St., Santa Ana. Open Tues.–Sun 10–4. Originally founded in 1936 by the city of Santa Ana, the organization closed its doors in the mid-1980s, reopening a decade later as a cultural center that includes a "Kidseum" for children and offering exhibitions, art classes for adults and children, and community lectures. In the past 15 or so years, the museum has hosted more than 50 special traveling exhibits. Look for Native American art, art and artifacts from the Pacific Islands, and pre-Columbian pottery. Adults $12, seniors and children $9.

✐ **Discovery Science Center** (714-542-2823), 2500 N. Main St., Santa Ana. Open daily 10–5. Just off the I-5 freeway, this distinctive building boasting a 100-foot-tall tilting cube up front offers hands-on exhibits especially appropriate for children 12 and younger. Among the highlights is a real bed of nails, to allow guests to explore the nature of force and weight for themselves. (Don't worry: my daughter promises this doesn't hurt.) There is also a 4-D movie theater (think 3-D but with special effects like fog and wind). Adults $12.95, children $9.95.

Irvine Museum (949-476-2565; www.irvinemuseum.org), 18881 Van Karman Ave., Suite 100, Irvine. Open Tues.–Sat. 11–5. This small museum features California art of the impressionist period (1890–1930) and highlights regional landscapes. New exhibits are featured every season. Admission is free.

✪ **Pretend City Children's Museum** (949-428-3900; www.pretendcity.org), 29 Hubble, Irvine. Open daily at 10 AM; closing hours vary. Young children (ages two to eight) have the chance to try on future careers at this new hands-on museum, 28,000 square feet of space that includes a pretend grocery store, farm, art studio, restaurant, lifeguard station, and doctor's office, among others. Adults and children $10.

✱ To Do

GOLF ✪ **Black Gold Golf Course** (714-961-0060), 1 Black Gold Dr., Yorba Linda. Located in Yorba Linda (northeast of Anaheim), Black Gold has raked in

THE NIXON PRESIDENTIAL LIBRARY AND MUSEUM

Although he might not fit the stereotype of a laid-back, beachgoing native, President Richard Nixon was a Southern Californian. He was born in inland Yorba Linda (northeast of Anaheim), and today the Nixon family's modest home is part of the Nixon Presidential Library (714-983-9120; www.nixon library.gov), 18001 Yorba Linda Boulevard. Also within the scope of this expansive and fascinating museum guests can view a replica of the Lincoln Sitting Room as it was decorated during Nixon's administration; a replica of the East Room of the White House; and *Army One,* the actual helicopter used by Presidents Kennedy, Johnson, Nixon, and Ford. The library has extensive research opportunities for scholars and also offers rotating exhibits that feature documents such as Nixon's daily diary; national security memos; and copies of every Nixon speech, message, and proclamation. Whatever your political leanings, this library and museum offers a rare peek into the inner workings of the political and personal life of one of the most compelling public figures of the 20th century.

the accolades over recent years: it has been voted one of the top two best municipal courses in Southern California by *Southland Golf Magazine,* rated four and a half stars by *Golf Digest,* and judged as a "hidden gem" by the *Orange County Register.* This par 72 course includes numerous water features, including a beautiful waterfall on the 18th green, and pretty views. Green fee: $75–115.

Coyote Hills Golf Course (714-672-6800; www.coyotehillsgc.com), 1440 E. Bastanchury Rd., Fullerton. This naturalistic course in Fullerton (north of Anaheim) has been tapped by *Golf for Women* as one of the "Top 100 Women Friendly Courses" in the country. Tee off at dawn or twilight and increase the possibility of seeing one of the namesake coyotes. Green fee: $69–110.

Oak Creek Golf Club (949-653-5300; www.oakcreekgolfclub.com), 1 Golf Club Dr., Irvine. In suburban Irvine, this Tom Fazio–designed course is named after the picturesque creek that cuts through. Look for well-manicured greens, bull-nose-carved bunkers, and tapered fairways. Green fee: $110–165.

Strawberry Farms Golf Course (949-551-1811; www.strawberryfarmsgolf.com), 11 Strawberry Farms Rd., Irvine. Strawberry Farms is a community course that offers championship golf in a rural setting. Green fee: $50–160.

✪ **Tustin Ranch Golf Club** (714-730-1611; www.tustinranchgolf.com), 12442 Tustin Ranch Rd., Tustin. East of Santa Ana, in suburban Tustin, this Ted Robinson–designed course is regularly chosen by *Golf Digest* as one of the best in Orange County. Green fee: $75–90.

THEME PARKS AND ZOOS See part 3 for extensive coverage of Anaheim's **Disneyland, Disney's California Adventure,** and **Downtown Disney.**

✪ 🖍 **Knott's Berry Farm** (714-220-5200; www.knotts.com), 8039 Beach Blvd., Buena Park. Open daily from 10 AM; closing times vary by season. Billing itself as

"America's First Amusement Park," Knott's Berry Farm started out just as the name implies—as a berry farm. In the 1930s, Walter and Cordelia Knott helped develop the boysenberry, a cross between a blackberry and a raspberry, and they became locally famous for selling jams and jellies from their farm stand. Farming was a tough business, however, especially during the Great Depression, so Cordelia augmented their income by selling chicken dinners—a business that grew exponentially from a few modest tables that could seat a dozen at a time into what is now known as **Mrs. Knott's Chicken Dinner Restaurant,** which serves more than 1.5 million guests every year. Because the chicken dinner restaurant quickly became popular (serving as many as four thousand dinners on Sun. by 1940), the Knott family developed an authentic Old West–themed ghost town to give waiting customers something to do; this highly authentic area eventually became the first of Knott's Berry Farm's six themed zones. Throughout the years, the Knott family added to the park, which today includes some of the best thrill rides in California, including the Corkscrew, the world's first looping roller coaster; Bigfoot Rapids, a wild white-water rafting ride; the GhostRider, one of the longest wooden roller coasters in the country; Montezooma's Revenge, which accelerates from 0 to 55 miles per hour in three seconds through a seven-story loop—both forward and backward; the Silver Bullet, a suspended coaster that corkscrews and spirals, with drops of as much as 100 feet; and the horrifying Supreme Scream, an attraction that plunges riders straight down 254 feet at more than 50 miles an hour. The park also has an extensive area for young children, the Camp Snoopy zone. Regardless of age, don't miss the Grand Sierra Scenic Railroad, a seven-minute ride aboard a replica of a steam locomotive that is prone to holdups by bandits. Although Knott's Berry Farm is much smaller than its more famous neighbor, The Disneyland® Resort, as a result Knott's tends to be much less crowded, even during the summer months—which is somewhat surprising given it is also much less expensive. Adults and children 12 and older $54, seniors and children 3–11 $24.

Knott's Soak City USA (714-220-5200; www.knotts.com), 8039 Beach Blvd., Buena Vista. Open daily at 10 AM, late May–early Sept.; closing hours vary. This expansive, colorful water park offers a variety of thrilling water slides and attractions, including the Old Man Falls, a series of three single-rider speed slides; the Banzai Falls, six multilane speed slides that are designed for a headfirst drop; Tidal Wave Bay, a 750,000-gallon pool with a variable wave machine; and the Sunset River, a 0.3-mile twisting, turning lazy river. The park also offers the Gremmie Lagoon, designed for young children. Beware of height restrictions at this park: many attractions require life jackets for anyone under 4 feet. Adults and children 12 and older $26, children 11 and younger $20.

Medieval Times (866-543-9637; www.medievaltimes.com), 7662 Beach Blvd., Buena Park. Step into the 11th century at this enormous dinner-theater venue that offers a four-course meal (roasted chicken, spare ribs, soup, garlic bread, dessert)—all to be

INSIDER TIP: Save time and money by purchasing Knott's Berry Farm tickets online, for a discount of as much as $22 for adults. There are also significant discounts for AAA members and Southern California residents.

enjoyed sans flatware—and an elaborate jousting tournament. Guests are seated in an amphitheater of sorts and assigned a knight to cheer on. The epic battles include horses, authentic weaponry, and a royal court presiding over the evening. Adults and children $35.

Pirates Dinner Adventure (714-690-1497; www.piratesdinneradventure.com), 7600 Beach Blvd., Buena Park. Another dinner-theater attraction, the Pirates Dinner Adventures is set aboard a replica 18th-century Spanish galleon that is anchored in a 250,000-gallon indoor lagoon. Seating surrounds the set in six additional ships. The show includes swashbuckling heroes, damsels in distress, sword fights, and cannon blasts, but the best part is the audience participation: more than 150 guests have the chance to play a role in each show. For an additional $15, guest can upgrade to front-row booths and the chance to share in the pirates' booty (a strand of beads). Adults and children $30.

✷ Lodging

PRICE KEY FOR A STANDARD ROOM:

$	$100 or less
$$	$101–150
$$$	$151–250
$$$$	$251 and up

The area most visited by travelers in inland Orange County surrounds The Disneyland® Resort and Knott's Berry Farm areas. Let me be blunt: Aside from a handful of lovely hotels in Anaheim (which are covered in part 3), the area is otherwise devoid of much beyond cheap motels and moderately priced chain hotels. In all good faith, I can recommend only one independent hotel, which is adjacent to Knott's Berry Farm, and although it is a bit pricier than the aforementioned options, it is also a bit more appealing.

Anaheim

See part 3 for coverage of hotels in The Disneyland® Resort and around Anaheim.

Buena Park

Knott's Berry Farm Resort Hotel (866-752-2444; www.knottshotel.com), 7675 Crescent Ave. Located on the grounds of **Knott's Berry Farm** and adjacent to **Knott's Soak City USA,** the modest family-friendly hotel is also close to **The Disneyland® Resort.** Standard rooms are basic and large enough to sleep a family in comfort. When traveling with young children, book a Camp Snoopy room, which is festive with Snoopy decorations throughout. The pool is large and inviting. The hotel offers a free shuttle to Disneyland. $$

KNOTT'S BERRY FARM RESORT HOTEL

© Knott's

✷ Where to Eat

DINING OUT

Anaheim

See part 3 for coverage of fine dining in The Disneyland® Resort and around Anaheim.

Buena Park

✪ **Mrs. Knott's Chicken Dinner Restaurant** (714-220-5080; www.knotts.com), 8039 Beach Blvd. Open daily for lunch and dinner. Just outside the park entrance, this homey restaurant's draw has long been some of the best fried chicken outside my mother's kitchen—along with Knott's famous boysenberry pie. This place is one of the worst-kept secrets in the area. Waits can be upwards of two hours on the weekends. The good news is they have counter service, too, so if you don't have the time to sit down and enjoy the nostalgic ambiance of the dining room, grab a bucket to go. $$

Irvine

Chakra (949-854-0009; www.chakracuisine.com), 4143 Campus Dr. Open daily for lunch and dinner. This elegant Indian restaurant offers a seductive, exotic interior and traditional recipes reinvented for Western palates. Favorites include tandoori rack of lamb, lobster in a coconut red curry, and my eternal favorite, chicken tikka masala. There are also ample choices for vegetarians, like paneer (yogurt cheese) in spicy Makhani sauce, or the "dal of the day"—an ever-changing variety of lentil soup. The restaurant offers a wide variety of wines, but I've never been successful at pairing wine with Indian food, so I stick with the Chakratinis. $$–$$$

MRS. KNOTT'S CHICKEN DINNER RESTAURANT

© Knott's

PRICE KEY FOR A TYPICAL ENTRÉE:

$	$10 and under
$$	$11–20
$$$	$21–30
$$$$	$31 and up

EATING OUT

Anaheim

See part 3 for coverage of casual dining in The Disneyland® Resort and around Anaheim.

Irvine

Ajisen Ramen (949-833-3288; www.ajisen-la.com), 2700 Alton Pkwy. Open daily for lunch and dinner. Part of a chain of dozens of Japanese noodle shops, Ajisen Ramen sells authentic chewy, thin ramen noodles served with a traditional tonkatsu soup base and paired with beef curry, spicy pork, pork ribs, and a handful of other meat and veggie combos. $$

Tia Juana's Long Bar (949-551-2998; www.tiajuanas.com), 14988 Sand Canyon Rd. Open daily for lunch and dinner. This casual Mexican restaurant is located in an old lima bean warehouse, in Old Town Irvine, in what was the sprawling Irvine Ranch. The historic atmosphere fits the rustic Baja fare, like carne asada steak, spicy short ribs diablo, and juicy carnitas. $$

✷ Entertainment

See also part 3 for specific coverage of The Disneyland® Resort and Anaheim.

THEATERS **Irvine Barclay Theater and Cheng Hall** (949-854-4607; www.thebarclay.org), 4242 Campus Dr., Irvine. On the campus of the University of California, Irvine, the Barclay is renowned for imaginative, world-class programming in theater, music, and dance, and is home to the likes of the Long Beach Opera, Community Youth Orchestra of Southern California, and the Festival Ballet Theater.

✪ **Orange County Performing Arts Center** (714-556-2787; www.ocpac.org), 600 Town Center Dr., Costa Mesa. This expansive center is one of the premier venues in Southern California, thanks to cutting-edge facilities and spectacular architecture. The center hosts Broadway shows, leading dance companies, and world-class touring artists, and offers a 3,000-seat opera house, a 2,000-seat concert hall, a 500-seat multipurpose theater, and a 250-seat intimate venue. The OC Performing Arts center is home to the Pacific Chorale, the Pacific Symphony, and the Philharmonic Society of Orange County.

✷ Selective Shopping

Inland, in Costa Mesa, the **South Coast Plaza** (800-782-8888), San Diego Freeway (I-405) at Bristol Street, is a favorite with the OC locals, offering upscale shopping with stores like Dolce & Gabbana, DKNY, Fendi, Giorgio Armani, Gucci, Michael Kors, and Versace. **The Lab** (714-966-6660), 2930 Bristol Street, Costa Mesa, will attract those whose tastes are more eclectic; it is anchored by ARTH, Black & Blue, and Urban Outfitters. The new **Shops at Anaheim GardenWalk,** 321 W. Katella Avenue, Anaheim, blend entertainment with shopping, offering retail stores, dining options, movie theaters, and an upscale bowling lounge. In Irvine, look for the **Irvine Spectrum Center** (949-753-5180), 71 Fortune Drive, Irvine, which also hosts retail and entertainment venues.

SANTA CATALINA ISLAND

Although Santa Catalina Island is only 22 miles off the coast (accessible via Dana Point and Newport Beach), it is worlds apart from mainland Southern California—and for that reason, an extremely popular weekend getaway for locals. The island, which aside from heavily populated Avalon (the ferry terminus city) is largely preserved and undeveloped, is surrounded by blue, clear water—so clear it's possible to stroll on the beach and see fish swimming underwater 10 feet from the shoreline. There is not one traffic light on the island—in fact, many residents don't have cars; most transportation is via golf cart, and although the sidewalks can get congested on summer weekends, there is no rush hour here.

The town of Avalon was founded as a resort in 1887. In 1919 William Wrigley Jr., chewing gum magnate, purchased the majority share of the conservancy company that manages the island. A few years later, he brought his baseball team, the Chicago Cubs, to the island for spring training, which was held here for the next 30 years. In 1972 the Catalina Island Conservancy bought 88 percent of the island, to protect it and restore the land. The island is now a haven for wildlife, including bald eagles and a large herd of bison—remnants of a small group of animals left behind on the island after a Western was filmed here in 1924.

Today visitors are sure to visit the picturesque Green Pleasure Pier, shop along the main drag in Avalon, stroll the pretty little beaches on Avalon Harbor, and check out the iconic Casino Building. On the western end of the island is Two Harbors, a small quiet village that offers premier camping. Lodging can be expensive, but thanks to regular ferry runs, this is an easy day trip from Orange County.

GETTING THERE *By air:* You can arrive in Catalina via helicopter for less cash than you might think (about $150 round-trip). The flight is a 15-minute trip aboard **Island Express Helicopters** (800-2AVALON; www.islandexpress.com), which depart hourly from San Pedro and Long Beach.

By ferry: Two ferry companies provide service to the island from Dana Point, Newport Beach, Long Beach, San Pedro, and Marina del Ray, and arrive at the hub of Avalon or Two Harbors, to the north. Guests may bring aboard luggage, but bicycles, camping gear, and larger sporting equipment is an extra cost. Ferries begin departing from the mainland at 9 AM and all leave Catalina by 4:30. Look for the schools of dolphins that regularly greet the ferries just off the coast of Catalina and escort the boats into the harbor. It takes about an hour and a half to reach

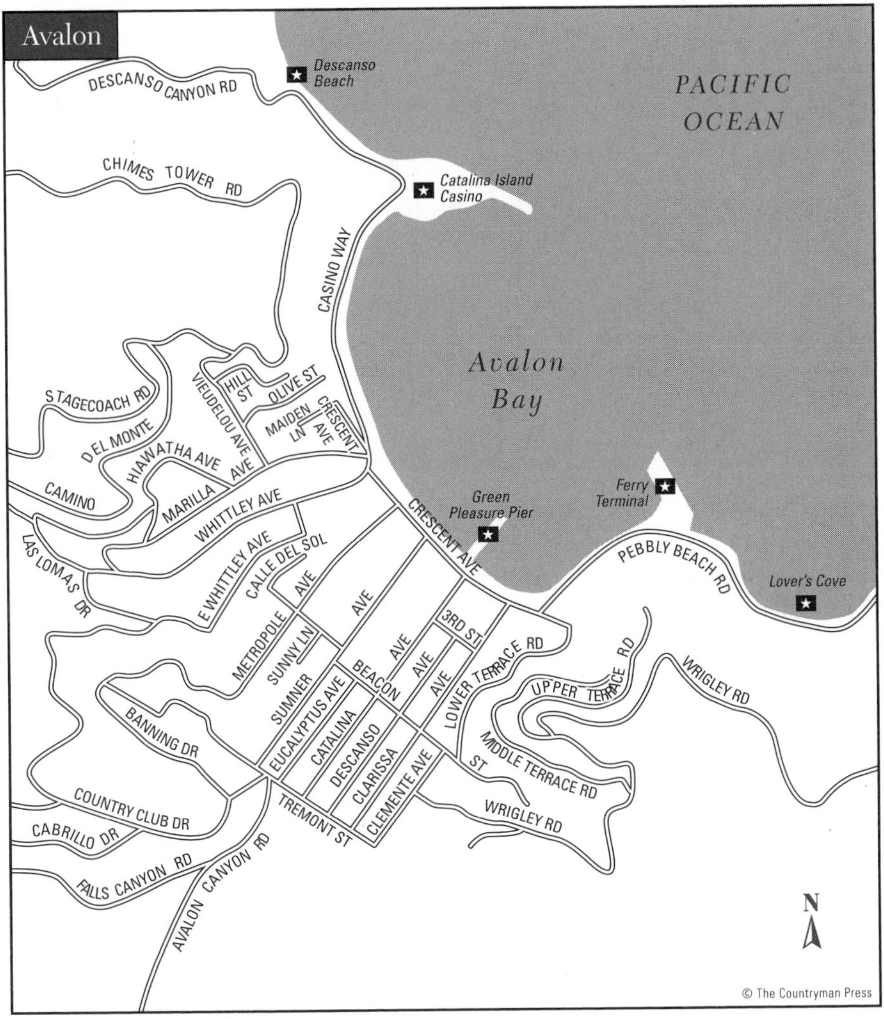

Catalina from Dana Point aboard one of these fast, people-only ferries, which make up to 30 round-trips a day, so arrival and departure times are flexible. **Catalina Express** (310-519-1212; www.catalinaexpress.com), $60 round-trip; **Catalina Flyer Express** (800-830-7744; www.catalinainfo.com), $57 round-trip.

✷ To See

HISTORICAL SITES Casino Building (310-510-2414). At the northeastern end of the bay, the eye-catching Casino Building, a circular art deco structure, is the jewel of Avalon Harbor. Don't bring your bucket of coins to gamble the night away here: in this instance, *casino* refers to the Italian word meaning "gathering place."

Courtesy Catalina Chamber of Commerce

DESCANSO BEACH, WITH THE CASINO IN THE BACKGROUND

In its heyday in the 1940s, this was the place to come for ballroom dancing to some of the most famous big bands of the era. Today, the building houses the **Catalina Island Museum,** the **Casino Art Gallery** (featuring a small collection of local artists), and the **Avalon Theater.**

✪ ✐ **Green Pleasure Pier.** At the center of Crescent Avenue in Avalon, this historic pier dates to about 1910 and is the jumping-off point for glass-bottom-boat and submarine tours, fishing trips (see *To Do*), and home to a handful of local fast-food outlets.

MUSEUMS Catalina Island Museum (310-510-2414; www.catalinamuseum.org). Open daily 10–4. In the picturesque Casino Building, the Catalina Island Museum features exhibits on local history and is worth a brief visit for first-timers. Adults $5.

Wrigley Memorial and Botanical Garden (310-510-2595; www.catalina.com/memorial.html), Avalon Canyon Rd., Avalon. Open daily 8–5. Just 2 miles from Avalon Bay, the Wrigley Memorial and Botanical Garden features a monument commissioned by the Wrigley family (the folks responsible for chewing gum and longtime owners of the Chicago Cubs), who lived part-time on the island for decades. The Spanish mausoleum is inlaid with Catalina tiles, which are now widely collected, and it is surrounded by a garden of native plants and cacti (including a type of wild tomato that grows only on Catalina). Oddly enough, no one from the Wrigley family is entombed here. Adults $5.

INSIDER TIP: The ferry trip over to Santa Catalina is usually choppy, and those prone to seasickness should take medication or wear motion-sickness wristbands, just in case. Many find sitting up top—outside, in the fresh air—helps with nausea, but it is also windy and sunny, so be sure to dress properly and wear sunscreen.

✷ To Do

Although there are independent tour companies on Catalina Island, the **Santa Catalina Island Company** (800-414-2754; www.visitcatalinaisland.com) offers the vast majority of such adventures, including an inland motor tour that will take guests from Avalon through the island preserve to the Airport in the Sky, Casino tours, glass-bottom boat tours, and a Seal Rocks tour. Discounts of as much as 25 percent are available from this organization when you book more than one tour.

BICYCLING Only locals are allowed to drive cars on the island—and even for them there is a years-long wait for a permit to do so. Transportation is thus by golf cart, foot, or bicycle. **Brown's Bikes** (310-510-0111), 301 Crescent Ave. and 107 Pebbly Beach Road, rents beach cruisers, tandem bikes, and mountain bikes. Note that to bike off-road in Catalina (i.e., all but the paved streets of Avalon), you must purchase an annual permit from the Catalina Conservancy (310-510-2595).

GOLF Despite the many golf carts on the island (as noted, the primary mode of transportation even for locals), there is really only one golf course in Avalon: **Catalina Island Golf Course** (310-510-0530), 1 Country Club Drive, a nine-hole executive course with small greens that offers a modest challenge for proficient golfers. Green fee: $39.

SPAS ❀ **Catalina Canyon Spa** (800-478-7829; www.catalinacanyonresort.com), 888 Country Club Dr., Avalon. This day spa, part of the **Catalina Canyon Resort,** offers herbal wraps and a large variety of massages and facials, all at relatively low rates. An 80-minute treatment can be under $150.

Catalina Sea Spa (310-510-1633; www.catalinaseaspa.com), 117 Clarissa Ave., Avalon. Look for the Goddess package at the Catalina Sea Spa, which includes a lavender facial massage, a peppermint scalp massage, and a 50-minute full-body massage.

✷ Water Sports

BOATING **Catalina Adventure Tours** (877-510-2888; www.catalinaadventuretours.com). If you don't want to get wet (or the water temps are just too chilly), book a trip aboard a real-life yellow submarine, or board a glass-bottom boat, for a peek into the clear Catalina waters.

Catalina Ocean Rafting (310-510-0211; www.catalinaoceanrafting.com). Tour the Avalon waterfront or Two Harbors aboard motor-powered inflatables, or book snorkeling trips to explore sea caves or frolic with dolphins. Whale-watching tours are available Jan.–Mar.

Descanso Beach Ocean Sports (310-510-1226; www.kayakcatalinaisland.com), P.O. Box 386, Avalon, CA 90704. This organization offers guided natural-history kayaking trips that include all equipment and instruction, as well as kayak and snorkel rentals.

DIVING AND SNORKELING The water is surprisingly clear surrounding Catalina—so much so that the ocean looks much more like the Caribbean than typical Southern California waters. **Lover's Cove** is excellent for snorkeling, with gentle waters and good visibility. Even beginners are sure to spot the native bright-orange Garibaldi—but watch out for glass-bottom boats and kayaks, which litter the area by midmorning. Certified divers will want to head to **Casino Point Underwater Park,** which offers a number of wrecks to explore.

Catalina Divers Supply (310-510-0330; www.catalinadiverssupply.com), P.O. Box 126, Avalon, CA 90704. Located at the Green Pleasure Pier in Avalon and at Casino Point, this organization offers scuba and snorkel tours of Avalon, for novices through masters. Be sure to call ahead for reservations. Certification classes are available.

FISHING ✐ **Afishinado Charters** (310-510-2440; www.fishcatalina.com). Charter fishing trips for families or expert anglers alike with Afishinado Charters, and expect to catch yellowtail tuna.

Scotty's Sportfishing (310-510-1570; www.scottyssportfishing.com). Charter a boat for private parties for fishing and sight-seeing.

✷ Green Space

BEACHES ✪ **Descanso Beach,** on the far end of Avalon Casino. This small, scenic beach offers prime swimming and snorkeling. Part of the Descanso Beach Club, there are ample facilities here, including outdoor showers, dressing rooms, and chair and umbrella rentals.

Middle Beach, just to the north of the Green Pleasure Pier. Scenic and central, Middle Beach offers clear waters and proximity to restaurants and water activities. This and South Beach are small and get quite crowded in the summer.

✐ **South Beach,** just south of the Green Pleasure Pier. This beach is at the heart of the action, near the many eateries in downtown Avalon and on the pier. The water is calm and deepens very gradually, which makes it ideal for children.

TWO HARBORS

Courtesy Catalina Chamber of Commerce

GARDENS Wrigley Memorial and Botanical Garden (310-510-2595; www.catalina.com/memorial.html), Avalon Canyon Rd., Avalon. Adults $5. See *To See—Museums* for a full description.

NATURE PRESERVES Casino Point Underwater Park, immediately in front of the Casino on the Avalon Harbor. This marine preserve disallows boating and fishing, thus making it a premier spot to scuba dive or snorkel in the surprisingly clear waters. Bright orange Garibaldi are the showiest residents, but also expect to see bat rays, Baja lobsters, and moray eels. Nearby **Lover's Cove** is shallower and thus better for snorkeling (no diving is allowed here)—but look out below: glass-bottom boats cruise these waters as well.

✷ Lodging

Avalon

In addition to a number of fine small hotels, Catalina Island offers several campsites that allow guests a true beach wilderness experience. These include **Boat-in Primitive Beach Camp Sites** (www.campingcatalinaisland.com), **Catalina Island Camping** (310-510-TENT; www.visitcatalinaisland.com), and **Hermit Gulch** (310-510-TENT; www.visitcatalinaisland.com).

Avalon Hotel (310-510-7070; www.theavalonhotel.com), 124 Whittley Ave. This historic lodging started out life as an exclusive gentleman's club in the pre–World War II era. Today, the small hotel off Avalon Harbor (an easy walk from the ferry landing) showcases the famous Catalina tile and fine wooden details in Craftsman style, with individually decorated rooms that are comfortable and plush. Amenities include thick robes, ocean views that won't stop, complimentary taxi pickup, and an extensive cold breakfast. My favorite room (Room 301) offers a wraparound balcony with stunning views of the harbor. $$$$

Catalina Canyon Resort (800-478-7829; www.catalinacanyonresort.com), 888 Country Club Dr. In the foothills, overlooking downtown Avalon, this relaxed, unfussy property is ideal for families traveling with children. Cheerful island décor and Mediterranean architecture, along with nicely landscaped grounds and a big pool, make this a good choice for those who want to unwind—and it is quite a bit less expensive than some of the smaller properties in downtown. $$

Hotel Metropole (310-510-1884; www.metropolemarketplace.com), 205 Crescent St. This tiny boutique hotel is awash in beachy, airy style; some rooms offer fireplaces, Jacuzzi tubs, ocean-view balconies, and spectacular harbor views. Recently renovated rooms in the VIP wing are especially luxurious, with rich wooden furniture and plenty of room to spread out. In addition to standard accommodations, the Metropole offers the adorably decorated Beach House, a spacious, separate two-bedroom, two-bath home complete with cozy living room and full kitchen. $$$$

Hotel St. Lauren (310-510-2299; www.stlauren.com), P.O. Box 2166,

PRICE KEY FOR A STANDARD ROOM:

$	$100 or less
$$	$101–150
$$$	$151–250
$$$$	$251 and up

Avalon, CA 90704. Although this hotel boasts entirely too much *pink* for my taste, the country interior décor and gingerbread-clad Victorian exterior give it an unmistakable romance. The hotel is located a block from the beach and the main drag of Avalon—and frankly it is a bit of a hike from the ferry landing. However, this lodging offers some real bargains, depending on room choice, view, and season. $–$$$

✪ **The Inn on Mt. Ada** (310-510-2030; www.innonmtada.com), P.O. Box 2560, Avalon, CA 90704. Listed on the National Register of Historic Places, and dating to 1921, this Georgian Colonial mansion (former home to William Wrigley, of chewing gum fame) is perched high on a hill overlooking Avalon Bay. A stay here feels very much like a visit with a well-heeled friend, thanks to the luxurious yet comfortable surroundings and the impeccable hospitality of the innkeepers. Public rooms offer cozy sitting nooks arrayed to make the most of the jaw-dropping views. Each guest accommodation is decorated individually (and named). If possible, secure the Queen's Aviary, formerly Mrs. Wrigley's room, which offers postcard-perfect views of Avalon, the harbor, and the Casino. A stay at the inn includes a complimentary golf cart, as well as a hearty breakfast and a light lunch (with a daily Mexican special). Meals can be enjoyed in the Federal-style dining room or on the outdoor patio, which is highly recommended on sunny days, because the views go for miles. Snacks are served throughout the day and might include mixed nuts, freshly baked cookies, or even ice cream sundaes. No children 13 years or younger are allowed. $$$$

Courtesy Catalina Chamber of Commerce

THE INN ON MT. ADA

✪ **Snug Harbor Inn** (310-510-8400; www.snugharbor-inn.com), 108 Sumner Ave. This tiny inn is in the very heart of Avalon, across from the beachfront and overlooking Avalon Bay. The half dozen accommodations have a Cape Cod feel and an understated nautical theme. All rooms come with fireplaces, DVD and CD players, oversized Jacuzzi tubs, and luxurious bath appointments. There is a movie library for guests, and the inn will loan out beach chairs and towels. Each evening guests are served wine and cheese, and a complimentary and customizable continental breakfast is delivered to the rooms each morning. This small property manages to be quaint without being overly precious and offers the unparalleled convenience of being right in town. $$–$$$

🏵 **Zane Grey Hotel** (310-510-0996; www.pueblo.com), 199 Chimes Tower Rd. High on a cliff overlooking the Casino, with lovely views of both the ocean and the mountains, this former home to Western novelist Zane Grey is a pueblo-style structure decorated with Southwestern flair. The lofty balcony off the guest living room is the ideal perch from which to watch the cruise ships sail in to the harbor or to watch hummingbirds flit from one native plant to another. The ambling property has pretty gardens, and there is a small (unheated) pool in the shape of an arrowhead. Beware: Guests at the Zane Grey have no choice but to be on island time. There are no clocks, no TVs, and no phones in the rooms. To keep the hotel as serene as possible, families with children are encouraged to lodge elsewhere. A small buffet breakfast is included. $$

✷ Where to Eat

DINING OUT

Santa Catalina Island

✪ **Armstrong's Fish Market and Seafood Restaurant** (310-510-0133; www.armstrongseafood.com), 306 Crescent Ave. Open daily for lunch and dinner. This is my favorite option for fresh seafood on Avalon Bay. The outdoor patio right off the water offers great views of the iconic Casino. Specialties include mesquite broiled seafood that is literally straight off the boats. Fresh ceviche comes in the form of tilapia marinated in lime juice and served with a generous portion of cilantro and jalapeño. Check out the ahi tuna, which can be prepared blackened, and don't miss the house garlic bread. $$$

Catalina Country Club (310-510-7404), 1 Country Club Dr. Open daily for lunch and dinner. Former clubhouse of the Chicago Cubs, who used to train on the island, this elegant, Spanish-style country club is now a restaurant specializing in steak and seafood. Specialties include sand dabs served with lemon caper sauce, hanger steak with udon noodles, and roasted quail with a goat cheese stuffing. For lunch, don't miss the clubhouse burger. $$$

✪ 🏵 🍸 **Lobster Trap** (310-510-8585; www.catalinalobstertrap.com), 128 Catalina St. Open daily for lunch and dinner. This might not qualify as a "fine" dining institution, because it is a bit of a dive, but the cuisine is top-notch, even if the ambiance is a little rough around the edges. Patrons can choose from a large selection of fresh fish (swordfish, halibut, tuna, etc.) and specify preparation (blackened, with macadamia nut breading, served with fresh mango salsa, etc.), or pick one of the house specialties, like cioppino (a tomato-based seafood stew) or local lobster, charbroiled and served with a garlic and basil butter. For those looking to economize, there are also $3 tacos (fish, shrimp, steak, or chicken). $–$$$

🍸 **Steve's Steakhouse** (310-510-0333; www.stevessteakhouse.com), 417 Crescent Ave. Open daily for lunch and dinner. This pricey yet casual steakhouse is sure to please carnivores with a wide variety of red meat, including a 1-pound T-bone, filet mignon with traditional béarnaise, baby back ribs, rack of lamb, plus myriad surf-and-turf options. For a lighter meal, try the Chinese chicken salad or the delicious Boston-style clam chowder. Steve's offers a full bar as well. $$$

EATING OUT

Santa Catalina Island

Antonio's Pizzeria (310-510-0060), 114 Sumner Ave. Open daily for breakfast, lunch, and dinner. This longtime island favorite offers tasty Neapolitan pizza (try a pie with Portuguese

PRICE KEY FOR A TYPICAL ENTRÉE:

$	$10 and under
$$	$11–20
$$$	$21–30
$$$$	$31 and up

sausage), antipasto, salads, pasta, and huge subs, to eat in or to go. If you dine inside the restaurant, check out the 1950s tunes on the old jukebox. Better yet, grab a table on the outside patio and enjoy premium harbor views. Although one wouldn't expect it of a pizzeria, Antonio's also offers stellar breakfasts. $$

✪ **Big Olaf's** (310-510-0798), 220 Crescent Ave. Open daily. Big Olaf's ice cream parlor sells the best ice cream on the island, served in huge house-made waffle cones. Don't miss the frozen bananas and the outrageous banana splits. Expect long lines on hot days (which is most every day in the summertime). $

Coyote Joe's (310-510-1176; www.coyotejoescatalina.com), 113 Catalina St. Open daily for lunch, and for breakfast and dinner on Sat. and Sun. in the summer. Near the foot of the Green Pleasure Pier, this casual restaurant and bar offers Mexican specialties (check out the Wet Burrito) as well as great burgers. Dine inside or out. Try a Buffalo Milk cocktail, a Catalina Island specialty, with crème de cacao, banana, and whipped cream. $$

ANTONIO'S

Courtesy Catalina Chamber of Commerce

Eric's on the Pier (310-510-0894), Green Pier No. 2. Open daily for lunch and dinner. Chow down on a buffalo burger or a tasty breakfast burrito at this snack shack on the water. Eric's also offers great soft tacos and fresh fish-and-chips. This place has been family run for more than 75 years and couldn't be more casual: don't be surprised to see guests pull up a stool in their bathing suits. $

Joe's Place (310-510-0491), 501 Crescent Ave. Open daily for breakfast, lunch, and dinner. At the foot of the Green Pleasure Pier, this is a favorite with locals, thanks in large part to awesome burgers, fast service, and extremely fair prices. $–$$

Lloyd's of Avalon Confectionary (310-510-7266; www.catalinacandy.com), corner of Crescent Ave. and Front St. Open daily. Get your sweet fix here, with traditional saltwater taffy, gooey caramel apples (the Maui Wowie with macadamia nuts and white and milk chocolates is especially good), fudge, peanut brittle, and other house-made treats that you can watch in production through the glass windows. $

✱ Entertainment

The bulk of visitors to Catalina leave with the last ferries by 4:30 PM, so the nightlife on the island is predictably a little sparse. Locals have their favorite watering holes, however, and the natives are friendly.

CLUBS **El Galleon Restaurant and Karaoke Lounge** (310-510-1188; www.catalinahotspots.com), 411 Crescent Ave., Avalon. This boisterous establishment is also a well-liked restaurant specializing in applewood-smoked barbecue ribs and abalone (a personal favorite), but when the sun goes down, the joint becomes a popular karaoke spot for the over-21 crowd.

TOP 10 DAY IN CATALINA ISLAND

1. Chow down on a breakfast burrito at Antonio's Pizzeria (see pp. 131–132)
2. Take a morning walk along quiet Descanso Beach (see p. 128)
3. Kayak with dolphins in Avalon Bay (see p. 127)
4. Munch on a burger at Joe's Place on the Green Pleasure Pier (see p. 132)
5. Stroll alongside the cacti at Wrigley Memorial and Botanical Garden (see p. 126)
6. Shop at the Metropole Marketplace (see p. 133)
7. Dine on halibut with macadamia nut crust at the Lobster Trap (see p. 131)
8. Take in the feature of the week at the Avalon Theater (see p. 133)
9. Sip a potent Buffalo Milk nightcap at Luau Larry's (see p. 133)
10. Overnight at the Inn on Mt. Ada (see p. 130)

Y **Luau Larry's** (310-510-1919), 509 Crescent Ave, Avalon. This tropical tiki bar is adjacent to the beach and offers better than decent pub grub. Specialty drinks include the Wiki Wacker, made from rum, brandy, and pineapple juice, and the Pago Pago planter's punch. Look for the fake parrots drinking beer, and expect the late-night crowd to get rowdy.

Y **Marlin Club** (310-510-0044; www.marlinclub.com), 108 Catalina Ave., Avalon. The oldest bar in town, this watering hole has been restored to its original 1946 décor—and this would seem to include some patrons who have been frequenting the place since midcentury as well.

THEATERS ✪ **Avalon Theater** (310-510-0179). This restored art deco theater on the ground floor of the iconic Casino shows first-run movies in a stylish setting. Features generally change every week, and the theater can accommodate more than 1,800 at a sitting. The colorful wall murals alone are worth the price of admission.

✷ Selective Shopping

There are plenty of shops to explore in downtown Avalon, within steps of the ferry port. In addition, check out **Metropole Marketplace** (310-510-1884), a quaint cobblestoned shopping area that offers shops and cafés.

✷ Special Events

(in Greater Orange County)

January: **Catalina Island Plein Air Painting Exhibition** (310-510-2414), in Santa Catalina, features local outdoor scenes from more than 20 artists.

February: During **Annual Avalon Harbor Underwater Cleanup** (www.catalinaconvervancy.org), in Catalina, more than five hundred volunteers collect debris on the only day that diving is allowed in Avalon Bay.

March: **Swallows Day Parade** (949-493-1976), in San Juan Capistrano, is a nonmotorized parade downtown that celebrates the famous birds who return to the region every year.

April: **Newport Beach Film Festival** (www.newportbeachfilmfest.com), the last week of the month, showcases studio and independent films from around the world. **Annual Rubber Ducky Derby** (310-510-0288), on South Beach, Santa Catalina, is a fundraiser that supports the local children's theater group.

May: **Doheny Blues Festival** (949-360-7800), south of Dana Point, has music and food over Memorial Day Weekend. **Newport Beach Annual Food and Wine Festival** (949-729-4400), at the Balboa Bay Club, celebrates fine food and wine with demonstrations and tastings.

June: **Sawdust Art Festival** (949-494-3030; www.sawdustartfestival.org), in Laguna Beach, beginning late in the month and running through the end of Aug., offers workshops, exhibits, and a chance to meet artists. **Art-a-Fair** (949-494-4514) is an art festival in Laguna Beach that runs from the end of the month through early Sept. **Summer Jazz Festival** (949-729-6400), in Newport Beach, starts this month and runs through early Oct., with music, food, and wine.

July: The **Victoria Skimboards World Championship** (www.victoriaskimboards.com) is held in Laguna Beach. Running from early July through the end of Aug., the world-famous **Pageant of the Masters** (949-494-1145), in Laguna Beach, is where classical and contemporary art comes to life in living, breathing creations; live models pose in an outdoor amphitheater, with the accompaniment of an orchestra and live narration.

August: **San Clemente Street Festival** (949-492-1131) has live music, food, arts and crafts, and a run/walk.

September: **Doheny Days** (949-360-7800), in Dana Point, is a two-day festival of reggae music, food, and arts

NEWPORT BEACH CHRISTMAS BOAT PARADE

Courtesy of Visit Newport Beach Inc.

and crafts vendors. At the **Annual Taste of Newport** (949-729-4400), a three-day event, more than 50 restaurants and wineries participate in a tasting festival.

October: **Laguna Dance Festival** (949-715-5578; www.lagunadancefestival.org), early in the month, offers myriad dance performances and educational opportunities. **Halloween Parade** (310-510-1520), down Crescent Ave., Santa Catalina, starts at 4 PM on Halloween. **Battle of the Mariachis,** in San Juan Capistrano, is held in the mission courtyard. **Old World Oktoberfest**, in Old World Village, Huntington Beach, has oompah music, German *wurst*, and plenty of beer.

December: At the **Newport Beach Christmas Boat Parade** (www.christmasboatparade.com), festooned boats and yachts ply the harbor in a nighttime parade. **New Year's Eve Celebration** (310-510-1520), Casino Ballroom, Santa Catalina, is a black-tie optional event (make reservations for this highly popular party as much as six months in advance).

3

The Disneyland® Resort

THE DISNEYLAND® RESORT

The most die-hard Disneyland® Resort fans want to believe that this small patch of real estate is its own sovereign country—or at least believe that it *ought* to be. On any given day, the population inside the gates of Disneyland is greater than most small U.S. cities. In reality, the resort falls within the borders of the city of Anaheim, in Orange County (see part 2), but the über-popular resort begs for more comprehensive discussion: The Disneyland® Resort is the most visited tourist attraction in California—and the sixth most visited attraction in the country.

The heart of the resort is Disneyland, the theme park most people think of when they think of The Disneyland® Resort. Just across from the entrance turnstiles is the 21st-century Disney's California Adventure theme park, and adjacent is a wildly popular shopping and entertainment complex called Downtown Disney. Also in the official reaches of The Disneyland® Resort are three Disney-owned hotels, all within walking distance to both theme parks.

WORLD OF DISNEY

DISNEYLAND

Mickey Mouse put Anaheim on the map. Sure, there were orange groves and a small suburban community in place before Walt Disney christened the "happiest place on earth" back in 1955, but it was Disneyland that made Anaheim the family-travel mecca that it is today. Although there is more to Anaheim than the pixie-dusted nirvana of this ultimate theme park, Disneyland remains at the heart of the city, and the prime reason many visitors to Southern California ever see it. Of the

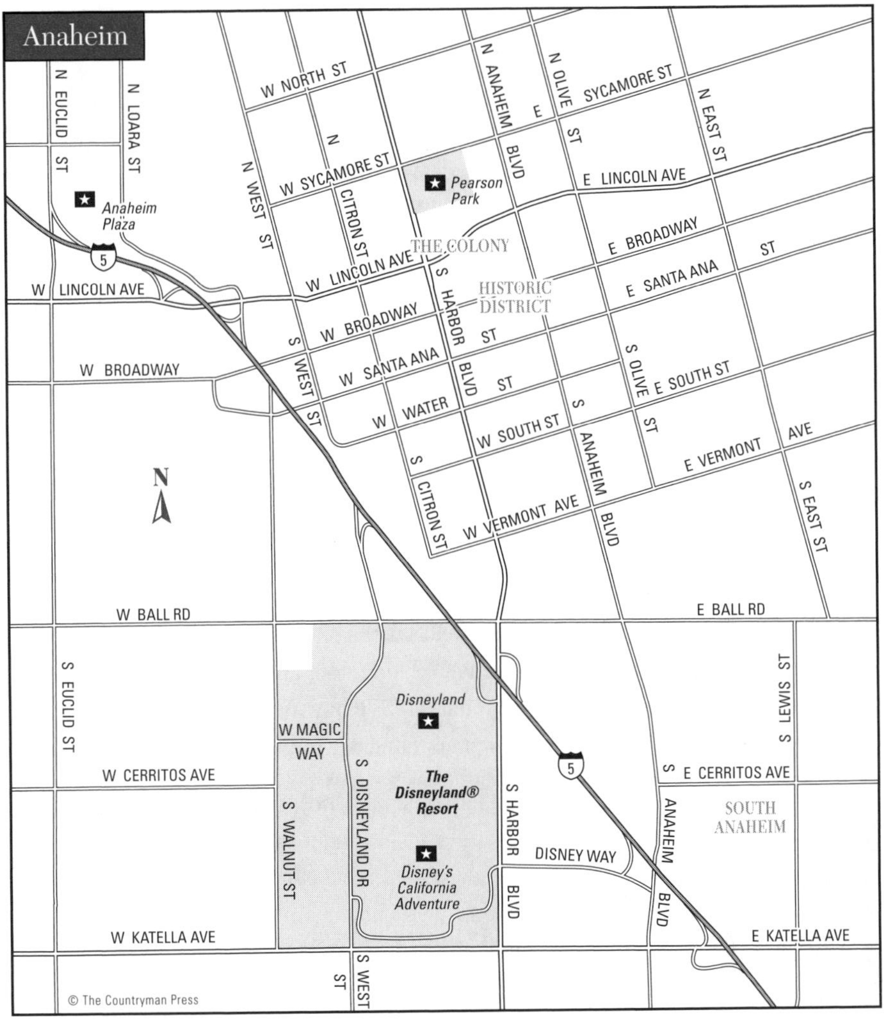

more than 15 million out-of-towners who come to Anaheim each year, 13 million of them spend at least one day in Disneyland. Over the years, more than 550 million visitors have passed through Disneyland's turnstiles, and the popularity of the park shows no signs of abating, despite a few hiccups during the recent economic downturn. Although it has its fair share of detractors, Disneyland really does offer something to enchant every visitor, from toddlers in strollers to thrill-seeking teenagers to nostalgic grandparents.

The 85-acre park is divided into various themed lands, which offer rides and attractions that build on a central theme, beginning with Main Street U.S.A., a re-creation of an idyllic Midwestern Victorian town built at three-quarter scale. This small stretch of faux Americana alone offers delights enough to amuse a visitor for the day, with myriad specialty shopping, vintage candy stores, and impeccably, pristinely, *fastidiously* clean facades. Everyone who arrives in this park does so via the quaint Main Street, which then spills into the centerpiece of the park, Sleeping Beauty Castle, modeled on actual castles in Bavaria, which rises above the surrounding trees and structures in a frothy pink and white architectural flourish. Each of the eight lands of Disneyland radiate out from this central castle. The elaborately themed zones include the rugged Adventureland, the toddler-friendly Fantasyland, the Old West Frontierland, the cartoon-inspired Mickey's Toontown, and the futuristic Tomorrowland. Live entertainment is available throughout the park, all day long, in the form of elaborate parades, Broadway-style shows, bands, seemingly impromptu street performances, and—when the sun goes down—spectacular fireworks displays. One-day entrance to Disneyland: 10 years and up $72, 3–9 years $62. Park Hopper day pass to both parks: 10 years and up $97, 3–9 years $87.

DISNEY'S CALIFORNIA ADVENTURE

To offer new entertainment possibilities and to ameliorate some of the crowding at the original park, in 2001 Disney opened Disney's California Adventure, a Golden

TIPS TO AVOID THE CROWDS AT DISNEYLAND

It's not always easy navigating Disneyland; the size and scope of the place can be daunting. This is compounded by the undeniable fact that the park is often overcrowded. To make the most out of a day at the theme park, and to avoid the worst of the park congestion, consider the following tips:

- Line up outside the gates at least 30 minutes before the posted park hours. The gates usually open earlier than advertised, although not every ride operates on this early morning schedule. Check the park schedule for specifics.
- Take advantage of "magic hours" offered to guests of the Disney resort hotels. On specified days (http://disneyland.disney.go.com/disneyland/en_US/calendar), a given park will be open an hour earlier to those who can prove (usually with a room key) that they are guests at a Disney hotel. This benefit is also open to certain multiday pass holders.
- Plan a trip Tuesday–Thursday to avoid the worst of the park congestion on weekends. Believe it or not, Monday is actually the most crowded day of the week. If a weekend day is unavoidable, choose Sunday over Saturday.
- Use the Disney FASTPASS to cut to the front of the line. This is a priority ticket offered at a handful of the most popular attractions in both theme parks. Obtain one by inserting a park pass into a distribution machine near the attraction entrance and receive a pass that will allow return during an hour-long window, during which

State–themed amusement park adjacent to Disneyland. (Note that Disney's California Adventure requires a separate, equally pricey entrance ticket; however, combination and Park Hopper passes can be purchased that are money savers for those wishing to visit both parks.) Like Disneyland, Disney's California Adventure is divided into themed areas that feature elaborately designed rides and attractions. Among these, guests will find Paradise Pier, a beach-themed zone that offers boardwalk rides and games and a coastal atmosphere; Hollywood Studios Backlot, a tinsel-town main street that offers a peek into the movie industry; and Golden State, a gold-country zone that is anchored by Grizzly Mountain, a landscape feature that is part of the white-water raft ride Grizzly River Run.

However, Disney's California Adventure hasn't met Disney's expectations for attendance, and as a result, the park is currently undergoing extensive renovations (set to be complete in 2012) to expand its offerings. One of the first attractions to open, **Toy Story Mania!** has received rave reviews thanks to truly impressive cutting-edge technology that allows guests to have an interactive experience unlike any available elsewhere in the parks. In addition, the **Games of the Boardwalk,** at Paradise Pier, have undergone upgrades, along with a nearby reinvented 150-

time it is possible to bypass the standby line and enter via a much shorter line. This generally cuts the wait by about 75 percent. However, there are a limited number of FASTPASS tickets available at any given time, and you can't acquire a new pass until the time frame of the previous one has expired.

- When congestion gets overwhelming, look for lesser known (less popular) attractions, like **Tarzan's Treehouse** in Adventureland and **Mr. Toad's Wild Ride** in Fantasyland, which are generally accessible even during the worst of the crowds.
- Consider breaking the day into chunks, to work around the busiest times at the parks. As noted, arrive early and stay until just before lunchtime, when crowds peak. Spend the afternoon shopping off-property, lounging by the hotel pool, or napping. Then return to enjoy the park at sunset, until closing, when many families with young children leave the parks for the day. (Note: Be sure to get a hand stamp on the way out, to facilitate easy return.)
- Eat during off hours—lunch before 11 or after 2, dinner before 4 or after 8—which will avoid long lines at cafés and snack shops. Alternatively, skip formal meals altogether and graze throughout the park. There are a number of healthy snack options available.
- Minimize the amount of time spent walking between attractions. Finish with the attractions at one "land" before moving on to another, to avoid zigzagging the park and getting into the inevitable foot traffic along the corridors that connect the various park locales.

foot Ferris wheel (now emblazoned with Mickey's face), and a telescoping swing structure in **Silly Symphony Swings** that is even more thrilling than the similar attraction it replaced. In 2011, expect a new attraction based on *The Little Mermaid* characters, as well as a completely redesigned main entrance called **Buena Vista Street.** To finish off the ambitious redo, in 2012 a new land with three new attractions is opening based on the movie *Cars.* The most ambitious of the changes at the park have to do with the dazzling nighttime spectacular, **World of Color,** which debuted in the summer of 2010. This water, laser, film, and music production has redefined multimedia entertainment, and its popularity draws huge crowds to view the spectacle.

Even before the finishing touches, this theme park is still well worth a visit, either in conjunction with Disneyland or on its own, both because it has unique, cutting-edge rides and attractions not available elsewhere (especially **Soarin' Over California** and the aforementioned **Toy Story Mania!**) and because the park is more expansive and was designed to accommodate 21st-century crowds, which makes it a good place to avoid the congestion of neighboring Disneyland park. One-day entrance to Disney's California Adventure: 10 years and up $72, 3–9 years $62. Park Hopper day pass to both parks: 10 years and up $97, 3–9 years $87.

DOWNTOWN DISNEY

Downtown Disney, a spectacularly designed shopping, entertainment, and dining complex, is conveniently located between the two theme parks, adjacent to the **Disneyland Hotel** and surrounding **Disney's Grand Californian Hotel.** The pedestrian-only thoroughfare is stunning, with eclectic and entertaining storefronts and whimsical landscaping, which is transported by hundreds of thousands of glittering lights once the sun sets. It's here guests will find the enormous **World of Disney**

MEETING MICKEY AND FRIENDS IN PERSON

If traveling with young children, be sure to meet Mickey and his gal pal, Minnie, in person, along with dozens of other Disney characters, who show up at various locations throughout the parks for 30 minutes at a time. Look for a schedule of Meet and Greets as you arrive in the park. Another surefire way to see characters is at a character breakfast at resort hotel restaurants (**Goofy's Kitchen** at the Disneyland Hotel, **Storyteller's Café** at Disney's Grand Californian, and **Disney's PCH Grill** at the Paradise Pier Hotel). Within the parks, look for **Minnie and Friends Breakfast** at the Plaza Inn restaurant (on Main Street in Disneyland) and **Ariel's Princess Celebration** at Ariel's Grotto restaurant (at Paradise Pier, Disney's California Adventure). These are popular restaurants (and surprisingly expensive, given most are buffets), and priority seating is highly recommended (call 714-781-3463 as much as 60 days in advance). Some kids like to purchase autograph books for their favorite characters to sign; in addition to a signature (or a paw print, in the case of Goofy and Pluto), some costumed cast members will add a sketch or cartoon of themselves as well.

© Disney Enterprises, Inc.

DISNEY'S CALIFORNIA ADVENTURE

store, which sells just about every imaginable item emblazoned with a Disney character, from ice cube trays in the shape of Mickey's ears to musical toasters that play "When You Wish Upon a Star," to boxer shorts emblazoned with the image of Cruella de Vil. Other favorites in Downtown Disney include the **Build-a-Bear Workshop,** where guests can stuff and then outfit their own plush animals; **Basin,** a fine bath products outlet; **Ridemakerz,** a store that lets children (and their parents) design and build remote-controlled cars; and **Disney Pin Traders,** which offers a bewildering number of character pins to collect, wear, and swap. Also in Downtown Disney are a number of dining options, from upscale restaurants like **Catal** and **Ralph Brennan's Jazz Kitchen** to casual diners like the **Rainforest Café** and the **House of Blues.**

Entertainment options include the aforementioned **House of Blues,** which offers live blues and jazz acts every evening; the **ESPN Sports Zone,** with myriad big-screen TVs and nonstop sports action; and the **AMC Theater** complex, which always features at least one family-friendly movie.

Downtown Disney does not require paid admission, so it is popular with locals who like to enjoy the Disney experience without the sticker shock. Not surprisingly, it can get uncomfortably crowded, especially on weekend evenings.

DOWNTOWN DISNEY

© Disney Enterprises, Inc.

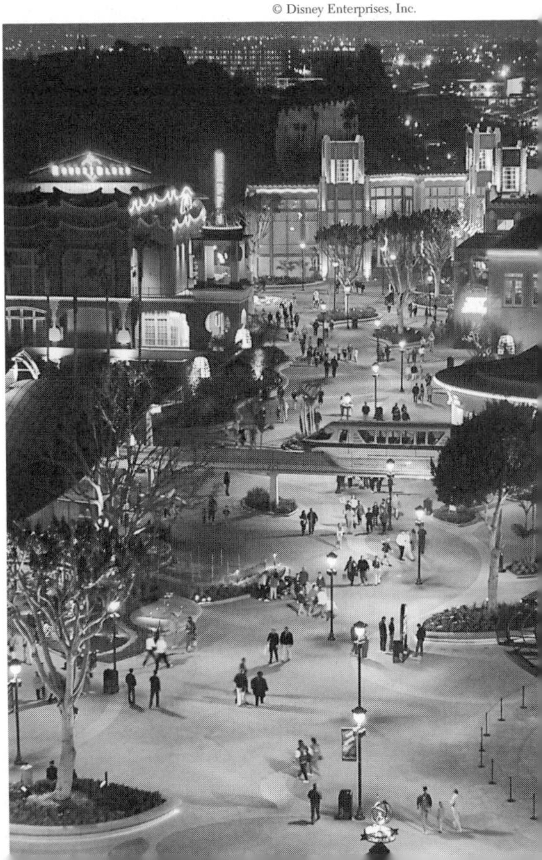

GETTING AROUND To explore both theme parks and Downtown Disney, plan to wear comfortable shoes: Most transportation within the park is via foot power. However, the 2-mile **Disneyland Monorail** serves as the resort's public transportation into and out of the Disneyland park. The monorail, opened in 1959, was the first single-rail transportation system in the United States. Today the monorail has two stops: at Downtown Disney (near the Disneyland Hotel) and in Tomorrowland.

There are also a number of happenstance transportation options within Disneyland, which are great choices if the timing is right—and the vehicle is going in the direction you want, at the time that you want. These include the **Disneyland Railroad,** which can be boarded at stations in Main Street, New Orleans Square, Tomorrowland, or Mickey's Toontown; horse-drawn streetcars that traverse Main Street; or the ***Mark Twain* Riverboat** in New Orleans Square.

RIDES AND ATTRACTIONS

There are dozens of rides and attractions, and a separate book could (and *has*) been written to enumerate each and every option. Following are my picks for must-sees, organized by the age group most likely to appreciate the attraction. Note, however, that The Disneyland® Resort can present sensory overload even for some older kids, who might not tolerate the attractions as well as a younger child who is less sensitive. Likewise, some older children (and adults) will find plenty to love about rides and shows that might have been designed for a younger audience. Such is the magic of Disney: it encourages everyone to be a kid again. Note that in addition to the speed and thrills that make some rides too much for some youngsters, many inside rides are often eerily dark and too loud for them. Thus, a seemingly innocent attraction like Snow White's Scary Adventures really is too scary for a lot of toddlers and young children. When in doubt, don't be afraid to ask the ride operators to explain the attraction, which will help you determine if this is something your child will enjoy. Also, be sure to check height restrictions before waiting in line.

✷ Disneyland

TODDLERS (AGES 2–3) ✐ **Alice in Wonderland,** in Fantasyland. Board an oversized caterpillar that inches its way through the rabbit hole at this Disney classic, a favorite with children for decades. Very young kids might be frightened at the appearance of the Queen of Hearts, who predictably yells out "off with their heads" when the ride passes by.

✐ **Casey Jr. Circus Train,** in Fantasyland. This little train is an original to the park and chugs around miniature villages made up of what look like charming dollhouses. Kids like to be seated in the animal cars, designed to look like cages. Come early to ride this attraction, because the wait times can be ridiculous by midday.

✐ **Dumbo,** in Fantasyland. Another original to the 1955 park. Guests climb into brightly colored Dumbo look-alikes for a (brief) flight aboard a flying elephant. Kids can control the height by moving a joystick that will make Dumbo climb or descend.

✐ **Finding Nemo Submarine Voyage,** in Tomorrowland. For years the lagoon that used to house the old Disney submarine ride was left unused. Recently, however, the ride was revamped to include scenes from *Finding Nemo,* and it has been a huge draw ever since, especially with fans of the movie. Boarding and unboarding is a bit cumbersome (guests have to walk up and down a very narrow winding staircase), which contributes to a *long* wait time. This is another ride best done early in the morning or late in the evening.

© Disney Enterprises, Inc.

DUMBO

✪ ✐ **"it's a small world,"** in Fantasyland. Although it is true that the music for this attraction is mind-numbingly unforgettable, the nearly 10-minute boat ride through the expansive collection of internationally costumed Audio-Animatronics dolls is not to be missed. The ride is even more impressive during the holidays, when the interior of the ride is transformed with Christmas and Hanukkah decorations and thousands of lights.

✐ **King Arthur Carrousel,** in Fantasyland. This attraction dates to the original park opening in 1955, but the ride is actually even older. The European hand-carved horses were crafted in the 19th century. Don't miss the Sword in the Stone, just behind the attraction. One lucky child a day actually manages to pull out the bejeweled blade.

✐ **Mad Tea Party,** in Fantasyland. Outside (and thus not too dark) and with cheery music (and thus not too scary), these oversized teacups spin and twirl underneath a canopy of lanterns that is especially lovely at night. Guests can control how fast they want to spin by turning the wheel (or not) inside the teacup. Note: Anyone with motion sickness should steer clear.

✐ **The Many Adventures of Winnie the Pooh,** in Critter Country. Guests hop aboard a beehive-shaped conveyance and voyage throughout the Hundred-Acre Wood to meet Kanga and Roo, Rabbit, and Piglet. Little kids *love* it when the ride starts to bounce like Tigger. This newer attraction was designed with tiny children in mind: it isn't terribly dark, and the music is not overly loud.

YOUNG CHILDREN (AGES 4–8) ✐ **Astro Orbitor,** in Tomorrowland. Step into individual rocket ships, which will circle and rise at the rider's command and which look very much like something out of a 1950s sci-fi movie. Ride this attraction after dark, and views of the nighttime park lights are inspiring.

✪ ✐ **Buzz Lightyear Astro Blasters,** in Tomorrowland. This newish attraction is like climbing into a video game: the interactive ride lets guests battle evil Emperor Zurg by shooting laser blasts at hundreds of targets throughout the colorful attraction while traveling in a moving Star Cruiser. Once the game is finished, riders are presented with their scores. Children especially love this, because they are generally better at video games than their parents.

✐ **Jungle Cruise,** in Adventureland. The guides on these faux African riverboats that travel through an imaginative safari have been telling the same stale jokes since I was a child—and yet I still laugh at them. Look for the wiggling-eared hippos in the river.

INSIDER TIP: To minimize wait times, when an attraction line splits off into two (as it does for the Jungle Cruise), move to the left side—which generally is shorter because Americans naturally tend to merge right.

Peter Pan's Flight, in Fantasyland. Guests climb aboard a flying sailboard and soar through the Darling children's bedroom, over London, and past the Lagoon of Mermaids in Never Land, to see Peter Pan battle it out with Captain Hook. Although it is dark inside, the ride is gentle enough even for the most timid kids.

Roger Rabbit's Car Toon Spin, in Toontown. Climb behind the wheel of an out-of-control taxi as it spins and jerks through the animated world of *Roger Rabbit.* I will be honest: this attraction is loud, obnoxious, and gives me a headache—and therefore is a *huge* favorite with young kids.

OLDER CHILDREN AND TEENAGERS (AGES 9 AND UP) ✪ **Big Thunder Mountain Railroad,** in Frontierland. This outdoor roller coaster, which is jarringly fast but without any major drops, depicts a runaway train through mine shafts, caverns, and past falling boulders. Look out for the rattlesnakes just before one of the biggest dips.

JUNGLE CRUISE

Haunted Mansion, in New Orleans Square. Climb aboard a "Doom Buggy" that takes guests through a creepy, cobwebby mansion that offers some pretty spectacular special effects, including a ballroom full of waltzing ghosts. Note: At the beginning of the attraction, the lights go out for a brief moment, which is startling to young children—and sure to induce blood curdling screams from silly teenagers.

✪ ***Indiana Jones* Adventure™,** in Adventureland. Disney is legend at creating a total experience, and nowhere is the company's creativity on better display than in the queue for this ride, which winds through authentic ruins and a forbidden temple, in this case making getting there half the fun. The ride itself is brilliant: thrilling, unexpected, and with stunning special effects.

Matterhorn Bobsleds, in Fantasyland. As a child, I always knew we were getting close to Disneyland when from the freeway I saw the peaks of the

Matterhorn, a fabricated "Swiss alp" that houses an indoor roller coaster. The looping, jostling bobsled ride slides past an abominable snowman that is little more than an oversized teddy bear—but it can be scary for youngsters.

Pirates of the Caribbean, in New Orleans Square. A shockingly accurate Johnny Depp/Captain Jack Sparrow figure (a new addition) presides over a voyage through a pirates' hideout that culminates in a cannon shootout between two opposing pirate ships. The lifelike Audio-Animatronics in this attraction are still amazing after 25 years.

© Disney Enterprises, Inc./Lucasfilm Ltd.

INDIANA JONES ADVENTURE™

✪ **Space Mountain,** in Tomorrowland. A high-speed indoor roller coaster through darkened passageways mimics hurtling through space, all to the accompaniment of a high-decibel soundtrack. This is another ride that makes the most of the queue space, which is convincingly staged to look like a space station.

Star Tours, in Tomorrowland. Fans of *Star Wars* will not want to miss this motion simulator ride, which takes guests on a tour to the Endor Moon, with R2-D2 as navigator. The attraction culminates in a spectacular battle on the infamous Death Star, as Jedi fighters dodge and maneuver. (Disneyland has plans to convert the attraction to 3-D soon.)

Tomorrowland Autopia, in Tomorrowland. Many Southern California drivers got their start in Autopia driving miniaturized gas-powered hot rods, which will accelerate and decelerate on command, and must be steered (even though they are on rails). The car route winds through a pleasant patch of trees, but the exhaust fumes can be heady.

✷ Disney's California Adventure

TODDLERS (AGES 2–3) **Flik's Flyers,** in A Bug's Land. One of many rides that rises up slightly and then spins in a gentle circle (à la Dumbo and Astro Blasters), Flik's Flyers lets guests ride inside an oversized raisin box, Chinese food take-out container, or juice box. Note: This ride, and many others in A Bug's Land zone, will make much more sense to children if they have seen the movie *A Bug's Life*.

> **INSIDER TIP:** At the beginning of the Pirates of the Caribbean, just as you float past the Blue Bayou restaurant, look up at the faux sky to catch a glimpse of a shooting star.

TOP 10 DAY IN DISNEYLAND

1. Enjoy Mickey Mouse–shaped waffles at Goofy's Kitchen (see p. 157)
2. Run from the entrance to the magical first ride of the day: Space Mountain (see p. 147)
3. Grab a FASTPASS to return later, then head to Star Tours (see p. 147)
4. Feast on a Monte Cristo sandwich and a virgin mint julep at the Blue Bayou (see p. 156)
5. Climb to the very top of Tarzan's Treehouse (see p. 141)
6. Grab a front seat on the *Indiana Jones* Adventure™ attraction (sitting on the left side to avoid the oversized snake) (see p. 146)
7. Stop for a slice and a soda at Red Rockett's Pizza Port (see p. 159)
8. Shop for Disney-themed clothing on Main Street U.S.A. (p. 139)
9. Stay up late to watch the fireworks extravaganza (see p. 151)
10. Overnight at the Disneyland Hotel (see p. 153)

✪ **Golden Zephyr,** at the Paradise Pier. This gliding 90-foot gondola floats along, suspended on cables that carry the cars over Paradise Bay, the central water feature of Disney's California Adventure. Note: The ride closes when the winds are strong.

Heimlich's Chew Chew Train, in A Bug's Land. Some rides at the two theme parks are designed for children and their parents. This slow-moving train ride is not: it will amuse toddlers to no end, but it will likely be somewhat tedious for anyone older than five or six.

King Triton's Carousel, at the Paradise Pier. This merry-go-round offers creatures of the sea—like otters, mermaids, and sea horses—instead of traditional carousel ponies. This is a great attraction for impatient little ones, because there is usually a very short wait to board.

YOUNG CHILDREN (AGES 4–8) **Grizzly River Run,** in the Golden State. A fast, thrilling water-rapids ride, Grizzly Run is especially popular in the hot summer months, because it is all but inevitable that riders will get *soaked.* There are lockers nearby to store any gear that is not waterproof.

Mickey's Fun Wheel, at Paradise Pier. This gigantic Ferris wheel has been transformed recently, so that it now features Mickey's face and tremendous views of the park and beyond. There are both stationary and rocking baskets, the latter of which can be horrifying for those of us with acrophobia.

Mullholland Madness, at Paradise Pier. A small roller coaster, this is in many ways more heart-pounding than **California Screamin',** because of the short hairpin turns that make you feel as if you're about to fly out of the car. Warning: Avoid this ride if you have back or neck problems, because it is very jerky.

Silly Symphony Swings, at Paradise Pier. Formerly styled as the Orange Zinger, these old-fashioned aerial swings are thrilling and offer good views from the top of Disney's California Adventure.

✪ ✐ **Soarin' Over California,** in the Golden State. This attraction is part movie, part moving attraction, set to mimic soaring in a hang glider over inspiring scenes filmed throughout the state of California, and it's one of my all-time favorite rides, appropriate for young children and elderly grandparents. (Hint: Try to smell the orange blossoms when flying over the citrus groves.)

✪ ✐ **Toy Story Mania!** at Paradise Pier. One of the newest attractions to come out of the ongoing renovations at Disney's California Adventure, this impressive 4-D attraction is interactive and wildly popular (i.e., expect a *long* wait in line). After donning 3-D glasses, guests use spring-action shooters to launch rings at aliens, darts at balloons, and eggs at various targets—which when hit result in special effects. The ride changes every time, and patrons can compete for the highest score.

OLDER CHILDREN AND TEENAGERS (AGES 9 AND UP) ✪ ✐ **California Screamin',** at Paradise Pier. This *fast* roller coaster ride, which features an inverted loop and plenty of hair-raising drops, takes off like a rocket and doesn't let up for a second. This is arguably the most thrilling of all rides in either theme park, but for some reason the lines are generally less oppressive than they are for roller coasters in the Disneyland park.

✐ **The Twilight Zone Tower of Terror,™** Hollywood Pictures Backlot. The premise of this thrill ride is of a runaway elevator in a haunted hotel. The attraction offers randomized drops from as much as 13 stories, so every ride is slightly different. The view from the top is spectacular.

TOY STORY MANIA!

✷ Entertainment

DISNEYLAND Note that Disneyland has live entertainment throughout the park, throughout the day, all year long, the highlights of which are the Main Street parades and the nighttime fireworks extravaganzas. Theatrical performances change regularly, but the shows listed below have been ongoing, in some form, for many years.

Billy Hill and the Hillbillies, in Frontierland. These four "brothers" (all named Billy) hang out in Frontierland, sometimes performing their bluegrass and comedy routine onstage at the **Golden Horseshoe** and sometimes playing to the crowds outdoors.

MONEY-SAVING TIPS IN THE DISNEY THEME PARKS

- Buy and print tickets online before arrival, which can save as much as $10 a day on multipark **Park Hopper** passes (which allow guests to move between Disneyland and Disney's California Adventure at a lower price than if tickets to both parks are purchased individually).
- If staying at the resort for more than one day, consider purchasing a package deal that includes tickets and accommodations, which generally offers a considerable discount. Look for special offers on the Disneyland Web site, http://disneyland.disney.go.com.
- Likewise, if visiting the parks for more than a few days, look into the yearly pass options, which in some cases can be less expensive than buying individual day passes. Annual passes also entitle the bearer to discounts in some restaurants, hotels, and resort shops. Beware: Some passes have blackout dates, generally prohibiting a visit during summertime months, the winter holidays, and many Saturdays.
- The cost of meals and snacks at the park can add up quickly. Consider bringing a picnic instead. There is a shaded picnic area near the Disneyland entrance to enjoy food from home. Or if this doesn't appeal, at least fill up on a large breakfast before entering the parks, so that the snacks aren't as immediately tempting.
- Tote a refillable water bottle to soothe thirsty Mousketeers, and fill up at any of a number of water fountains throughout the parks. Most concession stands also offer free ice water. Packets of iced tea or lemonade mix can be added if the tap water is not to your taste.
- Insist that children wait until the end of the day to purchase souvenirs. This will avoid having to carry purchases unnecessarily throughout the park, and it will give kiddos the chance to look around and find what they really want (rather than the first thing that catches their eye)—thus likely spending less overall.

The Disneyland Story Featuring Great Moments with Mr. Lincoln, at the Disneyland Story Theater on Main Street. After being retooled following the 50th-anniversary celebration, the incredibly lifelike Abe Lincoln Audio-Animatronic figure is back, narrating a patriotic story of American history. This is the perfect attraction to visit during midday, because it tends to be much less crowded than traditional rides, and the theater offers comfy seats and air-conditioning in which to relax.

Fantasmic! in Frontierland. Debuting in Walt Disney World Resort near Orlando, this fireworks, fiber optics, video, and water show is based on the premise that Mickey Mouse is battling evil forces and is derivative of the original movie *Fantasia*. The show operates seasonally and is incredibly popular. Arrive 45–60 minutes early to ensure the best view.

Fireworks Show, over Sleeping Beauty Castle in Fantasyland. Every few years, Disneyland changes the theme of the nightly fireworks show, but there are two constants in these shows: There will be a Mickey Mouse–shaped fireworks explosion at least once in the evening, and Tinker Bell will set off the festivities. Hours and days vary by season, but expect pyrotechnics every weekend evening, throughout the two-week traditional school winter holiday break, and throughout the summertime. Good views are available throughout the park, especially Main Street and Fantasyland. The best seats in the house are benches surrounding the Walt Disney statue in front of Sleeping Beauty Castle. I'm not a fan of the crowds that gather for these shows, and the crunch to exit the park immediately afterward is enough to trigger agoraphobia, but despite the hassles, for anyone who loves fireworks, this show is not to be missed.

Jedi Training Academy, at the Tomorrowland Terrace Stage, in Tomorrowland. In this show, performed every few hours throughout the day, Jedi masters pull a few lucky kids from the audience and teach them light saber skills, the mysteries of The Force, and then give them the opportunity to battle ultimate bad guy Darth Vader. Warning: As much fun as this is to watch, it can be painful for youngsters who aren't chosen, so be sure to prepare kids. Only a half dozen or so children are picked to participate.

Main Street Parade, along Main Street. Held once or twice a day (according to season), the Main Street Parade offers music, dancing, Disney characters, over-the-top floats, and plenty of exuberant cast members. Be sure to grab a seat at the curb at least 45–60 minutes in advance. For those who do not love a parade, be sure to be in the section of the park you want to remain until after the parade is over, because it is all but impossible to cross Main Street during the performance.

DISNEY'S CALIFORNIA ADVENTURE **High School Musical 3, Senior Year—Right Here, Right Now!** in Sunshine Plaza. Part parade, part concert, part dance recital, this outdoor performance is a hit with tweens who like the namesake movies. Some kids are pulled into the action for dancing sequences.

It's Tough to Be a Bug! in A Bug's Land. A 3-D film with "smellovision," this movie offers guests a bug's-eye view of the world. Without giving too much away, be forewarned: there are special effects that might freak out those of us who are not fans of bugs.

MuppetVision 3D, in Hollywood Pictures Backlot. A 3-D film starring Miss Piggy, Kermit the Frog, and other Muppet stars, MuppetVision 3D is entertaining even for children who don't know these characters, thanks to much silliness and slapstick humor, which manages to be entertaining for adults as well.

INSIDER TIP: Just in case your party gets separated, decide on a predetermined meeting place and time. Be sure to make it someplace easy to find—like the Matterhorn in Disneyland or Grizzly Mountain in Disney's California Adventure. Note that lost children are routinely taken by park personnel to City Hall on Main Street, U.S.A.

Playhouse Disney: Live on Stage! in Hollywood Pictures Backlot. Ideal for tiny kids who love Playhouse Disney, this 20-minute interactive show features singing and dancing from familiar characters like Handy Mandy. There are no chairs in this theater: guests sit on their bums, crisscross-applesauce style.

Turtle Talk with Crush, in Hollywood Pictures Backlot. I admit it: this show, starring the animated surfer-dude turtle Crush from *Finding Nemo,* is meant for little kids—but it fascinates me. The animated character actually interacts with audience members, changing facial expression and responding in real time to audience questions—and the character's speech and actions are specific to each audience. I don't know how they do it, but it sure is fun to watch.

World of Color, at Paradise Pier. New to Disney's California Adventure, the World of Color is a water, music, and lights spectacular staged on the Paradise Bay, in front of **California Screamin'.** Computer choreography coordinates nearly 1,200 water fountains, familiar Disney music, audio and visual effects, and projections of new animation on massive "screens" of water, offering perhaps the biggest nighttime draw of The Disneyland® Resort.

DOWNTOWN DISNEY AMC Theaters (888-262-4386). This multiplex, designed to mimic vintage theaters of midcentury but with cutting-edge

WORLD OF COLOR

technology, is near the **Disneyland Hotel** and offers 12 screens, all with 3-D capability. There is always at least one family-friendly alternative playing.

🍸 **Flambeaux's Jazz Club.** In **Ralph Brennan's Jazz Kitchen,** this New Orleans–style jazz club offers live music, authentic food, and a full bar.

🍸 **House of Blues** (714-788-2583). In addition to better-than-average grub, House of Blues offers live entertainment nightly, including reggae, blues, Latin, and hip-hop. Don't miss the Sunday Gospel Brunch, an all-you-can-eat Creole buffet with a panoply of live gospel performers.

✱ Lodging

In-Park Lodging

Yes, lodging in Disneyland is expensive—up to 50 percent more than comparable hotels in the immediate vicinity. But is it worth it? I think so. The heftier price tag buys unparalleled service and the attention to detail for which Disney is famous. Guests can arrange for a wake-up call from Mickey himself, balloons and other room decorations to celebrate a birthday or other special occasion, and plan to have all in-park purchases delivered directly to guest rooms. In addition, all three Disney lodges offer character dining on-site, kid-centric décor, guest rooms designed with families in mind (with beds enough for four or five), and Disney-character-themed pools. Rooms offer free Disney Channel and ESPN. And all guests staying on property can take advantage of the "magic hour," an early-morning entry available on certain days that will allow hotel guests to enjoy the park before the crowds.

PRICE KEY FOR A STANDARD ROOM:

$	$100 or less
$$	$101–150
$$$	$151–250
$$$$	$251 and up

✪ ✐ **Disneyland Hotel** (714-778-6600; www.disneyland.com), 1150 Magic Way. This is the oldest property, and my sentimental favorite, thanks to its kid-friendly extras. The enormous Never Land–themed pool with a pirate ship in the middle and a winding water slide that weaves through the lush landscape will entice children into taking a few hours off from the parks to enjoy it—not an easy feat. Also on-site are two smaller pools, an oversized koi pond with roaring waterfalls, and a playground perfect for toddlers. The guest rooms themselves are in one of several high-rise towers, some of which have stellar views of the nightly fireworks show. Guest rooms are adorned with wallpaper border starring Tinker Bell, with glow-in-the-dark pixie dust (although ongoing remodeling may replace this feature). Character dining is at the longtime favorite **Goofy's Kitchen.** Also on-site are a handful of other dining options, including **Steakhouse 55** (for steaks, naturally), **Hook's Pointe** (for seafood), and the **Coffeehouse** (for a quick breakfast or for pastries all day long). $$$

✪ ✐ **Disney's Grand Californian** (714-956-6425; www.disneyland.com), 1600 S. Disneyland Dr. The priciest, most elegant option at Disney, Disney's Grand Californian is located at the epicenter of the action, in the heart of Downtown Disney and just a short walk from the entrance of both Disneyland and Disney's California

© Disney Enterprises, Inc.

DISNEYLAND HOTEL

Adventure. The lobby décor is meant to mimic a historic national park lodge, with soaring timbers, a massive stone fireplace, and sophisticated Arts and Crafts furnishings. Guest rooms are chic, spacious, and comfortable; although patrons will still find subtle reminders that this is the house that Mickey built, the ambiance at this hotel is much more sophisticated than one might expect. Families will appreciate that some rooms offer bunk beds, a big hit with my daughter when she was younger. In addition, this property has a private entrance to Disney's California Adventure reserved just for hotel guests, which makes for a very quick entry. On-site dining is at the *fabulous* **Napa Rose,** as well as character dining at the **Storyteller's Café.** $$$$

Disney's Paradise Pier Hotel (714-999-0990; www.disneyland.com), 1717 S. Disneyland Dr. Although hardly a bargain, Paradise Pier offers the best in-park lodging choice for budget travelers, and there are often significant online discounts available during the off-season. The property is the farthest walk from the parks, although it *is* still walkable, and higher rooms overlook Disney's California Adventure park, which stays lighted well past closing time. Décor evokes the California beachside hotels of the 1940s, and although rooms here are slightly smaller and less opulent than the other two Disney properties, they still offer comfortable accommodations and a whimsical ambiance. Although the pool is less dramatic than those at the other two resort properties, it has a large twisty water slide. $$–$$$

Lodging Outside the Park

Neighboring hotels in Anaheim aren't as convenient to the parks and Downtown Disney, but many offer family-pleasing amenities, and these generally come at a much smaller price tag than Disney properties. Some off-property hotels claim to be within walking distance of the parks; in theory, this is true, but anything beyond a 15-minute walk to a park where I am bound to be on my feet for 12 hours straight is too much for me. For $3 per person, per day, anyone can purchase a hotel shuttle pass (operated by the city of Anaheim), which will ferry guests from the front entrance of most local hotels to the parks' entrances and back. Look for ticket kiosks outside most large hotels near the parks. (Be sure to allocate about 30 minutes to purchase tickets, wait for the shuttle, and make the ride over.)

DISNEY'S GRAND CALIFORNIAN

© Disney Enterprises, Inc.

INSIDER TIP: California residents are eligible for significant discounts when booking hotel and ticket packages, especially in January–March. If this applies to you, be sure to inquire about special offers when booking Disney properties.

The Anabella (714-905-1050; www.anabellahotel.com), 1030 W. Katella Ave., Anaheim. This elegant Spanish mission–style hotel is near both the Disney theme parks and the Anaheim Convention Center. The inviting ecofriendly property offers several suite configurations, which are designed with separate sleeping areas, making this ideal for families traveling with children (who may be on different bedtime schedules than their parents). Rooms are elegant and spacious, and some come with private balconies. The property has two large pools set amid lush landscaping. Parents will especially appreciate that this property presents a true bargain. $$

Hilton Anaheim (714-750-4321; http://www1.hilton.com/en_US/hi/hotel/SNAAHHH-Hilton-Anaheim-California/index.do), 777 Convention Way, Anaheim. I don't usually recommend big chain hotels (largely because for those who prefer the chains, it is easy enough to find them by searching the Internet), but the expansive Hilton Anaheim is a worthy exception. It is immediately next door to the Anaheim Convention Center; offers a quiet, relaxing atmosphere with a large pool deck with nary a Disney character in sight; and includes a well-equipped fitness club with basketball court, indoor pool and sauna, and yoga and Pilates classes for adults. Book an executive room on the 14th floor and the stay includes breakfast, complimentary hors d'oeuvres and cocktails in the evenings, and soft drinks 24 hours a day. For a very few dollars more, secure a room with a view to watch the evening fireworks over Disneyland. $$–$$$

Jolly Roger Inn (714-782-7500; www.jollyrogerinn.com), 640 W. Katella Ave., Anaheim. This small motel across the street from Disney's California Adventure is one of the few budget accommodations this close to The Disneyland® Resort. A longtime fixture in Anaheim, the 58-room lodging has been recently renovated, so that rooms are fresh and clean. There's a retro kidney-shaped pool, and refrigerators and microwaves are available for an additional cost. $

Portofino Inn and Suites (714-782-7600, www.portofinoinnanaheim.com), 1831 S. Harbor Blvd., Anaheim. A few blocks from the parks, this cheerful small Mediterranean-style property is designed for families traveling with young children. Guests can book "kid suites" that can sleep up to six people in two separate bedrooms, which are divided by glass doors, so parents can keep an eye on children. The kids' side of the suite is furnished with bunk beds, a mini-sized activity table and chairs, a sofa sleeper, and its own TV. The small outdoor pool offers little razzle-dazzle, but it is quiet and relatively uncrowded. $–$$

✱ Where to Eat

DINING OUT

Although most dining options within the theme parks and in Downtown Disney do not take reservations, some of the finer establishments will provide guests who call ahead (714-781-3463) with a priority seating time—which isn't quite the guarantee that a reservation provides, but it does mean that guests on the priority seating list will be seated well before folks just showing up. This service is not available at all restaurants, but it is well worth the effort when dining at popular places like Ariel's Grotto, Blue Bayou, Goofy's Kitchen, Napa Rose, and at Plaza Inn for the special character breakfast with Mickey and Minnie. Priority seating can be requested 60 days in advance.

Disneyland

✪ **Blue Bayou,** in New Orleans Square. Open daily for lunch and dinner. Waterside tables at this indoor fine-dining establishment overlook the start of the **Pirates of the Caribbean,** attraction, and even midday seems like twilight here, with a setting complete with romantic lanterns and twinkling fireflies. The enormous Monte Cristo sandwich is delicious and easily big enough to share. This is one of the most popular eateries in The Disneyland® Resort, and thus it is vital to secure priority seating well in advance. $$$–$$$$

BLUE BAYOU

PRICE KEY FOR A TYPICAL ENTRÉE:

$	$10 and under
$$	$11–20
$$$	$21–30
$$$$	$31 and up

Plaza Inn, on Main Street. Open daily for breakfast, lunch, and dinner. Although this cafeteria serves food buffet style, the opulent Victorian décor puts it a cut above most of the quick-bite joints in the park. Character dining is available at breakfast. $$–$$$

Disney's California Adventure

Ariel's Grotto, at the Paradise Pier. Open daily for lunch and dinner. Home of the Disney Princess Celebration, Ariel's Grotto offers character dining in a pleasant sit-down venue that overlooks the park's large human-made lake, Paradise Bay. Entrées include cioppino, roasted tri-tip, and herb-crusted chicken. Be sure to call ahead for priority seating, especially on weekends. $$$$

Wine Country Trattoria, in the Golden State. This wine-country restaurant could be in Napa, Santa Ynez, or Paso Robles: aside from the whimsical kids' menu, there is no clue this elegant eatery falls within a Disney theme park—and for that, many princess-weary parents are grateful. The chicken bruschetta salad is especially good when enjoyed with a glass of pinot grigio. $$–$$$

Downtown Disney

✪ **Catal Restaurant and Uva Bar** (714-774-4442), Downtown Disney. Open daily for lunch and dinner.

© Disney Enterprises, Inc.

WINE COUNTRY TRATTORIA

Upstairs in a tower dining room, Catal serves multicourse Mediterranean meals. Downstairs at the outdoor Uva Bar, guests can grab tapas, coffee, or dozens of tempting desserts: don't miss the trio of crème brûlée. $$$

✪ **Goofy's Kitchen,** on the ground floor of the Disneyland Hotel. Open daily for breakfast, lunch, and dinner. The beloved Goofy's Kitchen offers buffet-style meals hosted by Goofy, Mickey, and a handful of other costumed characters that roam the dining hall to pose for photographs and to sign autographs. Don't miss the peanut butter and jelly pizza and Mickey waffles for breakfast. $$$$

✪ **Napa Rose** (714-300-7170), 1600 S. Disneyland Dr., at the Grand California Hotel. Open daily for dinner. By far the finest dining experience on the Disneyland property, Napa Rose draws customers who aren't even visiting the theme parks. The sophisticated Arts and Crafts décor, seasonal wine-country cuisine, and extensive wine cellar have drawn rave reviews since the restaurant opened in 2002. Priority seating is highly recommended, as is casual elegant attire (i.e., shorts and a Mickey sweatshirt won't cut it here). $$$$

Y **Ralph Brennan's Jazz Kitchen,** Downtown Disney. Open daily for breakfast, lunch, and dinner. Creole- and Cajun-style cuisine predominate in this Big Easy–inspired restaurant, which offers live music in the evenings

DISNEY'S PHOTOPASS SERVICE

Disneyland and Disney's California Adventure are full of photo opportunities, so by all means bring along a camera. Guests will also find professional photographers stationed throughout both parks—generally at the front entrances and in conjunction with character Meet and Greets and character dining. Early in the day, ask any photographer for a pass card. Then reuse the card for every photo op. Afterward, download the photos at www.disneyphotopass.com within 30 days, at which point you can edit them, purchase prints and CDs, and order personalized products.

© Disney Enterprises, Inc.

NAPA ROSE

and cozy patio dining. Jambalaya is a specialty, and don't miss the chance to try the authentic morning beignets with chicory coffee. $$$

Storyteller's Café, on the ground floor of Disney's Grand Californian Hotel and Spa. Open daily for breakfast, lunch, and dinner. This elegant yet casual restaurant specializes in wood-fired pizzas, as well as salads, grilled fish, and steak. For breakfast, look for Chip, Dale (chipmunk characters), and other costumed friends. $$$

Nearby, but Outside the Parks

✪ **Anaheim White House** (714-772-1381; www.anaheimwhitehouse.com), 887 S. Anaheim Blvd., Anaheim. Open daily for lunch and dinner, brunch on Sun. A 1909 landmark a few miles from The Disneyland® Resort that really does look like the president's abode outside—with an interior opulent enough to host a State dinner—White House cuisine is mostly northern Italian, with an earthy *pasta e fagioli* soup, fragrant fettuccine with white truffle oil topped with black truffle shavings, and the strangely named *Filetto di Romeo and Juliet* (filet mignon topped with Gorgonzola cheese and served with polenta). $$$

Bubba Gump's Shrimp (714-635-4867; www.bubbagump.com), 321 W. Katalla Ave., Anaheim. Open daily for lunch and dinner. This is one of a handful of nationwide chains that celebrates the characters from one of my all-time favorite movies: *Forrest Gump.* It's hard for me to resist reading the menu items out loud, in my worst faux Southern accent: fried shrimp, broiled shrimp, chilled shrimp, coconut shrimp, shrimp and crab, etc. The fun, noisy restaurant also serves steaks, salads, and pasta. Save room for the wickedly rich cinnamon bread pudding. $$$

Luigi's d'Italia (714-490-0990; www.luigisditaliaoc.com), 801 S. State College, Anaheim. Open daily for lunch and dinner. This restaurant, with a loyal local following, has a casual atmosphere and fine-dining cuisine featuring authentic Italian specialties like baked cannelloni, the delicious sausage and peppers platter, and fresh handmade pizzas (as well as calzone, a stuffed turnover that tastes like an inside-out pizza). $$–$$$

EATING OUT

Disneyland

Carnation Café, on Main Street. Open daily for breakfast, lunch, and dinner. Although this vintage-style restaurant serves old-time specialties like chicken potpie and roast beef with whipped potatoes, I like to come here for the *massive* ice cream sundaes that are meant for two. (Sharing isn't mandatory.) $$

Rancho del Zocalo Restaurante, in Frontierland. Open daily for lunch and dinner. Mexican fast food like tacos and burritos are on offer at Rancho del Zocalo, a Spanish Colonial courtyard café that has a lovely outdoor dining patio. $$

Red Rockett's Pizza Port, in Tomorrowland. Open daily for lunch and dinner. It gets hot in Anaheim in the summertime, and this is one of the few fast-food restaurants in the park that offer indoor (air-conditioned) seats. The pizza is not bad, either, and service is especially fast—all the better to hurry back in line to nearby **Space Mountain.** $$

Tiki Juice Bar, in Adventureland. Open daily. The Tiki Bar isn't a full-service restaurant, but it offers among the healthiest snacks in Disneyland: fresh pineapple spears, fresh juice, and frothy pineapple whips. $

Disney's California Adventure

Lucky Fortune Cookery, in the Golden State. Open daily for lunch and dinner. This quick-service Asian diner sells healthy rice bowls (including many vegetarian options), which can be enjoyed outside on an expansive, colorful dining patio. The edamame here works well as a sensible snack on the go. $$

Pacific Wharf Café, in Golden State. Open daily for breakfast, lunch, and dinner. Another healthy dining option in Disney's California Adventure, Pacific Wharf sells nutritious soups and salads, served in authentic San Francisco sourdough bread bowls. A pleasant outdoor patio for dining overlooks the waterfront. $$

Pizza Oom Mow Mow, at the Paradise Pier. Open daily for lunch and dinner. When the kids want pizza and Mom and Dad want a fresh salad, this is the place to go to get both at one stop. Dining is outside on a surfing-themed patio. $$

Taste Pilots Grill, in Golden State. Open daily for breakfast, lunch, and dinner. Near **Soarin' Over California,** Taste Pilots Grill offers hamburgers,

TOP 10 DAY IN DISNEY'S CALIFORNIA ADVENTURE

1. Enjoy Chip 'n Dale's Critter Breakfast buffet at Storyteller's Café (see p. 158)
2. Go directly from the opening gates to Soarin' Over California; ride as many times as possible, then get a FASTPASS to come back and do it all again later (see p. 149)
3. Win an oversized stuffed Piglet at the Games of the Boardwalk (see p. 141)
4. Check out Turtle Talk with Crush (see p. 152)
5. Lunch on a garden salad in a sourdough bread bowl at the Pacific Wharf Café (see p. 159)
6. Throw caution to the wind and ride California Screamin' on a full stomach (see p. 149)
7. Follow up with a ride on the Silly Symphony Swings (see p. 149)
8. Feast on roasted herb chicken and a glass of merlot at Napa Rose at Disney's Grand Californian Hotel and Spa in Downtown Disney (see p. 157)
9. Return to the park for the World of Color extravaganza (see p. 152)
10. Overnight at Disney's Grand Californian (see pp. 153–154)

© Disney Enterprises, Inc.
FIREWORKS IN DISNEYLAND

ribs, chicken sandwiches, and chili fries. Unlike many fast-food diners at this park that funnel guests to outdoor dining venues, Taste Pilots offers extensive indoor seating—especially welcome in the hot summers or on rare chilly days. $$

✷ Special Events

(at The Disneyland® Resort)
April–May: **Disney's California Food and Wine Festival,** held daily throughout the resort from mid-April through the end of May, features culinary demonstrations, appearances by celebrity chefs, and wine seminars.

June–August: **Summer Nightastic,** in both theme parks, from mid-June through the end of August, features special fireworks extravaganzas and late-night entertainment.

Late November–early January: **Holidays at Disneyland Resort** features the transformation of many beloved attractions, including the Haunted Mansion, which transforms into a scene from *The Nightmare Before Christmas,* as well as hundreds of thousands of holiday decorations and lights, culminating in a "snow" fall on Main Street.

Los Angeles

4

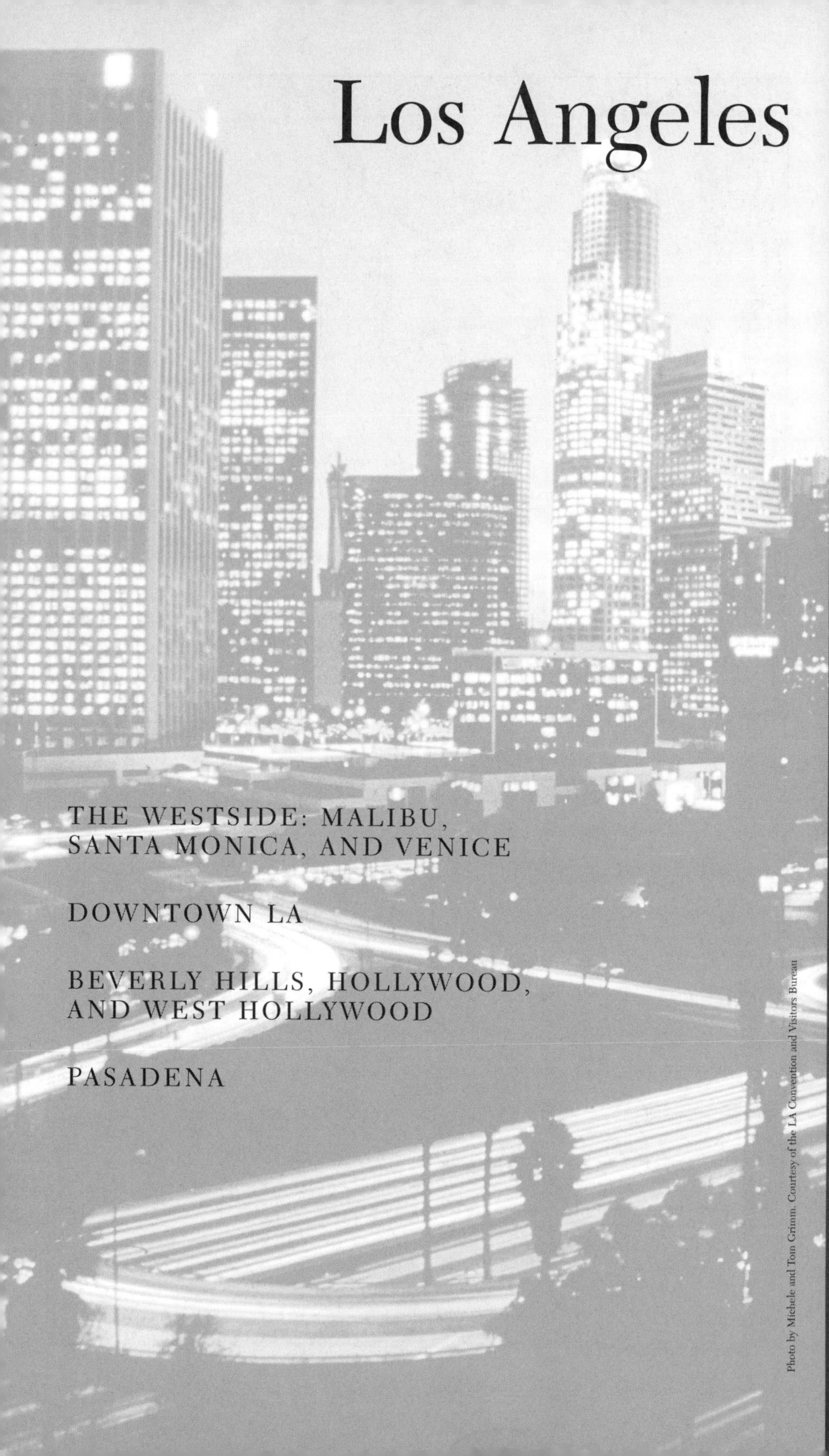

THE WESTSIDE: MALIBU, SANTA MONICA, AND VENICE

DOWNTOWN LA

BEVERLY HILLS, HOLLYWOOD, AND WEST HOLLYWOOD

PASADENA

Photo by Michele and Tom Grimm. Courtesy of the LA Convention and Visitors Bureau

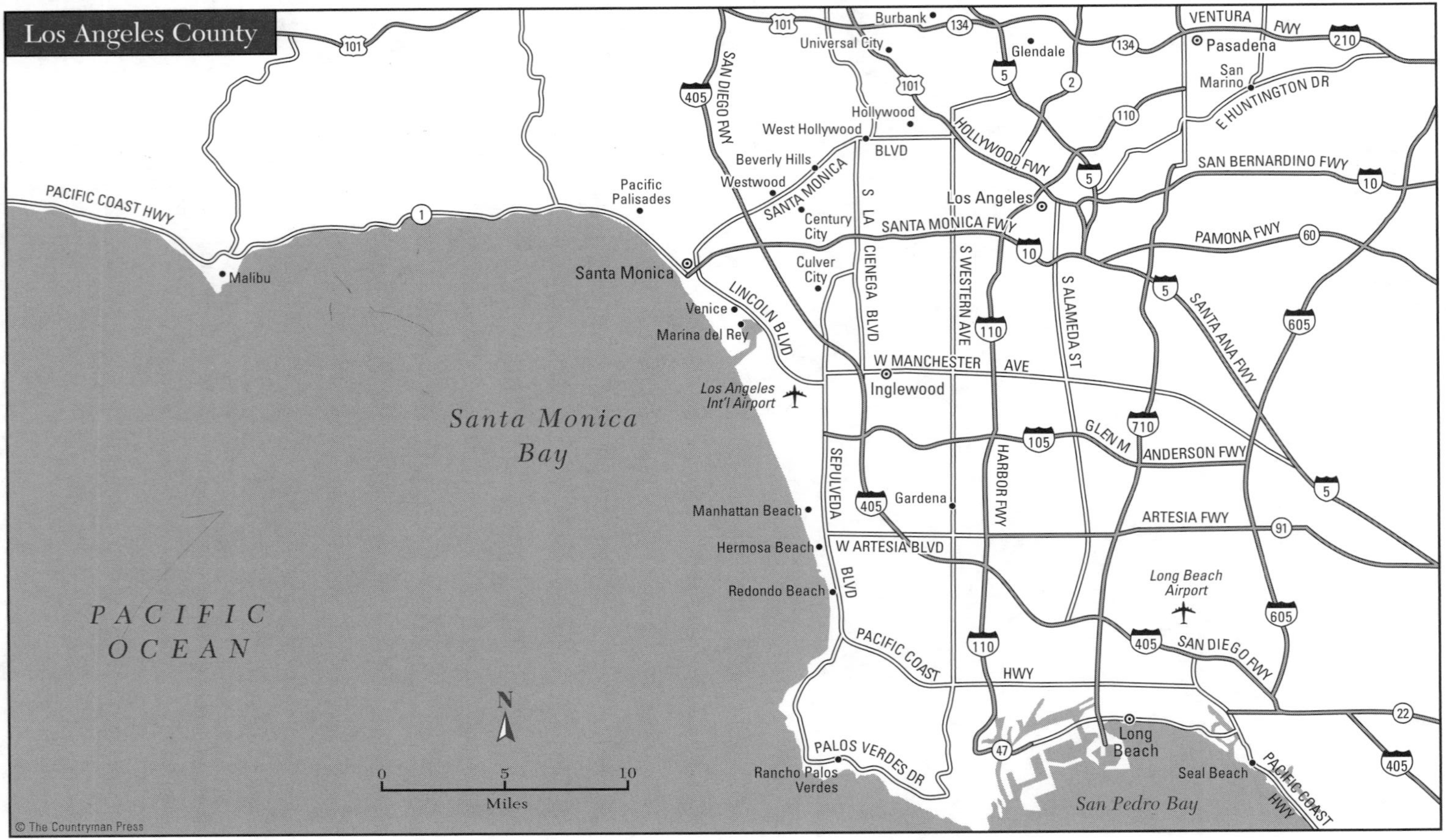
Los Angeles County
PACIFIC COAST HWY
Malibu
Pacific Palisades
Santa Monica
SAN DIEGO FWY
Westwood
Beverly Hills
West Hollywood
Hollywood
Universal City
Burbank
Glendale
Pasadena
San Marino
E HUNTINGTON DR
VENTURA FWY
HOLLYWOOD FWY
SANTA MONICA
BLVD
Century City
Culver City
Venice
Marina del Rey
LINCOLN BLVD
Los Angeles Int'l Airport
Los Angeles
SANTA MONICA FWY
SAN BERNARDINO FWY
PAMONA FWY
SANTA ANA FWY
S LA CIENEGA BLVD
S WESTERN AVE
S ALAMEDA ST
W MANCHESTER AVE
Inglewood
GLEN M ANDERSON FWY
HARBOR FWY
SEPULVEDA BLVD
Gardena
ARTESIA FWY
W ARTESIA BLVD
Manhattan Beach
Hermosa Beach
Redondo Beach
PACIFIC COAST HWY
Long Beach Airport
SAN DIEGO FWY
PALOS VERDES DR
Rancho Palos Verdes
Long Beach
Seal Beach
San Pedro Bay
Santa Monica Bay
PACIFIC OCEAN
N
0 5 10
Miles
101
134
210
405
5
2
110
10
60
605
710
105
91
22
47
1
© The Countryman Press

INTRODUCTION

To paraphrase one of my favorite movie characters, Los Angeles is like a box of chocolates: you never know what you're going to get. LA can be a dazzling, celebrity-infused orgy of highbrow and pop culture, gourmet dining, stunning coastline, idyllic weather, and nonstop entertainment. There are more than three hundred museums in the region, as well as a lion's share of live music venues and movie and television studios, hundreds of clubs featuring many performers on their way to superstardom, and dozens of internationally acclaimed chefs. The cherry on top? The area enjoys an average of 330 days of sun annually. On the other hand, LA can be chaotic; overwhelming in size; gritty; noisy; and hard to navigate, thanks to some of the most confusing surface streets in Southern California and the infamous, unrelenting traffic. In addition, the city is demarcated according to stark socioeconomic disparities, with the Haves living much different lives than the Have-Nots. Despite the inevitability of extremes—and the near certainty that visitors will either love or hate the city—LA is well worth the effort. This is one of the most vibrant, eclectic, exciting places in the world, and even with the gridlock, smog, and sprawling layout, the city has attractions and rewards like no other. Among the favorites that bring me back year after year are the treasures at the Getty Center in Malibu, the old-Hollywood glamour of the Beverly Hills Hotel, the powdery white sands of Zuma Beach, the charms of strolling along the Third Street Promenade in Santa Monica, the stunning architecture of downtown—the most audacious example of which is the newish Walt Disney Concert Hall—and foot-high pastrami at Cantor's Deli on the Miracle Mile near the LA County Museum.

The geography is almost incomprehensible in size: the city is 467 square miles, and the county comprises more than 4,000 square miles. There are 88 incorporated cities within LA County, including LA City, with a population of its own of nearly 4 million, making it the second-largest city in the nation. The county includes more than 10 million residents—more than most states. The geography is also incredibly diverse, bounded by the San Gabriel Mountain range and divided by the Santa Monica Mountains. The county boasts 75 miles of coastline and three major rivers (the Los Angeles River, the Rio Hondo, and the San Gabriel River). The terrain is often hilly and punctuated by canyons, which are responsible for the ubiquitous smog: these geographic depressions hold in the soot like a bowl.

To make a trip to LA comprehensible, focus on a couple of the most popular areas: (1) On the Westside is Venice, an infamous hangout for characters of all sorts; lovely, beachy Santa Monica, a longtime favorite of mine because of its relatively slower pace and its astonishing collection of world-class restaurants; and incomparable Malibu, an ultrapricey zip code that is home to the likes of Barbra Streisand, Cher, and Dustin Hoffman. (2) Inland is downtown LA, awash with dazzling skyscrapers, astonishing traffic, and a revitalized attitude that is attracting young adults by the droves to live and work there. (3) Inland are Hollywood, West Hollywood, and Beverly Hills, the renowned playgrounds of some of the most famous people in the world and the site of incomparable nightlife, dining, and shopping. (4) Pasadena—famous for being home to the Rose Bowl, the Rose Parade, and little old ladies (and less famous for being the birthplace of cooking icon Julia Child)—lies to the northeast and offers nostalgic charm in its quaint old town, stately homes along its tree-lined boulevards, and more than its fair share of eminent art museums. These four regions offer the biggest bang for the tourist buck in terms of attractions, natural beauty, abundance of hotels and dining, and ease of access, and for this reason I concentrate most of this chapter on these locales.

Don't let me discourage you from heading farther afield, however. Just over the hill from Hollywood, the San Fernando Valley made "Valley girls" and SoCal slang known worldwide, like, totally. My husband, who is a native of the San Fernando Valley, marvels over the revitalization most of the area has enjoyed in the past few decades, and despite a few neighborhoods that are still a little rough around the edges, the Valley is becoming a preferred neighborhood for young families. The big draw for visitors in the Valley is the proximity to the movie studios that flourish in Universal City and Burbank, as well as the historic Mission San Fernando Rey de España.

The south includes a handful of additional beach towns, each of which have their own attractions: Long Beach has long been industrial—and still hosts a huge number of unsightly smokestacks—but in recent years has spruced up with the Cabrillo Marine Aquarium, the stunning Long Beach Performing Arts Center, and fine dining on Belmont Shore and Pine Avenue. The grand old cruise ship the *Queen Mary* has been parked harborside for years. The South Bay includes Manhattan Beach, Redondo Beach, and Hermosa Beach, a string of small communities that offer the quintessential SoCal beach experience, with wide sands, ubiquitous surfing, and increasingly popular beach volleyball. (Misty May-Treanor and Kerri Walsh were once regulars at Manhattan Beach courts.) Along the waterfront are dozens of seafood restaurants and bars that offer astounding views of the Pacific. Nearby Marina del Rey offers one of the largest human-made harbors in the country and is thus wildly popular with the boating set—and also offers abundant water-view restaurants and bars.

GUIDANCE The Los Angeles Convention and Visitor's Bureau has two centers near Metro stations:

Hollywood and Highland Center, Convention and Visitors Bureau (323-467-6412), 6801 Hollywood Blvd., Hollywood.

Downtown, Convention and Visitors Bureau (213-689-8822), 685 S. Figueroa St., downtown.

There are also visitor kiosks at the Port of Los Angeles in San Pedro and inside the LA Convention Center.

SANTA MONICA PIER

Port of Los Angeles, Convention and Visitors Bureau (210-514-9484), Berth 93, Pacific Cruise Ship Terminal, San Pedro.

Many cities within Los Angeles County offer guidance as well:

Beverly Hills Conference and Visitors Bureau (800-345-2210; www.beverlyhillsbehere.com).

Pasadena Convention and Visitors Bureau (800-307-7977; www.visitpasadena.com).

Santa Monica Convention and Visitors Bureau (800-544-5319; www.santamonica.com).

West Hollywood Conference and Visitors Bureau (800-368-6020; www.visitwesthollywood.com).

MORE TELEPHONE NUMBERS Local time: 213-853-1212

Weather: 213-554-1212

Freeway conditions: 800-427-7623

MEDICAL EMERGENCIES For ambulance, fire, and police emergencies, call 911. There are literally hundreds of hospitals in the area—far too many to list. Below are a handful of the largest hospitals, listed in alphabetical order. For more information on local hospitals and emergency rooms, visit http://california.hometownlocator.com/features/cultural,class,hospital,scfips,06037.cfm.

Cedars-Sinai Medical Center (310-423-9964), 8700 Beverly Blvd., Los Angeles.

LA County/USC Medical Center (323-226-2622), 1200 N. State St., Los Angeles.

Memorial Medical Center of Long Beach (562-933-2000), 2801 Atlantic Ave., Long Beach.

Rancho Los Amigos Medical Center (562-401-7111), 7601 E. Imperial Hwy., Downey.

Courtesy of Jon Preimesberger

TOURING BEVERLY HILLS

St. Joseph Medical Center (818-843-5111), 501 N. Buena Vista St., Burbank.

UCLA Medical Center (800-UCL-AMD1), 10833 Le Conte Ave., Los Angeles.

GETTING THERE *By air:* Los Angeles is a major hub for most domestic airlines and many international ones, so it is easy to find flights getting to the city from just about anywhere in the world. The region is served by two large airports:

Los Angeles International Airport (313-646-5252; www.lawa.org), 1 World Way, Los Angeles.

Los Angeles Ontario International Airport (909-937-2700; www.lawa.org), 1923 E. Avion St., Ontario.

Two additional airports are nearby, the first in Santa Ana (which is in northern Orange County) and the second in Long Beach, which is south Los Angeles County.

John Wayne Airport (949-252-5200; www.ocair.com), 18601 Airport Way, Santa Ana.

Long Beach Airport (562-595-8564; www.longbeach.gov/airport), 4100 E. Donald Douglas Dr., Long Beach.

By car: The reputation of LA traffic is well known, and yes, it's as bad as everyone says. Worse, in fact. There doesn't seem to be a way around it anywhere in town, and there are no true rush hours: although typical commute times are heavier than normal, *all* hours of the day, and all days of the week, are ripe for traffic in this car-crazy city. Some trouble spots are predictable—the Sunset Strip in West Hollywood on Saturday night, for example, or Highway 1 going through Santa Monica and Malibu on a perfect beach day—and other trouble spots pop up mysteriously, with seemingly no reason to explain the congestion in a given area at a given time. Add to this the disrepair of many surface roads (even in posh neighborhoods like

Beverly Hills); the extensive, often confusing web of interconnecting freeways and highways; and the disturbingly narrow highway and freeway lanes, and you've got the perfect storm. Did I mention parking is difficult to find, and expensive, throughout the most popular parts of the city? With that said, it can be pricey to take taxis around town—it isn't easy to find cabs in the first place—and it can be slow to take public transportation. For those determined to have their own vehicle, I have only two words of advice when behind the wheel: be patient. Most Angelenos have learned to be. Although the city is a maze, it can be fun learning the ins and outs (just like it can be fun to solve a perplexing puzzle), and although traffic is

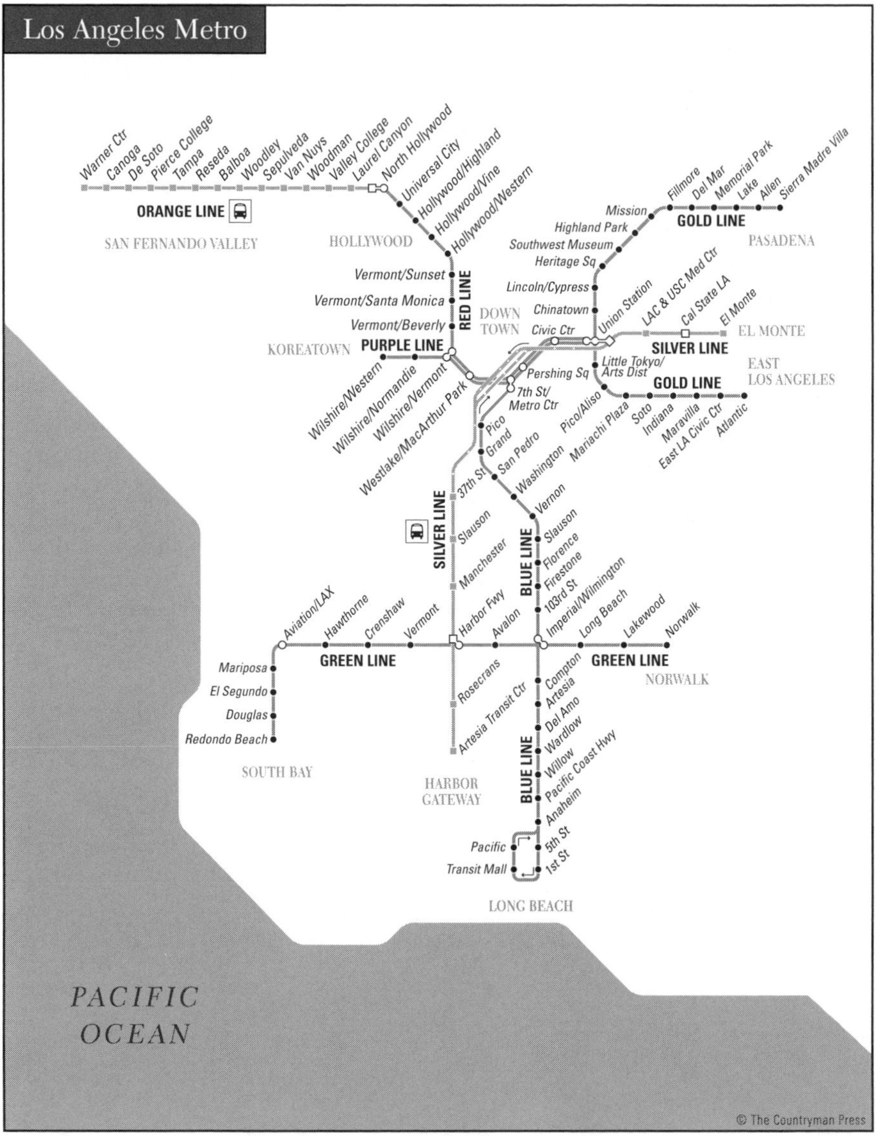

a major annoyance, visitors can comfort themselves with the thought that they don't have to deal with the congestion on an everyday basis.

By bus: **Greyhound Bus** serves the Los Angeles area, with stations in Hollywood (323-466-6381; 1715 N. Cahuenga Boulevard and 818-761-5110; 11239 Magnolia Boulevard), Long Beach (562-218-3011; 1498 Long Beach Boulevard), and downtown (213-629-8401; 1716 E. Seventh Street and 323-261-5522; 4910 E. Olympic Boulevard).

By train: **AMTRAK** (800-875-7245) serves the Los Angeles County area with a number of train stations, including downtown (213-683-6897; 800 N. Alameda Street), Burbank (3750 Empire Avenue), Fullerton (714-992-0530; 120 E. Santa Fe Avenue), Glendale (400 W. Cerritos Avenue), and Van Nuys (7724 Van Nuys Boulevard). Note that the *Pacific Surfliner* service runs from San Diego to San Luis Obispo, through Los Angeles, along a coastline route aboard bi-level cars with panoramic windows.

GETTING AROUND *By bus:* The **Metropolitan Transit Authority** (800-266-6883; www.mta.net) coordinates all public transportation in the city, including Metro rail and bus. Bus lines generally start at 4 AM and run past midnight, but for those traveling off hours, preplanning is essential because service is reduced in early morning and late-night hours. The MTA has an excellent trip-planning service, which is available online or by calling 323-GO-METRO. Agents can help over the telephone in planning routes, times, and coordinating transfers.

By subway: **Metro Rail** (800-266-6883; www.mta.net), the underground train system in Los Angeles, is limited but efficient. To get started, first purchase a ticket at a self-serve vending machine before boarding. Then, check the service maps to determine which train to take. It's as easy as knowing where you are and where you want to go, and then figuring out which line (designated by colors) going in which direction will take you there. For example, if you're in Hollywood at Hollywood and Highland and wish to travel to the civic center, you must board a redline train going in the direction of Union Station. Although subject to change, at the time this book went to press, the base fare was $1.25 (55 cents for seniors and disabled individuals), with increases based on length of travel and whether the trip is made during peak hours. A Metro day pass can be had for $5 ($1.80 for seniors and disabled individuals).

THE WESTSIDE: MALIBU, SANTA MONICA, AND VENICE

Santa Monica is as relaxed a place as you're apt to find in Los Angeles, offering a completely pleasant blend of laid-back beach culture and urban shopping and dining attractions, as well as some lovely oceanfront hotels. The iconic Santa Monica Pier offers amusement rides and a postcard-perfect nighttime scene, and the Third Street Promenade is an energetic, youthful, and entertaining pedestrian thoroughfare lined with restaurants and shops and accented with street performers. Northeast of Santa Monica (about halfway to Beverly Hills) is Westwood, a youth-centric district that offers several vintage movie theaters and the popular Westwood Village, teeming with inexpensive ethnic eateries. The area is also home to the massive campus of the University of California, Los Angeles.

Malibu is north of Santa Monica. Although undeniably posh, and the majority of residents unimaginably rich or famous (or both), the natural beauty of the 21 miles of coastline and wild bluffs has a primeval appeal to surfers and other beach

SANTA MONICA

lovers, even if our bank accounts don't allow residence here. Also nearby is the upscale neighborhood of Pacific Palisades, home to Pepperdine University, and Calabasas, the inland suburb made famous by the reality TV show *Meet the Kardashians.*

To the south is Venice: so named because of a series of canals that run through the neighborhood, this strip of coastline is infamous because of the cast of characters that call the area home. There are three distinct regions of Venice: downtown Venice Beach, home to a handful of nightclubs, art galleries, and bars; Venice Boardwalk, which offers prime souvenir shopping and people watching; and Muscle Beach, notorious as body-builder central, where bulging, oiled folks come to strut their stuff. Many might remember this stretch of sand as the former hangout of the California governator, Arnold Schwarzenegger, who pumped iron here before striking it rich in Hollywood (and then leaving it all behind for Sacramento). The famous oceanfront walk is a movable feast of humanity that includes fire jugglers, bikini-clad skateboarders, and rubber-snake charmers. Venice also offers eclectic boutique shopping and dining opportunities.

✷ To See

HISTORICAL SITES Malibu Pier (www.malibupier.com), 23000 Pacific Coast Hwy., Malibu. Dating to 1905, this recently renovated historic landmark is a favorite with locals out for a stroll—or for those hoping to catch a little local seafood. (No fishing license is required to cast off the pier.) The pier is home to restaurants like **Ruby's Shake Shack** and the **Beachcomber Café.** Also on the pier is the recently opened **Malibu Pier Surf Museum,** which houses surf memorabilia. If the museum inspires you to catch a wave for yourself, it's possible to rent boards at **Zuma Jay's.**

VENICE BOARDWALK
Photo Nadine Markora. Courtesy LA Convention and Visitors Bureau

✪ **Muscle Beach,** in Venice Beach, south of the volleyball courts. An outdoor gym area on Venice Beach, this place was made famous in the 1930s, when body builders like Jack LaLanne and Joe Gold (founder of Gold's Gym) used the open-air facilities to work out—often drawing a crowd to watch. Soon after, the beach attracted Hollywood luminaries and fitness buffs like Clark Gable and Kirk Douglas, who in turn attracted even larger crowds. The original Muscle Beach was closed in 1959, but it was re-created at this new site and features parallel bars, rings, and a padded gymnastics area for tumbling.

Ocean Front Walk, from Marine St. to the Venice Pier, on Venice Beach.

THE *QUEEN MARY* IN LONG BEACH

Moored since 1967 in Long Beach (about 25 miles south of Santa Monica), the once-fabulous *Queen Mary* cruise ship (877-342-0738; 1126 Queen's Highway, Long Beach) was originally built by Cunard in the mid-1930s as part of its luxury transatlantic ocean liners fleet. World War II put an end to pleasure travel between the United States and Europe, and the ship was commandeered by the U.S. government and used as a military transport from 1940 to 1946. During this period the ship carried more than 750,000 army and navy personnel to and from the war—ferrying as many as 15,000 troops at any given time, often cramming in soldiers into four-decker bunk beds. In 1947 the *Queen Mary* resumed its passenger service and sailed for 20 more years before being retired. The ship now serves as a museum and a hotel. Guests can take self-guided audio tours to explore the ship or enjoy more expansive guided walks, like the ever-popular Haunted Encounter Tour (to discover the ship's purported ghosts) and the World War II Tour (to learn about the *Grey Ghost,* as the ship was called during wartime, and its efforts to help the Allied forces). In addition, the *Queen Mary* offers three hundred original staterooms across three decks that are available as hotel lodging. The rooms offer period appointments and portholes, and people who believe in such things claim many of the hotel cabins are among the best places to observe paranormal activity.

This strip of boardwalk takes visitors past Muscle Beach, tattoo parlors, kamikaze skateboarders, street musicians, and some of the most eccentric folks you'll find (and that's putting it mildly). The boardwalk also attracts in-line skaters, skateboarders, bikers, and joggers. Venice Beach and its surrounds are iconic and entertaining, and it is well worth seeing, if only for out-of-towners to confirm their stereotypes about Southern California.

✪ **Santa Monica Pier** (310-458-8900; www.santamonicapier.org), off Colorado Ave., Santa Monica. The iconic Santa Monica Pier is a hot spot day and night, thanks to great views of the ocean and of Malibu to the north, as well as **Pacific Park,** a small amusement park atop the pier (complete with roller coaster and Ferris wheel, and plenty of fast-food options. If you can squeeze in, get a table overlooking the water at **Bubba Gump's.**

Venice Pier, at Washington Blvd. and Ocean Front Walk, Venice Beach. Venice Pier used to offer amusement park attractions in line with what guests can see on Santa Monica Pier. However, the former "pleasure pier" was damaged many times over due to storms and earthquakes. Today, the current 1,300-foot pier dates to 1997 and is a favorite with fishermen (no license is required). The pier provides accessible areas where those in wheelchairs can pull up comfortably and fish.

MUSEUMS ✪ **Getty Center** (310-440-7300; www.getty.edu), 1200 Getty Center Dr., Los Angeles. Open Tues.–Sun.; hours vary by season. This miraculous arts center compound, opened in 1997, is built on 750 acres amid the foothills of the Santa Monica Mountains, with views to Pacific Palisades and Malibu to the west and Century City and downtown to the east. Modernist architect Richard Meier designed the stunning array of curvy structures with rough-hewn travertine and glass, and punctuated the space between with soothing water fountains. The series of interconnecting galleries are light, bright, and surprisingly spacious, even when the museum is crowded. The permanent collection has much to offer, comprising a respectable collection of impressionist paintings, including the famously expensive *Irises* by Van Gogh. Other highlights include a collection of decorative arts and French antique furniture that is worthy of Versailles, a handful of Italian Renaissance paintings, venerable Dutch and Flemish works, and an outdoor sculpture garden. Kids will want to stop by the Family Room, which offers children ages 5–13 hands-on opportunities to create their own artwork. In addition, on the upper level of the East Pavilion, look for the Sketching Gallery, which provides patrons of all ages a sketch pad and pencils, and the opportunity to recreate works within the gallery. This huge complex also houses an auditorium, lecture hall, and research institute, as well as a full restaurant and a café on-site. Do not miss the stunning gardens at the back of the property, especially the astonishing flower maze with

INSIDER TIP: Arrive at the Getty Center 30 minutes before the museum opens. Early-morning trams are pleasantly empty, and it is possible to stroll the grounds and gardens before official opening times—which is much more enjoyable without the inevitable congestion later in the day.

GETTY CENTER

GETTY VILLA

more than four hundred azalea plants surrounded by a shallow pool of water. (Come in late Feb. to early Mar. to see the maze at its blooming peak.) Admission is free; on-site parking is $15 and includes a tram ride up the mountain from the parking structure at the bottom.

Getty Villa Malibu (310-440-7300; www.getty.edu), 17985 Pacific Coast Hwy., Malibu. Open Thurs.–Mon. 10–5, by reservation only. The Getty Villa was the one-time home of mogul J. Paul Getty and is modeled after a Roman country house near Pompeii. In keeping with its classical design, the newly renovated museum (reopened in 2006) is home to ancient Greek, Etruscan, and Roman artwork. Featured are an array of immaculately preserved Greek urns and glassware, sculptures, and mosaics. Look for the most famous piece in the collection, *The Victorious Youth,* salvaged from the Adriatic Sea off Italy and now residing in gallery 201—but be quick about it: Italy wants this particular piece back, claiming rightful ownership even though the piece is of Greek origin. Although the number and quality of antiquities at the Villa is astounding, the structure itself is perhaps the most appealing aspect of this museum, especially the stunning Outer Peristyle, which features a long narrow pool surrounded by statues and encircled by a formal garden. Children will enjoy the Family Forum, on the ground floor, which encourages hands-on participation with activities like sketching on a replica of an ancient urn. Admission is free; on-site parking $15.

Skirball Cultural Center (310-440-4500; www.skirball.org), 2701 N. Sepulveda Blvd., Los Angeles. Open Tues.–Fri. noon–5 and Sat.–Sun. 10–5. Located east of Malibu, the Skirball is a Jewish cultural institution that is part museum, part theater, part musical venue, and part event setting. Without a doubt, the highlight is the 8,000-square-foot Noah's Ark exhibit, which allows guests to walk through a wooden ark overflowing with fanciful animal re-creations (crafted with recycled materials like bottle caps and old bicycle parts). Patrons can help add on to the ark, interact with puppets, or "make" their own storms. **Zeidler's,** an on-site café, serves fresh salads, sandwiches, and a handful of hot entrées, and is worth a visit even without museum entrance. Adults $10, children $5.

THE RONALD REAGAN PRESIDENTIAL LIBRARY AND MUSEUM

At the Ronald Reagan Presidential Library (805-520-9702; www.reaganlibrary.com; 40 Presidential Dr., Simi Valley), in Simi Valley, north of Malibu, visitors can step aboard the actual Boeing 707 that was used as *Air Force One* during the tenure of seven presidents; view a Marine Helicopter Squadron One aircraft up close; and witness a U.S. Army MP patrol a re-creation of Checkpoint Charlie, the former border crossing of the Berlin Wall. Guests can also walk through an amazingly accurate re-creation of the Oval Office during the Reagan administration, complete with a jar of jelly beans on the desk and Reagan's collection of Remington bronze saddles on the bookshelves. The grounds of the library are open to explore, and those wishing to can pay their respects at President Reagan's gravesite. The library is also a repository for more than 60 million pages' worth of documents, more than 1.5 million photographs, tens of thousands of audio and videotapes, and more than 40,000 artifacts, some of which are on rotating display in the museum. The library hosts regular symposia, featuring guest speakers that have included former presidents, first ladies, and secretaries of state. Open daily 10–5. Adults $12, seniors $9, youth (11–17) $6, children 10 and under free.

PARKS ✐ **Chess Park,** along Ocean Front Walk, Santa Monica. This small park offers numerous permanent chessboards, along with a life-sized chessboard that is fun for kids. Tables are free and open to the public, and there are almost always willing opponents to be found.

Malibu Creek State Park, on Las Virgenes/Malibu Canyon Rd., 4 miles south of Hwy. 101, Malibu. Malibu Creek cuts through this expansive wild space, which offers hiking trails that trace the waterline, as well as fishing, picnicking, camping, and horseback riding opportunities. TV junkies will recognize the terrain as the backdrop for the 1970s television show *M*A*S*H.*

Solstice Canyon Park, on Coral Canyon Rd., 0.25 mile north of Hwy. 101, Malibu. Although heavily damaged by the fires that ravaged Malibu in fall 2007, Solstice Canyon Park has been reopened to visitors, who will find charred vegetation as well as numerous signs that the wildlife is returning to the area. The park features dozens of hiking trails, including an especially pretty one that leads to a small waterfall and pond.

✐ **Westwood Park,** 1350 Sepulveda Blvd., Westwood. In addition to a tranquil green space with picnic tables and barbecue pits, a pool, and tennis courts, Westwood Park is home to the amazing **Aidan's Place,** a wheelchair-accessible playground for children of all abilities that includes accessible slides, a sand castle play area, and a water play zone.

Will Rogers State Park (310-454-8212), 1501 Will Rodgers Park Rd., Pacific Palisades. Ranch house open for docent-led tours Thurs.–Fri. 11–2, Sat. and Sun.

10–4. Located in Pacific Palisades, the Will Rogers State Park started out as the sprawling ranch home belonging to Will Rogers, who in the 1930s was one of the most recognized actors in Hollywood. Often called the "cowboy philosopher," Oklahoma-born Rogers was also a columnist, radio personality, and a trick roper. On his death, the ranch was donated to the state, and today visitors can tour Rogers's one time home; hike a 3-mile loop to Inspiration Point, which has views to Santa Monica and sometimes, on really clear days, beyond to Catalina Island (see the "Santa Catalina Island" chapter); and bike the Backbone Trail into the Santa Monica Mountains.

✷ To Do

BICYCLING Bicycling in Los Angeles is a mixed bag: The good news is that a good chunk of the terrain is relatively flat, and there are bike paths along just about every street. The bad news is that car traffic is ubiquitous, and LA drivers are notoriously cranky about sharing the roadways. Beach pathways in Santa Monica and Malibu are among the best options for riders in the city. Especially good for those who don't mind dodging traffic are the lanes that run parallel to the waterfront along Ocean Avenue in Santa Monica. One of the best options for off-road biking is **Malibu Creek State Park,** which offers 15 miles of challenging trails.

STUDIO TOURS

Let's face it: most people come to Hollywood expecting to see movie and TV stars—and the studios that made them famous. Truth is, most of the major studios today are in the Valley, not Hollywood—and for a fee, many are kind enough to open their doors to visitors, who can get a backstage peek. It can be a bit disillusioning to look behind the curtains—the movie and TV business seem anything but glamorous in this light—but it is definitely interesting. Fans of the big and small screens shouldn't miss checking out at least one of these studio tours. (Note that Universal Studios is also a huge theme park, offering entertainment, dining, and thrill rides. See the "Beverly Hills, Hollywood, and West Hollywood" chapter.)

- **NBC Studios** (818-840-3537), 3000 W. Alameda Ave., Burbank. Admission to tapings free; tours $8.50.
- **Sony Pictures Studios** (310-244-TOUR), 10202 W. Washington Blvd., Culver City. Two-hour walking tour includes sets of TV shows and live productions. Must be 12 years or older. Advance reservations required (and be sure to bring a photo ID). Weekdays $28.
- **Universal Studios Hollywood** (818-622-3801; www.universalstudioshollywood.com), 100 Universal City Plaza, Universal City. Open daily at 10; close times vary by season.
- **Warner Brothers Studios** (818-972-8687; www.wbsf.com), 3400 W. Riverside Dr., Burbank. Open Mon.–Fri. 8:30–4. Admission $45.

Bike rental shops include **Blazing Saddles Bike Rentals** (310-393-9778), on the Santa Monica Pier; **Cycle Design of Malibu** (310-589-2048), 29575 Pacific Coast Highway, Malibu; and **Spokes 'n Stuff** (310-395-4748), 1715 Oceanfront Walk, Santa Monica.

GOLF The beachside communities featured in this chapter are jam-packed, and for this reason open space is at a premium. The majority of golf courses in this area are private, but there are a handful of public options.

Los Verdes Golf Course (310-377-7888; www.americangolf.com), 7000 W. Los Verdes Dr., Rancho Palos Verdes. Because this is the *only* inexpensive golf course in coastal LA—and views are stunning, especially from the 15th hole—it is imperative that golfers reserve tee times in advance. Green fee: $25.

Malibu Country Club (818-889-6980; www.malibucountryclub.net), 901 Encinal Canyon Rd., Malibu. Despite the exclusive moniker, Malibu Country Club is open to the public—and the course is one of the prettiest and most serene in the area, thanks to the abundant natural wilderness. Note that there is a dress code: no denim is allowed, and shirts with collars are required. Green fee: $75–100.

Riviera Country Club Pacific Palisades (310-454-6591; www.therivieracountryclub.com), 1250 Capri Dr., Pacific Palisades. *Golf Digest* ranks the Riviera Country Club in Pacific Palisades as one of the top one hundred golf courses in the country—and the stunning clubhouse and emerald greens do not disappoint. This is a private club, which means you'll need to befriend a member to gain entrance. Green fee: $200–250.

SPAS **Ai Spa** (818-225-8700; www.ai-spa.com), 4774 Park Granada, Suite 9, Calabasas. This Asian-inspired spa offers a fragrant Ginger Chocolate Body Wrap, a slimming Marine Lipo Body Wrap, and a refreshing RaVi Sugar Scrub, but for a true only-in-LA moment, check out the Golden Facial that includes application of 24-karat gold leaf.

Cure Spa at the Malibu Beach Inn (310-456-1499; http://spa.malibubeachinn.com), 22878 Pacific Coast Hwy., Malibu. It is hard to be anything but relaxed in Malibu, and the Cure Spa certainly encourages the Zen-like attitude of those who live here. The full-service facility offers typical massages, facials, and body wraps, as well as "finishing touches" like paraffin treatments, eyelash tinting, and eyebrow sculpting.

The Spa at Le Merigot (310-395-9700; http://lemerigothotel.com/spa.htm), 1740 Ocean Ave., Santa Monica. Part of **Le Merigot Hotel and Spa,** this full-service spa offers heavenly cranial massages (great for relieving stress headaches), a fragrant cucumber and mint wrap, and a luxurious caviar and pearl lifting facial to minimize fine lines—the latter of which actually provides instant results (although the fish-eggs treatment is a little stinky).

INSIDER TIP: Look for online specials at the Willow Spa, which often include a Monday special 50 percent discount on a facial when booked with an enzyme bath treatment.

Willow Spa (310-453-9004; www.willowspa.com), 3127 Santa Monica Blvd., Santa Monica. In addition to

PACIFIC PARK

traditional massages, facials, scrubs, and wraps, this day spa offers the surprisingly relaxing Willow Enzyme Bath: patrons climb into a huge wooden "dry tub," which is then filled with rice bran, vegetable and fruit enzymes, and wood shavings—imagine crawling into a compost pile—and the effect is a pleasant, very warm experience that is meant to detoxify and ease aching muscles. All treatments include a complimentary cup of tea and a foot massage.

THEME PARKS AND ZOOS ✪ ✐ ⇴ **Pacific Park** (www.pacpark.com), on Santa Monica Pier. Open daily; hours vary seasonally. This small, picture-postcard park is perched on the iconic Santa Monica Pier and offers spectacular views to Malibu and beyond from the Pacific Wheel, the world's only solar-powered Ferris wheel. (At night this "green" amusement ride lights up with energy-efficient LED lights in a computer-generated light show that is fun to watch from the pier or from a distance.) The gentle West Coaster roller coaster is another exclusive: it's the only oceanfront steel roller coaster on a pier on the West Coast. There are 10 other rides—most of which cater to the ankle-biter set—and 21 midway games. Riders can purchase tickets for individual rides or purchase a limitless pass for full access.

✷ Water Sports

BOATING There is no shortage of opportunities to be out on the water in Santa Monica and Malibu—and it is a special treat to view coastal Los Angeles from the vantage point of a boat. For kayak rentals, lessons, and guided tours through the abundant sea caves, check out **Malibu Ocean Sports** (310-456-6302; www.socal sail.com/bg/co/malibu-ocean-sports). For sailboat and powerboat rentals as well as charters, consider **Blue Pacific Boating** (310-398-8830; www.bluepacificboating .com). For those who prefer a full-service experience, don't miss **Hornblower**

Cruises (888-HORNBLOWER; www.hornblower.com/hce/home/mdr), which launches from nearby Marina del Rey and offers sunset dinner cruises, starlight cocktail cruises, and special-event trips like Fourth of July harbor fireworks tours.

DIVING AND SNORKELING Look for **Malibu Divers** (310-456-2396; www.malibudivers.com), **Ocean Adventures Dive Company** (310-578-9391; www.oceanadventuresdiveco.com), and **Scuba Haus** (310-828-2916; http://scubahaus.com) for scuba and snorkeling equipment and supplies, lessons and certification, and dive trips. These organizations offer local guided trips, as well as excursions to the Channel Islands (see part 6), Catalina Island (see the "Santa Catalina Island" chapter), and as far south as Baja Mexico.

FISHING Seasonal fish in the waters off Santa Monica include barracuda, calico bass, halibut, and yellowtail. Most fishing charters in the area set sail from the Marina del Rey harbor and fish the waters along the LA coastline. Check out **Marina del Rey Sportsfishing** (310-822-3625; http://marinadelreysportfishing.com), which provides equipment, tackle, and licenses. Half-day and full-day trips are available. Fishermen can also try their luck at the Santa Monica, Malibu, and Venice piers, no license required.

SURFING The California surfing culture got its start in Malibu, and these days it is nearly impossible to visit a beach on the West Coast without waves littered with hundreds of surfers, especially if you visit in the early morning hours; wind comes up later in the day and tends to flatten the swell, so diehards prefer hitting the beach at the crack of dawn. As with most beaches in Southern California, the locals in Malibu and Santa Monica are quite territorial. Only advanced surfers should head out on their own. Beginners and intermediates would do well getting the lay of the water with a certified instructor who is familiar with local etiquette, as well as currents and tides for local beaches. There are dozens of surf schools available, including **Malibu Long Boards Surf School** (310-467-6898; www.malibulongboards.com/lessons); **Malibu Surf Shack** (310-456-8508; www.malibusurfshack.com), 22935 Pacific Coast Highway, Malibu; and **Surfing LA** (310-663-0661; www.surfingla.com), Malibu.

✷ Green Space

BEACHES Los Angeles offers the widest expanses of shoreline on the West Coast. Although the acres of white sand and sparkling water are enchanting—especially on clear days—don't expect an intimate experience at any of these beaches. On warm weekends and throughout the late spring and summer, LA beaches are packed, and there is just no getting around the crowds. As when dealing with any congestion faced in the area in just about any circumstance, the best bet for the beaches is to arrive early—snag a limited parking spot and claim as much real estate as you can by spreading out blankets, towels, and beach chairs on the sand. Then wait through the morning haze to break and prepare for an onslaught of other beachgoers. Note that beach access in Malibu can be tricky, because so much of the coast is rimmed with high-end "stilt" homes that block immediate access. Look for signs along the road that say COASTAL ACCESS and follow the pathways to the shore. Otherwise, stick to the larger beaches (most of which offer paid parking and facilities).

El Matador Beach, 32215 Pacific Coast Hwy., 10 miles northwest of Malibu. Part of the Robert H. Meyer Memorial State Beach system, this secluded "pocket beach" with a rocky shoreline and crashing waves looks less like a beach in Southern California and more like a bit of secluded Mexican coastline, especially because of the large boulders that lie off the shoreline, which are reminiscent of Cabo San Lucas. Note that there are no facilities here, but plenty of cozy coves and some of the clearest water in LA. The small parking lot is open 8 AM–sunset. It is a bit of challenge to reach the shoreline: follow the signs to a steep dirt trail and then to some stairs.

Leo Carrillo State Beach, 35000 Pacific Coast Hwy., 30 miles north of Santa Monica. This state beach stretches more than a mile and offers sea caves, tide pools, picnic areas, and campsites. It is rocky in places, but it's picturesque and extremely popular with surfers. A small visitors center exhibits interpretive displays and offers guided walks and campfire programs.

Point Dume, south end of Westward Beach Rd., Malibu. Point Dume is a favorite with divers, surfers, and fishermen. It also offers good tidepooling, picnic tables, and restrooms with showers. Access is via a gradual ascending trail from the cul-de-sac at the end of Westward Beach Rd., which leads to a coastal bluff sand dune. It is worth visiting just to check out the views of the Santa Monica Bay and Santa Catalina Island in the distance.

✪ **Santa Monica State Beach,** along Pacific Coast Hwy., north of the Santa Monica Pier, Santa Monica. This very popular, very crowded beach is 2 miles long and offers spectacular views of Malibu in the distance. Because of the enormous size, it is possible to find a little elbow room here—especially if you set up closer to the roadway and farther from the water's edge.

SANTA MONICA BEACH

Surfrider Beach, 23050 Pacific Coast Hwy., Malibu. As the name suggests, this beach is highly popular with surfers, thanks to big breaks, especially in winter. Even those who don't surf will enjoy watching some of the best in the sport, who come here regularly. Check out the nearby **Malibu Lagoon Park and Pier** and the historic **Adamson House,** a showplace of Malibu artifacts.

Venice Beach, west of Pacific Ave., Venice. Although the surf and sand are lovely, the real treat in Venice is great people watching along Ocean Front Walk. Look for street performers like the locally famous Harry Perry, a turbaned guitar player on in-line skates; dozens of palm readers; chain-saw jugglers in Speedos; and the internationally famous rubber-snake wrangler.

Will Rogers State Beach, 2 miles north of the Santa Monica Pier, along Pacific Coast Hwy., Pacific Palisades. Find paid parking and a long, wide expanse of beach with premier views of Malibu to the north. There are seemingly endless numbers of beach volleyball courts here, and this is one of the most family-friendly of the LA beaches.

✪ **Zuma Beach,** 30000 block of Pacific Coast Hwy., Malibu. This very wide, very long, and very white sandy beach is my favorite in Los Angeles. It offers stunning wide-angle views; good sunbathing, wading, and swimming; volleyball courts; and is appropriate for families and singles alike. There is plentiful parking (for $6) and ample facilities—although despite the size, it can get mighty crowded, especially on holiday weekends.

GARDENS Mildred E. Mathias Botanical Garden (310-825-1260; www.botgard.ucla.edu), off Tiverton Ave., on the grounds of the University of California, Los Angeles. Tucked into the southeastern corner of the UCLA campus, this small exhibition garden features more than five thousand species of tropical and subtropical plants.

Self-Realization Fellowship Lake Shrine (310-454-4114; www.yogananda-srf.org), 17190 Sunset Blvd., Pacific Palisades. This 10-acre garden and memorial to

TOP 10 DAY IN SANTA MONICA

1. Wake up with hazelnut waffles with Nutella at FIG (see pp. 183–184)
2. Tour the Getty Center gardens in the early morning hours (see pp. 171–173)
3. Indulge in a cranial massage at the Spa at Le Merigot (see p. 176)
4. Lunch on an Office Burger and fries at Father's Office (see p. 185)
5. Sunbathe at Santa Monica State Beach (see p. 179)
6. Stroll along Ocean Front Walk, then stop by Chess Park for a leisurely game (p. 174)
7. Dine on butter-drenched lobster at Ocean Avenue Seafood (see p. 184)
8. Ride the LED-lighted Ferris wheel in Pacific Park at the Santa Monica Pier (see p. 177)
9. Sip a Kir Royale nightcap at the Veranda Bar (see p. 187)
10. Overnight in an ocean-view bungalow at the Fairmont Miramar Hotel (see p. 181)

Mahatma Gandhi comprises a serene, manicured botanical garden overlooking the coast.

South Coast Botanic Garden (310-544-1948; www.southcoastbotanicgarden.org), 26300 Crenshaw Blvd., Palos Verdes Peninsula. This garden boasts more than 2,500 plant species on nearly 90 acres. Highlights include a children's garden and a native draught-resistant exhibit.

✱ Lodging

Malibu

Malibu Beach Inn (310-456-6444; www.malibubeachinn.com), 22878 Pacific Coast Hwy. The Malibu Beach Inn is one of only a handful of truly beachfront properties in Los Angeles—the inn is built directly over a breakwater on the sand—and it is sited on one of the most exclusive stretches of shorefront in the world. The small property offers a variety of large accommodations, decorated in sophisticated beach chic design, with clean lines and muted tones. In addition to premium beach access, the hotel is also close to fine dining and shopping in Malibu and within easy access of the many amenities of nearby Santa Monica. The on-site **Carbon Beach Club Dining Room** has views that look directly over the water—about as close to the Pacific as you can get without being on a boat. $$$–$$$$

PRICE KEY FOR A STANDARD ROOM:

$	$100 or less
$$	$101–150
$$$	$151–250
$$$$	$251 and up

Santa Monica

✪ **Fairmont Miramar Hotel and Bungalows** (310-576-7777; www.fairmont.com/santamonica), 101 Wilshire Blvd. This classic beach hotel is just across from Santa Monica beach, with easy access to the pretty oceanfront pathway that runs parallel to Ocean Front Rd. The popular **Third Street Promenade** and the **Santa Monica Pier** are also within easy walking distance. The majority of accommodations at the Fairmont are available in the tower building, in which most rooms boast a spectacular view of the ocean. Clustered around a small pool and grassy lawn are also a handful of bungalows, all of which offer private patios and extra space. Service is attentive and friendly, and the on-site restaurant, **FIG,** offers pleasant surroundings and fine dining. $$$

Hotel Casa del Mar (310-581-5533; www.hotelcasadelmar.com), 1910 Ocean Front Way. This elegant seaside hotel was a favorite with Hollywood glitterati in the 1920s, and the meticulously

FAIRMONT HOTEL

refurbished and commodious suites (which have as many as four bedrooms) continue to be a hit with visiting dignitaries. The location is prime: on the beach, just south of the **Santa Monica Pier,** and close to fine dining and shopping. Gracious service harkens back to an earlier era, and guests really are treated like VIPs. $$$$

Le Merigot Beach Hotel (310-395-9700; www.lemerigothotel.com), 1740 Ocean Ave. A JW Marriott property, Le Merigot offers European elegance in a setting that is more formal than many others on the coastline. Italianate furniture, rich colors, and fine amenities are luxurious without being stuffy. Beach access is nearby, as are myriad wining, dining, and shopping opportunities. In addition, Le Merigot has a much-lauded spa (see *To Do*). The hotel offers a fun California Cruisin' package that includes a superior guest room and the use of either a Mercedes C class or BMW 300 series vehicle. $$$

✪ 🍸 ⚥ **Shutters on the Beach** (310-458-0030; www.shuttersonthebeach.com), 1 Pico Blvd. This is one of the few places in Los Angeles that caters to just about everyone, including tourists, dignitaries, Hollywood stars, and locals (who love cocktails in the lounge). The exclusive property offers light, breezy luxury, with spalike bathrooms, large guest rooms, and numerous inviting public spaces. The property sits on the beach, so views from most guest rooms are top-shelf. The inviting pool has private cabanas, for those who want to hide away, and the programmed activities include yoga on the beach, bicycle rentals, and surf lessons. Art lovers will enjoy the hotel's extensive collection of modern and contemporary art, which includes pieces by David Hockney, Roy Lichtenstein, and Richard Diebenkorn. $$$$

Westwood

✪ ⟴ **Hotel Palomar Los Angeles** (310-475-8711; www.thewestwoodhotel.com), 10740 Wilshire Blvd. I am a huge fan of the Kimpton Hotel line, and this stylish boutique property in Westwood, near UCLA, proves my point. Vibrant colors and bold design are the hotel's hallmark, which attracts a youthful, energetic clientele. The hotel features ecofriendly recycling bins in each room, energy-efficient lighting, and organic options in the minibar, and the on-site restaurant practices sustainable seafood guidelines. The key to the success of Kimpton hotels is their staff: the folks at Hotel Palomar are upbeat, helpful, engaged employees who make a stay here less businesslike and more personal. $$–$$$

✱ Where to Eat

DINING OUT

Century City

Craft Los Angeles (310-279-4180; www.craftrestaurant.com), 10100 Constellation Blvd. Open Mon.–Sat. for dinner. Celebrity chef Tom Colicchio (the tough judge on TV's *Top Chef*) recently opened this LA outpost of his very successful East Coast franchise.

> **INSIDER TIP:** If you'd like to soak up the ambiance of Shutters but can't afford the stiff rates, stop by for a drink on the poolside deck; or go to the lobby to pick up a brochure on the art collection, and then meander the public spaces to explore the impressive holdings.

Thanks to Colicchio's popularity, the place is booked solid weeks in advance, and there is a prevailing frenzy about getting in to see and be seen. But the cuisine rises above all the hype, and seasonal offerings of daring pairings like hush puppies served with smoked maple syrup, and roasted bone marrow with capers pull in die-hard foodies. $$$

Malibu

🍸 **Duke's Malibu** (310-317-0777; www.hulapie.com), 21150 Pacific Coast Hwy. Open daily for lunch and dinner. Although Los Angeles is increasingly becoming a gourmet haven, with both world-class dining and a plethora of ethnic cafés, sometimes a body just wants a good piece of fish served in a relaxed, friendly atmosphere, with an outstanding view of the Pacific Ocean. Duke's delivers, with patio dining boasting vistas that rival those of the most beautiful restaurants in the world. If you're just looking to unwind with a signature cocktail, like the Malibu Cooler (a blend of cranberry juice, pineapple juice, melon liqueur, and rum), try the on-site **Barefoot Bar,** which features Hawaiian dancers on Fri. and $4 mai tais every night. $$

Geoffrey's Malibu (310-457-1519; www.geoffreysmalibu.com), 27400 Pacific Coast Hwy. Open daily for lunch and dinner, brunch on Sun. This elegant, classic restaurant on the cliffs overlooking the sea offers a quintessential Southern California experience. Whether dining inside, in a sophisticated atmosphere that has attracted celebrities for decades, or outside, on the garden terrace with ocean views that go on for miles, Geoffrey's is true Malibu: upscale, casually opulent, and stunning in every way. Splurge on the surf-and-turf special: a petite filet in a cabernet reduction sauce alongside a 2-pound lobster in a subtle vanilla sauce. Locals have been celebrating special occasions at the Sun. brunch for years with lobster quiche and mimosas. $$$$

🍸 **Gladstone's 4 Fish** (310-454-3474; www.gladstones.com), 17300 Pacific Coast Hwy. Open daily for breakfast, lunch, and dinner. Directly on the beach, this casual seaside restaurant has the relaxed atmosphere of a crab shack on the East Coast—but, sadly, it has the prices of the oceanfront Malibu establishment that it is. Specialties include Alaskan king crab legs, Australian and Maine lobster, and scallops. Service is friendly, and the offerings are fresh—but know in advance that the real reason most people come to Gladstone's are the views, which are incomparable. $$$

Santa Monica

FIG (310-576-7777; www.fairmont.com/santamonica), 101 Wilshire Blvd. Open daily for breakfast, lunch, and dinner. Brunch after 11 on Sun. In the **Fairmont Santa Monica Hotel,** this small restaurant is named after the 130-year-old Australian fig that envelops the entryway. Breakfast items are especially tempting, like the lemon-ricotta blueberry pancakes with almond butter, the hazelnut waffles with a banana and Nutella compote, and house-made granola with Greek yogurt and strawberries. For dinner, try the delicious ice cream FIG bars for dessert. Don't come here in a

PRICE KEY FOR A TYPICAL ENTRÉE:

$	$10 and under
$$	$11–20
$$$	$21–30
$$$$	$31 and up

hurry, however: service can be leisurely. $$–$$$

✪ **Melisse** (310-395-0881; www.melisse.com), 1104 Wilshire Blvd. Open Tues.–Sat. for dinner. The exquisite Melisse is one of the top 10 tables in Los Angeles, and locals are in love with the French-inspired cuisine and the exclusive atmosphere that its sky-high prices have engendered. For about $25 each, choose a first course of Japanese unagi, wild mushroom ravioli, or blinis with Osetra caviar (the latter is closer to $150); for another $50 or so try entrées like Dover sole, rack of lamb, and rotisserie chicken stuffed with truffles. Prices this expensive make me nervous, so for those who are equally squeamish about the mounting costs in a high-end place like this, consider the four-course tasting menu, which at $105 per person is actually a relative bargain. $$$$

🍸 **Ocean Avenue Seafood** (310-394-5669; www.oceanave.com), 1401 Ocean Ave. Open daily for dinner. For my money, this restaurant offers the best oyster bar in Los Angeles, with the largest variety of oysters anywhere in the city. Those dining in a group of three or four shouldn't miss the deluxe iced shellfish platter, with oysters, clams, shrimp, mussels, lobster, and Dungeness crab enough to share—all for $70. The tall windows overlooking the ocean and Santa Monica Pier offer a popular place from which to watch the sunset, so expect crowds on weekends. $$

Westwood

Shaherzad (310-470-9131), 1422 Westwood Blvd. Open daily for lunch and dinner. There are a surprising number of Persian restaurants in the area, and Iranian friends swear by Shaherzad, raving especially about the tantalizing flatbread served piping hot and straight from an authentic tandour oven. Don't miss the *Shirin polo,* a rice dish with orange peel, almonds, pistachios, and a hint of rose water; or the savory *Fesenjan,* a chicken stew in a pomegranate sauce and served with walnuts. $$

EATING OUT

Malibu

✪ **Reel Inn** (310-456-8221), 18661 Pacific Coast Hwy. Open daily for lunch and dinner. Want delicious, fresh fish in Malibu for a bargain? This fish shack on the Pacific Coast Hwy. across the street from the ocean might be the best option in town. The slightly divey atmosphere is lively, with wooden picnic tables inside and surfboards hanging from the rafters; there's also a large outside patio. (Don't be surprised to see Hollywood luminaries here, looking for a good meal in a casual environment.) Order from a take-out window according to what's fresh for the day. Portions are gigantic and extremely well priced. Fish tacos and calamari steaks are popular, but I personally never bypass the fried oysters and chips. $–$$

Spruzzo Restaurant and Bar (310-457-8282), 29575 Pacific Coast Hwy.

REEL INN

Open daily for lunch and dinner. Across the street from Zuma Beach, Spruzzo offers outdoor rooftop dining overlooking the ocean and buzzing PCH. Guests can create their own pizza from more than a dozen different toppings, but sometimes simplicity is the best: try the plain Napoletana, with fresh tomato sauce and mozzarella. $$

Santa Monica

Cha Cha Chicken (310-581-1684), 1906 Ocean Ave. Open daily for lunch and dinner. This inexpensive Caribbean food stand specializes in spicy, crisp-skinned chicken, which is especially tasty when folded into a French roll with cheese and toasted on a sandwich press. Pick up food at a take-away stand and enjoy on picnic tables on a side patio. $

Earth, Wind, and Flour (301-829-7829; www.earthwindandflour.com), 2222 Wilshire Blvd. Open daily for lunch and dinner. Don't let the punny name fool you: this restaurant is an Italian bistro, and the handmade deep-dish pies are outrageous, especially the Hi-Tech Vegetarian, with eggplant, garlic, and basil. Guests will find a little bit of everything on offer, including pasta, sub sandwiches, salads, and the ever-popular Chocolate Suicide Cake. $$

Father's Office (310-736-2224; www.fathersoffice.com), 1018 Montana Ave. (with a second location downtown). Open Mon.–Fri. for dinner, Sat.–Sun. for lunch and dinner. This popular hangout for Hollywood A-listers serves up possibly the best burgers in town. Check out the Office Burger, with caramelized onions sautéed in bacon fat and adorned with Gruyère and blue cheeses. Sweet potato fries are an added bonus. $$

Randy's Donuts (310-645-4707; http://randys-donuts.com/frame.html), 805 W. Manchester Ave., Inglewood. Open 24 hours a day. South of Santa Monica, near the Los Angeles International Airport, Randy's Donuts (aka "The Big Donut") has been a mainstay in the city for more than 50 years. You can't miss the place: sitting atop the small streetside stand is a three-story sculpture of a giant donut. My husband, who is a self-proclaimed expert on donuts, insists that Los Angeles has *the* best in the country, and that Randy's is the cream of the crop. Favorites include the chocolate glazed, apple fritters, honey buns, and the wonderful raspberry-jelly filled. $

Real Food Daily (310-451-7544), 514 Santa Monica Blvd. Open daily for lunch and dinner. Real Food Daily offers vegan organic meals that are healthy and flavorful. Try the portobello mushroom sandwich, and save room for the dairy-free, gluten-free chocolate pudding. $–$$

Stephano's Pizza (310-587-2429), 1310 Third St. Promenade. Open daily for lunch and dinner. Stephano's offers a variety of pasta and sub items, but the favorite menu selection is the thin-crust pizzas—barbecue chicken and

RANDY'S DONUTS

Courtesy of Jon Preimesberger

vegetarian varieties are especially good. Service is fast, and there is a small outdoor patio where guests can enjoy the free entertainment of the Third Street Promenade while munching. $

Tacos Por Favor (310-392-5768), 1406 Olympic Blvd. Open daily for breakfast, lunch, and dinner. Taco stands are legendary in Southern California, and everyone has their own favorites. This slightly divey joint gets my vote for best carnitas and carne asada tacos on the Westside, served on delicious authentic tortillas that I imagine must have been made by somebody's grandmother. $

Westwood

Diddy Reise (310-208-0448; www.diddyriese.com/home.php), 926 Broxton Ave. Open daily 10 AM–midnight. Expect long lines to purchase the exceptionally inexpensive cookies (three for a dollar) from Diddy Reise, a local favorite, especially with students from nearby UCLA. Build your own ice cream sandwich with more than a dozen kinds of freshly baked classic cookies and a variety of ice creams. $

Lamonica's NY Pizza (301-208-8671), 1066 Galey Ave. Open daily for lunch and dinner. Lamonica's has been a Westwood staple for years, largely because of its crispy thin-crust pies—the white pizza with spinach is a must. Expect crowds, especially on weekends. The restaurant serves a college crowd, and perhaps because of this, and the resulting congestion, the service can be a little iffy. $

La Pain Quotidien (310-824-7900), 1055 Brockton Ave. Open daily for lunch and dinner; brunch on Sun. This Belgian bistro and bakery is an international chain and can be found in a number of locations throughout Los Angeles. Sandwiches and omelets are stellar, but as the name implies, the bread is the main draw: look for authentic French baguettes, flaky croissants, and organic brioche. Desserts are as beautiful as they are delicious, especially the pistachio marzipan tart. Grab a table outside on warm days. $

✷ Entertainment

CLUBS **Finn McCool's** (310-452-1734; www.finnmccoolsirishpub.com), 2702 Main St., Santa Monica. Owned by a true Irishwoman, Finn McGool's is an authentic Irish pub that has been reassembled from a dismantled bar imported straight out of Northern Ireland. For some reason, this aesthetic seems right at home in laid-back Santa Monica. The highlight is an evening of live music on Sun. (starting at 4 PM), which showcases traditional Irish ballads and jigs.

Hide Out (310-429-1851; www.santamonicahideout.com), 112 W. Channel Rd., Santa Monica. A neighborhood favorite, the Hide Out is a quiet, friendly sort of bar that allows you to do just that: relax here with friends in the comfortable, laid-back atmosphere and order a few well-mixed cocktails. Some nights feature karaoke.

House of Billiards (310-828-2120), 1901 Wilshire Blvd., Santa Monica. This relaxed pool hall also offers vintage pinball machines and inexpensive pitchers. It can get crowded on weekend evenings, but the wait for a table usually isn't too long—and there is generally someone friendly at the bar to chat with while you wait.

The Room Santa Monica (310-458-0707; www.theroomsantamonica.com), 1325 Santa Monica Blvd., Santa Monica. A trendy club that exists to be cool, Room offers DJs, dancing, and a place to see and be seen. Dress to impress, and expect drinks to be on the pricey side.

Y **Rusty's Surf Ranch** (310-393-7437; www.rustyssurfranch.com), 256 Santa Monica Pier, Santa Monica. Located on the Santa Monica Pier, beachy-themed Rusty's offers an eclectic mix of live music, including bluegrass and soft and hard rock.

Y **The Veranda Bar** (310-551-5533), 1910 Ocean Way, Santa Monica. The chic, tropical Veranda Bar at the **Hotel Casa del Mar** is a favorite seaside hangout for locals, many of whom are heavy hitters in the entertainment industry. Despite the moneyed clientele, the atmosphere isn't at all stuffy. This is a great place to relax with a Sundowner cocktail and enjoy the views over the ocean.

✷ Selective Shopping

It is almost easier to talk about where *not* to shop, because the West End—especially in Santa Monica—has world-class shopping in nearly limitless supply. To hit the highlights, try the **Westside Pavilion,** 10800 W. Pico Boulevard, east of Santa Monica, a tri-level retail center with entertainment and dining; the fabulous **Third Street Promenade** in Santa Monica, a pedestrian-only thoroughfare between Broadway and Wilshire that offers street performers, shopping, and restaurants; **Bergamot Station,** 2525 Michigan Avenue, a complex adjacent to the Santa Monica Museum of Art that comprises dozens of galleries and shops; and **Montana Avenue** (from Sixth to 17th streets), an open-air retail extravaganza in Santa Monica, with more than 150 shops and restaurants.

THIRD STREET PROMENADE

DOWNTOWN LA

The urban center of the city is in the midst of an exciting revitalization, and today downtown is one of the best places in Los Angeles to experience culture in all its forms. Highlights include the Frank Gehry–designed Walk Disney Concert Hall, home to the Los Angeles Philharmonic; the Museum of Contemporary Art; and multicultural neighborhoods like Olvera Street, which celebrates the city's Hispanic heritage, as well as Little Tokyo and Chinatown. This is also the place to enjoy some of the best inexpensive ethnic cuisine on the West Coast, as well as to experience live music and theater in one of a half dozen extraordinary venues. For those planning to lodge in downtown, beware: a good chunk of downtown still tends to roll up its sidewalks in the evenings and on weekends, with a few notable exceptions outlined below, and this, combined with the expanse of the area, makes this a less-appealing area to explore on foot. Choose downtown LA for the culture and restaurants, and plan to hit other neighborhoods (like West Hollywood and Santa Monica) for nightlife, shopping, and pedestrian-friendly streets.

✱ To See

HISTORICAL SITES **Cathedral of Our Lady of the Angels** (213-680-5200; www.olacathedral.org), 555 W. Temple St., Los Angeles. Open Mon.–Fri. 6:30–6, Sat. 9–6, Sun. 7–6. Free guided tours at 1 on weekdays. Opened in 2002, this massive modern structure was designed by noted Spanish architect Jose Rafael Morena. Look for an impressive collection of tapestries inside. The cathedral offers daily Mass.

Chinatown (www.chinatownla.com), between Cesar E. Chavez Ave. and Bernard St., Yale and Spring Streets, Los Angeles. Shops selling Chinese herbs, trinkets, and specialty food line the streets, and along Chung King Rd. it's possible to find fine antiques. On weekends, come for dim sum brunch (where the servers bring a cartload bounty of dumplings, soups, and other small dishes right to your table) at **Empress Pavilion** or **Ocean Seafood.** Look for the Chinatown Farmers' Market every Thurs. 3–7.

Olvera Street (213-628-1274; www.olvera-street.com), downtown Los Angeles. This open-air marketplace is overflowing with Mexican restaurants and strolling mariachis. Look for the **El Pueblo de Los Angeles,** the city's old town, which is home to 27 historic buildings, including the Avila Adobe, LA's oldest building (from 1818).

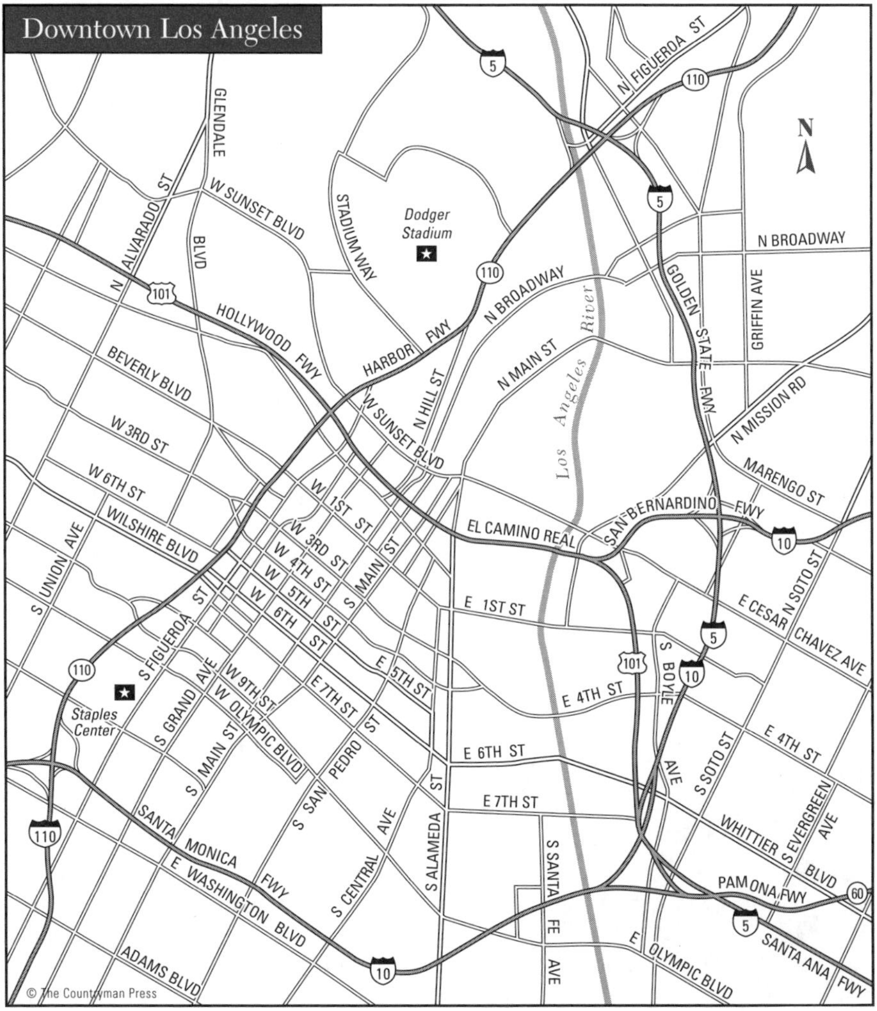

Downtown Los Angeles

MUSEUMS California African American Museum (213-744-7432; www.caa.museum.org), 600 State Dr., in Exposition Park, Los Angeles. Open Tues.–Sat. 10–5, Sun. 11–5. A 44,000-square-foot exhibition space that celebrates African American culture, art, and history, this museum includes a permanent collection of more than 3,500 art objects and more than 20,000 books. Admission $6.

✐ **California Science Center** (213-744-7400; www.casciencectr.org), 700 State Dr., in Exposition Park, Los Angeles. Open daily 10–5. Interactive exhibits and an IMAX theater focus on innovation in aeronautics and air and space engineering; a new exhibit in 2010 explores the world's ecosystems, including the environmental conditions found in Los Angeles. Admission is free.

Geffen Contemporary (213-626-6222; www.moca-la.org), 152 N. Central Ave., Los Angeles. Open Mon. and Fri. 11–5, Thurs. 11–8, Sat. and Sun. 11–6. Housed in a former police car garage in Little Tokyo, the Geffen is an offshoot of the nearby Museum of Contemporary Art (MOCA) and houses cutting-edge contemporary artwork as well as oversized pieces. Admission $8 (or free with same-day admission to MOCA).

Japanese American National Museum (213-625-0414; www.janm.org), 369 E. First St., downtown Los Angeles. Open Tues., Wed., Fri.–Sun. 11–5; Thurs. 11–8. This museum promotes appreciation of the Japanese American experience through cultural performances, artwork, and education. Exhibits include photography, film, and visual art. Don't miss the on-site **Chada Tearoom,** which offers more than three hundred varieties of tea. Admission $8.

✪ ✐ **LA Live's Grammy Museum** (213-765-6800; www.grammymuseum.org), 800 W. Olympic Blvd., in the LA Live complex, downtown Los Angeles. The 30,000-square-foot Grammy Museum at **LA Live,** a sports and entertainment complex in downtown, features exhibits on the art and technology of the recording process, as well as thematic collections, such as an exhibit of Michael Jackson's wardrobe (including an iconic single sequined glove) alongside an interactive dance floor; an audiovisual time line of music; and a collection of Neil Diamond memorabilia, including original handwritten lyrics and one of the performer's first guitars. This is the kind of museum that people who generally do not like museums will enjoy, especially if they are fans of music or pop culture. Adults $13, students and seniors $12, children $11.

WALT DISNEY CONCERT HALL

Courtesy LA Philharmonic

Museum of Contemporary Art (MOCA) (213-626-6222; www.moca-la.org), 250 S. Grand Ave., Los Angeles. Open Mon. and Fri. 11–5, Thurs. 11–8, Sat. and Sun. 11–6. MOCA offers a wide range of modern and contemporary art; the collection is often edgy and controversial, and always pushing the boundaries of traditional conceptions of art. MOCA also attracts some of the most important traveling exhibits of contemporary art. (See also the **Geffen Contemporary** location.) Admission $8.

✐ **Natural History Museum of Los Angeles County** (213-763-3466; www.nhm.org), 900 Exposition Blvd.,

INSIDER TIP: The National History Museum of Los Angeles County is free the first Tuesday of every month, and aside from the days on which this falls within traditional school holidays, this is a relatively uncrowded day to visit.

LOS ANGELES–AREA MISSIONS

The California chain of 21 coastal missions established between 1769 and 1823 was begun by Padre Junípero Serra, who was acting on behalf of Spain and the Catholic Church. The missions were placed a day's walk from each other and stretch from San Diego to Sonoma on a 650-mile route that is now known as El Camino Real. (The pathway today is marked with place markers sited along the roadway that depict a staff and mission bell.) Many of the missions have been relocated over the years, and most have been rebuilt because of fire or construction deficiencies, but each is a remarkable example of early architecture, and each is surprisingly unique. Los Angeles boasts three missions, and I highly recommend visiting at least one, not just because of their historical importance but also because they are truly beautiful structures, cared for lovingly through earthquakes, Native uprisings, and shifting political fortunes.

The **Mission San Gabriel Arcangel** (626-282-5191), 537 W. Mission Dr., San Gabriel, 9 miles east of downtown Los Angeles, is the oldest mission in the city, founded in 1771 by Father Serra as the fourth mission in the chain of 21. At one time the mission's real estate holdings covered more than 100,000 acres. Today the mission is unique for its structure: its fortresslike walls are 5 feet thick, and its windows are long and narrow, much like the design of California presidios that were built to protect the missions. On-site is a cemetery for nearly six thousand Native Gabrielino people, many of whom helped build and then staff the mission. The kitchen gardens and winery are intact, along with a small museum that exhibits Native American artwork and parchments as well as antique books.

Founded in 1782, the **Mission San Buenventura** (805-648-4496), 225 E. Main St., Ventura, about halfway between Los Angeles and Santa Barbara, is the ninth in line and the last mission to be personally founded by Father Serra. The pretty facade is triangular and opens onto gardens. An on-site museum displays two original wooden bells, believed to be the only ones of their kind in California. The mission continues to be a working church.

The **Mission San Fernando Rey de España** (818-361-0186), 15151 San Fernando Mission Blvd., Mission Hills (25 miles north of downtown in the San Fernando Valley), was founded in 1797 as the 17th in line, built after Father Serra's death. On-site is the *convento,* originally intended as a hospice for travelers, which is today the largest freestanding adobe structure in California. The statue of Saint Ferdinand that hangs above the church altar was brought from Spain three hundred years ago. Guests can also see the original flower-shaped fountain in the old mission plaza.

in Exposition Park, Los Angeles. Open Mon.–Fri. 9:30–5, Sat. and Sun. 10–5. This expansive natural-history museum is home to more than 35 million artifacts, including complete skeletons of several dinosaurs. Be sure to check out the Insect Zoo, which showcases live bugs from around the world—a real hit with the ankle-biter set. Adults $9, seniors and children $6.50.

PARKS **Exposition Park** (www.expositionpark.org), 700 Exposition Park, south of downtown Los Angeles. Founded in 1872 as an agricultural park, the 160-acre tract that is now a cultural and sports complex was reopened as Exposition Park in 1913. Today the park is one of Los Angeles's prime attractions, thanks in large part to the **Memorial Coliseum** and the Olympic Swim Stadium on-site, venues for both the 1932 and 1984 Summer Olympics held in LA. Other attractions in the park include the **California Science Center,** the **California African American Museum,** the **Los Angeles Sports Arena,** the **Exposition Park Rose Garden,** the **Natural History Museum of Los Angeles County,** and the **Science Center School and Amgen Center for Science Learning.**

MacArthur Park (www.laparks.org/dos/parks/facility/macArthurPk.htm), 2230 W. Sixth St., Westlake. West of downtown, MacArthur Park (formerly called Westlake Park) was a showpiece for Los Angeles urban living for many years. Sadly, by the end of the 20th century, the neighborhood took a turn for the worse, and crime was a major problem. Today, the community has embraced the scenic park again, and this pretty green oasis in the city has been cleaned up significantly. However, to be honest, this isn't someplace I would consider visiting at night—or by myself.

MACARTHUR PARK

Courtesy of Jon Preimesberger

DODGER STADIUM

Home to the LA Dodgers since 1962, the storied Dodger Stadium (855-DODGERS; http://losangeles.dodgers.mlb.com; 1000 Elysian Park Ave., Los Angeles) has seen eight National League pennants and four world championships. It has also hosted live performances by Michael Jackson, the Beatles, and Luciano Pavarotti. Pope John Paul II even celebrated Mass here. Dodger Stadium offers great views of the downtown skyline and, according to several of my in-laws, who are native Angelenos, the best ballpark hot dogs in the country. Fans can tour the ballpark to get an insider's view of restricted areas in a 90-minute tour that can include a trip to the field, a visit to the Dodger Dugout, and a stroll through the Vin Scully Press Box. Tours for adults $15, children $10, military personnel free.

The park today includes an amphitheater, playing fields, tot lot, and a beautiful small lake. The park is also home to Levitt Pavilion, a restored 1930s band shell that these days serves as the venue for 50 free concerts every summer. This is one of the best locations to get a truly fine glimpse at the downtown skyline.

✱ To Do

GOLF Real estate is precious in downtown LA, and serious local duffers generally head to Beverly Hills or Pacific Palisades, but there are a few options for those looking to get in a quick 18 holes without venturing too far afield.

The Links at Victoria Golf Club (310-323-6981, www.linksatvictoria.com), 340 E. 192nd St., Carson. About 10 miles from downtown, this simple but pleasant municipal course measures 6,800 yards and offers inexpensive play. Green fee: $20–25.

Rancho Park Golf Course (310-839-4374; www.lagolfclubs.com/clubs/NewHome.cfm/ClubID/29/Section/Home), 10460 W. Pico Blvd., Los Angeles. An extremely popular municipal course near downtown, Rancho Park is another true value—although getting a tee time can be challenging. Green fee: $17–25.

✱ Green Space

GARDENS **Exposition Park Rose Garden,** 701 State Dr., near downtown Los Angeles. Open daily 9–sunset. Near the University of Southern California in **Exposition Park,** the 7-acre Rose Garden has more than 20,000 bushes in nearly 200 varieties, arranged in a grass-enclosed oval around a central fountain (which makes a stunning background for family photographs). Peak blooming periods are early spring through summer. Note: The garden is closed Jan. 1–Mar. 15 for annual maintenance.

SIX FLAGS MAGIC MOUNTAIN

In Valencia, about an hour northwest of downtown Los Angeles, the Six Flags Magic Mountain park (661-255-4103; www.sixflags.com/magicmountain; 26101 Magic Mountain Parkway, Valencia) offers more scream than theme: this is the place to come if you're looking for adrenaline-pumping thrill rides, and it is a longtime favorite with teenagers and young adults throughout Southern California. The 260-acre park offers more than 100 attractions and includes some of the most exciting, hair-raising rides in the country. The Riddler is one of the few roller coasters in the world in which riders actually stand. The ride hurtles through six loops and over 1 mile of twisting inverted steel track at 65 miles per hour. Déjà Vu is a ski-lift-style roller coaster that allows guests to dangle their feet as the ride plunges from a 20-story tower, dangles guests facedown climbing a 90-degree tower, rockets them head over heels through a vertical loop—and then reverses and does the whole circuit again backward. Another thrilling coaster favorite, Tatsu barrels along more than 3500 feet of track at 62 miles per hour, treating riders to deep plunges and massive spirals. For astonishing speed, the Goliath is a massive 4,500-foot steel roller coaster that tops out at 85 miles per hour and features a 60 degree first drop and a half dozen zero-gravity floats. Because these rides aren't for the faint of heart (or for kiddos too short to ride safely), the park allows parents visting with youngsters to wait in line once and then swap out, so Mom and Dad can both ride. The park does offer a handful of gentler rides for young children—like the Merrie Melodies Carousel, the Thomas the Tank engine train ride, and the Sylvester's Pounce and Bounce, a tame drop ride—but Magic Mountain is really all about older kids (and the young at heart) who have a need for speed. Beyond the rides, the park offers a summer concert series, parade, children's karaoke, dance contests, and Looney Tunes characters that roam the thoroughfares. Congestion is less problematic at Magic Mountain than it is at other top parks in the area, but waits for the most popular rides can still back up by as much as an hour. To combat the traffic, the park offers Flash Passes that entitle the bearers to priority seating and front-of-the-line passes. The Flash Passes are sold for premium rates (on top of the cost of admission) at three levels: $41 will buy faster access to the most popular rides in the park, $69 offers the same faster access to even more rides, and $89 will buy a fast-access stand-in-line-once ride-twice privilege. Open daily; hours vary by season. Adults $60, children under 48 inches $34. (Significant discounts are often available for guests purchasing advance tickets online.)

✷ Lodging

PRICE KEY FOR A STANDARD ROOM:	
$	$100 or less
$$	$101–150
$$$	$151–250
$$$$	$251 and up

Downtown LA

Hilton Checkers Los Angeles (213-624-0000; www.hiltoncheckers.com), 535 S. Grand Ave. This historic four-diamond hotel in the downtown financial district dates to the 1920s. The soothing décor and spacious rooms are largely meant for business travelers (the hotel has especially comfortable and elegant meeting and conference rooms), but the tiny rooftop pool and even tinier Jacuzzi is romantic and especially fun for children, who will enjoy swimming under the bright lights of this big city. The hotel is within easy reach of the **Disney Concert Hall** and most of the other major venues in the theater district. The on-site restaurant **Checkers** offers an especially good breakfast: check out the Hawaiian French toast with caramelized pineapple and cinnamon butter. $$$

HILTON CHECKERS

⚤ **Kyoto Grand Hotel and Gardens** (213-629-1200; www.kyotograndhotel.com), 120 S. Los Angeles St. In the heart of Little Tokyo, this Asian-inspired 21-story mid-rise in the city offers something I've never seen before in a big-city hotel: a lush 0.5-acre rooftop Zen garden (on a third-floor terrace), complete with a small bamboo forest, flowering azaleas, bonsai, waterfalls, and tranquil ponds—which makes for a delightful oasis from the tumult and noise of the city. (Indeed, this is a favorite wedding spot for locals.) $$$

⚤ **Millennium Biltmore Hotel** (866-866-8086; www.millenniumhotels.com), 506 S. Grand Ave. Whereas many hotels in Los Angeles aim to sooth weary travelers with a minimalist vibe or a chic beach aesthetic, the venerable Millennium Biltmore is all about opulence and glamour. There is nothing subtle about the regal Biltmore: it screams privilege from the moment patrons walk into the soaring, gilded lobby. Guest rooms are only slightly less extravagant, although they manage to be welcoming and comfortable despite the pomp. Amenities include an indoor Roman-style pool, an extensive business center, and five massive ballrooms. On-site dining offers sushi and sashimi at **Sai Sai Restaurant** and Italian specialties at **La Bisteca.** $$$$

✪ Ÿ **The Standard** (213-892-8080; www.standardhotel.com), 550 S. Flower St. The chic, offbeat Standard is anything but. Clean-line décor and monochromatic color combine with whimsical contemporary art and furnishings. The sexy hotel seems to attract young, beautiful people in droves, likely because this is one hotel in downtown that seems to be more about fun and less about business. Especially popular is the **Lobby Lounge,** which features a 125-foot fuchsia sofa, a billiards table, and a kitschy photo-strip booth. On-site dining at the sunny **24/7 Restaurant** (literally named, because the kitchen never closes) offers California-inspired cuisine served amid lemon yellow booths and surrounded by bright yellow flooring, bright yellow ceilings, and a padded bright yellow bar counter. The rooftop pool is a geometric aqua jewel amid the high-rises. $$$–$$$$

Westin Bonaventure (213-624-1000; www.thebonaventure.com), 404 S. Figueroa St. This 35-story structure comprising several cylindrical glass towers is an architectural icon in downtown Los Angeles, offering surprisingly affordable accommodations that are close to the financial district and the downtown theaters. The huge property offers 1,400-plus guest rooms and suites, which are spacious and recently refurbished, and top floors offer stellar views of the city (and on those rare smog-free LA days, vistas all the way to the ocean). The 34th floor boasts a revolving cocktail lounge **(BonaVista Lounge)**, and the 35th floor offers **LA Prime,** a steak and lobster restaurant with killer views. Guests looking for a quick bite will find a food court downstairs, complete with an on-site Starbucks. The large outdoor deck and rooftop pool have commanding views of the neighboring high-rises. $$–$$$

PRICE KEY FOR A TYPICAL ENTRÉE:

$	$10 and under
$$	$11–20
$$$	$21–30
$$$$	$31 and up

✷ Where to Eat

DINING OUT

Downtown LA

Chaya (213-236-9577; www.thechaya.com), 525 S. Flower St. Open Mon.–Fri. for lunch and dinner, Sat. for dinner only. Chaya (with additional locations in Venice and Beverly Hills) is an oasis of calm in the middle of cacophonous downtown. The urbane

CHAYA

Courtesy of Chaya

ambiance is ideal for either a romantic dinner or a business lunch. In addition to a lovely dining room, the restaurant offers a full bar, lounge, quiet garden patio, and a sushi bar. The menu reflects a Continental influence on traditional Japanese cuisine, with multicultural delights like squid ink fettuccine with jumbo prawns and calamari, and miso-marinated white sea bass. Sushi lovers will not want to miss the Dragon Roll, spicy tuna, cucumber, and eel served with eel sauce. Happy hour deals are a steal: steamed edamame can be had for $3, spicy tuna rolls go for $4, and crab and scallop rolls for $6. $$$

Church and State Bistro (213-405-1434; www.churchandstatebistro.com), 1850 E. Industrial St. Open Mon.–Fri. for lunch and dinner, Sat. and Sun. for dinner only. Built into the loading dock of the original Nabisco Biscuit Company Building, which dates to 1925, this authentic French bistro delivers hearty, rich food worthy of a Parisian brasserie. Menu offerings include staples like garlicky escargots, French onion soup, cheese and mushroom tarts, gooey croque monsieurs (luscious grilled ham and cheese sandwiches), and unbelievable French fries fried in—yes!—lard. The tiny tables are jam packed—much like you would find in Paris or Lyon; service is helpful and friendly; and the inventive cocktails are handcrafted. Don't miss the fig tarts for dessert. $$

✪ 🍸 **Ciudad** (213-486-5171; www.ciudad-la.com), 445 S. Figueroa St. Open Mon.–Fri. for lunch and dinner, Sat.–Sun. for dinner. Owned by celebrity chefs Mary Sue Milliken and Susan Feniger (better known as the Food Network's "Too Hot Tamales"), this downtown restaurant combines Mexican cuisine with influences from Honduras, Argentina, Cuba, Spain, and Brazil. Sun. nights feature an extensive tapas menu and specials on Spanish wine by the glass. If you overindulge (and the unusual cocktails at Ciudad make this tempting), the restaurant offers a free shuttle to and from the Staples Center, Nokia Theater, the Dorothy Chandler Pavilion, the Mark Taper Forum, the Ahmanson Theater, and the Disney Concert Hall. In other words, this is a fantastic place to dine before a night out, because patrons only have to drive and park once, and then enjoy a cocktail, knowing there is no need to drive. $$$

✪ 🍸 **J Restaurant and Lounge** (213-746-7746; www.jloungela.com), 1119 Olive St. Open Mon.–Fri. for lunch; Mon.–Sat. for lunch and dinner. This wining, dining, and entertainment complex is *the* trendy choice for the young and beautiful crowd of LA today, and the eclectic ambiance and multiple venues promise it will continue to be a favorite for years. The industrial-loft space offers two floors, three lounges—one featuring a 30-foot granite bar—an open-air cigar lounge, and a huge patio with views of the downtown skyline. Expect live entertainment and DJs nightly. Menu options are sumptuous and rich, like the Madeira-braised veal cheeks with sautéed mushrooms and the organic grilled rib eye with horseradish gremolata. $$$

🍸 **Patina** (213-972-3331; www.patinagroup.com), 141 S. Grand Ave. Open Tues.–Sun. for dinner; closed Sun. in the summer. In the magnificent **Walt Disney Concert Hall,** this elegant restaurant offers an upscale option for theatergoers. (In addition to the Walt Disney Concert Hall, the Dorothy Chandler Pavilion, the Mark Taper Forum, and the Ahmanson are all right down the street.) Loire Valley–born chef Tony Esnault learned classic

French technique at the François Rabelais Culinary School, and his eclectic menu offers Continental treats like nettle velouté, butter-poached lobster, and squab with English peas. Patina offers seasonal tasting menus (one for vegetarians and one for carnivores), a wide selection of cheese, an impressive wine list, and a late-night cocktail bar. $$$–$$$$

Watergrill (213-891-0900; www.watergrill.com), 544 S. Grand. Open Mon.–Fri. for lunch and dinner, Sat.–Sun. for dinner. In the financial district of downtown LA, the Watergrill could very well be on the harbor, so impeccably fresh is the seafood here. Chef David LeFevre responds to the catch of the day by constantly changing the menu, which might include Alaskan halibut sautéed with lavender, Chilean sea bass braised with red chile marmalade, or seared big eye tuna. The raw bar is extensive and sells oysters by the half dozen, dozen, or individually—a nice way to try a wide variety of shellfish. Whatever is on offer for the day, finish off the meal with the decadent blueberry mascarpone cake. The colorful art deco interior is warm and friendly, and so are the servers. $$$

✪ **Wood Spoon** (213-629-1765), 107 W. Ninth St. Open Mon.–Sat. for lunch, Tues.–Sat. for dinner, brunch on Sun. This homey restaurant has Brazilian overtones, with specialties like salt cod croquettes, Portuguese sausage, and yucca fries, but it is famous for its chicken potpies, which are meaty and juicy, with a tender crust and interesting additions like olives and hearts of palm. Desserts are comforting yet eclectic, like Brazilian flan and passion fruit mousse. Believe it or not, some of the most interesting items on the menu are the house waters: they are flavored with cinnamon or mint or a handful of other herbs and fruits—very refreshing. $$

EATING OUT

Downtown LA

✪ ✐ **Nickel Diner** (213-623-8301; www.5cdiner.com), 524 S. Main St. Open Tues.–Sun. for breakfast and lunch, and Mon.–Sat. for dinner. Just thinking about the fun and inventive food at this restaurant makes my mouth water: imagine catfish with corn cakes and pecan sauce, homemade Pop Tarts and Ding Dongs, chocolate cake with peanut butter and potato-chip crust, and—the pièce de résistance—maple bacon donuts. Oh my! (Note: The neighborhood is a little iffy.) $

Pann's (323-776-3770; www.panns.com), 6710 La Tijera Blvd. Open daily for breakfast, lunch, and dinner. This classic '50s family diner has been serving the community since 1958. Breakfasts are legendary, likely because of the truly homemade-tasting biscuits that accompany belly busters like steak and eggs, Greek omelets (with spinach and feta), and fried chicken wings and waffles. $

Phillippe the Original (213-628-3781), 1001 N. Alameda St. Open daily for breakfast, lunch, and dinner. In business since 1908 (this is the oldest restaurant in Los Angeles), Phillippe's claim to fame is the French dip sandwich, reportedly invented here by mistake when the French-born owner accidentally dropped a roll in cooking juices as he prepared a beef sandwich. His obliging customer agreed to eat the sandwich as is—and the rest is history. You can order the famous sandwiches single-dipped or double-dipped, but you will not be served au jus on the side: the restaurant has only so much cooking juice to accompany its meaty sandwiches, and there is no extra to go around. The furnishings are nostalgic, and so is the price of a cup of coffee: still a dime. $

Sarita's Pupuseria (213-626-6320), 3175 Broadway. Open daily 9–6. In the Grand Central Market downtown, this Salvadoran food stand offers up *pupusas* in great variety—and for very little cash. For the uninitiated, *pupusas* are savory pies made from thick corn dough and stuffed with meat and cheese, generally served with cabbage. Sarita's is extremely popular, so the waits can be long, but for something this good and this cheap, it is well worth the wait. $

✷ Entertainment

CLUBS **The Edison** (213-613-0000; www.edisondowntown.com), 108 W. Second St., Suite 101, Los Angeles. Featuring handcrafted cocktails, live music, a small menu of bar food, a house DJ, and billiards, the Edison has something for everyone—including a virtual history museum of historic Los Angeles artifacts.

Library Bar (213-614-0053; www.librarybarla.com), 630 W. Sixth St., Suite 116-A, Los Angeles. Forget about drinking overpriced coffee in a bookstore; come to the Library Bar to be surrounded by books and drink Belgian beers or dirty martinis. This swanky cocktail lounge in the financial district is known for its wide-ranging brew and wine selection.

The Varnish (213-622-9999), 118 E. Sixth St., Los Angeles. This speakeasy looks to be straight out of central casting in Hollywood, so nostalgic and mysterious is the vibe. In truth, Varnish is a tiny downtown bar dedicated to the art of the cocktail. The bar has no stools—just padded edges, to make it easy on the elbows—and wood banquettes that resemble streetcars (an homage to Varnish's historic building's past as a Pacific Electric trolley terminal). This is a fine place to have a masterful cocktail and a quiet conversation.

AHMANSON THEATRE AND MARK TAPER FORUM

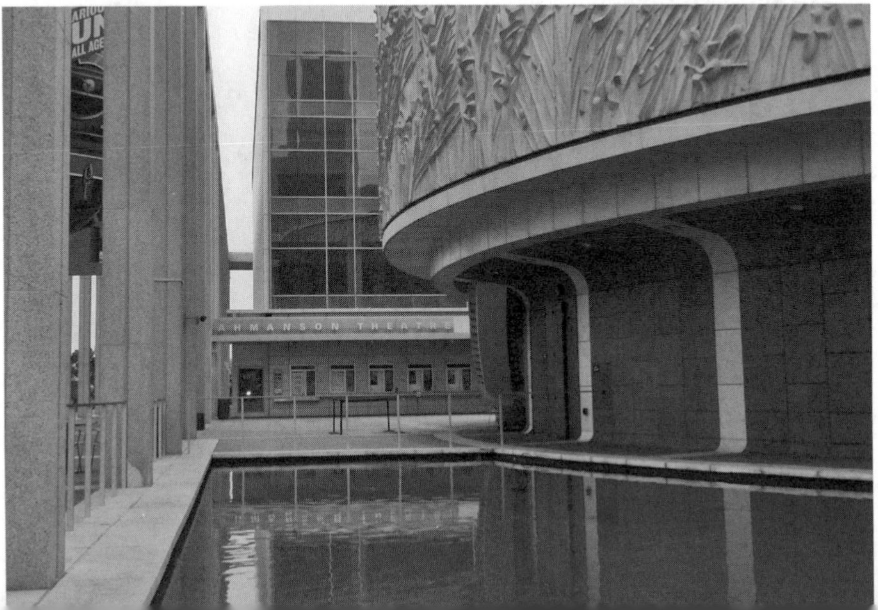

THEATERS **Ahmanson Theatre** (213-628-2772; www.centertheatregroup.org), 135 N. Grand Ave., Los Angeles. Home to live theater, the Ahmanson has staged *Dreamgirls, Mary Poppins,* and *The Color Purple* in recent years. The elegant Ahmanson is part of a large complex of theatrical venues located side by side, including the **Mark Taper Forum,** the **Dorothy Chandler Pavilion,** and the **Walt Disney Concert Hall,** collectively known as the "Music Center."

Dorothy Chandler Pavilion (213-972-0711; www.musiccenter.org), 135 N. Grand Ave., Los Angeles. Home of the LA Opera, directed by Placido Domingo, the Dorothy Chandler Pavilion also hosts touring dance and music companies like the Kirov Ballet, Alvin Ailey American Dance Theater, and the American Ballet Theatre.

✪ **LA Live Sports and Entertainment District** (213-763-LIVE), 800 W. Olympic Blvd., Los Angeles. This expansive sports, dining, and entertainment complex is the site of major concerts and sporting events, and draws big crowds. The complex is home to the **Nokia Theatre, Staples Center, LA Live Grammy Museum, ESPN Zone, Club Nokia, Lucky Strikes Lanes** (an upscale bowling alley), and the **Conga Room,** as well as dozens of restaurants, movie theaters, and shops. There is even on-site lodging at the **Ritz-Carlton.**

INSIDER TIP: Purchase half-price tickets for live performances throughout the city up to a week in advance from the LA Stage Alliance (www.lastagealliance.com). Tickets are released for the week on Tuesday and may be purchased online by credit card and then picked up the day of the performance at the Will Call window.

DOROTHY CHANDLER PAVILION

Courtesy of AEG

LA LIVE/STAPLES CENTER

Mark Taper Forum (213-628-2772; www.centertheatregroup.org), 135 Grand Ave., Los Angeles. A small live-theater venue in the heart of the theater district of downtown, the Taper has staged *Harps and Angels, Children of a Lesser God,* and *The Glass Menagerie* in recent years.

Staples Center (213-742-7100; www.staplescenter.com), 1111 S. Figueroa, Los Angeles. Part of the massive **LA Live** complex, the Staples Center is home to the LA Lakers and a handful of other professional sports teams, and also hosts major concerts for the likes of Madonna, Justin Timberlake, and John Mayer.

LOS ANGELES BALLET

There is no shortage of jokes about the lack of cultural opportunities in Southern California—many of which are perpetuated by folks from the northern half of the state, who are understandably proud of the heritage of San Francisco. But don't believe these stereotypes about SoCal: Los Angeles is most definitely *not* a cultural wasteland, and as proof, check out the new Los Angeles Ballet (301-477-7411; www.losangelesballet.org), which boasts a large corps of talented dancers from around the country. The relatively new company performs classical ballet at a handful of venues around town, in an effort to reach out to communities throughout the region. Recent offerings have included *The Nutcracker, La Sylphide,* and *Ballachine's See the Music, Hear the Dance.* Deeply discounted tickets for students are available for some performances.

TOP 10 DAY IN DOWNTOWN LOS ANGELES

1. Relish homemade Pop Tarts from Nickel Diner (see p. 198)
2. Tour the Cathedral of Our Lady of the Angels (see p. 188)
3. Head to LA Live's Grammy Museum (see p. 190)
4. Lunch on chicken potpie and cinnamon water at Wood Spoon (see p. 198)
5. Window-shop on Olvera Street (see p. 188)
6. Stroll through the Rose Garden in Exposition Park (see p. 193)
7. Dine on chorizo-crusted diver scallops at Ciudad (see p. 197)
8. Marvel at the LA downtown skyline at night
9. Savor a Belgian cherry beer at the Library Bar (see p. 199)
10. Overnight at The Standard (see p. 196)

✪ **Walt Disney Concert Hall** (213-972-4399; www.musiccenter.org), 135 N. Grand Ave., Los Angeles. Free tours Tues.–Fri. 10–1:30, Sat. 10–noon. The curvy steel exterior of the Walt Disney Concert Hall was designed by Frank Gehry, and since opening in 2003 it has become both an architectural landmark of downtown and a premier performing arts center, which is the permanent home to the Los Angeles Philharmonic. On-site is the acclaimed **Patina.**

✸ Selective Shopping

Fashionistas flock to the downtown **Fashion District** (213-488-1153; www.fashiondistrict.org), between Main and San Pedro streets and Seventh and Olympic Boulevard. There are more than a thousand stores here that sell at up to 70 percent discounts on clothing, accessories, and fabrics. The **Grand Central Market** (317 S. Broadway, Los Angeles) is the largest open-air food market in Los Angeles and has been a local favorite since 1917. It is great fun to wander the aisles to see beautiful produce, ethnic food stands, and the parade of humanity that enjoys the market. Look for Japanese bento boxes, Mexican street-style tacos, El Salvadoran pastries, chop suey stands, and juice bars.

BEVERLY HILLS, HOLLYWOOD, AND WEST HOLLYWOOD

Boasting perhaps the most famous zip code in the country (90210), Beverly Hills is synonymous with opulence, offering some of the finest (and most expensive) shopping, dining, and lodging in the world. The most exclusive part of the city is known as the Golden Triangle, which is bordered by Wilshire and Santa Monica boulevards and Rexford Drive. You'll find the bulk of restaurants along La Cienega Boulevard nearby, on Restaurant Row. Nearby are the über-expensive residential areas of Beverly Hills and adjacent Holmby Hills and Bel-Air, which offer tony zip codes in their own right.

Just to the east is Hollywood, long synonymous with the entertainment industry. This famous area is home to the immense Hollywood and Highland Center, a shopping and dining complex that houses the Kodak Theatre (venue for the Academy Awards). Not surprisingly, this neighborhood offers some the best movie-watching opportunities in the city, including the ArcLight Cinema and the glitzy El Capitan Theatre. Emblematic tourist attractions include Grauman's Chinese Theatre and the Hollywood Walk of Fame. The Hollywood streets are a little seedier than out-of-towners might expect, and frankly some areas of town are unsavory (and unsafe at night), but the area is a must-see destination—even if it is seen from the confines of a double-decker tour bus.

Despite the name, the 2-square-mile neighborhood of West Hollywood shouldn't be confused with Hollywood; in fact, the area is closer to an offshoot of Beverly Hills, thanks to eclectic shopping on W. Third Street and Beverly Boulevard and at The Grove retail shopping and entertainment complex. This is one of the best places in the city for upscale dining and is home to some of the hottest clubs in the city, including the legendary Roxy and Whisky a Go-Go on the famous Sunset Strip. A third of the residents are gay or lesbian, and 12 percent are recent immigrants from the former Soviet Union. This is the place to see and be seen, and is a favorite with young Hollywood. Without having statistics to back up my claims, I'm willing to bet that this neighborhood has the highest ratio of billboards to buildings as any in the country—and plenty of neon to light up the nighttime streets as well.

✱ To See

HISTORICAL SITES Capitol Records Tower, 1750 N. Vine St., Hollywood. This iconic structure looks like nothing so much as a stack of LPs (kids, ask your

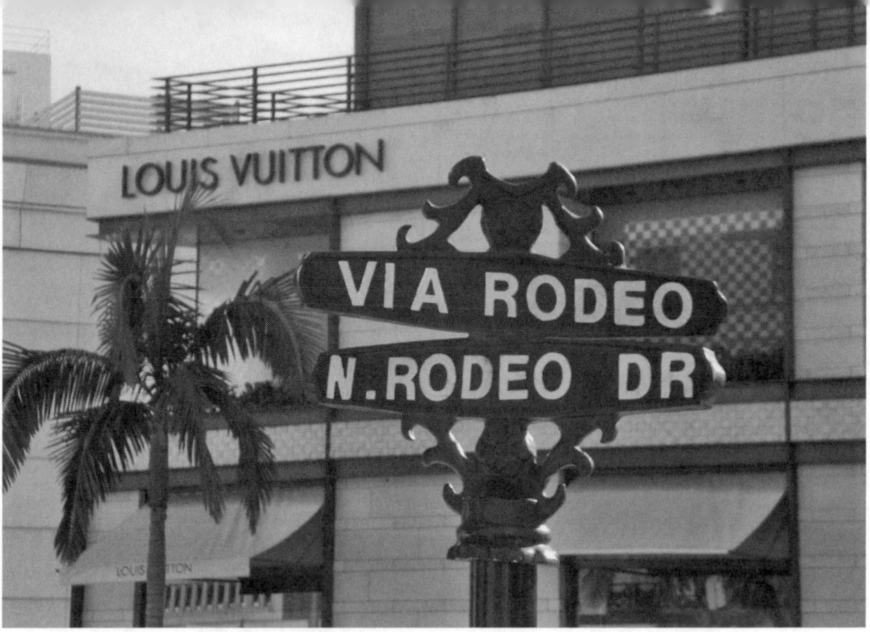

RODEO DRIVE IN BEVERLY HILLS

parents what this means). The building is still home to a working studio (which in its heyday hosted the Beatles, Frank Sinatra, and Billie Holiday). Today the property is closed to tours, but it makes for a great photo op. At night, a blinking light at the top of the high-rise spells out *Hollywood* in Morse code.

✪ ✐ **Grauman's Chinese Theatre** (323-461-3331; www.manntheaters.com), 6925 Hollywood Blvd., Hollywood. Since 1927, celebrities have been leaving their hand- and footprints in the concrete on the patio in front of this theater (which is now a multiplex), and doting fans have flocked here to see them. Today luminaries like Cary Grant, George Clooney, and the young cast of *Harry Potter* have left their mark—1940s bombshell Betty Grable even left an imprint of her calf. Look for the costumed characters (like Marilyn Monroe and Elvis impersonators) who hang out nearby and will pose for photos—for a price.

GRAUMAN'S CHINESE THEATRE

⚥ **Greystone Estate** (310-285-6830), 905 Loma Vista Dr., Beverly Hills. Open daily 10–5. This mansion, built in 1927 (and at the time comprising 415 acres), is the single largest family estate in Beverly Hills history. In the late 1970s, the mansion and grounds became a public park. The formal gardens are particularly lovely, highlighting an original fountain. It has also been the backdrop of dozens of Hollywood films, including *National*

Treasure 2, X-Men, and *Indecent Proposal.* Visitors can enjoy a self-guided tour through the formal gardens and estate.

✪ **Hollywood Sign** (www.hollywoodsign.org). The Hollywood Sign is best viewed from afar via the courtyard of the Hollywood and Highland retail complex. The sign itself is secured with a high fence and security surveillance, which makes it hard to get up close. The iconic sign originally read HOLLYWOODLAND, to advertise a nearby development. Fifty-foot white metal letters replaced the much-vandalized wooden originals in the 1970s. It is currently under threat, as developers are hoping to build on the hill where the sign resides—although this seems unlikely, given how much affection the sign enjoys worldwide.

Hollywood Walk of Fame (www.hollywoodchamber.net). On Hollywood Blvd., between La Brea Ave. and Gower St. and on Vine St. between Yucca and Sunset Blvd., the sidewalks are emblazoned with stars commemorating old Hollywood, like Bob Hope and Bing Crosby, as well as more recent luminaries like Cameron Diaz and Glenn Close.

🍸 ▼ **Sunset Strip,** the nearly 2 miles of Sunset Blvd. between Doheny Dr. in the west and Crescent Heights Blvd. in the east. Look for music venues that are legend, including **Whisky a Go-Go, The Viper Room,** and **The Roxy** (310-276-2222; www.theroxyonsunset.com). The area offers a bewildering display of billboards and hellish traffic on weekend nights.

MUSEUMS **Academy of Motion Picture Arts and Sciences** (310-247-3600; www.oscars.org), 8949 Wilshire Blvd., Beverly Hills. Hours vary based on exhibits. This is the headquarters for the group that nominates and chooses the Oscar winners, and visitors will find galleries and theaters that host film-related exhibitions and lectures on acting, screenwriting, and cinematography.

Hammer Museum (310-443-7000; www.hammer.ucla.edu), 10899 Wilshire Blvd., Westwood. Open Tues.–Sun. 11–7. Known for its impressive collection of

HOLLYWOOD SIGN

impressionist and postimpressionist paintings, the Hammer Museum is also home to the new Billy Wilder Theater, which is the venue for the UCLA Film and Television Archive screenings. Adults $7, seniors $5, students free.

✪ **Hollywood Museum** (323-464-7776; www.thehollywoodmuseum.com), 1660 N. Highland Ave., Hollywood. Open Wed.–Sun. 10–5. With more than five thousand artifacts from films, including costumes, movie posters, and props, the Hollywood Museum is a must-see for silver-screen buffs. Look for Rocky's boxing gloves and Marilyn Monroe's honeymoon dress. Visitors can also see the famous Max Factor makeup room where Lucille Ball became a redhead. Adults $15, seniors $12, children under 12 free.

> **INSIDER TIP:** To get an insider's view of Hollywood, and to save a little money to boot, purchase a Hollywood CityPass (www.citypass.com) for about $50, which includes admission to the Hollywood Wax Museum, a two-hour Starline Movie Stars' Homes Tour, a Hollywood Behind-the-Scenes Tour with Red Line Tours, and a choice between a guided tour of the Kodak Theatre or the Max Factor Building.

✐ **Hollywood Wax Museum** (323-462-5991; www.hollywoodwax.com), 6767 Hollywood Blvd., Hollywood. Open daily 10 AM–midnight. Although Madame Tussauds is a newcomer to the area, the Hollywood Wax Museum has offered lifelike re-creations of entertainment-industry stars since 1962. Look for Marilyn Monroe, Julia Roberts, and Angelina Jolie—and look out for "sculptures" who will jump out at unsuspecting visitors to give them a fright. Adults $15.95, children $8.95.

✐ **La Brea Tar Pits** (www.tarpits.org), Hancock Park, on the Miracle Mile, across from the Los Angeles County Museum of Art. Open daily. Tar has been bubbling up in the springs in La Brea for millennia, and in prehistoric times, animals like

LA BREA TAR PITS

woolly mammoths and saber-toothed tigers got stuck in the muck. Today archaeologists painstakingly pick through the black goo and over the years have amassed a huge collection of prehistoric skeletons, many of which are displayed at the nearby **Page Museum.** Although in decades past, the neighborhood has been less than appealing, these days the adjacent Hancock Park on the Miracle Mile is clean, attractive, and safe (in daylight hours, anyhow). Admission is free.

Los Angeles County Museum of Art (LACMA) (323-857-6000; www.lacma.org), 5905 Wilshire Blvd., on the Miracle Mile. Open Mon., Tues., and Thurs. noon–8; Fri. noon–9; Sat. and Sun. 11–8. This stunning complex is the largest art museum in the western United States, housing more than 100,000 pieces, including an extensive collection of art from the Americas, as well as a substantial collection of Korean and Japanese artwork. The compound of galleries includes the Ahmanson Building, the Art of the Americas Building, the new Broad Contemporary Art Museum, and the even newer Resnick Exhibition Pavilion. Also on-site is the Bing Theater, which screens foreign and indie films. Admission $12.

Madame Tussauds Hollywood (323-798-1670; www.madametussauds.com), 6933 Hollywood Blvd., Hollywood. Open daily 10–6 (except for the Sun. of the Academy Awards). Madame Tussauds, next to **Grauman's Chinese Theatre,** is the place to get close to more than one hundred top celebrities, like Beyoncé, Nicole Kidman, and Johnny Depp. Guests can pose for photographs with the wax creations. Adults $25, children $18.

Museum of Tolerance (310-553-8403; www.museumoftolerance.com), 9786 W. Pico Blvd., south of Beverly Hills. Open Sun.–Thurs. 11–4, Fri. 11–3. This newly remodeled space houses powerful exhibits on the Holocaust, as well as on human rights, immigration, and family violence. Admission $13.

The Paley Center for Media (310-786-1000; www.paleycenter.org), 465 N. Beverly Dr., Beverly Hills. Open Wed.–Sun. noon–5. Formerly known as the Museum of Television and Radio, this interactive museum allows guests to choose from among thousands of television programs, radio shows, and vintage commercials to view. The center also hosts lectures and symposia. By donation.

✐ **Ripley's Believe It or Not! Odditorium** (323-466-6335; www.ripleys.com), 6780 Hollywood Blvd., Hollywood. Open daily; hours vary. More than three hundred exhibits greet visitors to this museum dedicated to the bizarre. Adults $15, children $9.

PARKS ✐ **Griffith Park** (323-644-6661), from the 134 freeway at Victory Blvd. or off Los Feliz Blvd. at Western Canyon Ave. Open daily 5 AM–10 PM. The country's largest municipal park, at more than 4,200 acres, Griffith Park offers picnic areas, playgrounds, and natural areas that are ideal for hiking. The park is home to the **Griffith Observatory,** the **Los Angeles Zoo and Botanical Gardens,** the Greek Theatre, the Travel Town railroad museum, and the Autry National Center's Museum of the American West. There is also a merry-go-round on-site, along with pony rides.

✷ To Do

GOLF Bel-Air Country Club (310-440-2423; www.bel-aircc.org), 10768 Bellagio Rd., Bel-Air. This is one of the finest courses in the country and unbelievably

STARGAZING AT GRIFFITH PARK OBSERVATORY
Overlooking all of Los Angeles, the Griffith Observatory is perhaps most famous for its appearance in *Rebel without a Cause,* starring Hollywood bad boy James Dean. Located within Griffith Park (at 2800 E. Observatory Road), the observatory is actually one of the finest planetariums in the world. The star projector at the Samuel Oschi Planetarium can re-create a 360-degree view of the night sky at any time in history. Also on-site is the Richard and Lois Gunther Depths of Space exhibit. Open Tuesday–Friday noon–10, Saturday and Sunday 10–10. Admission is free. For more information call 213-473-0800 or log on to www.griffithsorb.org.

exclusive. Forget Spago and The Ivy: if you want to see Hollywood elite, this is the place. This is one of many private clubs in the city, which means you'll only get an invite if you can make friends with a member. Although it is a long shot, if you are set on trying this course, it is worth checking with your hotel concierge about guest passes.

Griffith Park Golf Course (323-664-2255; www.griffithparkgolfshop.com), 4730 Crystal Springs Dr., Los Angeles. The oldest and one of the best municipal courses in the city, Griffith Park Golf Course offers two 18-hole courses at an astonishing bargain. Green fee: $10–25.

SPAS **Beverly Hills Hotel Spa by La Prairie** (310-887-2505; www.beverlyhillshotel.com), 9641 Sunset Blvd., Beverly Hills. This tiny spa in the ultraexclusive **Beverly Hills Hotel** offers customized service and delightfully decadent, upscale products. I cannot imagine a place that smells better than this one. Check out the Caviar Firming Facial for true indulgence.

Bliss Hollywood (877-862-5477; www.blissworld.com), 6250 Hollywood Blvd., Hollywood. At the **W Hollywood** hotel, this Bliss outlet allows patrons to watch movies while they get manicured, complete with personal plasma TVs, headphones, and a DVD library. Look for the Hangover Herbie, a gentle massage, body wrap of invigorating essential oils, a revitalizing face mask, a 15-minute foot massage, and an oxygen spray—all designed to undo any damage done the night before.

Le Petite Retreat (323-466-1028; www.lprdayspa.com), 331 N. Larchmont Blvd., near Hollywood. This popular day spa is well known for its hydrotherapy baths in gigantic copper tubs big enough for two. The Peppermint Ginger Plunge includes a 30-minute soak in warm water infused with eucalyptus oil, peppermint, and ginger; the Green Tea Escape features lavender-scented water to soak in and antioxidant green tea to sip. Couples can indulge in a Swedish massage or hot-stone massage, either before or after a soak.

LeSpa at Sofitel (310-228-6777; www.lespala.com), 8555 Beverly Blvd., Beverly Hills. Part of the **Sofitel Hotel,** near the Beverly Center, LeSpa offers standard massage, scrubs, wraps, facials, and full-service salon treatments, as well as a few upscale items that are fitting for the upscale neighborhood: try the Liquid Pearl treatment, a scented milk bath, or the Liquid Gold treatment, a bath rich in essential oils and tinted the color of 14 karat gold.

Paint Shop Beverly Hills (310-652-5563; http://paintshopbeverlyhills.com), 319½ S. Robertson Blvd., Beverly Hills. This is unlike any other mani and pedi shop: patrons get their nails done while enjoying a cocktail. Check out the 'Ritas and Rocks Pedicure, which uses margarita salt as an exfoliator and lime oils for aromatherapy—all performed while the lucky guest sips on a real margarita.

Spa Montage Beverly Hills (310-860-7800; www.spamontage.com/beverlyhills), 225 N. Canon Dr., Beverly Hills. Part of the fabulous **Montage Beverly Hills** property, this 20,000-square-foot relaxation den is Moorish in design and offers luxuries like underwater massages, jasmine footbaths, and Dead Sea salt scrubs.

THEME PARKS AND ZOOS ✐ **Los Angeles Zoo and Botanical Gardens** (323-644-4200; www.lazoo.org), 5333 Zoo Dr., Los Angeles. Open daily 10–5. Home to more than 1,200 animals and 7,000 plants, the LA Zoo offers the Animals & You Program, a chance to pet animals in the Winnick Family Children's Zoo; the California Condor Rescue Zone, an interactive environment where children can learn about protecting endangered species; the Neil Papiano Play Park, an animal-themed climbing structure and toddler area designed to be accessible to children with physical disabilities; and the World of Birds Show, featuring rare birds of prey. The zoo recently opened a new habitat for seven African lowland gorillas, known as Campo Gorilla Reserves, in which a glassed-in viewing area and a moat is all that stands between visitors and these animals. Other favorites within the park include the Australia zone, home to the zoo's koalas, wallabies, and echidnas; Chimpanzees of Mahale Mountains, a 1-acre habitat for chimpanzees designed to mimic their native environment in Tanzania; the Dragons of Komodo, an enclosure for a pair of Komodo dragons, the world's largest lizards; and the ever-entertaining Red Ape Rain Forest, a multilevel habitat in which guests can be surrounded by a re-created Southeast Asian rain forest of bamboo and fruit trees as fellow primates jump through trees at eye level. Adults $14, children $9.

✪ ✐ **Universal Studios Hollywood** (800-UNIVERSAL; www.universalstudios hollywood.com), 1000 Universal Center Dr., Universal City. Open daily; hours vary by season. Just north of downtown LA, Universal Studios Hollywood is a fascinating mix of movie-themed thrill park and real working studio. (*Desperate Housewives* is filmed here, as are many other television shows and movies, and guests have the chance to see the real Wisteria Lane—and on rare occasions, the actresses and actors who make it come to life.) It would be easy to spend several days exploring Universal Studios, which offers nearly limitless entertainment possibilities. Admission to the park includes a full studio tour (which offers a peek of the sets used in Steven Speilberg's *War of the Worlds*, the facade of the Bates Motel from the

> **INSIDER TIP:** For an additional $60 ($50 for children), guests of Universal Studios Hollywood can purchase a Front of the Line Pass, which includes priority access to rides and priority seating at shows—which translates into vastly less waiting time and preferential treatment throughout the park.

CITYWALK, UNIVERSAL STUDIOS HOLLYWOOD

classic film *Psycho,* and Skull Island from *King Kong*); access to the adjacent shopping and dining complex **CityWalk;** admission to live-action shows like *Waterworld* and the new *Creature from the Black Lagoon: The Musical;* and unlimited passes to the many thrill rides, like the exhilarating Revenge of the Mummy (which takes off faster than any other ride I can think of), Jurassic Park: The Ride, and the new Simpson's Ride. CityWalk comprises 65 entertainment-themed restaurants, nightclubs, shops, and entertainment options, including a 19-screen movie theater (one of which is a huge IMAX theater), virtual NASCAR racing, iFLY Hollywood (a simulated skydiving experience), upscale bowling, and even the chance to ride a mechanical bull. Admission for five years and older $74. (Residents of Southern California are eligible for significant discounts.)

✷ Green Space

GARDENS Beverly Gardens Park, along the north side of Santa Monica Blvd., in Beverly Hills. Established in 1911, this linear park runs along 14 blocks and comprises a cactus garden, a rose garden, fountains, arbors, a jogging path, and the 40-foot-long BEVERLY HILLS sign.

Franklin Canyon, 2600 Franklin Canyon Dr. Adjacent to Beverly Hills, Franklin Canyon has hiking trails, picnic sites, and a large grass lawn. There's a small duck pond to the west and a lake picnic zone.

✷ Lodging

Beverly Hills

✪ ♂ **Beverly Hills Hotel and Bungalows** (800-283-8885; www.beverlyhillshotel.com), 9641 Sunset Blvd. If these walls could talk: This historic "pink palace" brings out my inner Lucy Ricardo. I want nothing more than to hide behind a dark pair of shades and stalk celebrities (something that the omnipresent hotel security would never allow, by the way). In addition to more than 200 elegant guest rooms and suites, there are 21 coveted bungalows, each designed like private residences. These lovely accommodations have been the home away from home for Golden Age Hollywood A-listers like Marilyn Monroe (who favored Bungalows 1 and 6), Elizabeth Taylor (who grew up on the property—her father ran a boutique off the lobby when she was a child, and she later celebrated six of her eight honeymoons here), and the elusive Howard Hughes (who spent the better part of 30 years hiding out in Bungalow 14). The stories go on and on: Katharine Hepburn played tennis regularly with paramour Spencer Tracey on the grounds; Marlene Dietrich sought sanctuary in a bungalow outfitted with an extra-large bed; the publicity-weary Beatles snuck into the pool wearing fake beards and top hats; Robert Kennedy's family was on property when they learned of Bobby's assassination; Warren Beatty made the acquaintance of many young starlets in the "Bachelor's Bungalows" at the back of the property, etc. Despite the rarified status of most guests today and all the Hollywood history, don't worry that this upscale icon will be stuffy: service is surprisingly friendly and personalized, and discretion is the word of the day—so whether you head to the pool in Manolos or Target flip-flops, you'll be treated kindly. On-site is the legendary **Polo Lounge,** which has both history and an enormous celebrity following today. For those who can afford it, the picture-perfect ballrooms and small private gardens make an idyllic wedding location. $$$$

PRICE KEY FOR A STANDARD ROOM:

$	$100 or less
$$	$101–150
$$$	$151–250
$$$$	$251 and up

The Beverly Hilton (310-274-7777; www.beverlyhilton.com), 9876 Wilshire Blvd. Opened in 1955—and recently renovated to make the accommodations even more plush—the Beverly Hilton is home to some of the most important red-carpet events in the city, including the annual Golden Globe Awards, which are held in the expansive International Ballroom. Guest room décor is perfectly tailored, conservative, and manly, with spacious bathrooms and luxurious amenities. The Penthouse Collection suites are several notches up from the standard accommodations and have hosted

INSIDER TIP: Guests who cannot afford the luxury accommodations at the Beverly Hills Hotel can still enjoy the ambiance of the property. The Fountain Room, a 60-year-old 20-seat counter diner just downstairs from the main lobby, serves affordable, freshly prepared food for breakfast, lunch, and dinner, offering an insider glimpse into working Hollywood.

presidents and A-listers. The hotel is home to the famous **Trader Vic's Lounge,** where legend has it the mai tai was born, and offers the largest pool in Beverly Hills (originally christened by Ester Williams herself, who used to offer impromptu swimming lessons on-site). Dining is at the well-regarded **Circa 55.** $$$$

Beverly Wilshire (310-275-5200; www.fourseasons.com/beverlywilshire), 9500 Wilshire Blvd. At the foot of famous Rodeo Dr., in the heart of Beverly Hills, the Beverly Wilshire is probably the best-located accommodation in the city, especially for those who want to do some serious shopping. The elegant hotel comprises two sections, the 10-story historic wing and the more contemporary 14-story wing, which together offer views of Rodeo Dr., the Hollywood Hills, and the Los Angeles skyline. Accommodations are spacious, opulent, and decorated in soothing cream tones, with Italian marble bathrooms that include deep soaking tubs. For anyone who believes the glamour of Hollywood is reserved for the older properties in town, be assured that this property has its own storied past: Warren Beatty called one of the suites here home for 10 years, and this is where Julia Roberts and Richard Gere filmed *Pretty Woman.* $$$$

Peninsula Beverly Hills (310-551-2888; www.beverlyhills.peninsula.com), 9882 S. Santa Monica Blvd. This elegant property looks and feels like a residential home, and service is discreet and professional—ensuring privacy and VIP treatment for hotel guests, be they overworked Hollywood glitterati or businesspeople in town for the night. The unique 24-hour stay policy allows guests to lodge for a full day, regardless of the check-in time: guests who check in at 6 PM aren't required to

BEVERLY WILSHIRE

check out until 6 PM the following day. On-site dining is at the acclaimed **Belvedere.** Don't miss the chocolate dim sum, a plate of crispy sweet dumplings filled with white and dark chocolate and served with a trio of fruit-flavored dipping sauces (available in the restaurant and via room service). $$$$

West Hollywood

✪ 🍸 **Andaz WeHo** (323-656-1234; http://westhollywood.hyatt.com/hyatt/hotels/index.jsp), 8401 Sunset Blvd. This sleek, sexy, newly revamped property reflects the youthful energy of the rock and roll crowd that still cruises this portion of the Sunset Strip—home to clubs like the **Whisky a Go-Go, The Roxy,** and **The Viper Room** (see *Entertainment*). This Hyatt-managed hotel has been in the thick of the action since rock god Jim Morrison of the Doors hung by his fingertips from an upper-floor room and Keith Richards of the Rolling Stones smashed a TV by tossing it out a window. Back in the day when this hotel was *the* place for rowdy rockers to party, the place was known as the Riot House; today the on-site restaurant **RH** pays homage to the legacy by carrying these initials. Upper-story rooms have astounding views of downtown LA and the Hollywood Hills, as does the pretty rooftop deck (complete with semiprivate cabanas). My favorite thing about this hotel? There is no check-in desk and no lines: guests are greeted on arrival by "hosts" who will offer complimentary beverages and See's candy, and then sit down in the comfy, hip "living room" to check in patrons via laptop. $$$

Le Montrose (310-855-1115; www.lemontrose.com/), 900 Hammond St. This all-suites property is a block off the famous Sunset Strip in West Hollywood and a close drive to Beverly Hills. Sleek accommodations include studio and one-bedroom suites, which incorporate an Asian style and midcentury-modern aesthetic. Most offer fireplaces, kitchenettes, and balconies. On-site dining is at the hip **Privato Restaurant,** which is reserved exclusively for hotel guests. There is also a small rooftop pool. $$$

The London West Hollywood (866-282-4560; www.thelondonwesthollywood.com/), 1020 N. San Vincente Blvd. Formerly the famed Bel Age Hotel, the London reopened in 2008 and has been transformed into suites-only lodging that is elegant, youthful, and trendy—perfect for the rock and roll neighborhood (the property is just off the Sunset Strip). The pool deck, 10 stories high, offers tremendous views and is one of many favorite places to see and be seen by young Hollywood. Celebrity chef enfant terrible Gordon Ramsay manages the on-site restaurant, the **Boxwood.** $$$

🍸 **Mondrian Los Angeles** (323-650-8999; www.mondrianhotel.com/#/home/), 8440 Sunset Blvd. As the artsy name suggests, this property is contemporary, minimalist, and extremely high style—yet it manages to be cozy and

ANDAZ WEHO

Courtesy of Andaz WeHo

welcoming, too, thanks to impeccable service and professional staff. Public and private spaces boast museum-quality modern furniture, a sunny palette, and an extremely hip vibe. Supermodels and rock stars are sure to feel right at home here—as would anyone young and fabulous. The rooftop pool is one of the coolest in the city, with an outdoor-room feel, spectacular deck furniture, and views of the Hollywood Hills. The supremely popular **SkyBar** draws residents from around the city for nightlife. $$$

Sunset Marquis (310-657-1333; http://sunsetmarquis.com/), 1200 Alta Loma Rd. This luxurious hotel has been a favorite rock-star hideout since 1963, when it opened its doors to the likes of Jimi Hendrix, the Rolling Stones, and the Who. Today music royalty such as U2, Green Day, and John Mayer haunt the halls—fitting, because the property is near the famed rock and roll playground, the **Sunset Strip.** The 14 private villas have enticed superstars of film, too. (George Clooney and Brad Pitt are said to have enjoyed the Sunset Marquis—under appropriately anonymous pseudonyms.) Accommodations vary widely, from standard rooms to the aforementioned commodious villas, and all feature an Asian aesthetic with eclectic furnishings, surprising artwork, and a youthful vibe. Dining is at **The Restaurant.** Sun seekers won't be disappointed with the opulent pool, complete with private cabanas, all the better to hide from paparazzi (who, by the way, would never be allowed on the grounds, thanks to the hotel's relentless security and dedication to its guests' privacy). $$$$

Sunset Tower Hotel (323-654-7100; http://sunsettowerhotel.com/), 8358 Sunset Blvd. This high-rise art deco landmark has been reinvented for a new generation. Formerly a posh apartment building that was home to silver screen icons like Marilyn Monroe, John Wayne (who reputedly kept a cow on his balcony), Greta Garbo, Mae West, Elizabeth Taylor, and Clark Gable, today the Sunset Tower offers commodious accommodations in a clubby, grown-up atmosphere. Floor-to-ceiling windows make the most of the views of nearby Beverly Hills and Hollywood, and elegant bathrooms offer movie-star pampering space. Dining is at the sophisticated **Tower Bar.** $$$

✷ Where to Eat

DINING OUT

Beverly Hills

✪ **Bouchon Bistro** (310-271-9910; www.bouchonbistro.com), 235 N. Canon Dr. Open daily for lunch and dinner. The brainchild of the extraordinary Thomas Keller, of French Laundry (Napa/Yountville) fame, this classic French brasserie offers ambiance to spare, with an authentic zinc counter, cane chairs, and high ceilings—and a virtual who's who of Los Angeles in the dining room. Expect hearty French favorites like trout almandine served with haricots verts; roasted duck breast with fennel puree, and roasted leg of lamb with artichokes, each prepared with a grace, passion, and artistry that is surprising. Desserts are equally divine, especially the lemon tarts. The bistro offers a wide selection of carafe

PRICE KEY FOR A TYPICAL ENTRÉE:

$	$10 and under
$$	$11–20
$$$	$21–30
$$$$	$31 and up

wines as well as reserve list bottles. This is one of the hottest tickets in town, so make reservations well in advance (at least two weeks). $$$$

Crustacean Restaurant (310-205-8990; www.anfamily.com/portalpage.html), 9646 Little Santa Monica Blvd. Open daily for dinner. This French-inspired Vietnamese restaurant is popular with the Hollywood set—and just about everyone else. It always seems to be packed, so it isn't the best choice for an intimate conversation. However, the place delivers on theatricality: patrons are literally encouraged to walk on water as they enter the place—over a glassed-in river full of koi that runs through the restaurant. As the name implies, favorite entrées include the Dungeness crab and coconut shrimp, but the garlic noodles are equally crave-worthy. Try the lychee martini for an unusual treat. $$$

Cut (310-276-8500; www.wolfgangpuck.com), 9500 Wilshire Blvd. Open Mon.–Sat. for dinner. Cut steakhouse is one of the many powerhouse restaurants owned by celebrity chef Wolfgang Puck and is part of the **Beverly Wilshire,** which sits at the foot of the famed shopping district on Rodeo Dr.—so it's clear this place is going to attract a posh crowd. Although it is unlikely Puck will be on the premises, this is another favorite with the Hollywood glitterati set, who come for the impeccable corn-fed porterhouse, Wagyu filet mignon, and the slow-roasted Kobe beef short ribs. Try the bone-marrow flan with custard served in the bone (trust me). $$$$

Il Cielo (310-276-9990; www.ilcielo.com), 9018 Burton Dr. Open daily for lunch and dinner. Known as one of the most romantic garden restaurants in the city, Il Cielo is ablaze with glittering lights in the evening. The welcoming restaurant features Tuscan cuisine and house-made pasta, like the *Ravioli ai Funghi Porcini con Zucca e Salvia* (ravioli with porcini mushrooms and butternut squash), *Pasta all Chitarra al Pesto* (pasta with a creamy fresh pesto sauce), and *Sciagliatelli con Melanzane e Ricotta Infornata* (fettuccine with eggplant and tomato sauce). Given the lovely setting—and expensive zip code—Il Cielo is a relative bargain, with most pasta dishes going for less than $15. $$–$$$

The Ivy (310-274-8303), 113 N. Robertson Blvd. Open Mon.–Sat. for lunch and dinner, Sun. for brunch and dinner. A current favorite with the Hollywood crowd, The Ivy has a surprisingly homey, country-chic aesthetic, with rustic antiques and fat fragrant roses blooming on the brick patio (the favored seating for the biggest stars). Cuisine is finely prepared, although simple—like the classic crabcakes, corn chowder, and even an exceptional hamburger. This is *the* place to spot celebs, and The Ivy is known for treating the occasional less-than-famous guest less than hospitably. Although the reputation for snobbery is not completely unwarranted, this is an upscale restaurant, and oftentimes professional service is misinterpreted as

CUT RESTAURANT

Courtesy of the Beverly Wilshire. Photo by Timothy Griffith.

unfriendly. However, do be sure to dress appropriately, to minimize the chance of getting the cold shoulder, and don't take any snubs to heart. Personally, I can endure a little attitude if I'm seated at a table next to George Clooney. $$$$

Mr. Chow (310-278-9911; www.mrchow.com), 344 N. Camden Dr. Open daily for dinner. An upscale Chinese restaurant in Beverly Hills, this is yet another Hollywood favorite—and a great place for celebrity watching. The crisp formal black-and-white interior is dramatic, and the nightly "noodle show"—in which a talented chef spins and twirls a bit of dough until it transforms into perfect strands of noodles—is worthy entertainment. The cuisine is mandarin style and includes an authentic Peking duck, unusual green prawns, and a variety of pleasing dumplings. Avoid disappointment and make reservations well in advance, especially on weekends. $$$

Polo Lounge (310-276-2251; www.beverlyhills.hotel.com), 9641 Sunset Blvd. Open daily for breakfast, lunch, and dinner. At the world-renowned **Beverly Hills Hotel,** the Polo Lounge has stories to tell. Back in the heyday of Hollywood, W. C. Fields, Humphrey Bogart, and Frank Sinatra had a standing reservation at the bar every evening, and Charlie Chaplin had his own booth for lunch every day. Nowadays, the cushy half-moon booths are the coveted makeshift offices of Hollywood movers and shakers, and it is typical to find A-listers like Jennifer Aniston and Gwen Stefani noshing in a dark corner. Service is discreet and professional, and the food is surprisingly good (it wouldn't have to be, given the status of the place): the eggs Benedict is sublime, as is the classic tenderloin steak tartar served with French fries and toast points. There are also much-loved daily specials, such as lobster thermidor on Fri. and steak with peppercorn sauce on Wed. On warm days, outdoor garden dining is lovely as well. $$$

Spago (310-385-0880; www.wolfgangpuck.com), 176 N. Canon Dr. Open daily for dinner, Mon.–Sat. for lunch. It's hard to imagine a more quintessentially LA restaurant than Spago, the eatery that helped make Wolfgang Puck a household name. Don't expect to see the celebrity chef at the restaurant—and although other celebrities do still drop in, this upscale eatery attracts more curious out-of-towners than Hollywood glitterati these days. However, the food is equal to the hype, regardless of who's enjoying it. Save room for the Kaiserschmarrn for dessert: fluffy pancakes drenched in strawberries. $$$–$$$$

Urasawa (310-247-8939), 218 N. Rodeo Dr. Open for lunch and dinner by appointment only. Given the top-dollar real estate this exclusive sushi bar occupies, it is no surprise that this is among the most expensive restaurants in LA. The tiny space can accommodate only a handful of people at a time at the two tables and wooden counter. Renowned chef Hiroyuki Urasawa creates a completely unique experience for his patrons every evening—and true aficionados claim that the nearly $300 tab per person (not including drinks or tip) is worth every penny. $$$$

West Hollywood

BLT Steak (310-360-1950; www.bltsteak.com), 8720 Sunset Blvd. Open daily for dinner. Don't expect bacon, lettuce, and tomato sandwiches at this upscale steak restaurant on the Sunset Strip: the acronym stands for Bistro Laurent Tourondel, marking this as one of Chef Tourondel's many culinary endeavors throughout the world.

Although it claims to be a "modern American steakhouse," the ambiance is more French bistro—and offers exquisite steaks prepared simply (and perfectly), along with fabulous house-made popovers and surely the city's best onion rings (oversized, well seasoned, and crispy). $$$

Boxwood Café (310-358-7788; www.thelondonwesthollywood.com/gordon_ramsay/Boxwood_cafe.cfm), 1020 N. San Vincente. Open daily for breakfast, lunch, dinner, and afternoon tea. At the **London West Hollywood Hotel,** the casual Boxwood Café is under the command of famously irritable Chef Gordon Ramsay of TV's *Hell's Kitchen* fame. Despite the cranky chef's reputation for tantrums, the restaurant is actually quite welcoming and friendly, and offers dishes like black cod marinated in sake, slow-roasted chicken with polenta, and the famous Prime London burger. Don't miss the strawberry and champagne zabaglione for dessert. $$$

Il Sole (310-657-1182), 8741 W. Sunset Blvd. Open daily for dinner. A cozy Italian eatery specializing in pasta and fish, Il Sole is another big stop on the celebrity circuit, especially for young Hollywood. The hip, beautiful crowd noshes on risotto with porcini mushrooms and truffle oil, spaghetti with lobster, and spoon-tended Dover sole. The price point is rather astonishing for predominately pasta, but portions are large, and the outdoor sidewalk dining patio is relaxing on a warm day. Note that paparazzi tend to hang out outside, which can be a little annoying—except for those looking for their 15 minutes of fame. $$$$

Ketchup (310-289-8590; www.dolcegroup.com), 8590 Sunset Blvd. Open Mon.–Fri. for lunch and dinner, Sat.–Sun. for dinner. This modernist upscale diner is owned in part by the multitalented Ashton Kutcher, whose whimsical sense of humor is reflected in both the playful décor and the entertaining menu. The clean-lined interior is white on white, with the expected splashes of red, with Warhol-esque art featuring—what else?—ketchup bottles. The cuisine is reinvented American comfort food, like fried green tomatoes served with a red pepper coulis and Shake 'n Bake, pistachio-encrusted chicken served with garlic mashed potatoes and mushroom gravy. Do not miss the side of mac and cheese, served with white truffles and crab. $$–$$$

Saddle Ranch Chop House (323-656-2007; www.srrestaurants.com), 8371 Sunset Blvd. Open daily for lunch and dinner, Sat. and Sun. for breakfast. On the Sunset Strip, the rustic, noisy Saddle Ranch is a fun, rock-and-roll chophouse that doesn't take itself too seriously. Dine on double-cut pork chops with apple bourbon sauce, real Southern fried chicken served with wickedly good bacon gravy, and cowboy cut prime rib. For dessert, don't miss the 3-foot-tall cotton candy treat adorned with bits of chocolate cake, cookies, berries, and cream. Or if that sounds like too much, the restaurant offers outdoor fire pits that allow diners to toast their own s'mores. The place even features a mechanical bull. $$$

EATING OUT

Beverly Hills

Frankie and Johnnie's (310-860-1155), 9533 Little Santa Monica Blvd. Open daily for lunch and dinner. Just off Rodeo Dr. (and down the street from the ever-popular cupcake joint, **Sprinkles**), F&J's offers the best dining bargain in Beverly Hills: pizza by the slice for $4. Eat in the tiny café or take away. $

Fulfilled (310-860-0776; www.fulfilledpastries.com), 9405 S. Santa

Monica Blvd. Open daily for lunch and dinner. This pretty shop serves small traditional Japanese pastries called Imagawa-yaki (or Ima). These pancake-style pastries are traditionally filled with sweet bean paste—but are also available with stuffings like Nutella and banana, and apple chicken sausage. Either way, they are addicting. $

Nate n' Al's (310-274-0101), 414 N. Beverly Dr. Open daily for breakfast, lunch, and dinner. This deli has been in business for more than 60 years, and in a town that sees trends come and go seasonally, its longevity is remarkable. Don't miss the stuffed cabbage and the fantastic chicken matzo soup. $

Sprinkles Cupcakes (310-274-8765; www.sprinkles.com), 9635 S. Santa Monica Blvd. Open Mon.–Sat. 9–7, Sun. 10–6. Expect a long line out the door every day at this tiny, wildly popular cupcake shop near Rodeo Dr. Specialties include the dark chocolate with chocolate sprinkles, red velvet cakes, and coconut confections. For a more immediate sugar rush, get a "frosting shot" for 75 cents. $

Hollywood

Cantor's Deli (323-651-2030; www.cantersdeli.com), 419 N. Fairfax Ave., Los Angeles. Open daily 24 hours. Near the Miracle Mile and Hollywood, this 50-year-old local favorite offers good French dip and giant pastrami sandwiches. Service is friendly, and the dining room is huge. There's also a nice bakery up front. $$

PASTRAMI AT CANTOR'S

Pizzeria Mozza (323-297-0100; www.mozza-la.com), 641 N. Highland Ave. Open daily noon–midnight. Owned in part by celebrity chef Mario Batali, Mozza features pies with light, thin, slightly charred crust that is almost good enough to eat plain, but try it topped with pureed anchovy paste and a fried egg: *very* Italian. $$

Roscoe's House of Chicken and Waffles (323-466-7453; www.roscoeschickenandwaffles.com), 1514 N. Gower St. Open daily for lunch and dinner. World-famous Roscoe's serves all manner of Southern comfort food, but the reason to visit is the namesake chicken and waffles, a surprisingly melodious combination. $

West Hollywood

Mel's Diner (310-854-7200), 8585 W. Sunset Blvd. Open daily 24 hours. This fun 1950s-themed diner offers breakfast all day, drawing a family crowd during daylight hours and club hoppers in the twilight hours. The small sidewalk patio is nice for people watching. Don't miss the thick chocolate shakes. $

Millions of Milkshakes (213-387-4253; www.millionsofmilkshakes.com), 8910 Santa Monica Blvd. Open daily until 2 AM. The owners weren't kidding when they named this place: with more than one hundred ingredients to blend into ice cream, yogurt, and soy-based gelato, there *are* millions of milk shake combinations possible. This is a favorite with young Hollywood, and as a result, tabloid photographers often hang out nearby. $

Courtesy of Jon Preimesberger

PINK'S HOT DOGS

✪ 🏅 ✐ **Pink's Hot Dogs** (323-931-4223), 709 N. La Brea Ave., La Brea. Open daily for lunch and dinner, until 3 AM on weekends. Since 1939, anyone who's anyone in Los Angeles has lined up at this hot dog stand near West Hollywood—and do expect to stand in line at this ever-popular joint, where Orson Welles once downed 18 dogs at one sitting. Try the chili dog with onions or the Martha Stewart dog (really!). $

Urth Caffé (310-205-9311), 8565 Melrose. Open daily for breakfast, lunch, and dinner. Best known as a backdrop for the LA-based TV show *Entourage,* this organic coffee and tea shop also serves sandwiches, salads, and fresh soups. The streetside outdoor dining patio overflows for breakfast and lunch. $$

✷ Entertainment

CLUBS In entertainment-obsessed Los Angeles, where a voracious crowd is always on the lookout for the hottest, most exclusive hangouts, clubs come and go in the blink of an eye. This is especially so in Hollywood and its immediate environs. With this in mind, represented here are some old standbys as well as some newcomers that promise lasting power. *Diversity* is the word, and locals and visitors alike are sure to find a watering hole and/or dance club to call home—assuming they can get past the velvet rope line.

Beverly Hills

🍸 **Stone Rose Lounge** (310-228-6677; www.gerberbars.com), 8555 Beverly Blvd. Part of the **Sofitel Los Angeles** hotel, the Stone Rose is a postmodern cocktail lounge that offers multiple venues to suit any mood: For an intimate setting, check out the VIP zone, complete with comfy sofas and leather walls. For a more casual atmosphere, try the outdoor patio, equipped with oversized beds, cabanas, and a huge outdoor fire pit. For making the scene, stick to the main lounge, which boasts a U-shaped bar with velvet seating. The grapefruit basil martini is yummy.

Hollywood

✪ 🍸 **Cat and Fiddle** (323-468-3800; www.thecatandfiddle.com), 6530 Sunset Blvd. This British pub offers a nice dart room, inviting patio, and traditional steak and kidney pie (okay, so maybe the food isn't the real draw). The live music here has been known to attract

INSIDER TIP: Getting into a hot nightclub in Los Angeles can be like high school all over again: beautiful, rich people have all the breaks, and the rest of us are likely to cool our heels indefinitely in a long line of hopefuls. To decrease wait time, dress as expensively and stylishly as possible. It also helps to show up unfashionably early, before crowds increase the competition.

aging (and painfully famous) Brit rock stars to listen and sometimes to join in.

🍸 **The Frolic Room** (323-462-5890), 6245 Hollywood Blvd. Next to the lovely **Pantages Theater,** this is a favorite after-show hangout that stays open late. The small, slightly divey place is enlivened with a mural of old Hollywood celebs.

✪ 🍸 **Lucky Strike Lane** (323-467-7776; www.bowlluckystrike.com), 6801 Hollywood Blvd., Suite 143. Come to this upscale bowling alley in the Hollywood and Highland complex if you "strike out" gaining admittance to exclusive clubs in town: Everyone gets in, and it is likely you'll spot a celebrity here.

🍸 **Red Buddha Lounge** (323-962-2913), 6423 Yucca Blvd. This upscale, Asian-inspired lounge is a relative newcomer but has become popular with a posh crowd. Dress to impress.

West Hollywood

✪ 🍸 **Comedy Store** (323-650-6268), 8433 W. Sunset Blvd. On the Sunset Strip, the Comedy Store has been hosting up-and-comers and big-name acts for years. Jim Carrey got his start here, as did Michael Keaton. The club is owned by Mizi Shore, the mother of comedian Pauly Shore, who is often in the house.

WHISKEY A GO-GO

🍸 ▼ **East/West Lounge** (310-360-6186; www.eastwestlounge.com), 8851 Santa Monica Blvd. Considered one of

TOP 10 DAY IN HOLLYWOOD AND BEVERLY HILLS

1. Power-breakfast on eggs Benedict at the Polo Lounge (see p. 216)
2. Mug for a photo in front of the HOLLYWOOD sign, visible from the Hollywood and Highland Center (see p. 205)
3. Compare handprints with the stars at Grauman's Chinese Theatre (see p. 204)
4. Catch a matinee at the ornate El Capitan Theatre (see pp. 221–222)
5. Lunch on a slice of sausage and pepper pie at Frankie and Johnnie's (see p. 217)
6. Top it off with a coconut cupcake for dessert at Sprinkles (see p. 218)
7. Window-shop on Rodeo Drive (see p. 223)
8. Indulge in steak and *frites* at the sublime Bouchon Bistro (see pp. 214–215)
9. Sip a nightcap at the Stone Rose Lounge (see p. 219)
10. Overnight in the Beverly Hills Hotel (see p. 211)

BE A MEMBER OF THE STUDIO AUDIENCE

Most television shows offer free tickets to their tapings, which is an opportunity not to be missed. Secure tickets directly from studios or from companies that distribute for the studios:

- **Audiences Unlimited** (818-506-0043; www.tvtickets.com), 100 Universal City Plaza, Universal City. Distributes free advanced tickets for TV tapings.
- **CBS Television City** (323-575-2458), 7800 Beverly Blvd., Los Angeles. Get tickets to game shows like *The Price Is Right.* Must be 18 or older.
- **NBC Television** (818-840-3537), 3000 W. Alameda Ave., Burbank. Reserve seats for sitcoms the day of the show; two tickets per person, on a first-come, first-served basis.
- **On-Camera Audiences** (818-295-2700; www.ocatv.com). Free tickets available for live tapings for shows like *American Idol* and *The Family Feud.*
- **Paramount Studios** (323-956-1777; www. paramount.com), 5555 Melrose Ave., Hollywood. Tickets available five days in advance, in person or via the Web site.

the best lesbian and gay bars in town, the East/West has a lively happy hour and offers truly inventive cocktails. Try the Spring Fling: champagne, vodka, and watermelon liqueur.

🍸 **The Viper Room** (310-652-4202; www.viperroom.com), 8901 W. Sunset Blvd. This small music club that features local bands hides behind an unimpressive storefront on the Sunset Strip, but despite the lack of curb appeal, it attracts big crowds on the weekends, including a who's who of young Hollywood celebrities.

✪ 🍸 **Whisky a Go-Go** (310-652-4202; www.whiskyagogo.com), 8901 W. Sunset Blvd. This iconic music club was the epicenter of the rock scene in the late 1960s and into the 1970s. Jim Morrison and the Doors were once the house band.

THEATERS ✪ **ArcLight/Cinerama Dome** (323-464-4226; www.arclight cinemas.com), 6360 Sunset Blvd., Hollywood. At $14 a pop, ticket prices at the ArcLight (an upscale movie theater) are steep, but the establishment offers reservations, extraordinary sound, and spacious seating, which are well worth the premium.

Cinespace (323-817-3456; www.cine space.info/welcome.html), 6356 Hollywood Blvd., Hollywood. This highly stylized nightclub/restaurant/lounge/movie theater seeks to be all things to all people—and manages to deliver, with an emphasis on emerging films.

El Capitan Theatre (323-467-7674; http://disney.go.com/disneypictures/el-capitan), 6838 Hollywood Blvd., Hollywood. The gorgeous, lavish El Capital opened in 1926, and for years it served as a movie theater and as a live theater

Courtesy LA Philharmonic

HOLLYWOOD BOWL

venue. Today the El Cap (which is across the street from the Kodak Theatre—home to the Oscars) serves as an exclusive first-run theater for Disney movies. It is also currently the taping venue for *Larry Kimmel Live.*

Hollywood Bowl (323-850-2000; www.hollywoodbowl.org), 2301 N. Highland Ave., Hollywood. This astonishing outdoor amphitheater is designed to seat 18,000 and offers premier views and sound. The LA Philharmonic plays their Summer Pops program at the Hollywood Bowl, offering jazz, classical, and Broadway tunes. Boxes within the orchestra section have tables that pop up, to allow patrons to bring their own picnics.

Kodak Theatre (323-308-6300; www.kodaktheatre.com), 6801 Hollywood Blvd., Hollywood. Open for tours daily 10:30–2:30. Part of the Hollywood and Highland Center (a good place to catch a peek of the HOLLYWOOD sign), this 3,400-seat theater is the home of the Academy Awards. Fans of the Oscars will be surprised to see that the Kodak Theatre does not have a grand entrance with a 0.25-mile approach that television makes it seem; instead, it's tucked into a multistory mall and surrounded by retail stores—which during the awards ceremony are hidden with elaborate draping. Tours: $15.

Pantages Theater (323-468-1770; www.broadwayla.org), 6233 Hollywood Blvd., Hollywood. This old-school movie theater hosts live musical and theatrical presentations in a historic setting. The art deco lobby has been lovingly restored and gives a glimpse into vintage Hollywood.

✷ Selective Shopping

Avenues of Art and Design, in West Hollywood, is a high-style pedestrian-friendly district encompassing upscale fashion businesses, interior design and contemporary furniture stores, and art galleries. Look for hot boutiques like Stella McCartney, Balenciaga, Alberta Ferretti, Maxfield, and John Varvatos. **The Grove Farmers Market** in West Hollywood is more than just a place to buy great local tomatoes and strawberries in season; this cobblestoned complex offers major retail stores like Barneys New York and Crate & Barrel; restaurants like Loteria Grill and the Cheesecake Factory; and free live entertainment. **Sunset Plaza,** on Sunset Boulevard in West Hollywood, offers luxury brands and designer names like Badgley Mischka, Catherine Malandrino, Nicole Miller, Armani, and Hugo Boss. If you work up an appetite spending money, dine at a handful of chic restaurants, many of which offer outdoor patio spaces that are perfect for people watching. Check out favorites like **Chin Chin Grill, Café Med,** and **Le Clafoutis.** Of course, **Rodeo Drive,** in Beverly Hills, is a must-see, even for those of us whose pockets aren't deep enough to buy a thing there. Indulge in some of the most tantalizing window-shopping you'll ever experience. Don't miss big-name shops like Harry Winston, Dolce & Gabbana, Prada, Jimmy Choo, Valentino, and the ever-popular Versace. **Two Rodeo,** on Rodeo Drive and Wilshire Boulevard in Beverly Hills, comprises a pretty cobbled pedestrian street lined with high-end boutiques and eateries. Look for the much-photographed "Spanish Steps," which ascend from Wilshire to Via Rodeo.

PASADENA

In many ways Pasadena (nicknamed the Rose City) is a throwback to simpler times, thanks to the calm suburban vibe, pristine tree-lined streets, and Arts and Crafts architecture that gives Old Town a historic look and feel. Beyond the annual Rose Bowl and Rose Parade, the area has undeniable charm. Old Pasadena offers plenty of boutique shopping and upscale dining, as well as what seems like a vintage movie theater on every corner. Nearby upscale San Marino is home to the immense gardens and art collection that are part of one of my favorite museums in the world: the Huntington Library.

Pasadena is also known for being home to some of the most prestigious research institutions in the country, including the California Institute of Technology (CalTech—ranked as being one of the top 10 most difficult universities in the world to gain admittance) and the Jet Propulsion Laboratory (JPL), the organization responsible for constructing robotic aircraft for NASA.

Geographically, Pasadena is just northeast of downtown Los Angeles, at the foot of the San Gabriel Mountains, and this somewhat sleepy residential enclave comprises three main areas. The 12 blocks that make up art deco Old Town Pasadena are immaculately clean and pedestrian friendly, and offer trendy boutiques, vintage theaters, and plenty of dining options. The South Lake Avenue district is home to upscale boutiques and retail chains like Anthropology. The Pasadena Playhouse district is a 1920s-era art-centric neighborhood that houses the namesake theater, as well as **Vroman's Bookstore,** the oldest independent bookseller in Southern California.

✱ To See

HISTORICAL SITES Colorado Street Bridge, spanning the Arroyo Seco. This graceful, landmark bridge was constructed in 1913.

Fenyes Mansion (626-577-1660), 470 W. Walnut, Pasadena. Opening hours vary. This 1906 Beaux-Arts building sits on what used to be Pasadena's Millionaires' Row, a lovely historic part of town. Visitors can explore the mansion via docent-led tours, which allow for a peek into the period-furnished rooms. Adults $5.

Gamble House (626-793-3334; www.gamblehouse.org), 4 Westmoreland Pl., Pasadena. Open Thurs.–Sun. noon–3. A stellar example of the Arts and Crafts architecture and design movement, the Gamble House, designed by architects Greene and Greene, is one of the most famous architectural sites in Los Angeles County. Adults $10.

Courtesy of Pasadena Convention and Visitors Bureau

TOURNAMENT HOUSE

✪ **Jet Propulsion Laboratory** (818-354-4321; www.jpl.nasa.gov), 4800 Oak Grove Dr., Pasadena. Open for tours several times a month; call in advance to schedule. This research lab, which is responsible for designing and building spacecraft for NASA, offers two-hour public tours that provide an overview of JPL's accomplishments and gives guests a peek at the Space Flight Operations Center and the Spacecraft Assembly Center, both of which are fascinating to anyone interested in science and engineering. All U.S.-resident guests older than 18 must bring a passport or driver's license as identification; guests from outside the United States must bring a passport or green card. Tours are free.

COLORADO STREET BRIDGE

Courtesy of the Pasadena Convention and Visitors Bureau

Tournament of Roses House and Wrigley Gardens (626-449-4100), 391 S. Orange Grove Blvd., Pasadena. Open for tours Thurs. 2–4; closed the entire month of Sept. Part of Millionaires' Row, this gorgeous white Italian Renaissance–style mansion and one-time home to William Wrigley Jr. (chewing gum magnate) is now the headquarters for the Pasadena Tournament of Roses Association. The beautiful interior boasts inlaid marble floors and ornate plaster ceilings. On display are the tiaras worn by former Rose

Parade queens and their royal court princesses, along with other parade memorabilia. The 4.5-acre garden in the back is abloom with a magnificent display of more than 1,500 varieties of roses and camellias. Tours are free Feb.–Aug.

MUSEUMS ✪ **The Huntington Library, Art Collection, and Botanical Gardens** (626-405-2100; www.huntington.org), 1151 Oxford Rd., San Marino. Open Mon., Wed.–Fri. noon–4:30; Sat. and Sun. 10:30–4:30. The 120 lavish acres of gardens that boast more than 14,000 kinds of plants would be reason enough to visit this magnificent estate, which once belonged to the über-wealthy railroad titan Henry Huntington: the rose garden alone has more than 1,200 species, displayed in historical progression. The new Chinese garden, appropriately named the Garden of Flowing Fragrance, showcases a lake, arching bridges, an authentic teahouse, a restaurant (try the dim sum!), and native Chinese plants and stones. But beyond the overflowing flower collections, expansive lawns, and full-grown forests, the Huntington also offers four art galleries (home to Gainsborough's *The Blue Boy* and Lawrence's *Pinkie*, hung across from each other in a long gallery of other British portraits) and arguably the most extensive collection of rare books on the West Coast. Bibliophiles will not want to miss the chance to see a Gutenberg Bible (ca. 1455), early folios of Shakespeare, and original letters written by the likes of George Washington, Benjamin Franklin, and Charlotte Brontë. On sunny weekends, arrive as the gates open. Crowds (and the heat in spring and summer) can be oppressive by early afternoon. Weekend admissions: Adults $20, seniors $15, students $10, children 5–11 $6, under 5 free. Discounts apply on weekdays and for group rates. Admission is free on the first Thurs. of each month with preregistered tickets.

✪ **Norton Simon Museum** (626-449-6840; www.nortonsimon.org), 411 W. Colorado Blvd., Pasadena. Open Wed., Thurs., Sat.–Mon. noon–6; Fri. noon–9. Fans of the annual Rose Bowl Parade will recognize the Frank O. Gehry exterior of this small museum, because it is directly on the parade route and often ends up on television as a result. The permanent collection offers Renaissance pieces to 20th-century masterpieces, including Van Gogh, Degas, and Monet. There is also a serene sculpture garden. Adults $8.

Pasadena Museum of California Art (626-568-3665; www.pmcaonline.org), 490 E. Union St., Pasadena. Open Wed.–Sun. 10–5. This museum is devoted exclusively to California architecture, design, and art, which is particularly salient in a city that is passionate about historic preservation. Adults $7, seniors and children $5.

✱ To Do

GOLF Brookside Golf Club (626-796-0177; www.americangolf.com), 1133 Rosemont Ave., Pasadena. This club offers two 18-hole championship courses—the more challenging of the two being the parklike No. 1. Note: Duffers should stay away the first day of the year, when the fairways are used for Rose Bowl parking. Green fee: $38–53.

Eaton Canyon Golf Course (626-794-6773; www.eatoncanyongc.com), 1150 Sierra Madre Villa Ave., Pasadena. This small executive course offers nine holes, with a clubhouse, driving range, and putting greens. Green fee: $50.

SPAS **Burke Williams** (310-966-4098; www.burkewilliamsspa.com), 39 Mills Pl., Pasadena. An opulent day spa with locations throughout Southern California, Burke Williams offers signature treatments like Savannah's Surrender, a mineral salts scrub followed by a warm mud application and finished with a peppermint moisturizer; and Harmony, a vibration treatment that includes an exfoliating massage and a hot and cold stone therapy, concluding with a piece of delicious dark chocolate.

Huntington Spa (626-568-3700; www.pasadena.langhamhotels.com), 1401 S. Oak Knoll Ave., Pasadena. Voted one of the top 10 hotel spas in the United States by *Travel + Leisure* magazine, the Huntington Spa is part of the lovely **Langham Huntington Hotel.** The opulent, newly refurbished spa incorporates traditional Chinese medicine into signature treatments that include breathing rituals and acupressure.

✷ Green Space

GARDENS **Descanso Gardens** (818-952-4400; www.descansogardens.org), 1418 Descanso Dr., La Canada Flintridge, northwest of Pasadena. Open for tram tours Tues.–Fri. 1–3, Sat.–Sun. 11–3. Although a bit far-flung, Descanso Gardens has 150 acres of native chaparral and woodland, along with 40,000 camellia bushes that bloom from late fall through winter. The lovely gardens are the site of regular summer concerts, as well as special events throughout the year. Guided tram tours are available. Admission $4.

✪ **The Huntington Library and Botanical Gardens** (626-405-2100; www.huntington.org), 1151 Oxford Rd., San Marino. The lovely botanical gardens at the Huntington Library feature 120 landscaped acres with more than a dozen themed gardens and a conservatory. Walking tours are available. For the full listing, see *Museums*.

⚣ **Los Angeles County Arboretum and Botanic Gardens** (301-821-3222; www.arboretum.org), 301 N. Baldwin Ave., Arcadia (southeast of Pasadena). Open

CHINESE GARDEN, HUNTINGTON LIBRARY

TOP 10 DAY IN PASADENA

1. Enjoy a house-made pecan roll at Pie and Burger (see p. 230)
2. Tour the Gamble House (see p. 224)
3. Wander the rose garden of the Huntington Library (see p. 226)
4. Head inside the Huntington and peruse the antique manuscripts (see p. 226)
5. Lunch on an organic turkey burger at Smitty's (see p. 230)
6. Hunt for antiques in the Fair Oaks district (see p. 231)
7. Admire more roses at the Wrigley Gardens (see pp. 225–226)
8. Dine on fois gras *frito* with pickled blueberries at the Dining Room (see pp. 229–230)
9. Take in a blockbuster movie at the Gold Class Cinema (see p. 231)
10. Overnight at the Langham Huntington Hotel (see p. 228)

daily 9–5. Guests will find 127 acres of trees and shrubs, and more than 30,000 plants from around the world, arranged by continent of origin. The arboretum is also home to exhibits that portray major phases of California history. Note that the arboretum hosts the California Philharmonic Concerts on the Green in the summer; on concert days, the gardens close at 3:30. Adults $8, students and seniors $6, children 5–12 $3.

Wrigley Gardens (626-449-4100; www.tournamentofroses.com), 391 S. Orange Grove Blvd., Pasadena. For the full listing, see *Historical Sites.*

✷ Lodging

Pasadena

✪ **The Langham Huntington Hotel and Spa** (626-568-3900; www.langhamhotels.com), 1401 S. Oak Knoll Ave. Most recently known as the Ritz-Carlton, the palatial Langham is the finest accommodation in Pasadena and offers the look and feel of a residential mansion. Dating to 1865, the hotel is sited on 23 immaculately landscaped acres overlooking the tony San Marino suburb. Accommodations are traditional, with period furnishings, opulent linens, rich oil paintings, and Italian marble bathrooms. The property offers a gracious pool, tennis courts, a full-service spa (see *Spas*), and on-site dining at **The Dining Room,** headed up by *Top Chef* winner Michael Voltaggio. $$$$

PRICE KEY FOR A STANDARD ROOM:

$	$100 or less
$$	$101–150
$$$	$151–250
$$$$	$251 and up

Sheraton Pasadena (626-449-4000; www.starwoodhotels.com/sheraton), 303 E. Cordova St. Although somewhat cookie-cutter in design, the Sheraton Pasadena is in the heart of Old Pasadena, within walking distance of great shopping, dining, and vintage movie houses. The hotel offers a full-service exercise facility, a pool, on-site dining, and a free shuttle to local attractions. $$–$$$

Westin Pasadena (626-792-2727; www.starwoodhotels.com/westin), 191 N. Los Robles. This stylish chain property boasts an Arts and Crafts design, with commodious guest rooms, a heated outdoor pool, sauna, workout facilities, hot tub, and in-room safes. Dining is at **Ventanas,** which offers California cuisine for breakfast and lunch, and at the **Living Room Lobby and Bar,** a clubby restaurant open for dinner. $$$

✷ Where to Eat

DINING OUT

Pasadena

Arroyo Chop House (626-577-7463; www.arroyochophouse.com), 536 S. Arroyo Pkwy. Open daily for dinner. This is a steak and martinis kind of place, and the locals like it that way. The restaurant offers an extensive wine list, a relaxing patio for outdoor dining, and live piano music nightly. Start with the pancetta-wrapped scallops or the classic chopped salad with hunks of bacon and blue cheese. For an entrée, choose among a Kansas City New York rib eye, double-cut lamb chops, or a whole main lobster. Items are à la carte, so round out the meal with Lyonnaise potatoes or the dreamy mac and cheese with Black Forest ham. All desserts are created in-house, so save room for the ultrarich chocolate pecan pie. $$$

PRICE KEY FOR A TYPICAL ENTRÉE:

$	$10 and under
$$	$11–20
$$$	$21–30
$$$$	$31 and up

Bistro 45 (626-795-2478; www.bistro45.com), 45 S. Mentor Ave. Open daily for lunch and dinner. This lovely bistro has the look and feel of a European eatery and the charm of a small-town café. Order favorites like braised short ribs served with creamed spinach and roasted mushrooms, bouillabaisse that is thick with shellfish, and classic steak and fries served with French green beans. This restaurant enhances the cozy atmosphere by banning cell phone conversations in the dining room—a welcome rule, in my book, but beware if this presents a problem for you. $$–$$$

Bistro 561 (626-405-1561; www.561restaurant.com), 561 Green St. Open Mon.–Fri. for lunch and dinner. Staffed by culinary students from the local Le Cordon Bleu College of Culinary Arts, 561 is a teaching restaurant that offers patrons the chance to experience up-and-coming culinary talents, who work in the restaurant as a prerequisite for graduation. Menus change regularly, but the focus is on California cuisine, healthy cooking, environmental sustainability, and classic French techniques. Tips from diners go to the school's scholarship fund. As one might imagine, the quality varies, but thanks to the stewardship of the instructors, the level of creativity and passion for food is uniformly high. $$$

✪ **The Dining Room** (626-568-3700; www.pasadena.langhamhotels.com), 1401 S. Oak Knoll Ave. Open Tues.–Sat. for dinner. Fans of TV's *Top Chef* will remember Chef Michael Voltaggio, who just edged out his brother to win the high-stakes cooking competition. It seems a bit incongruous that this brash maverick chef is at the helm of The Dining Room, part of the spectacular **Langham Huntington Hotel and Spa,** which exudes tradition and staid propriety, whereas Voltaggio seems to be all about pushing the envelope. Four- and eight-course tasting menus show off Voltaggio's skills at molecular gastronomy, but a quick peek at the menu confirms that this talented young culinary artist has managed to balance the offerings, so that there is something to please every palate: Traditionalists will find comforting favorites like suckling pig with polenta, lamb served with young chickpeas, and dreamy chocolate soufflé. Experimentalists will thrill to pork belly with sweet potato preserves and peanut butter powder, beef cheeks with garlic froth, and veal sweetbreads tempura with kale puree. The food takes center stage, and together with the elegant surroundings and gracious service explain why this is a Michelin-starred restaurant. $$$$

El Portal (626-795-8553; www.elportalrestaurant.com), 695 E. Green St. Open daily for dinner, Mon. for lunch only. In the Playhouse district, this Mexican restaurant offers specialties like halibut steak with guacamole, shrimp enchiladas, and Yucatan-style tamales. Be sure to try the unusual *panuchos,* small corn tortillas filled with black beans, fried, and smothered in grilled chicken and avocado slices. The restaurant features mariachis every Fri. and Sat. evening. $$

Yujean Kang's (626-585-0855; www.yujeankangs.com), 67 N. Raymond Ave. Open daily for lunch and dinner. In Old Pasadena, Yujean Kang's offers gourmet Chinese food that is fresh and inventive. There are many options for vegetarians here: try the Chinese risotto with black mushrooms and mustard greens or the cleverly named Ants on a Tree—spicy glass noodles accented with black sesame seeds. Carnivores shouldn't miss the crispy fried fish with garlic and spinach. The restaurant offers a nice wine and beer selection, and the desserts are intriguing, especially the warm red bean pancake served with ice cream. $$

EATING OUT

Pasadena

✪ **Pie and Burger** (626-795-1123; www.pienburger.com), 913 E. California Blvd. Open daily for breakfast, lunch, and dinner. This old-fashioned diner opened in 1963 and hasn't changed much since: there's even a waitress who's been with the place since the beginning. As the name implies, the joint is locally famous for burgers and pie, especially the seasonal strawberry pies. $

🍸 **Red White & Bluezz** (626-792-4441; www.redwhitebluezz.com), 70 S. Raymond Ave. Open daily for lunch and dinner. In Old Pasadena, this restaurant/wine bar/jazz lounge offers live music, a wide-ranging wine list, and amazing salads and sandwiches, like the barbecue chicken sandwich with maple barbecue sauce, applewood bacon, and sweet potato fries. $–$$

🍸 **Smitty's Grill** (626-792-9999; www.smittysgrill.com), 110 S. Lake Ave. Open Mon.–Fri. for lunch, daily for dinner. In the South Lake district, Smitty's offers comfort food in a homey atmosphere (which could well qualify as fine dining). Specialties include chicken potpie, cornmeal-crusted rainbow trout, liver and onions, and organic turkey burgers. $$

✷ Entertainment

CLUBS 🍸 **The Bar** (626-568-3700; www.pasadena.langhamhotels.com), 1401 S. Oak Knoll Ave., Pasadena. At the **Langham Huntington Hotel,** this elegant watering hole is perfect for quiet conversation over well-crafted cocktails like the Pasadena Sidecar and the refreshing Bangkok Basil.

Y **The Ice House Comedy Club** (626-577-1894; www.icehousecomedy.com), 24 N. Mentor Ave., Pasadena. Established in 1960, and one time venue for Robin Williams, Lily Tomlin, and Steve Martin, the Ice House still draws top comics and big crowds.

Y **Lucky Baldwin's** (626-795-0652; www.luckybaldwins.com), 17 S. Raymond Ave., Pasadena. This traditional British pub offers a huge selection of beers and nice fish-and-chips.

THEATERS ✪ Y **Gold Class Cinema** (626-639-2260; www.goldclasscinema.com), 42 Miller Alley, Pasadena. Pasadena offers a number of vintage movie theaters, but this one has added value: the seats are large comfy recliners equipped with pillows and blankets, and unobtrusive servers will bring drinks and dinner while you watch the latest flicks.

Pasadena Civic Auditorium (626-449-7360; www.thepasadenacivic.com), 300 E. Green St., Pasadena. This three-thousand-seat theater dating to 1931 is home to the Pasadena Symphony. The Civic is also the venue for Broadway musicals and international ballet companies, and has hosted the People's Choice Awards and the Emmy Awards.

Pasadena Playhouse (626-356-PLAY; www.pasadenaplayhouse.org), 39 S. El Molino Ave., Pasadena. The historic 1924 Pasadena Playhouse is a lovely small venue that hosts acclaimed regional theatrical performances. Sadly, as this book went to press, the playhouse was suffering serious financial problems. Check the Web site for up-to-date information on the status of ongoing performances.

✷ Selective Shopping

Pasadena is an antiques lover's dream, thanks to hundreds of dealers in the city. Fair Oaks Avenue and Green Street offer the greatest concentration of shops in the area, with the **Pasadena Antique Center and Annex** boasting 33,000 square feet of furniture, jewelry, and rare books. Throughout Old

DOWNTOWN PASADENA

Courtesy of Pasadena Convention and Visitors Bureau

Pasadena visitors will find boutique shops and major retail stores. Notable shopping districts include the **Paseo Colorado,** an open-air complex of more than 50 streetfront shops, and **One Colorado,** a courtyard-style shopping and entertainment complex.

✷ Special Events

(in the Greater Los Angeles Area)

January: **Tournament of Roses** (626-449-ROSE, www.tournamentofroses.com), better known as the Rose Parade, in Pasadena; reserve bleacher seating well in advance, or camp out overnight along the parade route on Colorado Blvd. **Australia Week** (www.australia-week.com) is a weeklong celebration of everything Aussie in West Hollywood.

February: **The Oscars** (www.oscars.org), the fabulous Academy Awards ceremony at the Kodak Theatre in Hollywood; lucky lottery winners can line the red carpet route and watch A-listers arrive in all their finery.

March: **Lantern Festival** (213-485-8567), downtown, marks the end of the Chinese New Year Celebration with lantern-making workshops and traditional food and entertainment. The **Los Angeles Marathon** (www.lamarathon.com), throughout the city, is the fourth-largest marathon in the country, drawing more than 25,000 runners a year.

April: **Blessing of the Animals** (213-625-5045; www.olvera-street.com/html/fiestas.html), downtown, is an Olvera St. tradition. On the day before Easter, pet owners line up at La Placita at El Pueblo Historic Monument for a sprinkling of holy water for their furry friends. **Cherry Blossom Festival Southern California** (www.cherryblossomfestivalsocal.org), along the streets of Little Tokyo in downtown, includes live taiko drumming, kimono fashion shows, and cultural craft activities, in addition to a huge assortment of food. At the **Sonkran Festival** (www.watthaiusa.com), the Thai New

ROSE PARADE

Courtesy of Pasadena Convention and Visitors Bureau

LOS ANGELES COUNTY MARATHON

Year, fireworks punctuate a three-day celebration throughout the streets of Hollywood.

May: The **Russian Cultural Festival** (www.weho.org/russianculturalmonth) is a family-friendly free day of entertainment, music, Russian crafts, and food sampling in West Hollywood. **Cinco de Mayo Celebration** (213-628-1274; www.olvera-street.com/fiestas.html), at La Placita in El Pueblo de Los Angeles, downtown, celebrates the Mexican victory over the French in 1862, including folk music, piñata breakings, and tons of food.

June: **Los Angeles Gay Pride Festival and Parade** (www.lapride.org) is a two-day celebration of diversity that culminates in a parade down Santa Monica Blvd. in West Hollywood. **Los Angeles Film Festival** (866-345-6337; www.lafilmfest.com), in Westwood, is a 10-day festival held in historic movie theaters in Westwood Village as well as theaters on the UCLA campus, showcasing the best in independent film.

July: **July Fourth Fireworks Spectacular** (www.hollywoodbowl.com) is a patriotic concert at the Hollywood Bowl capped off by a spectacular fireworks display in the skies over Hollywood. The **Lotus Festival** (213-485-1310, www.laparks.org), held at the lotus grove at the lake in Echo Park, celebrates Asian and Pacific Islander culture, including music, food, dance, and dragon boats.

August: **Nisei Week Japanese Festival** (213-687-7193), in Little Tokyo (downtown), includes exhibits of anime, taiko drumming, food, and a parade.

October: **West Hollywood Halloween Carnival** (www.westhollywoodhalloween.com), in West Hollywood, is perhaps the wildest Halloween celebration in the city.

December: ***The Nutcracker*** (www.losangelesballet.org) is performed annually by the LA Ballet at a handful of venues around town.

Palm Springs 5

PALM SPRINGS

A glimpse of the ubiquitous midcentury modern architecture and the Las Vegas aura that is an integral part of the ambiance of Palm Springs, and it's hard not to think of Frank Sinatra, Sammy Davis Jr., and the rest of the Rat Pack hanging out at some swanky bar, drinking martinis and smoking too much, as they did in the early days of Palm Springs. But the times have changed, the area has exploded in population and in number of visitors, and the vibe is more welcoming than ever before of alternative lifestyles. Nevertheless, the romance of the area still resonates. TV and movie A-listers continue to flock to the desert to chill out—as do couples and families from Southern California who are looking for a quick and easy getaway. In addition, the area is extremely welcoming to (and popular with) the LGBT community.

The diversions in the area have morphed over the past few decades to reflect the new, broader appeal of the valley, and in addition to plenty of sun-drenched pools and hip lounge spaces, now Palm Springs and the other desert cities nearby offer even more world-class dining, four-star resorts, and a fair share of culture to balance out the otherwise overwhelmingly hedonistic pleasures. There are numerous outdoor activities here, including an embarrassment of riches when it comes to golf courses; hiking in some of the loveliest high-desert scenery anywhere in the world; and plenty of flat terrain for biking. Especially in the family-friendly resorts to the east of Palm Springs (e.g., Indian Wells), families will find lots to entertain themselves, from outrageous water parks (some contained within the confines of expansive resort properties), to educational zoos and museums, to fun accommodation options designed with kids in mind.

MT. SAN JACINTO IN THE SNOW

Families will also appreciate the friendly atmosphere. Maybe it's the clean, dry air; maybe it's being surrounded by gorgeous mountains and

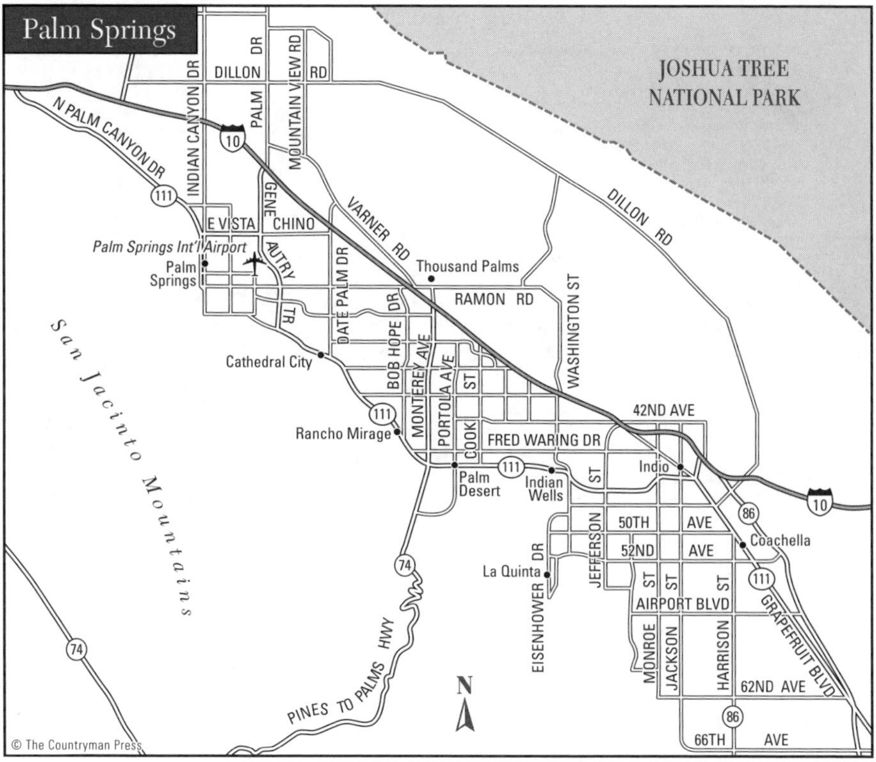

blue sky every day. Whatever the explanation, people in Palm Springs are uncommonly nice. Service in restaurants, bars, hotels, and shops is almost always personal and unhurried, and it isn't at all uncommon to strike up a conversation with total strangers over the juiciest steak in town, the most relaxing pool, or the most entertaining cabaret show.

Of course, it's not just the people who are warm: the weather in the desert is almost always between 10–30 degrees warmer than on the coast. Most days in winter and early spring, this means toasty days by the pool when on the same days in LA or San Diego you'd be bundled up and indoors. (On those rare occasions when it is too cold to be outside, the sidewalk cafés and pool decks of Palm Springs are well equipped with fire pits and outdoor heat lamps.) In late spring through early fall, this means *swelter*. Temperatures can top out at 120 degrees Fahrenheit, and although locals will assure you that because it is a "dry heat" it is more bearable than more humid climes, hot is hot. To ameliorate the worst of the season, most businesses have installed misters that will spray you with cool vapors as you walk by on the sidewalks in front, and all major resorts employ similar misters to make sitting by the pool bearable. Of course, a frozen cocktail in hand doesn't hurt, either.

GUIDANCE **Palm Desert Visitor Center** (760-568-1441; www.palm-desert.org), 72-567 CA 111, at El Paseo Intersection 59. Open daily 9–5. Find maps and

DOWNTOWN PALM SPRINGS

information on attractions, shopping, hiking, and dining here. There is also a gift shop on the property.

MORE PHONE NUMBERS Fire/medical assistance: 760-323-8181

Road conditions: 800-427-7623

Sheriff/police: 760-323-8116

Weather: 760-345-3711

MEDICAL EMERGENCIES For immediate emergency assistance, dial 911. For other medical emergencies, consult the local hospitals:

Eisenhower Medical Center (760-837-8953), 74785 CA 111, Suite 100, Indian Wells.

Eisenhower Medical Center (760-340-3911), 39-000 Bob Hope Dr., Rancho Mirage.

Desert Regional Medical Center (760-323-6511), 150 N. Indian Canyon Dr., Palm Springs.

GETTING THERE *By air:* Visitors can fly directly to the area via the **Palm Springs International Airport** (760-318-3800), 3400 E. Tahquitz Canyon Way, Palm Springs. Most guests flying in, however, arrive through Los Angeles (about 100 miles away) or Las Vegas (about 250 miles away) and drive from there.

By bus: **Greyhound** buses arrive in Palm Springs via routes from Los Angeles, San Diego, Phoenix, Las Vegas, and a number of smaller cities.

By car: To reach Palm Springs from Southern California, most folks drive in via I-10, exiting on CA 111, which drops down from the mountain pass into the Coachella Valley. Running along CA 111 (which changes in town to Palm Canyon Drive) southeast from Palm Springs are Cathedral City, a largely residential area;

Rancho Mirage; Palm Desert; Indian Wells, an upscale, family-friendly resort; and La Quinta, a recent favorite with golfers.

By train: **AMTRAK** trains run from the west via the *Southwest Chief* line, with stops in San Bernardino, Barstow, and Victorville. You can also take the *Sunset Limited* line, which runs from LA three times a week and arrives directly in Palm Springs in about two and a half hours.

GETTING AROUND *By bus:* The **Sunline Transit Agency** (760-343-3451; www.sunline.org) serves the greater Coachella Valley, from Palm Springs south to Indian Wells and beyond to farther-flung cities like Indio and Oasis. Fares range from $1 for adults to 50 cents for seniors, with additional discounts for disabled bus riders. Be sure to have exact fare, because bus drivers can't make change.

By car: Palm Springs and the surrounding cities are extraordinarily easy to navigate. The main corridor through all the cities is CA 111, which turns into Palm Canyon Dr. The road cuts through the heart of downtown Palm Springs and provides entry to the other desert cities as well. Exits are well marked, and there is plenty of parking, both on the street and in off-site parking garages. Note that for a few miles downtown, the road is one-way (running south). You are likely to hit a bit of evening rush-hour traffic on weekdays, especially driving into the outlying cities like Rancho Mirage and Indian Wells, but aside from frequent stops on Palm Canyon Drive because of ubiquitous traffic lights, it isn't something anyone who has experienced *true* traffic in Southern California should be concerned about.

✷ To See

HISTORICAL SITES ✐ **Cornelia White House** (760-323-8276), in the Village Green Heritage Center, 219-223 S. Palm Canyon Dr., Palm Springs. Open Wed. and Sun. noon–3, Thurs.–Sat. 10–4. Built in 1893, this one time home to early Palm Springs pioneer Cornelia White is made entirely of railroad ties. Inside are period furnishings, including one of the first telephones in Palm Springs. Adults $1, children free.

✐ **McCallum Adobe** (760-323-8276), in the Village Green Heritage Center, 219-223 S. Palm Canyon Dr., Palm Springs. Open Wed. and Sun. noon–3, Thurs.–Sat. 10–4. The oldest remaining structure in Palm Springs, the McCallum Adobe was built in 1884 for the first permanent nonnative settler to the region, John McCallum. Inside find a collection of vintage photographs, tools, books, and native handicrafts. Adults $1, children free.

AQUA CALIENTE CULTURAL MUSEUM

MUSEUMS ✐ **Aqua Caliente Cultural Museum** (760-778-1079), in the Village Green Heritage Center, 219-223 S. Palm Canyon Dr., Palm Springs. Open Wed.–Sat. 10–5, Sun.

noon–5. This tiny museum in downtown Palm Springs offers rotating exhibits highlighting the history and culture of the Agua Caliente band of Cahuilla Indians. Admission is free.

✐ **Children's Discovery Museum of the Desert** (760-321-0602; www.cdmod.com), 71701 Gerald Ford Dr., Rancho Mirage. Open daily 10–5; closed Mon. May–Dec. Find more than 50 hands-on exhibits for the ankle-biter set; among the most popular activities in the museum is the chance to dress up and act the role of a pizza maker, veterinarian, or motorcycle police offer. Admission $8.

✐ **Palm Springs Air Museum** (760-778-6262; www.palmspringsairmuseum.org), 745 N. Gene Autry Trail, Palm Springs. Open daily 10–5. Check out the extensive collection of World War II combat aircraft, as well as photographs and other memorabilia of the era. Kids will enjoy the flight simulators and planned children's activities (scheduled somewhat sporadically). Adults $12, children $10.

✪ **Palm Springs Art Museum** (760-322-4800; www.psmuseum.org), 101 Museum Dr., Palm Springs. Open Tues.–Sun. 10–5, with occasional late hours on Thurs. Permanent collections as well as temporary exhibits include modern and contemporary art, Native American art, and Mesoamerican artifacts. Be sure to check out the dazzling contemporary glass art in the permanent collection. Also on-site is the Annenberg Theater, which offers free films and lectures, and a charming outdoor sculpture garden. Adults $12.50, seniors $10.50, students $5, children under 12 free.

✐ **Ruddy's General Store Museum** (760-327-2156), in the Village Green Heritage Center, 219-223 S. Palm Canyon Dr., Palm Springs. Open Thurs.–Sun. Oct.–June and Sat.–Sun. July–Sept. This re-creation of a 1930s general store features barrels filled with crackers, bottles of sarsaparilla, and display cases full of unctions, balms, and tinctures—all original items that would have been for sale in a general store in this era. Admission $1.

✷ To Do

BICYCLING The valley throughout the Palm Springs area is flat, making it ideal for bicycling—and you'll find the activity is popular with athletes as well as families out for a little fun. Well-marked bike trails crisscross Palm Springs and neighboring cities; pick up detailed bike lane maps at the Palm Springs Leisure Center (760-323-4712), 401 S. Pavilion Way. If you prefer to head out with a group, check out these tour agencies:

Adventure Bike Tours (760-328-0282), 70250 Chappel Rd., Rancho Mirage. Rent a wide variety of bikes, including two-seaters and baby sidecars, at Adventure Bike Tours, and then sign up for an easy tour of the backstreets of Palm Springs or more rigorous adventures that traverse the desert scenery.

Big Wheel Bike Tours (760-779-1837; www.bwbtours.com). P.O. Box 4185, Palm Springs, CA 92263. The price of a tour with this group includes bikes, helmets, snacks, and a Palm Springs specialty: a date shake. An interesting tour option is the Earthquake Canyon Express, which is a 20-mile trip through the San Andreas fault zone amid typical desert scenery.

GOLF Thanks to 350 days of sunshine and spectacular scenery, the Palm Springs area is a golf haven, with dozens of courses to meet the expectations of duffers of all skill levels. This list of my favorites represents only a fraction of what's available in the valley.

WIND POWER

Driving into the Coachella Valley from the west, visitors are often struck by the array of huge white wind turbines that are scattered in abundance on either side of the highway. Along the San Gorgonio Mountain pass and stretching to the San Bernardino Mountains, there are more than four thousand of the turbines, which are actually quite lovely when in motion, resembling giant kinetic sculptures. Wind turbines are a type of windmill that is an increasingly popular source of alternative energy, the largest of which is 150 feet tall, with blades as wide. A typical wind turbine can produce 300 kilowatts of power a day, enough to power the average household for about a week.

Classic Club (760-601-3600; www.classicclubgolf.com), 75-200 Classic Club Blvd., Palm Desert. Considered among the top golf courses in the country by publications like *Golfweek* and *Golfweek Travel Annual,* Classic Club offers a full-service golf shop and two premium courses (somewhat archaically designated as the men's course and the ladies' course). Green fee: $125.

⇻ **Desert Willow Golf Resort** (760-346-7060; www.desertwillow.com), 38-995 Desert Willow Rd., Palm Desert. Voted one of the best places to play by *Golf Digest,* this club offers two challenging courses landscaped with native plants and irrigated using recycled water. On-site is the well-respected **Palm Desert Golf Academy,** which offers comprehensive programs for all skill levels. Green fee: $65–100.

CLASSIC CLUB

Photo by Chris Miller

Mountain Vista Golf Club at Sun City (760-200-2200; www.scpdca.com/golf), 38-246 Del Webb Blvd., Palm Desert. This expansive course offers 36 holes designed by golf legend Billy Casper. The course is home to a fall and winter golf clinic, which offers classes in putting, bunker play, and pitching, all for the low cost of $30 per week. Green fee: $81.

INSIDER TIP: Tee times and discounted green fees are available at most golf resorts (see *Lodging*), even for the most popular courses. Check with your hotel concierge for preferred reservations.

✪ **PGA West Resort Courses** (760-564-5729; www.pgawest.com), 56-150 PGA Blvd., La Quinta. Home of the annual Bob Hope Classic, the PGA West Resort stretches out over more than 2,000 acres and offers six courses and 109 holes of championship golf, designed by the likes of Arnold Palmer, Pete Dye, and Greg Norman. The surroundings are breathtakingly beautiful, nestled next to Coral Mountain and adorned with lush landscaping and abundant water features. Green fee varies by course.

Rancho Mirage Country Club (760-324-4711; www.ranchomiragegolf.com), 38-500 Bob Hope Dr., Rancho Mirage. Ideal for the beginner and the more experienced player alike, this beautiful course offers unexpected challenges and stunning desert scenery. Green fee: $25–59.

Silver Rock Resort (760-777-8884; www.palmsprings.com/golf/silverrock), 78179 Ahmanson Lane, La Quinta. An Arnold Palmer Classic Course, the relatively new (ca. 2005) 18-hole Silver Rock offers the longest layout in Palm Springs, with challenging holes and plenty of water play. Green fee: $85–135.

Tahquitz Creek Legend (760-328-1005; www.tahquitzgolfresort.com), 1885 Golf Club Dr., Palm Springs. Two 18-hole golf courses, with stunning views of the San Jacinto Mountains, represent a relative bargain for desert golfing. Guests will find more than 60 bunkers and an island fairway on this mature course, which is a favorite with locals. Green fee: $35–74.

✪ **The Trilogy at La Quinta** (760-771-0707; www.palmsprings.com/golf/intrawest), 60-151 Trilogy Pkwy., La Quinta. At the base of the Santa Rosa Mountains, the Trilogy at La Quinta has been awarded four stars by *Golf Digest.* The 18-hole course offers five sets of tees, which ensures a challenge for every skill level. Green fee: $79–89.

SPAS ✪ **Aqua Serena Spa and Salon** (760-674-4100; www.grandchampions.hyatt.com), 44600 Indian Wells Lane, Indian Wells. On-site at the **Hyatt Grand Champions Resort,** the Aqua Serena Spa uses indigenous botanicals and natural remedies from the desert to soothe away stress and promote relaxation. The spa is surrounded by calming, cooling water and highlights clean-lined décor. Specialty treatments include a date and sugar massage, a self-heating desert mud wrap, and a highly recommended desert stone massage.

Estrella Spa (760-318-3000; www.viceroypalmsprings.com/spa), 415 S. Belardo Rd., Palm Springs. At the **Viceroy,** the Estrella Spa specializes in numerous aromatherapy treatments, including the cinnamon and vanilla exfoliation and massage package; the Estrella Scrub, with sage, lemongrass, and lavender; and the white tea and ginseng facial for men.

PALM SPRINGS AERIAL TRAMWAY

One of the magical aspects of Southern California is the spectacular variety of scenery and terrain, and nowhere is this variety more striking than in Palm Springs, where you can move from the desert floor to the top of Mount San Jacinto at 8,500 feet in less than 10 minutes via the world's largest rotating suspended tram. Catch the tram northwest of downtown Palm Springs, at the end of Chino Canyon (off CA 111; 760-325-1391; www.pstramway.com). You'll purchase a ticket for a given tram, scheduled every 10 minutes, and wait in a somewhat crowded lobby to board. Once you step inside, don't worry about getting the "best spot"; the tram floor constantly rotates, so your view will change as you travel along the cable. And what a view it is—whether looking down into the valley or up into the craggy mountain, when visibility is good, views are astonishing. Although getting there is half the fun, the destination isn't bad, either: at the top you'll find the Santa Rosa and San Jacinto Mountains National Monument, just miles from the mountaintop resort of Idyllwild. There are more than 50 miles of trails, perfect for hiking in the warm weather and even better for snowshoeing or cross-country skiing in the winter. Hint: It can be as much as 30 degrees cooler on the top of the mountain than at the foot, so dress accordingly. Open 8–5 (last tram up is at 4). Adults $22.95, children $15.95.

PALM SPRINGS AERIAL TRAMWAY

Photo courtesy of Jon Preimesberger

✪ **Parker Palm Springs Spa** (760-770-5000; www.theparkerpalmsprings.com /spa), 4200 E. Palm Canyon Dr., Palm Springs. Rated by *Condé Nast Traveler* as one of the 10 best spas in the country, this hotel spa in the **Parker** bills itself as the only "yacht club" in the desert. Spa personnel greet guests with "welcome aboard," and the nautical theme carries throughout the décor. The real draw is the amazing indoor pool with a Moroccan ambiance and indoor cabana. In addition to traditional treatments, the spa offers free yoga classes for guests.

SpaTerre (760-778-6690; www.psriviera.com/riviera_spa.aspx), 1600 N. Indian Canyon Dr., Palm Springs. Located in the **Riviera Resort and Spa,** this lovely facility offers full-service treatments, including massages, facials, wraps, and scrubs. Particularly enchanting is the whirlpool room that is available to patrons before or after treatments, which includes two large heated pools, light steam rooms with aromatherapy, and surprisingly comfortable (and popular) stone lounging benches.

✪ **The Well Spa** (760-837-1652; www.miramonteresort.com/luxury-spa-resort /palm-desert-spas.php), 45000 Indian Wells Lane, Indian Wells. Part of the **Miramonte Resort and Spa,** this luxury facility offers unusual treatments like Watsu, which is a massage while immersed in warm shallow water; wine baths; and the Pittura Festa, which is described as a "colored mud-painting party." The Tuscan-style surroundings and exceptional service make this one of the top spas in the country.

THEME PARKS AND ZOOS ✐ **Knott's Soak City Palm Springs** (760-327-0499; www.knotts.com/public/park/soakcity/palmsprings), 1500 S. Gene Autry Trail, Palm Springs. Open times and days vary by season. This expansive water park is *heaven* during the sweltering desert summer (temperatures in the Coachella Valley can top out at 120 degrees!), especially for tweens and teens. Favorite thrill rides include the seven-story Tidal Wave Tower (a near-vertical water slide), the ever-popular 600-foot lazy Sunset River, and the 50-foot Sea Snake tube slide. Adults $31, children 11 and under $20.

✪ ✐ **The Living Desert** (760-346-5694; www.livingdesert.org), 47900 Portola Ave., Palm Springs. Open daily 9–5. This combination zoo and botanical garden is home to more than 450 animals indigenous to the deserts of North America and Africa, including bighorn sheep, mountain lions, and cheetahs. Also on display are hundreds of species of cacti and other plants native to the desert, arranged in thematic zones, such as the Butterfly Garden, the Barrel Cactus Garden, and the Cahuilla Indian Ethnobotanical Garden. Children should not miss the large model-train display and the fanciful merry-go-round. Adults $12.50, children $7.50.

> **INSIDER TIP:** Visit the Living Desert first thing in the morning, before temperatures soar in the largely shadeless park. Morning is the best time to see the animals as well, as many of them are lethargic in the heat.

✱ Green Space

GARDENS **Moorten Botanical Garden** (760-327-6555), 1701 S. Palm Canyon Dr., Palm Springs. Open daily 10–4; closed Wed. Look for more than three thousand plant varieties, crystal exhibits, and Native American artifacts. Adults $3, children $1.50.

NATURE PRESERVES **Coachella Valley Preserve** (760-343-1234; www.coachellavalleypreserve.org), Ramon Rd., off I-10, Thousand Palms Canyon. This 20,000-acre nature preserve system was designed to protect the Coachella Valley fringe-toed lizard, which is found nowhere else in the world. Visitors will find three separate sand dune ecosystems within the preserve, the largest of which cuts through the Indio Hills in Thousand Palms Canyon, at the north of the valley. The other two systems are at the western end of the valley, north of Palm Springs. Within each dune system are microecosystems that include creosote bush scrub, mesquite hummocks, and a variety of palm oases, the latter of which are lush green areas sometimes with small streams. Guests may visit the palm oases via a series of hiking paths, but the fragile dunes are protected from access. Admission is free.

Santa Rosa and San Jacinto National Monument (760-862-9984). One of the most striking natural features of the Palm Springs area are the rugged mountains that rise up dramatically from the desert floor. The Santa Rosa and San Jacinto Mountains top out at 10,834 feet. The national monument comprises 272,000

JOSHUA TREE NATIONAL PARK

Joshua Tree National Park is an easy day trip from Palm Springs. The park comprises more than a million acres that are sited between the high Mojave Desert and the low Colorado Desert, which happens to be the perfect habitat for the rare preserved Joshua trees for which the park is named. Wildlife abounds in this seemingly barren locale, including bobcats, bighorn sheep, and roadrunners. Favorite tourist sites include the Keys View vista point, which on clear days extends to the Salton Sea; Skull Rock, a spooky outcropping that really does look like its name implies; Cottonwood Springs, which in wetter months offers a small gushing waterfall; and Covington Flats, which contains some of the largest Joshua trees in the park. In springtime the park offers prime wildflower viewing, which generally begins with the large creamy blossoms (known as "candles") of the Joshua trees in late February. Colorful ground flowers come in by mid-March, and showy, waxy cacti bloom in late April or May. Year-round the park attracts thousands of rock climbers, who can find nearly limitless challenges here. And because of its remote location, this is also one of the best places in Southern California to observe the nighttime sky and is a favorite spot to watch meteor showers. For guests looking to experience the park for longer than a day trip, there are a handful of excellent campgrounds, but consider roughing it by backcountry camping: Joshua Tree has fewer camping restrictions than most national parks and will allow sites just about anywhere in the park, as long as they are at least 1 mile off the roadways and 500 feet from any trail. (Be sure to register for a free backcountry permit.) Single-day entry $5; seven-day vehicle pass $15.

acres and the two named distinct wilderness areas, and offers educational, biological, geological, and recreational resources, including extensive hiking trails, which in the snowy winter months provide prime cross-country skiing and snowshoeing opportunities. The easiest way to access the area from Palm Springs is via the **Palm Springs Aerial Tramway** (see the sidebar of the same name in this chapter). Admission included with the tram ride.

✱ Lodging

Indian Wells

✪ ✐ **Hyatt Grand Champions** (760-341-1000; www.grandchampions.hyatt.com), 44-600 Indian Wells Lane. Located adjacent to the magnificent 36-hole **Indian Wells Golf Resort,** this expansive resort is the epitome of desert relaxation. The extensive grounds, landscaped lushly with drought-resistant native plants and a generous helping of towering palm trees, are punctuated by seven pools, including a kids' pool with a water slide and an adults-only pool lined with private cabanas. Standard guest accommodations are spacious, light, and bright, with private balcony or patio, flat-screen TVs, and spalike bathrooms. The real delight here are the villas, private one- and two-bedroom options that include a dining area, a large living room with seating enough to entertain, and surprisingly large patios that are equipped with abundant outdoor furniture and private Jacuzzis. Many offer stunning views of the nearby San Jacinto Mountains, the lush golf course, and a human-made pond. On-site fine dining is at **Lantana,** which offers pleasant outdoor patio dining. $$$

PRICE KEY FOR A STANDARD ROOM:

$	$100 or less
$$	$101–150
$$$	$151–250
$$$$	$251 and up

OASIS POOL, HYATT GRAND CHAMPIONS

✐ **Renaissance Esmeralda Resort and Spa** (760-773-4444; www.renaissanceesmeralda.com), 44-400 Indian Wells Lane. In the exclusive Indian Wells resort, the four-star Renaissance Esmeralda delivers unparalleled amenities, including a full-service spa; 36 holes of championship golf; two fine-dining restaurants, the Italian **Sirocco** and **Cava,** which features California cuisine; three gorgeous swimming pools, including one that offers a sandy bottom; tennis courts; a state-of-the-art fitness facility; and lushly landscaped grounds with views of the Santa Rosa Mountains. The resort also offers a well-attended kids club, which entertains children with arts, crafts, cooking, games, and nature walks. Guest rooms are elegant and designed with clean lines and luxury in mind. $$$–$$$$

Palm Springs

▼ **Andreas Hotel** (760-327-5701; www.andreashotel.com), 227 N. Indian Canyon Dr. This 25-room historic hotel in downtown Palm Springs dates to 1935 and balances original architecture with Spanish-modern style. Rooms are cozy, and all offer fireplaces. Suites come equipped with oversized jetted tubs and patios. The lovely pool is literally outside the door of many of the rooms, and because the property is intimate in size, the lounge area and game room is generally quiet and reflective—unlike some larger properties, which can become party central during high season. The location is prime: walk to many of the best restaurants and bars in downtown Palm Springs. $$

▼ **Hotel California** (760-322-8855; www.palmspringshotelcalifornia.com), 424 E. Palm Canyon Dr. "You can check in anytime you like" into this tiny, charming hotel, which is a real bargain given its central location downtown. Rooms are large and furnished simply. The pool and spa are relaxing and quiet, and unlike some of the larger properties in the area, it is easy to secure a lounge chair. $–$$

🍸 **Hotel Zoso** (760-325-9676; www.hotelzoso.com), 150 S. Indian Canyon Dr. This edgy boutique hotel in the heart of downtown Palm Springs is all about clean lines, sensual pleasures, and high style. Contemporary furnishings, eye-catching artwork, and an abundance of space define both the public and private areas, which are simultaneously youthful and sophisticated. In short: this isn't your father's Palm Springs hotel. Summer pool parties attract a beautiful, hip crowd, and the on-site **Zlounge Supper Club and Cabaret** is a hot nightspot for locals and visitors. $$$

✪ **Parker Palm Springs** (760-321-4611; www.theparkerpalmsprings.com), 4200 E. Palm Canyon Dr. This chic property was once film star Gene Autry's private estate, and it retains an air of residential comfort in its overflowing gardens and private bungalows—but unless you are a guest, you will never have the chance to explore the property: this is where the Hollywood elite come for their privacy, and the Parker makes sure even the richest and most famous guests can unwind here without being bothered. Famed designer Jonathan Adler is responsible for the eclectic midcentury modern chic aesthetic. Check out the amazing on-site **Norma's** for breakfast and lunch, and the atmospheric **Mr. Parker's** for dinner, the latter of which is designed to look like Mick Jagger's moody 1979 Scottish castle. $$$$

🍸 ▼ **Riviera Resort and Spa** (760-327-8311; www.psriviera.com), 1600 N. Indian Canyon Dr. Located in downtown Palm Springs, this revitalized, rambling 1950s-era resort is the very definition of *fabulosity*. Low-slung two-story buildings radiate outward like spokes on a wheel, encircling the expansive free-form pool, which is the heart of the action, day and night. Comfy, brightly colored lounge furniture rings the water's edge, including lounge beds with canopies and overstuffed wicker pod chairs arranged around inviting fire pits. Public spaces are flamboyant, with glowing red lights and lots of glitz. Private spaces are just this side of overdone, with red faux-leather walls and oversized headboards. Bathrooms are well appointed, including many with deep soaking tubs and large showers (although don't expect multiple showerheads in

RIVIERA RESORT

this water-conserving desert oasis). Check out the on-site **Circa 59 Restaurant** and the decadent **Spa-Terre.** $$–$$$

Rancho Mirage

✪ ✐ **Rancho Los Palmas Resort and Spa** (866-423-1195; www.rancholaspalmas.com), 41-000 Bob Hope Dr. This kid-friendly resort offers opulent Tuscan décor that is sophisticated without being fussy, along with plenty of amenities for everyone in the family. For adults there is upscale dining at the **bluEmber,** which showcases fresh local ingredients in a California fusion style; relaxing adults-only pools and lushly landscaped grounds; as well as the fabulous **Spa Las Palmas,** which specializes in detoxifying desert mud treatments and antiaging facials. For children there is Spashtopia, a self-contained water park on the property that includes a 400-foot lazy river, two 100-foot water slides, a sandy beach for making sand castles, and water play zones for tiny ones. Best of all, the large resort wraps around the premier 27-hole Ted Robinson–designed golf course, which makes for stunning views even if no one in your party golfs. $$$–$$$$

Westin Mission Hills Resort and Spa (760-328-5955; www.starwoodhotels.com/westin), 21333 Dinah Shore Dr. This all-inclusive resort offers enough amenities to keep guests on the property throughout their visit, and the sophisticated, vaguely Asian-influenced design ensures that a stay of any length will be restful. The jewels of the property are two spectacular golf courses, one of which is the only Gary Player Signature course in the area. The serene grounds are heavily

CLOTHING-OPTIONAL RESORTS

There are a number of clothing-optional resorts in the Palm Springs area—some targeted to straight couples and some toward gay men. (Needless to say, these resorts do not allow children.) If no tan lines appeals to you, here are a couple of options:

- **CCBC Resort** (760-324-1350), 68-369 Sunair Rd., Cathedral City. For men.
- **Living Waters Spa** (866-329-9988), 13340 Mountain View Rd., Desert Hot Springs. For straight couples.
- **Sea Mountain Resort** (877-928-2827), Palm Springs (address is provided only to those with secured reservations). For straight couples.
- **The Terra Cotta Inn** (760-322-6059; www.sunnyfun.com), 2388 E. Racquet Club Rd., Palm Springs. For straight couples.
- **Triangle Inn** (800-732-7555; www.triangle-inn.com), Palm Springs (address is provided only to those with secured reservations). For men.

Courtesy of Rancho Los Palmas Resort and Spa
RANCHO LOS PALMAS RESORT

adorned with palms and water features, including three lovely pools (one for adults only) that are maintained at a comfortable 84 degrees year-round. The family-friendly free-form pool offers a 60-foot water slide, as well as private cabanas and poolside dining. There are seven impeccably maintained lighted tennis courts on property, as well as world-class workout facilities and the expansive **Spa at Mission Hills.** Every evening the hotel features Native American storytelling in the lobby lounge and patio, and in summer offers a kids' program that includes crafts, board games, and sports. $$$

✷ Where to Eat

DINING OUT

Indian Wells

The Grove Artisan Kitchen (760-341-7200), 45000 Indian Wells Lane. Open daily for breakfast, lunch, and dinner. Sustainable cuisine is all the rage throughout California, and the new Grove Artisan Kitchen in the **Miramonte Resort** leads the trend by promising farm-to-table freshness, organic produce, Pacific seafood, and free-range meats. Expect menus to change regularly, as ingredient availability varies, but when you can find them, don't miss the delicate Dungeness crabcake appetizers, the wild mushroom risotto, and the juicy lamb osso buco. If you save room for dessert, the strawberry shortcake is sublime. On Thurs. the restaurant features a tapas menu of small plates that offer a variety of treats, like candied walnuts with triple-cream Brie, braised short rib *shui mai* (delicate dumplings served with an Asian dipping sauce), and lobster quesadillas. $$–$$$

Le St. Germain (760-773-6511; www.lestgermain.com), 74985 CA 111. Open daily for dinner. A small shopping mall off the main highway going to Indian Wells seems an unlikely location for fine French cuisine, but Le St. Germain is full of surprises. The interior is a bit drab and, frankly, a little uninviting, but step outside to the adorable outdoor patio and dine beneath a canopy of trees in a setting that is reminiscent of the Luxembourg Gardens in Paris. There are traditional French dishes on offer, like bouillabaisse, wild mushroom soup, and garlicky escargots, but California-French fusion predominates; the chef offers twists on old favorites, like Maine lobster cocktail with mango, papaya, and passion fruit sauce; veal sweetbreads crusted with mustard and herbs; and pineapple-glazed duck breast. $$$$

Palmie (760-341-3200), 44491 Town Center Way. Open Mon.–Sat. for

PRICE KEY FOR A TYPICAL ENTRÉE:

$	$10 and under
$$	$11–20
$$$	$21–30
$$$$	$31 and up

dinner. This French bistro is also tucked into a strip mall in Indian Wells, behind a bland storefront facade. Although lacking in ambiance, the Francophile comfort food at Palmie makes the effort to find the place well worth it. (Coming north on Town Center, make your first left into the mall.) Try the two-cheese soufflé or the lobster ravioli for a meal, or come just for dessert: there are fresh creations daily, but look for the triplets of crème brûlée and the chocolate mousse. $$$

✪ **Sirocco** (760-346-9308), 44-400 Indian Wells Lane. Open daily for dinner. Located on the property of the pretty **Esmeralda Resort** in Indian Wells, Sirocco serves fine Italian cuisine in a sophisticated, formal atmosphere—with hefty prices to match. Service in the elegant dining room is stellar, making this one of the premier dining attractions in the Coachella Valley. True to its Venetian roots, Sirocco specializes in seafood, which is highlighted in the delicate saffron fettuccine with roasted sautéed shrimp, lobster, and crab, and in the incomparable Dover sole stuffed with lump crab. Venetians love their sweets, too: try the chocolate *panna cotta* with white chocolate cream, or the moist pound cake layered with cream and chocolate hazelnut filling and served with a chocolate liqueur sauce. $$$$

La Quinta

Amorè (760-777-1315; www.amore-dining.com), 47474 Washington St. Open daily for dinner. The exterior architecture of this upscale Italian bistro looks like something out of the *Jetsons*—all glass and odd angles. The interior is warmer and more welcoming, although evening crowds can be off-putting. The menu is extensive at Amorè, boasting versions of everyone's favorite Italian dishes, like tender rolled eggplant stuffed with ricotta cheese and fresh herbs that is baked in a tangy marinara; handmade pastas like the nostalgic linguine with white clam sauce; tender veal Piccata; and a melt-on-your-tongue lobster gnocchi. Carnivores will not want to miss the filet mignon, which is wrapped in a crispy thin pastry dough and served with melted Gorgonzola sauce. $$$

✪ Y **Arnold Palmer's Restaurant** (760-771-4653; www.arnoldpalmersrestaurant.com), 78164 Ave. 52. Open daily for dinner. The golf legend who owns this fine-dining establishment has left his mark on the décor, with trophies and personal memorabilia. The clubby atmosphere also boasts a fireplace in every room, stacked-stone walls, and sports-themed artwork floor to ceiling. Palmer himself comes here often, so if you're a fan, keep your eyes open for his private wine room and bar located within the restaurant. The seasonal menu includes fine steakhouse offerings in addition to favorites like sautéed sand dabs and Australian lamb chops. Don't miss the vanilla pound cake with apple sorbet and caramelized apples for dessert. The restaurant offers an extensive wine menu, including Arnold Palmer's own label. $$$

Palm Desert

Café des Beaux-Arts (760-346-0669; www.cafedesbeauxarts.com), 73640 El Paseo. Hours and days vary by season. This family-owned French sidewalk café across from the Gardens on El Paseo highlights fine art as well as fine food. A changing exhibit by local artists defines the décor, and a seasonal menu ensures that visitors never have the same experience twice. Start with traditional escargots bourguignon or mussels *marinière;* entrées include exceptional duck à l'orange and coquilles St. Jacques. A French café wouldn't be complete without decadent desserts: luscious options include chocolate profiteroles and crêpes suzette. $$–$$$

Palm Springs

✪ 🍸 **Circa 59** (760-327-8311; www.psriviera.com), 1600 N. Indian Canyon Dr. Open daily for breakfast, lunch, and dinner. Part of the **Riviera Hotel,** this glamorous restaurant offers three dining venues: an outside space overlooking the sparkling pool (especially pretty when lit at night by the numerous fire pits), a romantic covered patio with gauzy curtains, and the over-the-top retro-chic interior space that boasts red walls and black chandeliers. Service in this nostalgic property is exceptional. Don't miss the signature chorizo-stuffed dates wrapped in bacon and served in a tangy tomato sauce to start. Fun, reinterpreted side dishes include truffle French fries and the lobster mac and cheese. Although there are plentiful fish and even vegetarian options, at heart, this place is a steakhouse and offers up a succulent Roquefort-encrusted filet mignon served with whipped potatoes and asparagus tips, and rich short ribs served with sautéed mushrooms. Portions aren't overwhelming, so dessert remains a possibility: the hot chocolate cake with a side of bananas Foster offers the best of two dessert worlds. $$$

🍸 **Las Casuelas Terraza** (760-778-6744; www.lascasuelas.com), 222 S. Palm Canyon Dr. Days and hours vary by season. This festive restaurant boasts a colorful interior and outdoor patio dining in a 1920s-era Palm Springs casa. The family-owned restaurant has been serving up authentic and inventive Mexican specialties for more than 30 years, including *albondingas* soup with Mexican meatballs, fresh tamales (including my favorite sweet variety—with pineapple), pomegranate guacamole (with tangy pomegranate seeds mixed in with the avocado), and a wide variety of traditional soft tacos. Large portions ensure that no one goes home hungry, and live nightly entertainment makes dinner here an event. $$

✪ **Norma's** (760-770-5000; www.theparkerpalmsprings.com), 4200 E. Palm Canyon Dr. Open daily for breakfast and lunch. Located at the exclusive **Parker** hotel, Norma's has possibly the coolest breakfast menu ever. Ordering is ridiculously difficult, because what's not to love? Start with an order of Norma's donuts: tiny round versions of Mexican churros, dusted with sugar and cinnamon and served with freshly made lemon curd and blueberry jam. Then there's mango-papaya brown-butter cinnamon crêpes, seared lobster and asparagus omelets, lemon griddle cakes served with Devonshire cream, a chocolate Belgian waffle with a peanut butter and toffee crunch filling, eggs Benedict served with smoked salmon, and the decadent zillion-dollar lobster frittata—for $100 with 1 ounce of Sevruga caviar and $1,000 with 10 ounces. There is a small indoor dining area and a more expansive outdoor patio, which has lovely views to the Parker's exclusive grounds (which are otherwise off-limits to anyone but hotel guests). $$$

Rancho Mirage

🖉 **Babe's Bar-B-Que Grill and Brewhouse** (760-346-8738), 71800 CA 111. Open Mon.–Sat. for dinner. Inspired by the movie *Babe* (really!), this pig-centric restaurant serves up regional barbecue from around the country in a warm, inviting atmosphere. Try the Texas-inspired brisket, North Carolina–style pulled pork, and Kansas City baby back ribs, and wash it down with highbrow ales or a glass of

California wine from Napa, Temecula, or Paso Robles. Save room for a slice of bananas Foster cream pie or an old-fashioned biscuit shortcake drenched in seasonal fruit. $$

Kobe Japanese Steak House (760-324-1717; www.koberanchomirage.com), 69838 CA 111. Open daily for dinner. Enter this lovely Asian diner via a pathway that leads you past a serene Japanese garden and koi pond, musical water fountain, and a temple garden bell to a replica of a Japanese country inn. Inside the restaurant are entertaining teppanyaki-style grill-at-your table entrées like tiger prawns, Angus steak, and teriyaki chicken, served with vegetables, rice, miso soup, and green tea. $$$

EATING OUT

Cathedral City

Big Mama's Soul Food (760-324-8116), 68510 E. Palm Canyon Dr. Hours and days vary by season. Tucked into a strip mall amid car dealerships and fast-food chains (and on the way from downtown Palm Springs to the pricey Indian Wells resort area), this small restaurant serves authentic Southern-style food at modest prices. Specialties include baby back ribs (smoked on the property), deep-fried chicken wings, collard greens, fried okra (my personal favorite), and peach cobbler. The sweet tea is straight out of Alabama. $

Palm Springs

Blue Coyote Bar and Grill (760-327-1196; www.bluecoyote-grill.com), 445 N. Palm Canyon Dr. Open daily for lunch and dinner. Great Mexican cuisine and outdoor patio dining go hand in hand, and this restaurant in downtown Palm Springs offers both. In addition to killer margaritas, Blue Coyote offers specialties like *pollo* cilantro, a butterflied chicken breast stuffed

TOP 10 DAY IN PALM SPRINGS

1. Feast on chocolate, peanut butter, and toffee waffles at Norma's (see p. 251)
2. Ride the Palm Springs Aerial Tramway to the top of Mount San Jacinto (see p. 243)
3. Shop for antiques along Palm Canyon Drive in downtown Palm Springs (see p. 256)
4. Stroll through the photography exhibit at the Palm Springs Art Museum (see p. 240)
5. Lunch on mussels and fries on the sidewalk patio of Pomme Frite (see p. 253)
6. Slurp a frozen drink beside just about any pool at just about any resort (see pp. 246–249)
7. Luxuriate in a milk and honey body wrap and sugar exfoliation at Spa-Terre in the Riviera Resort (see p. 244)
8. Sup on steak and martinis at a poolside table at Circa 59 (see p. 251)
9. Stargaze in the evening
10. Overnight at a private villa at the Hyatt Grand Champions Resort (see p. 246)

with cheese; whiskey scallops; and Yucatan-style charbroiled lamb marinated in grapefruit juice. The restaurant offers live music in the evenings and three-course specials for under $30. $$

▼ **Hamburger Mary's** (760-778-6279; www.hamburgermarysps.com), 415 Palm Canyon Dr. Open daily for lunch and dinner. This kooky diner bills itself as a family restaurant "no matter who's in your family." The atmosphere is fun and kitschy, but the quality of the food is taken seriously: nearly everything is made fresh daily on the premises. As the name implies, hamburgers are the thing: the outrageous Buffy the Hamburger Slayer is a 0.5 pound of meaty goodness interspersed with garlic cloves and drizzled with red wine; the equally sublime Mac and Cheese Burger is a charbroiled patty topped with a hearty serving of homemade macaroni and cheese. There are even wild boar and antelope burgers here, as well as salmon patties and shrimp burgers. $$

▼ **Koffi** (760-322-7776; www.koffi coffee.com), 1700 S. Camino Real at E. Palm Canyon Dr. (second location at 515 N. Palm Canyon at Alejo). Open daily 5:30 AM–8 PM. An espresso café in chic surrounds, this neighborhood hangout has exceptional coffee, tea lattes, bakery items, and free Wi-Fi. $

Y **Pomme Frite** (760-778-3727; www.pomme-frite.com), 256 S. Palm Canyon Rd. Open daily for lunch and dinner. This friendly café on the main drag of Palm Springs offers up French and Belgian bistro food. When the weather is temperate, eat outside on the sidewalk café. Specialties include authentic country-style pâté with cornichons, mussels steamed in white wine and tomatoes, and hearty bouillabaisse. What really brings me to my knees are the authentic fries (any good Belgian can tell you that "French" fries are a misnomer—true fries originated in Belgium): they are fluffy and steaming on the inside and crispy and salty on the outside. $$

Rick's Restaurant (760-416-0090; www.ricksrestaurant.biz), 1973 N. Palm Canyon Dr. Open daily for breakfast and lunch. At this quintessential breakfast diner you'll be served a cup of coffee before you've even had the chance to open your menu. There are down-home specials like grits and biscuits and gravy, along with monster-sized cinnamon rolls, Eggs Norwegian (two poached eggs, lox, sliced tomato on an English muffin and topped with homemade hollandaise), and corned beef hash. Lunchtime specials include soup, salad, sandwiches, and burgers. This is where the locals go, and the staff treats everyone like a neighbor. $

Spunky Monkey Café (760-327-6415), 370 N. Palm Canyon Dr. Open daily for lunch and dinner. Look for the crazy green jungle facade on the main drag in Palm Springs, and you've found this tiny café, which specializes in juices and smoothies, as well as "jungle crust" pizzas and Caesar salad. Try the Pink Flamingo—strawberry, banana, and apple juice—or if you need a pick-me-up, check out Monkey

SPUNKY MONKEY CAFÉ

Dirt: a milk shake flavored with fresh espresso grounds. Very nice people run the place, but service can be slow. $

✷ Entertainment

CLUBS 🍸 ▼ **The Falls Martini Bar** (760-416-8664; www.palmsprings.com/dine/thefalls), 155 S. Palm Canyon Dr., Palm Springs. Inside the Falls Prime Steakhouse, this is a popular nightspot, especially during happy hour (5:30–7:30 Mon.–Sat. and all night on Sun.). Don't miss the dirty martini.

🍸 **Hair of the Dog** (760-323-9890; www.thehairofthedog.net), 238 N. Palm Canyon Dr., Palm Springs. The only English pub in Palm Springs, the Hair is a comfortable place to knock back a pint or two with friends, any time of day or night.

🍸 ▼ **Hunters** (760-323-0700; www.huntersnightclubs.com/palm_springs), 302 E. Arenas Dr., Palm Springs. Open daily. This popular gay video and dance bar keeps guests mingling with "show your undies" on Wed., "hottest man" contests on Fri., and a Sat. night special bottomless glass of champagne for $10.

🍸 ▼ **Peabody's Karoake Club** (760-322-1877), 134 S. Palm Canyon Dr., Palm Springs. Coffee bar and sidewalk café by day, Peabody's opens for karaoke Thurs.–Sat.

🍸 **Village Pub** (760-323-2375; www.palmspringsvillagepub.com), 266 S. Palm Canyon Dr., Palm Springs. This casual club offers live music seven days a week, dancing, big-screen TVs for catching sports action, pool tables, and foosball. There's no cover charge, and the pub grub is better than average.

THEATERS Annenberg Theater (760-325-4490), 101 Museum Dr., Palm Springs. Part of the **Palm Springs Art Museum** complex, the Annenberg is a moderate-sized venue that showcases music, dance, and theater productions.

Palm Canyon Theatre (760-323-5123; www.palmcanyontheatre.org), 538 N. Palm Canyon Dr., Palm

PALM SPRINGS CHORUS LINE

Courtesy Palm Springs Convention and Visitors Bureau

Springs. Offering affordable access to live theater, the Palm Canyon has been the venue for musicals, comedy improves, and Shakespeare for the past decade.

✪ **Plaza Theater** (760-327-0225; www.psfollies.com), 128 S. Palm Canyon Dr., Palm Springs. The historic Plaza in downtown Palm Springs is home to the infamous **Palm Springs Follies,** a Las Vegas–style music, dance, and comedy revue that features showgirls well into their golden years (although through the magic of make-up, good lighting, and even better genetics, guests would be hard-pressed to see any signs of aging among this energetic crew).

Range Rider's Cowboy Dinner Theater (760-329-0189; www.cowboydiners.com). With the promise of bringing singing cowboys back to the desert, the Range Riders offer a full meal with beverages, and a live musical revue starring Stetson-wearing cowpokes (and cowgirls). The show is staged at rotating venues throughout Palm Springs.

▼ **Thorny Theater** (760-325-0853), 2500 N. Palm Canyon Dr., Palm Springs. This small, alternative theater stages eclectic productions aimed at a gay audience. *All* shows include nudity and adult subject matter.

FEELING LUCKY? CASINOS IN PALM SPRINGS

It used to be that Southern Californians had to drive to Las Vegas to risk it all in the desert. In the past decade or so, however, Indian gaming casinos have sprung up throughout the Coachella Valley, and many offer world-class concert venues, hotels, and restaurants as well. Although this list isn't exhaustive (largely because new casinos seem to spring up overnight), these are among the largest and most popular in the area:

- **Aqua Caliente Casino Resort and Spa** (760-321-2000; www.hotwatercasino.com), 32250 Bob Hope Dr., Rancho Mirage. With nearly two thousand slot machines and video poker, high-limit gaming, and many wining and dining venues, this resort offers a true Vegas-style experience.
- **Morongo Casino, Resort and Spa** (888-667-6646; www.morongocasino.com), 49500 Seminole Dr., Coachella. In addition to traditional gaming machines and poker tables, guests will find a lazy river water feature on the property, along with a penthouse nightclub and bowling alley.
- **Spa Resort Casino** (888-999-1995; www.hotwatercasino.com), 100 N. Canyon Dr., Palm Springs. Located in downtown Palm Springs, this casino offers baccarat, poker, and high-stakes gaming tables.
- **Spotlight 29 Casino** (866-878-6729; www.spotlight29.com), 46200 Harrison Pl., Coachella. This large casino boasts more than 2,000 slot machines, 30 game tables, a lounge, and a spectacular concert showroom.

✷ Selective Shopping

Palm Springs and the surrounding neighborhoods of Palm Desert and Indian Wells are a mecca for shopaholics. Expect great antiques shopping along Palm Canyon Drive (the main drag of Palm Springs); check out the tiny **L. Smith Home Antiques** (760-844-2477), 861 N. Palm Canyon Drive, and the huge, museum-like **House 849** (760-325-7854; www.house849.com), 849 N. Palm Canyon Drive, just next door. Find luxury shopping that rivals Rodeo Drive on **El Paseo,** with three hundred specialty boutiques—including many jewelers—and upscale labels like Gucci, Tiffany, Brooks Brothers, and Coach. Slightly more affordable are the shops at **Westfield Palm Desert,** on CA 111 in Palm Desert, with favorites like Macy's and JCPenney. In Rancho Mirage, **The River** (760-341-2711; www.theriveratranchomirage.com), 71-800 CA 111, is a mixed-use entertainment and shopping venue that is built along a pretty waterway, which makes for a pleasurable browsing experience at such places as Bang and Olufsen, Bobby Chan's, and Borders Books and Music. Look for free concerts here throughout the year.

L. SMITH HOME ANTIQUES

✷ Special Events

(in Greater Palm Springs)

Note that every Thurs. evening (excluding holidays), the **Palm Springs Villagefest** closes down North Palm Canyon Dr. (between Amado and Baristo) to automobiles so that visitors and locals can stroll the streets in a party atmosphere.

January: **Bob Hope Chrysler Classic** (www.bhcc.com) in La Quinta is one of the largest, best-attended celebrity golf events in the country. **Palm Springs International Film Festival** (800-898-7256; www.psfilmfest.org) presents a great opportunity to see Hollywood A-listers.

February: **Desert Concours d'Elegance** (www.desertconcours.com), at the end of the month in La Quinta, draws hundreds of rare cars, including Aston Martins, Duesenbergs, and classic Packards.

March: **Festival of Native Film and Culture** (www.accmuseum.org) at the Aqua Caliente Cultural Museum in Palm Springs showcases films by Native Americans. **Dinah Shore Weekend** (www.clubskirts.com), in Palm Springs, is a four-day party that attracts thousands of lesbians from around the country.

April: The **White Party** (www.jeffreysanker.com), in midmonth in Palm Springs, is one of the largest, most exuberant gay festivals in the country, with more than 20,000 gay men in attendance, all wearing white, enjoying good company, music, and dancing.

May: The **Smooth Jazz Festival,** in Palm Springs, offers music and dinner under the stars.

GALLERY CRAWLING

Known as the "valley of art," thanks in large part to the extraordinary light that has attracted artists and art lovers for a century, Palm Desert is home to many fine galleries. If you're looking for an investment piece or just something that will look good over the sofa, check out the following: **Adagio Galleries** (800-268-2230; www.adagiogalleries.com), 73300 El Paseo; **Coda Gallery** (800-700-4661; www.codagallery.com), 73151 El Paseo; **Denise Roberge Gallery** (760-340-5045), 73995 El Paseo; **J. Willott Gallery** (760-568-3180; www.jwillott.com), 73190 El Paseo; and the **Edenhurst Gallery of Fine Art** (760-346-7900; www.edenhurstgallery.com), 73660 El Paseo.

September: The **Cinema Diverse** (www.cinemadiverse.org), presented by the Palm Springs Cultural Center, showcases LGBT filmmaking at its best.

December: **Festival of Lights Parade** (760-325-5749), in early Dec., runs through downtown Palm Springs and features lighted floats, festive music, and blinged-out tractors; arrive early to claim a spot (locals bring beach chairs by noon).

Santa Barbara 6

SANTA BARBARA

SANTA YNEZ VALLEY
WINE COUNTRY

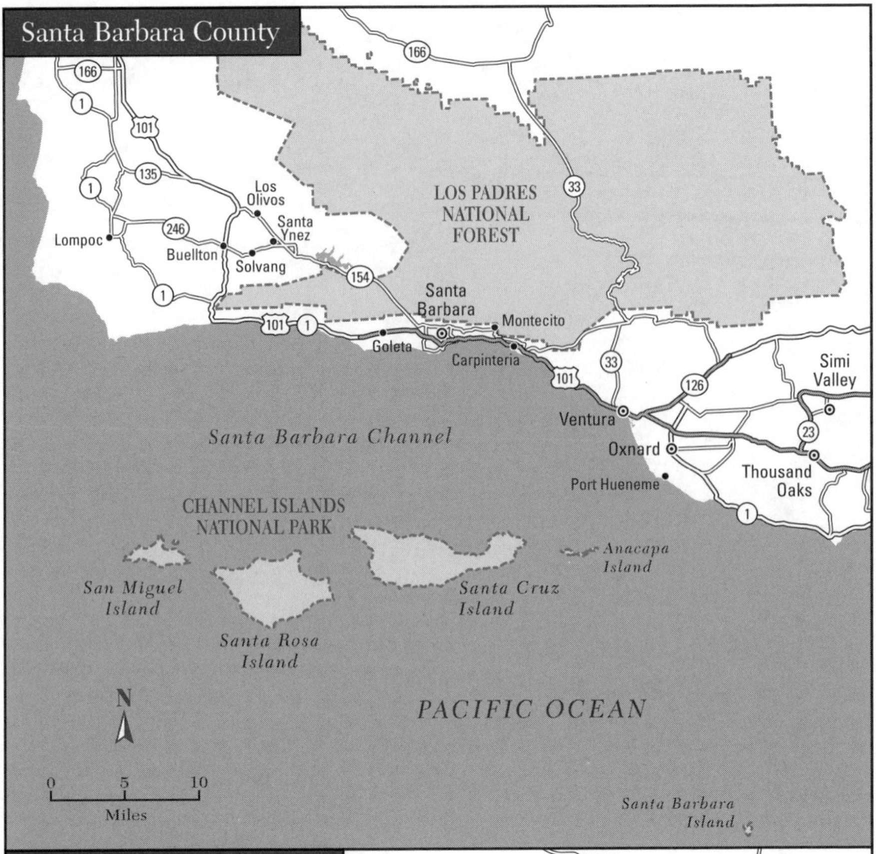
Santa Barbara County
166
1
101
135
246
154
33
126
23
Los Olivos
Santa Ynez
Lompoc
Buellton
Solvang
LOS PADRES NATIONAL FOREST
Santa Barbara
Montecito
Goleta
Carpinteria
Simi Valley
Ventura
Oxnard
Thousand Oaks
Port Hueneme
Santa Barbara Channel
CHANNEL ISLANDS NATIONAL PARK
San Miguel Island
Santa Rosa Island
Santa Cruz Island
Anacapa Island
PACIFIC OCEAN
Santa Barbara Island
N
0
5
10
Miles

Downtown Santa Barbara
ALAMEDA PADRES SERRA
SANTA BARBARA ST
E ANAPAMU ST
N MILPAS ST
W MISSION ST
STATE ST
DE LA VINA ST
S SALINAS ST
E MASON ST
E HALEY ST
E GUTIERREZ ST
101
SAN ANDRES ST
GARDEN ST
E YANONALI ST
E CABRILLO BLVD
W HALEY ST
CASTILLO ST
LOMA ALTA DR
W CARILLO ST
Stearns Wharf
Santa Barbara Harbor
PACIFIC OCEAN
SHORELINE DR
CLIFF DR
© The Countryman Press

INTRODUCTION

Santa Barbara is the stuff of movies: charming red-roofed Spanish architecture tucked between the blue Pacific and the nearby mountains; a scenic wharf and harbor sprinkled with sailboats and yachts; gorgeous beaches; and a generous share of parks and gardens overflowing with flowers that bloom year-round, thanks to idyllic weather. Add to the mix a local community with a passionate commitment to the environment and the friendly, laid-back demeanor for which Southern Californians are known, and the result is one of the most beautiful, welcoming cities in the country and a favorite weekend getaway for folks from Los Angeles and San Diego.

Just to the south of Santa Barbara is Montecito, a sleepy upscale suburb that offers boutique shopping, galleries, and a handful of fine-dining options. Montecito is home to the lovely Butterfly Beach and the five-star Four Seasons Biltmore Resort, both of which attract an elite crowd. Summerland is farther south still and has an impressive collection of cozy restaurants and upscale antiques stores, many of which specialize in Italian antiquities. Goleta to the north is home to the University of California, Santa Barbara—surely one of the most vista-blessed institutions of higher learning in California: the campus sits right on the coastline, and students have only a quick five-minute walk to Goleta Beach.

To the north is the distinct wine country region of Santa Barbara County. The inland Santa Ynez Valley is impossibly beautiful, with rolling hills and massive oak trees that look to have been sculpted in place. Patches of orderly vineyard and rocky mountains in the distance are reminiscent of Tuscany, and the whole is evocative of a Van Gogh landscape. The area is largely rural and boasts a burgeoning wine industry that specializes in pinot noirs and chardonnays. The charming small town of Santa Ynez is nostalgic and maintains historic false-front buildings to preserve its Old West heritage. Los Olivos is an even tinier, picture-perfect small town that boasts several fine restaurants. So enchanting is the place that it was the one time home of Michael Jackson, who built his Neverland Ranch just beyond the town limits. Buellton is a contemporary town of chain fast-food outlets and car lots—and it is also home to some fun fine dining (such as the Hitching Post II, made famous by the 2004 film *Sideways*).

Nearby Solvang offers a little bit of Europe in the Southern California hills: *Solvang* means "sunny fields" in Danish, and this stylized village looks to be straight out of 19th-century Scandinavia, with thatched roofs, windmills, fairy-tale

SANTA BARBARA HARBOR

cottages, and a half dozen authentic Danish bakeries. The tiny pedestrian-friendly city was founded by Danish American educators in 1911 and today is known as the Danish Capital of America. Visitors will find more than 100 themed boutiques and restaurants, a dozen wine tasting rooms, and major crowds every weekend to enjoy them.

GUIDANCE **Santa Barbara Conference and Visitors Bureau and Film Commission** (805-966-9222; www.santabarbaraca.com), 1601 Anacapa St., Santa Barbara.

Santa Barbara Visitors Center (805-965-3021), 1 Garden St., Santa Barbara.

Solvang Conference and Visitors Bureau (805-688-6144), 1511-A Mission Dr., Solvang.

MORE WEB SITES Car-Free Santa Barbara: www.santabarbaracarfree.org

Experience Santa Barbara: www.santabarbaradowntown.com

Santa Barbara County Vintners Association: www.sbcountywines.com

Santa Ynez Valley Wine Country Association: www.santaynezwinecountry.com

Solvang city page: www.cityofsolvang.com

MEDICAL EMERGENCIES As with all medical emergencies in Southern California, dial 911 for immediate assistance. Hospital and emergency clinics include:

Cottage Health System (805-569-7201), 320 W. Pueblo St., Santa Barbara.

Santa Ynez Valley Cottage Hospital (805-688-6431), 2050 Viborg Rd., Solvang.

GETTING THERE *By air:* The greater Santa Barbara area is served by the Santa Barbara Airport (805-967-7111;www.flysba), a regional terminal just outside of the city.

By bus: The **Greyhound** bus station is in the heart of downtown Santa Barbara, off State Street and Carrillo (34 W. Carrillo Street). Connections are available to the Santa Ynez Valley wine country and to Solvang.

By train: **AMTRAK** serves Santa Barbara via the *Coast Starlight,* which runs from Los Angeles to Seattle, and the *Pacific Surfliner,* which runs from San Diego to San Luis Obispo. Both trains are comfortable and offer scenic vistas aboard bi-level cars. Ask for a Transit Transfer Pass for two free rides on the Santa Barbara Metropolitan Transit District (MTD) buses and shuttles. The AMTRAK train station is near Stearns Wharf, just off State St.

GETTING AROUND The city is dedicated to reducing carbon emissions, and as part of that green movement has sponsored **Car-Free Santa Barbara** (www.santabarbaracarfree.org), an organization that helps visitors find their way around the city using inexpensive public transportation and alternative transportation. Two MTD electric shuttle routes serve the most popular tourist destinations of the city: downtown (via State Street) and the waterfront (via Cabrillo Boulevard); these shuttles are 25 cents per ride, with free transfers. The shuttles run frequently throughout the day and are easy to use. Car-Free Santa Barbara encourages guests to explore the Santa Ynez Valley wine country (see *To Do—Wineries* in the "Santa Ynez Valley Wine Country" chapter) without a private car as well. There are a number of private wine tour companies that will pick up at hotels or the train station.

> **INSIDER TIP:** Downtown offers 75 minutes of free parking at select lots throughout the city. Look for lots along State Street, from Guitierrez Street to Micheltorena Street.

By bus: As noted earlier, visitors to Santa Barbara can tour the area in open-air, quiet, electric shuttles for 25 cents. Shuttles run until 6 PM year-round, and until 9 PM on Friday and Saturday from April through October.

By car: Santa Barbara is an easy city to navigate: it is compact, streets are well marked, and aside from the popular downtown–State Street corridor (which can be congested), parking is readily available. Traffic getting into (and out of) the city is a problem, however, as it is with many Southern California cities, especially during traditional rush hours.

SANTA BARBARA

Santa Barbara is a surprisingly compact city, with major attractions located in concentrated regions downtown and along the waterfront. Downtown is a pedestrian-friendly zone, anchored by the 1929 Moorish Santa Barbara County Courthouse and boasting myriad restaurants, bars, clubs, boutiques, and pubs, especially along popular State St. The waterfront region along Cabrillo Boulevard, which runs parallel to the ocean, is home to the landmark Stearns Wharf, site of the Ty Warner Sea Center and a handful of restaurants and shops. The expansive wharf is also a favorite with local fishermen. North of downtown is the Santa Barbara Mission, the lovely Queen of the Missions, which sits atop a hill overlooking a well-tended rose garden and has as its backdrop lush mountains and a stunning historic neighborhood. The pink-hued mission is both a historic treasure and an architectural icon for Santa Barbara, and it is the site of city celebrations and festivals year-round.

✷ To See

HISTORICAL SITES **Casa de la Guerra Historic House** (805-965-0093; www.sbthp.org), 15 E. de la Guerra St., Montecito. Open weekends noon–4. Once belonging to one of Santa Barbara's most influential early citizens, this 1820s adobe features period-decorated rooms and historical and art exhibits. Adults $5 (or free with admission to El Presidio de Santa Barbara State Historic Park).

✐ **El Presidio de Santa Barbara State Historic Park** (805-965-0093; www.sbthp.org), 123 E. Cañon Perdido St., Santa Barbara. Open daily 10:30–4:30. A reconstruction of the original Spanish fort founded in 1782, the presidio comprises a beautiful chapel and bell tower, and living quarters for the presidio commander, his lieutenants, and the padres. There are two original portions standing: the **El Cuartel** (the oldest adobe building in Santa Barbara) and parts of the **Cañedo Adobe.** The whitewashed buildings were originally constructed of sun-dried adobe bricks (basically, mud and straw), and timbers from the nearby Los Padres forest were used to support the roof. Adults $5 (or free with admission to the Casa de le Guerra Historic House).

✪ ✐ **Santa Barbara Mission** (805-682-4713; www.santabarbaramission.org), 2201 Laguna St., Santa Barbara. Considered among the most beautiful of the 21 Spanish missions in California, this Queen of the Missions was founded in 1786. It is particularly striking because of the graceful lines of the main chapel and the muted

SANTA BARBARA BIKE PATH

shades of pink on the exterior. Built atop a hill, the church offers a view of the ocean and the nearby mountains. The current structure dates to 1820. The original mission buildings were small adobe structures, which over time were replaced and rebuilt bigger and more grandly. The current church is the fourth version of the mission. The lovely 1808 fountain in the front survived an earthquake in 1812 that destroyed an earlier structure. Today the mission continues to be home to a community of Franciscan friars, who operate a retreat center on the premises. The church is also an active parish. Visitors can tour the stunning church interior, walk through the fascinating cemetery and mausoleum, and enjoy 10 acres of lush manicured gardens. Be sure to visit the nearby **Mission Rose Garden** as well. Adults $5, children $1.

✪ ✐ **Stearns Wharf** (805-897-2683), Cabrillo Blvd., at the foot of State St., Santa Barbara. This historic landmark dates to 1872 and is one of the loveliest places to stroll in the city, offering views of the ocean, the city, and the mountains beyond. There are plenty of shopping and dining opportunities on the pier, and there is never a shortage of people taking advantage of the offerings. Also here is the **Ty Warner Sea Center.**

SANTA BARBARA MISSION

MUSEUMS ✐ **Carriage and Western Art Museum** (805-962-2353; www.carriagemuseum.org), 129 Castillo St., Santa Barbara. Open weekdays 9–3. Find the largest collection of horse-drawn conveyances in North America here, including humble buggies and workaday stagecoaches. Admission is free.

INSIDER TIP: The downloadable Red Tile Walking Tour (www.santabarbaraca.com/podcasts) will lead visitors through more than 70 historic landmarks throughout a 12-block area of downtown. This 16-minute video is optimized for viewing on a video iPod or iPhone.

✪ **Karpeles Manuscript Library Museum** (805-962-5322; www.karpeles.com), 21 W. Anapamu St., Santa Barbara. Open daily 10–4. This museum exhibits the largest private collection of original documents and manuscripts, including works on music, literature, art, and science. Look for original letters by Abraham Lincoln, Charles Darwin, and Albert Einstein. Admission is free.

Santa Barbara Historical Museum (805-966-1601; www.santabarbaramuseum.com), 136 E. de la Guerra St., Santa Barbara. Open Tues.–Sat. 10–5, Sun. noon–5. This small museum chronicles the history of Santa Barbara through costume and furniture exhibits in "The Story of Santa Barbara." By donation.

✪ **Santa Barbara Maritime Museum** (805-962-8404; www.sbmm.org), 113 Harbor Way, Santa Barbara. Open days and hours vary seasonally. Located on the Santa Barbara Harbor, this interactive maritime museum offers fun and educational exhibits that, among other things, let guests experience how it feels to catch a big fish, sail a tall ship, and surf a big wave. The museum also includes three historic ships, including a 28-foot fishing boat built in 1926, all of which are available for tour. Admission $7.

Santa Barbara Museum of Art (805-963-4364; www.sbma.net), 1130 State St., Santa Barbara. Open Tues.–Sun. 11–5. In addition to attracting some of the most important touring exhibits, the Santa Barbara Museum of Art has an impressive permanent collection that includes antiquities, impressionist and expressionist works, and contemporary pieces from around the world. If traveling with kids, don't miss the interactive children's gallery. Adults $9; seniors, students, and children $6. (Admission is free on Sun.)

Santa Barbara Museum of Natural History (805-682-4711; www.sbnature.org), 2559 Puesta del Sol Rd., Santa Barbara. Open daily 10–5. Tucked away into a residential part of town, near the mission, this informative museum is generally crowded with children on the weekends, who particularly enjoy exploring the exhibits dedicated to insects, mammals, marine life, fossils, and native Americans. The 72-foot blue whale skeleton is a favorite exhibit. Also on-site is the Gladwin Planetarium, the Museum Library, and the nature trail that follows Mission Creek. Admission $10.

Santa Barbara Surfing Museum (805-962-9048; www.sbsurfingmuseum.com), 16-A Helena Ave. #6, Santa Barbara. Open Sun. noon–5. Near the Stearns Wharf, this small collection features vintage surfboards, skateboards, photographs, surf-themed art, and films. Admission is free.

INSIDER TIP: The first Thursday of every month in downtown Santa Barbara, galleries and other cultural venues throw open their doors and offer free access to the public 5–8 pm. This festive celebration of the arts also includes live music, wine tastings, and artist receptions.

TY WARNER SEA CENTER

Ty Warner Sea Center (805-962-2526; www.sbnature.org), 211 Stearns Wharf, Santa Barbara. Open daily 10–5. A satellite of the **Santa Barbara Museum of Natural History,** this aquarium on Stearns Wharf offers interactive exhibits, a 1,500-gallon tide pool tank, and a live-shark touching pool. Children will not want to miss the chance to crawl through a tube that snakes through the tide pool. Admission $8.

PARKS ✪ **Alameda Park,** 1400 Santa Barbara St., Santa Barbara. This 2-block park offers flowering trees and shrubs, a romantic gazebo, and a pond with lilies and resident turtles and koi. This is also home to **Kids' World,** a massive playground with swings, slides, a castle, a fort, climbing structures, and picnic areas.

Chase Palmer Park, both sides of E. Cabrillo Blvd., near Stearns Wharf, Santa Barbara. Running along the waterfront, this narrow park is adjacent to **East Beach,** with a bike path and walkway. Across the street is a 10-acre addition that offers a carousel, lagoon, fountains, and a large grassy area that is the site of a summertime concert series.

Shoreline Park, Shoreline Dr. and La Marina, Santa Barbara. This scenic park perched on the cliffs overlooks the beach and harbor and features walking paths, a children's playground, and large grassy areas for picnicking and kite flying.

Skaters' Point, south of Stearns Wharf, Santa Barbara. Skaters' Point

ALAMEDA PARK

attracts mostly teenage boys on skates and bikes, with a few in-line skaters showing up to enjoy bowl riding. The popular park attracts some real talent, and it's fun to watch the action.

✷ To Do

BICYCLING Santa Barbara has one of the prettiest, most extensive systems of level bike paths in California. The two-lane, 3-mile **Cabrillo Bike Lane** follows the shoreline and offers terrific views of the water and of the **Andree Clark Bird Refuge.** Marked paths extend west to Goleta and the University of California, Santa Barbara (UCSB). For a free bike path map, visit www.trafficsolutions.info/biking.htm. Rent bicycles or family-friendly seated pedicabs at **Wheelfun Rentals** (805-966-2282), 23 E. Cabrillo Boulevard; **Isla Vista Bicycles** (805-968-3339), near UCSB; **Open Air Bicycles** (805-962-7000); and **Santa Barbara Bikes to Go** (805-617-3362), which offers free delivery to hotels and the AMTRAK station.

GOLF **Rancho San Marcos** (805-683-6334; www.rsm1804.com), 4600 CA 154, Santa Barbara. A little more than 10 miles outside downtown Santa Barbara, well-respected Rancho San Marcos is set in the mountains, amid abundant natural beauty. Green fee: $95–120.

Sandpiper Golf Club (805-968-1541; www.sandpipergolf.com), 7925 Hollister Ave., Santa Barbara. This public course offers premier ocean views on a challenging course that has hosted the PGA Tournament Players Series and the LPGA Tour. The 18-hole, par 72 course was designed by William F. Bell and offers rolling fairways. Green fee: $139–159.

SPAS ✪ **Bacara Spa** (877-422-4245; www.barcararesort.com), 8301 Hollister Ave., Santa Barbara. Part of the exclusive **Bacara Resort,** this luxurious hotel spa offers myriad ways for guests to pamper themselves. Among the best (and most expensive, at nearly $400) is the Bacara Crème de la Crème treatment, which starts with a moisturizing soak in a vanilla milk bath, followed by a lime scalp treatment, a full-body espresso mud-mask exfoliation, a full body massage, and a paraffin treatment for hands and feet. Patrons are invited to enjoy a eucalyptus steam, sauna, Jacuzzi, or water treatments available before massages and facials as part of the total package.

Float (805-845-7777; www.floatluxuryspa.com), 18 E. Cañon Perdido St., Santa Barbara. A pretty day spa in downtown, Float offers a bright, airy space and indulgences like the Thai massage, in which a technician guides guests through yoga-style stretches; and the Ultimate Body Facial, starting with a full-body exfoliation using antioxidant grape seeds, followed up with a green tea and ginger enzyme wrap, and then a massage with protein lotion and a final application of glycolic peppermint cream.

Spa Del Mar (805-884-8540; www.santabarbaraspadelmar.com), 633 E. Cabrillo Blvd., Santa Barbara. A bright, cheerful spa reflective of Santa Barbara's Spanish colonial roots, the Spa Del Mar at the **Fess Parker Doubletree Resort** offers inventive treatments like the Almond Glow, an exfoliation treatment done with a concoction of crushed almonds, milk, and honey, followed by a facial and scalp and foot massage; and the blissfully noncaloric Chocolate Paradise, starting with a chocolate sugar scrub, followed by a full-body massage using chocolate crème lotion.

✪ **Spa at the Four Seasons Biltmore** (805-969-2261; www.fourseasons.com/santabarbara/spa), 1260 Channel Dr., Montecito. At the heavenly **Four Seasons Biltmore,** this opulent seaside spa offers treatments in private suites with fireplaces and ocean views. Signature treatments include the Moor Mud Mask, which starts with a full-body brushing, followed by an aromatic wrap and facial, and finishing with a massage done with oils customized for each patron; or the fabulous Sunset Sanctuary, an inclusive (and spendy) package that offers a hand and foot reflexology treatment, a couples stone-therapy massage, all topped off with a three-course dinner for two on the terrace of a private spa suite, complete with champagne and dessert.

THEME PARKS AND ZOOS **Santa Barbara Zoo** (805-962-6310; www.santabarbarazoo.org), 500 Niños Dr., Santa Barbara. Open daily 10–5. More than 160 species of animals are exhibited in naturalized habitats that stretch over 30 acres, which also comprise formal gardens, cacti and succulent collections, and exotic flowering plants. Popular zones within the park include the African Veldt, which houses the giraffes, meerkats, and African tortoises; the California Trails, which is home to bald eagles, California condors (the Santa Barbara Zoo is only one of two zoos in the country that display these large birds), and Channel Island fox; and the Crawford Family Penguin House, which premiered in 2006 with a collection of warm-weather Humboldt penguins. The zoo offers educational, hands-on opportunities throughout the year, including zoo camps for children and Family Zoo Snooze nights, which offer the chance to pitch a tent and spend the night in the park. Adults $12, children $10.

✷ Water Sports

BOATING **Aquasports** (800-773-2309), 111 Verona Ave., Goleta. This well-respected group leads guided sea kayaking trips along the Santa Barbara coastline and into the **Channel Islands National Park.** This is a good option for those wishing to try out kayaking for the first time or for those who aren't able to participate in extremely rigorous sports: Aquasports trips tend to be less demanding than many other kayaking options in the city.

Captain Jack's Santa Barbara Tours (805-564-1819), 415 E. Montecito St., Santa Barbara. Captain Jack's offers a huge variety of boating options, including guided kayak tours, sunset sailboat cruises, kayak and biking tours, and kayaking and horseback riding tours.

✪ **Condor Cruises** (805-882-0088), 301 W. Cabrillo Blvd., Santa Barbara. Guests sail aboard comfortable vessels for premier whale-watching tours, dinner cruises, excursions to the **Channel Islands,** kayaking tours, and birding excursions that offer the chance to view pterodromas and other exotic species.

Santa Barbara Adventure Company (805-884-WAVE), various venues throughout Santa Barbara. This organization offers a number of exciting outdoor activities, including horseback riding, rock climbing, paragliding, and fabulous coastal kayaking tours. Check out the Sea Cave Kayaking option that leaves from Ventura Harbor; guests ride onboard a power boat to the **Channel Islands National Park,** and from there paddle among the coves and sea caves of Santa Cruz Island.

Santa Barbara Sailing Center (805-962-2826), Santa Barbara Harbor. The Santa Barbara Sailing Center offers sailing classes, kayaking excursions, sunset cruises, powerboat rentals, and whale-watching tours aboard a speedy catamaran. The company also charters an 85-foot luxury catamaran for private events.

Sunset Kidd Sailing Charters (805-962-8222), 125 Harbor Way, Santa Barbara. This business provides a number of chartered cruises, including two-hour morning cruises, sunset cocktail cruises, and overnighters to the Channel Islands. Once a month Sunset Kidd offers full-moon cruises as well.

DIVING AND SNORKELING **Anacapa Dive Center** (805-963-8917), 22 Anacapa St., Santa Barbara. The Anacapa Dive Center teaches scuba classes for all levels, including basic open water classes to technical and refresher courses, and offers dive tours along the Santa Barbara coast and off the Channel Islands.

Blue Whale Hunter (800-452-6696), 117-D Harbor Way, Santa Barbara. The Blue Whale specializes in free diving and spearfishing tours, some overnighters, including dive trips to the Channel Islands and lobster spearfishing in Santa Rosa.

FISHING Sportfishing charters depart from the Santa Barbara harbor. Note that fishing is allowed from Stearns Wharf; no fishing license is required.

Sea Landing Sport Fishing (805-963-3564), 301 W. Cabrillo Blvd., Santa Barbara. Sea Landing caters to beginners and experts and offers half-day trips that are ideal for families (although I recommend this be reserved for children 12 and older). Equipment, bait, and tackle are provided, and guests can expect to reel in calico bass, halibut, and rockfish.

SURFING The best time to surf the beaches near Santa Barbara County is winter, thanks to storms during this season that generate the big waves. Swells are largest near the tip of Point Conception or in Ventura, to the south, but there are a number of well-known surfing destinations closer in. Perhaps the best known is **Rincon,** which falls between Ventura and Santa Barbara counties and is home to some of the biggest, best-formed waves—and draws the biggest crowds as well. Other favorites include **Hammonds Reef,** in Montecito; **Leadbetter Point,** past Stearns Wharf in Santa Barbara proper; and **The Ranch,** an all-but-inaccessible stretch that fronts private land and runs from Gaviota State Beach to Point Conception. Good surfing instruction is available from **Santa Barbara Surf School** (805-745-8877) and **Surf Happens** (805-451-7568). To get in on the latest trend of paddle surfing, check out **Blueline Paddle Surf** (www.bluelinepaddlesurf.com), which offers rentals and lessons.

✷ Green Space

BEACHES ✪ **Butterfly Beach,** off Hwy. 101 at Olive Mill Rd., Montecito. Across from the **Four Seasons Biltmore,** this west-facing beach is secluded (thanks to the cliffs), scenic, and offers good swimming and great people watching: Perhaps because of the proximity to the pricey Biltmore and other wallet-busting resorts, this beach is popular with celebrities. Parking is limited.

Carpinteria Beach, off Hwy. 101 at Bates Rd., Carpinteria. A favorite beach in the area, Carpinteria offers dunes and a long expanse of sand. Facilities include showers, restrooms, and volleyball nets. The tidepooling is especially good here, although note that part of the beach is closed during seal-birthing season.

✐ **East Beach,** between Stearns Wharf and the Andree Bird Refuge, off Cabrillo Blvd., Santa Barbara. This long stretch of sand in the heart of Santa Barbara is adjacent to a popular bike path and offers volleyball courts and a play area. The beach faces south, which makes for mild waves that are good for young children (but the beach is not so great for watching sunsets).

El Capitan State Beach, look for signs off 101, north of Goleta. With great views of the Channel Islands, this somewhat isolated and rocky beach could be an idyllic oasis, although the vistas are somewhat marred by the ubiquitous oil rigs offshore.

Goleta Beach, off Hwy. 101 at Sandspit Rd. North of Santa Barbara proper and at the foot of the University of California, Santa Barbara, campus, this beach offers a sandy area with play zone and picnic grounds, as well as a fishing pier, volleyball nets, and a snack bar. Parking can be tight.

Refugio State Beach, off Hwy. 101 at Refugio Rd. To the north of Santa Barbara, on the other side of railroad tracks that run along the tops of the steep cliffs that back the beach, this somewhat rocky beach looks and feels distinctly different from most Southern California beaches and resembles the more rugged beaches of northern California. There is nearby camping, hiking, and biking, and facilities include a general store (open weekends only) and restrooms.

✪ **Rincon Beach,** off Hwy. 101 at Bates Rd. South of Santa Barbara, Rincon is one of the most popular surfing spots in Southern California, because this relatively small beach is angled perfectly to face the incoming waves. The sand is narrow (and all but disappears during high tide), and the water is usually too rough for swimming, so this beach is best reserved for boarders and those who like to watch them. Adjacent **Rincon Point** is accessible via a sloping path and is a more appropriate beach for sunbathers.

GARDENS 🐾 **Mission Rose Garden,** 2201 Laguna St., Santa Barbara. At the foot of a grassy hill that fronts the **Santa Barbara Mission,** the Mission Rose Garden offers hundreds of rose varieties in well-tended beds. There is a central water fountain and benches, as well as a large expanse of grass that is popular with dog owners.

✪ ✐ **Santa Barbara Botanic Garden** (805-682-4726; www.sbbg.org), 1212 Mission Canyon Rd., Santa Barbara. Open daily 9–5. On 65 acres just miles from downtown and adjacent to the 1806 Mission Dam, a restored aqueduct that once supplied water to the expansive Mission Santa Barbara, these botanic gardens are the pride of the city. The showiest of the exhibits, and one of the first things a visitor will see on entering the gardens, the Meadow is a representative California grassland that is especially dazzling in the spring, when a huge number of California poppies are in bloom. Also of special interest is the Ceanothus Exhibit, which comprises species of California lilac; the Desert Exhibit, which features the California fan palm, a native to the state; and the Manzanita Exhibit, which collects these small shrubs and trees, also natives of California. Throughout are contemplative pathways and trails. Adults $8, seniors and students $6, children $4.

NATURE PRESERVES **Andree Clark Bird Refuge,** 1400 E. Cabrillo Blvd., Santa Barbara. Open daily. In addition to bike trails and hiking paths, birders will appreciate the wide array of native and migratory birds that frequent the lagoon. Look for interpretive signs along pathways. Admission is free.

SANTA BARBARA BOTANIC GARDEN

✷ Lodging

Montecito

✪ **Four Seasons Biltmore** (805-969-2261; www.fourseasons.com/santabarbara), 1260 Channel Dr. Off the beaten track, several miles outside downtown Santa Barbara, this very private estate property is one of the finest in the city, with stunning views of the ocean and luxury accommodations. Décor is Spanish Colonial, and the property is lushly landscaped with winding pathways and cozy private

CHANNEL ISLANDS NATIONAL PARK

Twenty-five miles off the coast of Ventura and Santa Barbara, the Channel Islands National Park comprises five nearly undeveloped islands (Anacapa, Santa Cruz, Santa Rosa, San Miguel, and Santa Barbara) that are easily visible from the Santa Barbara coastline. The park encompasses nearly 250,000 acres—half of which are underwater. The islands' relative isolation has preserved the native flora and fauna, many of which are unique. This is an especially good place to view sea lions, harbor seals, and northern elephant seals. San Miguel is also home to northern fur seals and the rare Guadalupe fur seals. In addition, this volcanic archipelago is a favorite with birders, who can expect to view sea- and shorebirds like bald eagles, oystercatchers, and three kinds of cormorants. Santa Cruz island is the only place in the world to see island scrub jay. For plant lovers, in early springtime, all five islands are covered in wildflowers. The islands are also popular with hikers, kayakers, campers, snorkelers, and fishermen, who appreciate the unspoiled surroundings and find nearly limitless sporting opportunities. The islands can be reached via boat trips that originate from Santa Barbara Harbor (see *Boating*) or via the Ventura-based **Island Packers** (805-642-1393; www.islandpackers.com). There are no entrance fees to visit the park.

sitting areas. On-site dining is at **Bella Vista,** which offers patio seating, breathtaking views, and a fabulous Thurs. seafood buffet with sushi, lobster, and freshly shucked oysters. The property is adjacent to beautiful **Butterfly Beach,** a favorite with locals. $$$$

Montecito Inn (805-969-7854; www.montecitoinn.com), 1295 Coast Village Rd. Four miles east of downtown Santa Barbara, this historic inn, built in 1928 by silver-screen star Charlie Chaplin, offers tiny rooms and even tinier baths in tony Montecito. The petite accommodations include antiques and plenty of charm, despite the limited space. There is a small pool on-site, along with an ancient elevator. A minimal breakfast is included. $$$

Santa Barbara

Cabrillo Inn (805-966-1641; www.cabrilloinn.com), 931 E. Cabrillo Blvd. Just south of Stearns Wharf, this small motel is well located, across the road from the beach and within easy walking distance of great bike paths, restaurants, and the pier. The interior is dated and a little worse for wear, and views are ideal only from upper-floor rooms (which cannot be guaranteed), but depending on the season and the room, rates can be a steal. A stay also includes a modest continental breakfast. $–$$$

Canary Hotel (805-884-0300; www.canarysantabarbara.com), 31 W. Carrillo St. This eclectic boutique hotel is near State St. and Stearns Wharf, and close enough to walk to fine dining. The charming rooftop pool and extensive sundeck offers views to the mountains, the Channel Islands, and all of downtown Santa Barbara. Guest room décor is bright and light, with a touch of Colonial design in the dark wood beds and side tables, and each accommodation is thoughtfully equipped with field guides and binoculars. Dog lovers will especially appreciate Club Canario, a canine program that offers a dog bed, food and water bowls, a dog treat, a hotel Frisbee, and a personal grooming kit for your pooch. $$$$

PRICE KEY FOR A STANDARD ROOM:

$	$100 or less
$$	$101–150
$$$	$151–250
$$$$	$251 and up

Fess Parker Double Tree Resort (805-564-4333; www.fessparkersantabarbarahotel.com), 633 E. Cabrillo Blvd. Located across the street from the beach, south of Stearns Wharf, this huge resort has something for everyone in the family. The property features four on-site restaurants, an extensive fitness facility, shuffleboard, a heated pool (that really *is* warm year-round), tennis courts, the beautiful **Spa Del Mar,** and a full-service

FOUR SEASONS BILTMORE
Courtesy of the Four Seasons Biltmore

beauty salon. Rooms are spacious, and many offer cozy balconies with views of the gardens or the ocean. $$$

✪ **Harbor View Inn** (800-755-0222; www.harborviewinnsb.com), 28 W. Cabrillo Blvd. Immediately across from the beach and Stearns Wharf, this charming, moderately sized property offers quintessential Santa Barbara style at a reasonable price. Guest rooms are casually elegant, all are equipped with spacious balconies or patios, and many boast superior ocean views and fireplaces. Harbor-front dining is within easy walking distance, and the popular heart of downtown, on State St., is less than a mile away. The hotel offers a pretty pool with ocean view, a spa, on-site restaurant, and underground parking. $$$

🐾 **Hotel Mar Monte** (805-963-0744; www.hotelmarmonte.com), 1111 E. Cabrillo Blvd. The classic Colonial Hotel Mar Monte was built in 1931 and remains an architectural icon in Santa Barbara, its Moorish-style tower visible from many parts of the city. The historic property is known first and foremost for its impeccable service and second for its premier location: the hotel is across the street from **East Beach** and close to fine dining at the harbor and on State St. On-site is the **Spa Mar Monte,** dining at **Bistro Eleven,** and an outdoor pool and whirlpool. The Hotel Mar Monte is 100 percent smoke-free, and dogs are welcome. $$–$$$

FESS PARKER RESORT
Courtesy Santa Barbara Convention and Visitors Bureau

Hotel Santa Barbara (805-957-9300; www.hotelsantabarbara.com), 533 State St. The small Hotel Santa Barbara is in the heart of downtown, steps from the many fine dining options on State St., but still within easy reach of the beaches. The newly renovated, charming French Country décor is cozy, and the rooms are comfortable and quiet, albeit on the small side. A stay includes a complimentary continental breakfast with make-your-own waffles. Hotel staff is friendly and helpful. $$$

✪ **Inn of the Spanish Garden** (805-564-4700; www.spanishgardeninn.com), 915 Garden St. A luxury boutique property in the center of downtown, this small, elegant hotel is sophisticated and romantic. The inn is in the Presidio district, surrounded by historic architecture and within easy reach of the action on popular State St. Guest rooms are well appointed, with fine Frette linens, French press coffee makers, and fluffy robes. All rooms include either a private garden patio or a balcony. The grounds are replete with native landscaping, soothing fountains, and a communal fire pit in the courtyard. The hotel offers a wine bar every evening, featuring the best of nearby Santa Ynez wineries. There is a lap pool on-site, and a continental breakfast is included. $$$$

Santa Barbara Inn (800-231-0431; www.santabarbarainn.com), 901 E. Cabrillo Blvd. Across the street from the beach, the exterior of the Santa Barbara Inn has the look of a sprawling motel, but the interior is surprisingly exotic and elegant, with striking tropical fabrics and furnishings, and each guest room has a balcony or patio, many with premium views of the ocean. The property is committed to protecting the environment: management is passionate about recycling and conservation, and the city's electric shuttle (see *Getting Around* in the introduction to part 6) stops at the front of the property every half hour, encouraging guests to visit the city car-free. The hotel offers great package deals with **Condor Express** for Channel Island excursions and year-round whale-watching tours. A stay includes a continental breakfast. $$$

✪ **Simpson House Inn** (800-676-1280; www.simpsonhouseinn), 121 E. Arrellaga. This 15-room bed & breakfast is in a historic neighborhood, tucked behind tall hedges and amid an acre of manicured English gardens. The property includes an 1874 Victorian home, a restored 1878 barn, and three idyllic garden cottages. The Simpson House repeatedly earns a five-diamond rating from AAA, thanks to impeccable service and hospitality. Each room is individually decorated with period furniture and charming Victorian details. A stay includes a gourmet vegetarian breakfast and wine tastings and hors d'oeuvres in the evening. $$$$

✷ Where to Eat

DINING OUT

Santa Barbara

Blue Agave (805-899-4694; www.blueagavesb.com), 20 E. Cota St. Open daily for dinner. It's difficult to pin a label on this eclectic restaurant, which offers variety even in the choice of seating (a garden patio or rustic country interior with cozy fireplace and open kitchen). As the name implies, this organic restaurant offers myriad brands of tequila (made from the agave plant). Spanish-style tapas are served 5:30–11 every night—including treats like spicy turkey meatballs in an olive oil tomato sauce and shrimp wrapped in crispy prosciutto. Entrées reflect several cuisine traditions and include lamb burgers, chicken mole enchiladas, French-style steak with black peppercorn sauce, and lemony fettuccine Alfredo with mushrooms. $$–$$$

PRICE KEY FOR A TYPICAL ENTRÉE:

$	$10 and under
$$	$11–20
$$$	$21–30
$$$$	$31 and up

Bouchon Santa Barbara (805-730-1160; www.bouchon.net), 9 W. Victoria St. Open daily for dinner. The menus of Bouchon Santa Barbara reflect the freshest local ingredients and a fanciful imagination. Depending on the season, expect unusual preparations like tangerine-seared sea scallops with sautéed pea tendrils and tarragon cream, and blood-orange and mint marinated rack of lamb with herbed barley. The brasserie has an extensive cheese

FARE FROM BOUCHON
Courtesy Santa Barbara Convention and Visitors Bureau

selection, good wine collection, and desserts worthy of the French moniker: don't miss the blueberry upside-down cake with lemon zest ice cream. $$$

✪ **Downey's** (805-966-5006; www.downeyssb.com), 1305 State St. Open daily for dinner. Downey's downtown is an upscale mom-and-pop restaurant (owned and managed by the Downeys) that offers fresh local ingredients in a pleasant, relaxing environment. When available, check out the flavorful wild king salmon with sorrel sauce, served with artichoke hearts and parsley potatoes. The wine list is extensive and features the best of California vintners, including many choices from the nearby Santa Ynez Valley. For the very reasonable price of $50, enjoy a Taste of Santa Barbara, a four-course meal that highlights produce from the local farmer's market. $$$

✪ **Kai** (805-560-8777; www.kaisushishabushabu.com), 738 State St. Open daily for lunch and dinner. This small restaurant in downtown offers a wide range of Japanese cuisine, including exotic shabu shabu–style dining, which means guests get to cook their own dinner in a pot right at the table. Paper-thin slices of Kobe beef or chicken are dipped into bubbling kombu broth for only a few seconds, and then consumed on the spot. Kai also offers an extensive selection of sushi, salad, cold ramen dishes, teriyaki dishes, and tempura. $$–$$$

Opal Restaurant (805-966-9676; www.opalrestaurantandbar.com), 1325 State St. Open Mon.–Sat. for lunch and dinner. A charming bistro in downtown, Opal features wood-fired pizzas that are well loved by locals, especially the smoked chicken with chipotle glaze. Vegetarians will find several good choices, too, including the vegetable napoleon with wild mushrooms on a Gorgonzola potato cake, and the Arborio risotto with wild mushrooms, asparagus, and artichokes served with toasted walnuts and a parmigiano cream. The menu changes frequently, but when available, don't miss the macadamia-nut-crusted halibut with a mango-orange salsa. $$–$$$

✪ 🍸 **Pierre Lafond Wine Bistro** (805-963-1455; www.pierrelafond.com), 516 State St. Open daily for breakfast, lunch, and dinner. Although a wine bistro wouldn't seem to be an obvious breakfast choice, Pierre Lafond offers several early-morning treats, like the fabulous breakfast bruschetta with prosciutto, fried eggs, mozzarella, pesto, and tomatoes, or the cheese blintzes with strawberry rhubarb compote. Lunch and dinner options are designed to pair perfectly with wine and include an equal measure of chicken, beef, seafood, and vegetarian options. The restaurant offers boxed lunch and picnic baskets to go—perfect for folks looking to make a day of it in the nearby Santa Ynez Valley wine country. Don't miss Passport to the World of Wine on the first Wed. of every month, which features little-known varietals. And comfort-food addicts take note: every Thurs. is grilled cheese day. $$–$$$

Stella Mare's (805-969-6705; www.stellamares.com), 50 Los Patos Way. Open daily for lunch and dinner, brunch on Sun. Housed in a historic home that dates to 1872, this country French restaurant is elegant and comfortable, with several small rooms within the rambling building for intimate gatherings. The menu offerings are traditional and include coquilles St. Jacques (baked scallops with mushrooms, bay shrimp, and cream sauce); cassoulet and duck confit (a slow-cooked white bean casserole with

SANTA BARBARA SEAFOOD SPECIALTIES

Look for four local seafood specialties Santa Barbara fishermen haul in:

- Rock crab, harvested all year, are similar to Dungeness.
- Santa Barbara spot prawns, harvested early spring through midfall, are especially sweet and highly coveted by local chefs.
- Sea urchin, harvested all year, are buttery, sweet, and briny, and can be found in local sushi bars.
- Spiny lobster, harvested fall through early spring, are clawless and yield sweet, firm flesh.

These delicacies, and much more, can be found at the **Fishermen's Market,** at the Santa Barbara Harbor, on Saturday 7:30–11:30 AM.

sausage and shredded duck); *boeuf Bourguignon* (a hearty French beef stew with pearl onions, carrots, and pleasantly lumpy mashed potatoes); and *canard à l'orange* (duck breast with orange sauce served with potato mousseline). Don't miss the creamed spinach as an à la carte side. $$$

🍸 **Wine Cask** (805-966-9463; www.winecask.com), 813 Anacapa St. Open daily for dinner. The Wine Cask comprises a restaurant, bar, and tasting room that highlights the best of the Central Coast wines. Dining options include the braised lamb shank with asparagus risotto, the smoked pork chop with house-cured bacon and creamy potatoes gratin, and the pan-seared wild salmon with fava beans and Meyer lemon yogurt. Save room for the bread pudding with bourbon salted caramel. $$$

EATING OUT

Santa Barbara

🍸 **Dargan's Irish Pub and Restaurant** (805-568-0702; www.dargans.com), 18 E. Ortega St. Open daily for lunch and dinner, with happy hour 4:30–7. This bar offers decent pub grub, including very tasty beer-battered fish sandwiches, and a convivial atmosphere. Dine on the outside patio, or enjoy the pool tables and fireplace indoors. Dargan's offers live folk music every Thurs. and Sat. $

✪ **Moby Dick** (805-965-0549), 220 Stearns Wharf. Open daily for breakfast, lunch, and dinner. This rustic, nautical-themed restaurant is located toward the end of Stearns Wharf and used to be owned by old-time actors James Cagney and Ronald Coleman. These days, the views over the water are the stars. Look for happy hour

DARGAN'S

Courtesy Santa Barbara Convention and Visitors Bureau

deals Mon.–Fri. 4–7. The calamari is fresh, and the clam chowder is well above average. $$–$$$

Rusty's Pizza Parlor (805-564-1111), 232 W. Cabrillo Blvd. Open daily for lunch and dinner. Look for the faux lighthouse across the street from Stearns Wharf to find one outpost of Rusty's, a small local pizza parlor chain. If you like it hot, don't miss the El Diablo Fuego pie, with chiles, spicy chorizo sausage, pepperoni, bacon, and jalapeños. $

Saigon (805-966-0909; http://saigon-restaurants.com), 1230A State St. Open daily for lunch and dinner. This small local chain offers authentic Vietnamese food in a casual atmosphere. The papaya salad with shrimp, chicken, mint, and peanuts is refreshing; the spicy seafood soup hot pot is tongue scorching (in a good way). $$

Sambo's (805-965-3269; www.sambosrestaurant.com), 216 W. Cabrillo Blvd. Open daily for breakfast and lunch. Across from the beach for more than 50 years, Sambo's is *the* place for pancakes: try the banana caramel pecan stack or the classic buttermilk pancakes with strawberries on the side. The atmosphere is especially family friendly. $

Zen Yai Thai (805-957-1102), 425 State St. Open daily for dinner, Tues.–Fri. for lunch. This inexpensive Thai restaurant in downtown has exceptional chicken sate and traditional spicy Tom Yum soup; be sure to check out the authentic basil salmon in a spicy sauce, too. $$

✱ Entertainment

CLUBS **Café Buenos Aires** (805-963-0242; www.cafebuenosaires.com), 1316 State St., Santa Barbara. Open daily. Downtown, this popular restaurant in the Historic Arts District serves traditional Argentine cuisine, and—by evening—transforms into a hot music and dancing destination, with a professional tango show on Wed., Argentine folklore dance with live musicals on Thurs., and a live Latin jazz band on Sat.

Indochine (805-962-0154; www.indochinebar.com), 434 State St., Santa Barbara. This stylish, high-energy nightclub is a favorite with young adults looking to dance and mingle. Dress to impress and expect crowds—although it is possible to reserve a table for larger parties (for a price that can be applied to the bar tab).

The James Joyce (805-962-2688), 513 State St., Santa Barbara. A festive Irish pub in downtown Santa Barbara, the James Joyce offers live music, pool tables, dartboards, a big barrel of peanuts, and jovial compatriots who enjoy a good pint or three.

Santa Barbara Brewing Company (805-730-1040; www.sbbrewco.com), 501 State St., Santa Barbara. Open daily 11 AM–midnight. This gastropub offers award-winning handcrafted beers, local wines, large HDTVs, pool tables, and a casual atmosphere.

SohO (805-962-7776; www.sohosb.com), 1221 State St., Santa Barbara. A comfortable restaurant and music/dancing venue, SohO aims to create a New York City vibe that welcomes a mature crowd (i.e., not college kids). The establishment offers live music every day (jazz on Sun.).

Whiskey Richards (805-963-1786), 435 State St., Santa Barbara. Envision black walls, neon signs, a small dance floor, and live rock music: Whiskey Richards is a bit of a dive, but it attracts a friendly crowd, both in its patrons and its employees.

THEATERS **Arlington Center for the Performing Arts** (805-963-4408),

STATE STREET

1317 State St., Santa Barbara. Home to the Santa Barbara Symphony, the beautiful Arlington Center also hosts plays, ballets, movie premieres, and first-run Hollywood hits.

Center Stage Theater (805-963-0408), 700 State St., Santa Barbara. The Center Stage is an intimate black box theater, upstairs in the Paseo Nuevo Shopping Center, in downtown Santa Barbara.

Grenada Theater (805-899-2222), 1214 State St., Santa Barbara. Restored to its 1924 grandeur, this

TOP 10 DAY IN SANTA BARBARA

1. Belly up to the Mama Mumbo pancake special at Sambo's (see p. 278)
2. Take a morning tour of the Santa Barbara Mission (see pp. 264–265)
3. Bike along Cabrillo Bike Lane to the Andree Clark Bird Refuge (see pp. 268, 271)
4. Walk to the end of Stearns Wharf to catch the views (see p. 265)
5. Munch on fried calamari at Moby Dick (see pp. 277–278)
6. Feed the koi at Alameda Park (see p. 267)
7. Hike the Meadow Trail at the Santa Barbara Botanic Garden (see p. 271)
8. Dine on shabu shabu beef and tempura shrimp at Kai (see p. 276)
9. Throw darts and enjoy a pint at the James Joyce (see p. 278)
10. Overnight at the Harbor View Inn (see p. 274)

historic movie house hosts local performing arts and national touring acts. The Grenada is also home to **Opera Santa Barbara.**

Lobero Theater (805-963-0761), 33 E. Cañon Perdido St., Santa Barbara. Dating to 1873 (and rebuilt in 1924), the Lobero is the oldest continuously operating theater in California. Today the venue hosts the **Opera Santa Barbara,** State Street Ballet, the Santa Barbara Chamber Orchestra, and the Flamenco Arts Festival, among others.

Opera Santa Barbara (805-899-2222; www.operasb.org), 1214 State St., Santa Barbara. Performing at the **Grenada Theater** and the **Lobero Theater,** the Opera Santa Barbara stages several shows a year. Note that all final dress rehearsals are open and free to students of all ages.

Santa Barbara Symphony (805-898-9626; www.thesymphony.org), 1214 State St., Santa Barbara. Performing at the **Grenada Theater,** this regional orchestra performs from mid-Oct. through mid-May, including a New Year's Eve pops concert.

* Selective Shopping

Eclectic shops and mainstream chains can be found along popular **State Street** in downtown Santa Barbara. Look also for **Paseo Nuevo,** between the 700 and 800 blocks of State Street, an open-air retail mall. Also popular is **El Paseo,** between State and Anacapa streets on Cañon Perdido, a beautiful Spanish-style arcade that boasts galleries and artsy shops. Antiques lovers will not want to miss the upscale neighborhoods of Montecito and Summerland, to the south of the city, the latter of which offers amazing (but blisteringly expensive) Italian and Etruscan antiquities.

SANTA YNEZ VALLEY WINE COUNTRY

The Santa Ynez Valley comprises five increasingly important wine-growing regions and a handful of charming small towns. Santa Ynez proper is a quaint, tiny place filled with meticulously maintained yards behind tidy white picket fences. The small town offers drop-dead views of the mountains in the distance, with some upscale winery-related businesses near the **Chumash Casino.** Los Olivos is uniformly charming, with antiques shops, restaurants, and lots of wine-tasting bars. Buellton is perhaps less romantic, thanks to strip malls and chain restaurants, but the town still offers some outrageous views of the mountains. Finally, Solvang is a slightly strange little Danish town that until recently was given over to kitschy shopping and an overabundance of bakeries. In the past several years, however, several high-style accommodations have come to town, to cater to the wine-tasting crowds. Although these establishments still read Danish outside, interiors are boutique-y—yet at a fraction of the cost of similar accommodations in Napa or Sonoma, the better-known wine destinations in the northern half of the state.

✷ To See

HISTORICAL SITES **Bethania Lutheran Church,** 603 Atterdag, Solvang. This historic church dates to 1927 and features Danish-style architecture, stained-glass windows, and a ship hanging in the nave—said to be a good omen for safe crossing over the "waters of life."

Little Mermaid **Sculpture,** on the corner of Mission Dr. and Alisal Rd., Solvang. This half-sized replica of the famous *Little Mermaid* sculpture in the Copenhagen harbor pays homage to the famous fairy tale by Danish writer Hans Christian Andersen.

✪ **Old Mission Santa Inés** (www.missionsantaines.org), 1760 Mission Dr., Solvang. Established in 1804, the Santa Ynez mission was the 19th California mission built in the state and continues as an active parish. On-site is a small museum featuring interactive displays of Chumash artifacts and a pretty garden. An audio tour is available from the gift shop. By donation.

MUSEUMS ✪ 🖍 **Elverhoj Museum of History and Art** (805-686-1211; www.elverhoj.org), 1624 Elverhoy Way, Solvang. Open Wed.–Sun. 1–4. This small

LAFOND VINEYARD

museum is housed in what was once the home of two Danish artists and today is dedicated to all things Danish. Exhibits showcase Danish folk arts like paper cutting, needlework, and lace making. Costumed docents demonstrate crafts and offer guided tours through the museum and art gallery. Admission is free.

Hans Christian Andersen Museum (www.solvangca.com/museum), 1680 Mission Dr., Solvang. Open daily 10–5. The small museum, just upstairs from **The Book Loft,** offers exhibits that include first-edition books, Andersen's sketchbooks, and photos. Admission is free.

Historical Museum and Carriage House (805-688-7889; www.santaynez museum.org), corner of Sagunto and Faraday streets, Santa Ynez. Open Wed.–Sun. noon–4. Operated by the Santa Ynez Historical Society, this small museum showcases carriages and stagecoaches of the Old West, as well as saddles, antique clothing, and Native American artifacts. Adults $4, children free.

OLD MISSION SANTA INÉS

✷ To Do

BICYCLING For biking through the Santa Ynez Valley wine country, check out **Wine Country Cycling** (888-557-8687; www.winecountrycycling.com).

GOLF La Purisima Golf Course (805-735-8395; www.lapurisimagolf.com), 3455 CA 246, Lompoc. In the Santa Ynez Valley, outside Lompoc, this 18-hole, par 72 public course is a favorite with locals, who appreciate the reasonable rates. Green fee: $60–78.

✪ **River Course at the Alisal** (805-688-6042; www.rivercourse.com), 150 Alisal Rd., Solvang. This public course was featured in the 2004 movie *Sideways* (see *Wineries*) and offers beautiful views of the Santa Ynez Mountains and central proximity to both Santa Barbara and the Santa Ynez Valley. Green fee: $50–60.

WINERIES The wine country of Santa Ynez Valley was made famous by the 2004 film *Sideways*, which chronicles the wine-tasting and romantic adventures of two men who explore the best of the area. There are five distinct winemaking regions: Santa Maria Valley, Santa Ynez Valley, Santa Rita Hills, Los Alamos Valley, and Happy Canyon. There are dozens of wineries in each region, most of which boast tasting rooms. The cost of tastings averages about $10 for five to six wines. Tasting rooms generally open at 10 or 11 AM and remain open until 4:30 or 5 PM. The region is growing fast, and the following represent only a handful of the best wineries.

🍸 **Bridalwood Winery** (805-688-9000; www.bridlewoodwinery.com), 3555 Roblar Ave., Santa Ynez. Approach this lovely winery via a long, tree-lined drive and discover a tasting-room complex that looks like a Spanish mission. The tasting room is huge by Santa Ynez Valley standards, with high ceilings, open beams, and plenty of tasting stations. The winery specializes in Syrahs and boasts "old-world wine making techniques and new-world vineyard management."

WINE TASTING 101

Wine tasting doesn't have to be intimidating or snobbish. The point is to find favorite wines and favorite wineries, and there is no "wrong" choice. Every expert agrees: drink what you like, and don't worry about what is *supposed* to be best. For those who are new to wine tasting, follow these tips to look like a pro:

1. After receiving a partial glass for tasting (usually filled only about an inch), look at the wine, noting its color and clarity.
2. Gently swirl the wine inside the glass for about five seconds: the point is to aerate the wine.
3. Sniff the wine: try to detect the smell of fruit, herbs, or spices, which provide a clue to the taste.
4. Sip the wine. Don't be shy about slurping: this additional aerating will open up the flavors.

If you don't like the wine, swallow the first sip and dump out the rest in the dump bucket. (This isn't considered rude.) Be sure to follow the winery's suggested order for wines (usually sparkling, white, rosé, then red), and cleanse the palate between tastings with crackers or bread. Drink plenty of water to avoid headaches, and designate a nontaster to drive from one tasting site to the next.

ZACA MESA WINERY

🍸 **Cambria Estate Winery** (805-938-7318; www.cambriawines.com), 5475 Chardonnay Lane, Santa Maria. Specializing in chardonnay, pinot gris, pinot noir, and viognier, far-flung Cambria Estate is in the northeastern-most portion of Santa Barbara County. Glass windows in the tasting room offer a peek into the winery operations, and the pretty tasting room is often crowded.

🍸 **Fess Parker Winery** (805-688-1545; www.fessparker.com), 6200 Foxen Canyon Rd., Los Olivos. Fess Parker of TV's *Daniel Boone* fame owned and operated this winery until his death in 2010. The winery specializes in Burgundian and Rhône varietals, and offers an extensive gift shop and a large grassy picnic area. The rambling estate hosts summer performances by the Shakespeare Santa Barbara Theater.

✪ 🍸 **Lafond Winery** (805-688-7921; www.lafondwinery.com), 6855 Santa Rosa Rd., Buellton. The exterior that fronts the popular Santa Rosa Rd. wine trail is modest, but the views of the vineyards and bucolic mountains behind the tasting room are some of the prettiest in the valley. Service is friendly and knowledgeable, and the wine is exceptional, especially the pinot noir.

🍸 **Sanford Winery** (800-426-9463; www.sanfordwinery.com), 5010 Santa Rosa Rd., Lompoc. This Tuscan-style tasting room at the foothills of the Santa Rita Hills is surrounded by wildflower gardens with vineyards in the back, along with an inviting outdoor fireplace and picnic tables.

✪ 🍸 **Zaca Mesa Winery** (805-688-9339; www.zacamesa.com), 6905 Foxen Canyon Rd., Los Olivos. Located along the scenic Foxen Canyon wine trail, Zaca Mesa offers a simple tasting room with an appealing metal bar, friendly pourers, and among the most drinkable wines in the valley. After sampling the wares, take the nearby Windmill Trail (accessible from the winery parking lot) up a short, very steep hike for views of the vineyards and the mountains in the distance. Bring along a picnic (the winery sells cheese, crackers, and salami) to enjoy at a table beneath a grapevine-covered pergola.

✷ Lodging

Los Olivos

🍸 **Fess Parker Wine Country Inn and Spa** (805-688-7788; www.fessparker.com), 2860 Grand Ave. Located in the heart of the pretty, small town of Los Olivos, the Fess Parker Inn is a

PRICE KEY FOR A STANDARD ROOM:

$	$100 or less
$$	$101–150
$$$	$151–250
$$$$	$251 and up

rambling Victorian with commodious rooms adorned with floral fabrics and cozy fireplaces. On arrival, guests will receive a half bottle of Fess Parker wine, as well as a complimentary wine tasting for two at the nearby **Fess Parker Winery.** The location is unbeatable: close driving distance to Santa Ynez Valley wineries and walking distance to a dozen wine-tasting rooms in town. $$$$

Santa Ynez

✪ Y ⚥ **Santa Ynez Inn** (805-688-5588; www.santaynezinn.com), 3627 Sagunto St. This beautiful new Victorian inn boasts over-the-top Queen Anne décor with rich details that include massive chandeliers and lots of polished dark wood. Beyond the large bathrooms and roomy closets (a dead giveaway of a modern design), it's hard to tell this isn't a historic property. Some rooms include fireplaces and huge Jacuzzi tubs. The inn offers a fabulous hot breakfast in a cozy dining room with a fireplace and hosts evening wine tastings in the quaint parlor. The romantic ambiance is perfect for a cozy weekend getaway. For a small fee, the inn will arrange in-room delivery of red roses, chocolate-covered strawberries, or a bottle of champagne on ice. $$$$

Solvang

✪ **Hadsten House** (805-688-3210; www.hadstenhouse.com), 1450 Mission Dr. Don't let the exterior fool you: what looks like a typical 1960s-era motel (with the Danish half-timber exterior that Solvang mandates) has been transformed inside to a surprisingly chic boutique lodging. Rooms are small but well appointed, with comfortable couches, fireplaces, flat-screen TVs, fine linens, and very stylish interior designs in black and white with punches of red. Because this is on the edge of town, this is a particularly appealing option for wine tasters who want the convenience of overnighting in the larger city of Solvang but who don't want to be in the thick of the tourist congestion. The on-site restaurant is one of the best in the area (see *Dining Out*). $$–$$$

Hotel Corque (805-688-8000; www.hotelcorque.com), 400 Alisal Rd. The Chumash Nation recently bought this large property—formerly known as the Royal Scandinavian—and undertook a massive renovation of the space. Interiors now appeal to the wine-country crowd with upscale, modern design that is chic and comfortable. Each guest room is slightly different, but expect soothing earth tones, rich woods, and luxurious linens. Bathrooms offer soaking tubs or extra-large showers with oversized shower heads. Each room features original artwork and an oversized flat-screen TV. Rates are astonishingly low, given the high style and exceptional level of service. On-site dining is at the upscale **Root 246.** $$

HADSTEN HOUSE

✷ Where to Eat

DINING OUT

PRICE KEY FOR A TYPICAL ENTRÉE:	
$	$10 and under
$$	$11–20
$$$	$21–30
$$$$	$31 and up

Buellton

🍸 **The Hitching Post II** (805-688-0676; www.hitchingpost2.com), 406 E. CA 246. Open daily for dinner. Just west of Solvang, the Hitching Post II is renowned for oak-wood-grilled steaks and an impressive wine collection, including particularly fine pinot noirs (including Hitching Post wines bottled by the restaurant's own winemakers). Locals come for the grilled artichokes served with smoky ancho chile aioli. Flank steaks and t-bones are juicy and flavorful (although cooked a bit rarer than one might normally expect: if you want what is typically medium, order medium well). Specials include ostrich steaks raised on a nearby ranch. Although the interior is homey and unassuming, the place attracts foodies from around the country. $$

Los Olivos

🍸 **Los Olivos Café** (888-WINES4U; www.losolivoscafe.com), 2879 Grand Ave. Open daily for lunch and dinner. Made famous in the 2004 film *Sideways* as the site of Paul Giamatti's infamous drunken phone call, Los Olivos Café is a relaxed and comfortable restaurant featuring wine-country cuisine and an impressive wine collection, with more than five hundred varieties. Outside is a lovely vine-covered patio, which makes for a romantic evening meal when the weather is warm. Start with the baked Brie in pastry crust topped with a sweet port-wine reduction, and for the main course, don't miss the spoon-tender pot roast piled high with sweet potato chips. The restaurant is famous for their "scream cake," presumably the reaction the first bite elicits: a decadent flourless brownie is topped with a generous portion of homemade vanilla ice cream that is drizzled with caramel sauce—maybe not worthy of a scream, but certainly a groan of delight. $$

WINE WELL AT LOS OLIVOS CAFÉ

Santa Ynez

🍸 **Dos Carlitos** (805-688-0033; www.doscarlitosrestaurant.com), 3544 Sagunto St. Open daily for dinner. This colorful Mexican bistro is fronted by an extensive outdoor patio adorned with bright umbrellas and an old-growth oak tree. Inside there is an extensive tequila bar, open-beamed ceilings, and warm décor. Vegetarians will appreciate the roasted eggplant, tomato, and basil quesadilla with asadero cheese served with cilantro pesto. Carnivores will delight in the sizzling fajitas platter, overflowing with mesquite-grilled chicken and steak and served with handmade corn tortillas. Another house specialty is the authentic grilled chicken breast with mole poblano. $$

🍸 **Vineyard House Restaurant** (805-688-2886; www.thevineyardhouse.com), 3631 Sagunto St. Open Wed.–Mon. for lunch and dinner, brunch on Sun. Part of the **Santa Ynez Inn,** this wine-country restaurant has a country-style dining room and an extensive outdoor patio. Dinner specials include crispy buttermilk chicken with onion gravy, charbroiled rib eye with onion rings, and butternut squash ravioli with a roasted cream sauce. Sun. brunch features crabcakes Benedict and chilaquile frittatas. $$$

Solvang

✪ 🍸 **Hadsten House Restaurant** (805-688-3210; www.hadstenhouse.com), 1450 Mission Dr. Open daily for breakfast, lunch, and dinner. Like the hotel this restaurant serves, the Hadsten House Restaurant is unassuming on the outside: it's easy to bypass, given there is no large sign on the exterior—just a side door beyond the hotel's main entrance. Also like the hotel, the restaurant holds myriad surprises. Step into a moody, elegant dining space with large leather sofas clustered around a fireplace, intimate booths and tables, and an inviting bar. The dinner menu offers delights like dreamy macaroni and cheese with lobster, and a Hadsten House monster burger that comes with several kinds of cheeses, sautéed spinach, mushrooms, and a fried egg (be sure to order the homemade truffle chips as an accompaniment). Desserts are huge and well worth the calories: try the bananas Foster, served with puff pastry and homemade vanilla ice cream. $$

Heidelberg Inn (805-688-6213; www.theheidelberginn.com), 1618 Copenhagen Dr. Open daily for lunch and dinner. Specializing in German (and some Danish) dishes, the Heidelberg Inn offers authentic bratwurst, sauerbraten, and jagerschnitzel, and more than 20 beers. Be sure to save room for the homemade apple strudel, which is served with warm vanilla sauce and is alone worth the visit. $$

DOS CARLITOS

✪ 🍸 **Root 246** (805-688-9003; www.root-246.com), 420 Alisal Rd. Open daily for dinner, lunch on the weekends. A Bradley Ogden restaurant, upscale Root 246 specializes in local, organic ingredients and is easily the finest dining option in touristy Solvang. The chic dining room is blissfully lacking Danish knickknackery, instead offering an opulent, high-style lounge in which to enjoy the chef's farm-to-table approach to cuisine. Menus change regularly but might include options like pumpkin ravioli with pomegranate cream and fried shallots; a short rib stew with crispy sweetbreads; or local snapper with mushrooms and a citrus emulsion. Be sure to try the house-made ice creams and sorbets. $$$$

EATING OUT

Buellton

🖍 **A.J. Spurs** (805-686-1655), 350 E. CA 246. Open daily for lunch and dinner. This restaurant looks like something out of a Wild West movie: there are a couple of stagecoaches on the roof, taxidermied buffalo and bears inside this log-cabin structure, and wagon wheels in just about every nook and cranny. The ambiance and the cuisine are family friendly, and the place specializes in oak pit barbecue and massive portions. The aptly named Twin Peaks dish is two bacon-wrapped filets served with two different sauces—and is easily enough for two people to share. (Note, however, that the restaurant charges a hefty fee to split entrées.) Try to save room for the root beer float. $$

Pea Soup Andersen's (805-688-5581; www.peasoupandersens.com), 376 Ave. of the Flags. Open daily for lunch and dinner. The original Pea Soup Andersen's, this expansive place serves the specialty pea soup, as well as burgers and salads. Stop by the in-house bakery on the way out for Danish pastries. $

Solvang

Big Bopper Drive-In (805-688-6018), 1510 Mission Dr. Open daily for lunch and dinner. A '50s-style drive-in, the Big Bopper offers burgers, fries, and a few Mexican fast-food specialties. Try the peanut butter shake. $

Bit O' Denmark Restaurant and Bar (805-688-5426), 473 Alisal Rd. Open daily for lunch and dinner. For more than 40 years, Bit O' Denmark has been serving Danish specialties like *medisterpolse* (Danish sausage), *frikadeller* (meatballs), and *rodkaal* (red cabbage). Danish friends tell me the cuisine is authentic, although Scandinavian food is definitely not to everyone's taste. Warning: Service can be slow. $$

Mortensen's Danish Bakery (805-688-8373), 1588 Mission Dr. Open daily. Pastry chefs bake homemade pumpernickel bread and mounds of sweet treats every day for hungry tourists, who flock to this place likes flies to—well, Danish pastry. $

✪ **Olsen's Danish Bakery and Coffee Shop** (805-688-6314), 1529 Mission Dr. Open daily. My favorite bakery among nearly a dozen in this small town, family-owned Olsen's (now run by the fourth generation) offers authentic almond custard kringle pastries that are to die for. The shop also sells some of the best Kranskage (almond horn-shaped cookies) in the city. $

Red Viking (805-688-6610; www.theredvikingrestaurant.com), 1684 Copenhagen Dr. Open daily 8–8. Specializing in Danish dishes, Wiener schnitzel, and Danish smorgasbord, the Red Viking is locally famous for its huge open-faced roast beef sandwiches served with horseradish and Danish cucumbers. $$

✪ **Solvang Restaurant** (805-688-4645; www.solvangrestaurant.com), 1672 Copenhagen Dr. Open daily for breakfast, lunch, and dinner. This unpretentious diner specializes in round Danish pancakes called Aebelskiver, which are served hot, smothered

OLSEN'S BAKERY

AEBELSKIVER, SOLVANG RESTAURANT

in raspberry jam, and dusted with powdered sugar. Aebelskiver are made to order, but if you're in a hurry, the Solvang Restaurant has a to-go window, and the cook will gladly make you an order "to walk." $

✷ Entertainment

CLUBS 🍸 **Maverick's Saloon** (805-686-4785), 3687 Sagunto St., Santa Ynez. A historic Old West–themed restaurant, bar, and dance club, Maverick's is housed in a building that has been the site of a saloon since the early 1900s. The place features live music and dancing in a friendly atmosphere that falls somewhere between honky-tonk and barn dance. What's most fun about this place is that it attracts an eclectic crowd of all ages, from locals to wine tourists, from farmers to students.

THEATERS Solvang Festival Theater (805-686-1789), 420 Second St., Solvang. A seven-hundred-seat open-air arena theater, this venue hosts the Pacific Conservatory for the Performing Arts festival in the summer. The theater also host workshops for students.

✷ Selective Shopping

Wandering the tiny boutiques in Solvang is fun, and there are plenty of wine rooms featuring the products of local wineries, but there's no getting around the fact that shopping in this region tends toward kitschy souvenirs and wine. Beyond these two extremes, in Solvang, seek out **Vinhus** (805-688-7117), 440 Alisal Road, the best place in the valley to purchase gourmet picnic fixings to bring along on vineyard tours. Other good options include the Christmas-themed **Jule Hus** (805-688-6601; www.solvangchristmashouse.com), 1580 Mission Drive; **The Book Loft** (805-688-9930), 1680 Mission Drive; **Clock Shop Jewelers** (800-939-5426), 467 Alisal Road; and the European import shop **Gaveaesken** (805-686-5699), 433 Alisal Road. And although it takes some effort to find the place, the **Clairmont Lavender Farms** (805-688-7505), 2480 Roblar Avenue, in Los Olivos, is a lovely place to visit during peak blooming season (in late June) and a good place year-round to purchase culinary lavender, scented soaps, and pretty sachets—perfect for freshening a suitcase full of laundry.

CLAIRMONT LAVENDER FARMS

TOP 10 DAY IN SANTA YNEZ WINE COUNTRY

1. Dive into the gooey goodness of a slice of kringle from Olsen's (see p. 288)
2. Take a morning tour of the Elverhoj Museum (see pp. 281–282)
3. Hit the wine trail in Santa Ynez Valley (see p. 283)
4. Picnic on wine and cheese at Zaca Mesa (see p. 284)
5. Play eighteen holes at the River Course at the Alisal (see p. 283)
6. Arrange a photo op with the *Little Mermaid* statue in Solvang (see p. 281)
7. Dine on a soft-shell crab sandwich with a side of truffle fries at Hadsten House Restaurant (see p. 287)
8. Shoot tequila at Dos Carlitos (see p. 286)
9. Two-step at Maverick's Saloon (see p. 289)
10. Overnight at the Santa Ynez Inn (see p. 285)

✷ Special Events

(in Greater Santa Barbara)

January: **Santa Barbara International Film Festival** (www.sbfilmfestival.org), with more than 250 screenings of movies from around the world.

March: **Annual Taste of Solvang Food and Wine Festival** (805-688-6144), toward midmonth, features a Walking Smorgasbord with more than 50 tasting sites throughout downtown Solvang. **Santa Barbara International Orchid Show** (www.sborchidshow.com), in Santa Barbara, also in mid-month, exhibits thousands of orchids.

April: **Vintners' Festival** (www.sbcountywines.com), in Santa Barbara, offers wine tastings, winemaker dinners, and entertainment.

May: **I Madonnari Italian Street Painting Festival** (www.imadonnarifestival.com), over Memorial Day, features more than two hundred chalk paintings at the plaza of the Santa Barbara Mission in Santa Barbara.

June: Running through the end of Sept., **Solvang's Pacific Conservatory of Performing Arts Theaterfest Live Performances** has shows under the stars at the Solvang Festival Theater.

July: **French Festival** (www.frenchfestival.com), in Santa Barbara, on or near Bastille Day, has food, music, and other live entertainment.

August: **Old Spanish Days Fiesta** (www.oldspanishdays-fiesta.org), a city-wide celebration in Santa Barbara, has food, wine, music, and a dance rodeo.

September: **Annual Solvang Danish Days Celebration** includes Hans Christian Andersen storytelling sessions, parades, live entertainment, and plenty of Danish food. **Book and Author Festival,** Santa Barbara, features book signings, panel discussions, and the chance to meet authors.

October: **Harbor and Seafood Festival** (www.santabarbara.gov) celebrates the fruits of the sea in Santa Barbara.

November: **California Indian Festival,** at the Santa Barbara Museum of Natural History, includes Native American storytelling, dancing, children's crafts, and music.

December: **Downtown Holiday Parade** (www.santabarbaradowntown.com), in downtown Santa Barbara early in the month, stars Santa himself.

San Luis Obispo 7

SAN LUIS OBISPO

PISMO BEACH, MORRO BAY, AND CAMBRIA

PASO ROBLES

San Luis Obispo County

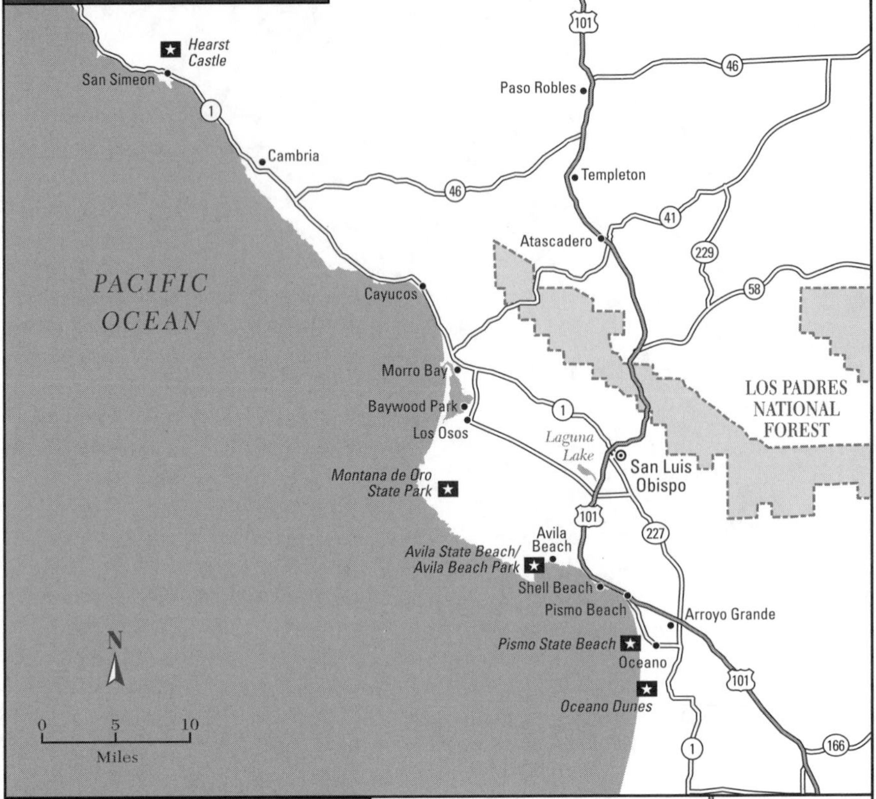
Hearst Castle
San Simeon
Cambria
Paso Robles
Templeton
Atascadero
PACIFIC OCEAN
Cayucos
Morro Bay
Baywood Park
Los Osos
Laguna Lake
San Luis Obispo
LOS PADRES NATIONAL FOREST
Montana de Oro State Park
Avila Beach
Avila State Beach/ Avila Beach Park
Shell Beach
Pismo Beach
Arroyo Grande
Pismo State Beach
Oceano
Oceano Dunes
101
46
1
41
229
58
227
166
N
0 5 10
Miles

Downtown San Luis Obispo

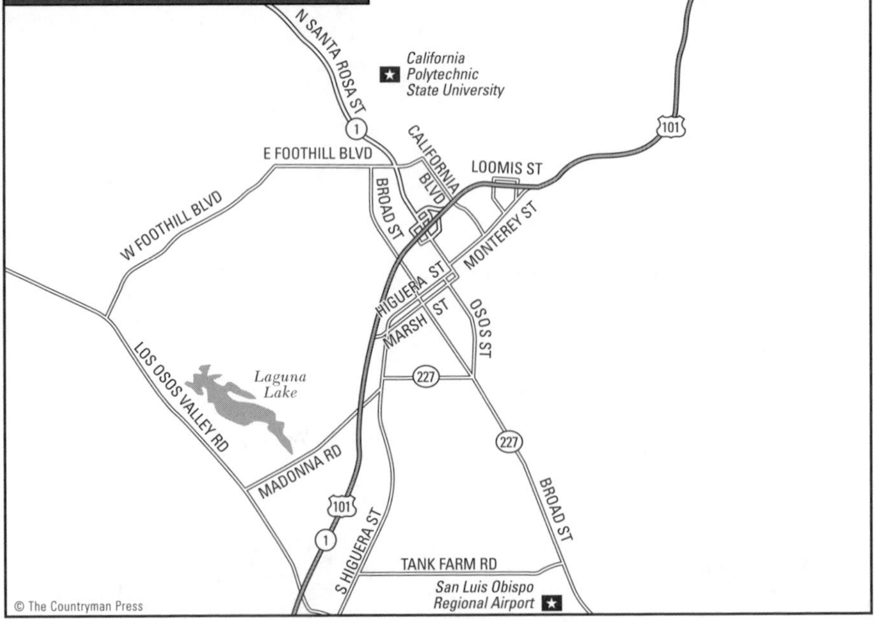
N SANTA ROSA ST
California Polytechnic State University
E FOOTHILL BLVD
CALIFORNIA BLVD
LOOMIS ST
BROAD ST
W FOOTHILL BLVD
MONTEREY ST
HIGUERA ST
MARSH ST
OSOS ST
LOS OSOS VALLEY RD
Laguna Lake
MADONNA RD
S HIGUERA ST
TANK FARM RD
San Luis Obispo Regional Airport
101
1
227
© The Countryman Press

INTRODUCTION

Located slightly inland, east of historic Highway 101 and about three and a half hours north of Los Angeles, San Luis Obispo is in the heart of the Central Coast. Even though San Luis Obispo does fall in the lower half of the state (and thus is included in this book), this area is a distinct region, with a feeling apart from the sprawling expanse of San Diego, the congestion of Los Angeles, and the sophistication and moneyed ambiance of Santa Barbara. Driving north into San Luis Obispo on historic Highway 101, the road cuts through rolling hills that go on for miles, with little evidence of development. It isn't unusual to see cows grazing on the lush, bucolic foothills—and it's easy to imagine these as the infamous "happy cows" of California. The small city of San Luis Obispo nestles in a valley at the foot of the pretty hills and offers a compact, imminently livable enclave for the artsy, health-conscious, environmentally aware population. At heart a college town (home of California Polytechnic State College—CalPoly), the pace is relaxed, congestion is rare, and the locals epitomize laid-back. Even the abbreviation of the town name—SLO, which is appended to myriad businesses throughout town—points to the unrushed pace of life here.

The downtown center is walkable, vibrant, and diverse, offering cultural treats such as historic movie theaters, creekside dining, and a crazy alleyway completely paved over with chewed gum. An added bonus for visitors is the ample public parking, either streetside or in lots with meters. And the city is lovely, thanks to the quaint architecture and the predominant natural feature: a river runs through it (or at least a creek). The San Luis Creek downtown is a favorite with children and makes for a picturesque backdrop for a handful of restaurants with outdoor patios that back to the small waterway.

Just north of SLO is the small-town community of Atascadero. To the southwest are Pismo Beach and Avila Beach, and just to the northwest of these is Morro Bay (home to a national estuary and Morro Rock, a state historical monument often called the Gibraltar of the Pacific). Heading still farther north, along the coast, is Cayucos (a favorite for surfers and fishermen, and home to the Cayucos Pier) and Cambria. Cambria is an artsy village nestled between the hillsides and the ocean, and offers two downtown sections: historic East Village and the newer West Village. Nearby is tiny San Simeon (home of the famous Hearst Castle). Eastward is Paso Robles, one of the best winemaking regions in the state (many say second only to Napa and Sonoma) and a lovely region that offers rolling hills paved over with vineyards, quaint architecture, and a rural feel.

SAN LUIS CREEK

GUIDANCE Atascadero Visitors Bureau (805-466-2044; www.visitatascadero.com).

Paso Robles Chamber of Commerce (www.pasorobleschamber.com/).

Pismo Beach Information (805-773-4382; www.classiccalifornia.com), 581 Dolliver St., Pismo Beach.

Welcome to San Luis Obispo County (805-541-8000; www.sanluisobispocounty.com), 811 El Capitan Way, San Luis Obispo.

MEDICAL EMERGENCIES As with all cities in Southern California, dial 911 for medical emergencies. Local hospitals include the following:

French Hospital Medical Center (805-543-5353), 1911 Johnson Ave., San Luis Obispo.

Santa Maria Care Center (805-925-8877), 820 W. Cook St., Santa Maria.

Sierra Vista Regional Medical Center (805-546-7600), 1010 Murray Ave., San Luis Obispo.

Twin Cities Community Hospital (805-434-2500), 1100 Las Tablas Rd., Templeton.

GETTING THERE *By bus:* The **Greyhound Bus** line serves San Luis Obispo county with stations in Arroyo Grande, Atascadero, Paso Robles, and San Luis Obispo proper.

By plane: **San Luis Obispo Regional Airport** (805-781-5205; http://sloairport.com), 903-5 Airport Dr., San Luis Obispo. South of the city of San Luis Obispo, this airport serves the Central Coast via two commercial airlines that fly in from Los Angeles, Phoenix, and San Francisco.

By train: **AMTRAK** offers service along the Central Coast via the *Coast Starlight* and the *Pacific Surfliner* trains, with depots in San Luis Obispo, Paso Robles, and nearby Grover Beach.

GETTING AROUND *By bus:* The **San Luis Obispo Regional Transit Authority** (RTA) coordinates all public transportation in the area. RTA buses run from the city of San Luis Obispo along the coast northward to Morro Bay, Cambria, and San Simeon; south to Pismo Beach; and north to Paso Robles.

By car: San Luis Obispo County is the least-congested region covered in this book and as a result is one of the easiest to drive. Traffic is rare, roadways are scenic, and parking is abundant, even in downtown SLO.

By trolley: Avila Beach and Cambria offer trolley services. The **Avila Beach Trolley** runs through Avila and Shell Beach on weekends 9–6 and is free to all riders. The **Cambria Trolley** operates Friday–Sunday 9–6 and runs from Cambria to San Simeon and Hearst Castle. Rides are 50 cents.

SAN LUIS OBISPO

San Luis Obispo is a bit of a throwback—and I mean that in the best possible sense: the downtown has a comfortable, small-town feel; the pace is notoriously "SLO"; and the mellow vibe is vaguely hipster. The storefronts downtown are tidy, the streets are safe and clean, and the ambiance is friendly. Nearby CalPoly and its students keep the population youthful, and likely for this reason, there are numerous opportunities throughout town to listen to live music, drink beer, and catch poetry readings. This is also a great place to eat healthy, because there are a number of vegetarian eateries, a ridiculously large number of farmer's markets, and a growing number of restaurants that practice sustainable cooking using organic ingredients. Best of all, this is one of the few cities in Southern California that is compact and easily accessible: you can tour the place in a few days without feeling overwhelmed, and it is next to impossible to get lost.

✱ To See

HISTORICAL SITES ✐ **Bubblegum Alley,** off Higuera St., between Garden and Broad streets, San Luis Obispo. Maybe Bubble Gum Alley doesn't qualify as historical, but it is definitely a "site." This narrow alleyway is covered inches deep in chewed gum, from the bottom of the walls about 7 feet up, stretching the length of the approximately 20-foot alley. It is artistic in a creepy, sticky way, and a definite must-see for visitors with children, who will surely want to add to the collection.

BUBBLEGUM ALLEY

✪ **Mission San Luis Obispo de Tolosa** (805-543-6850), 751 Palm St., San Luis Obispo. Open daily 9–4. Founded in 1772, the San Luis mission is unique in that it continues to be completely ensconced in the old part of downtown San Luis Obispo, and thus continues to be a vital part of city life. Learn about native Chumash

MISSION SAN LUIS OBISPO

Indians and California history in the tiny museum, and then step inside the pretty working church. Note that there is a daily Mass at noon, during which the chapel is closed to tourists. By donation.

MUSEUMS Jack House (805-781-7308), 535 Marsh St., San Luis Obispo. Open for tours Sun. 1–4.This property dates to 1870, when the Jack family (of local banking fame) called it home (remaining there for nearly 90 years); the Victorian house is now a living museum, with rooms filled with original furnishings, utensils, tools, and artwork. The library is especially interesting, with more than two thousand volumes, many of which are first editions. Admission $4.

FREMONT THEATER

San Luis Obispo Children's Museum (805-544-KIDS; www.slocm.org), 1010 Nipoma St., San Luis Obispo. Open Tues.–Sun.; hours vary by season. Young kids will enjoy more than 20 hands-on exhibits that include singing and dancing on a performance stage, fighting "fires" at the Fire Station, and serving a meal at the Cosmic Café. Onsite is a 17-foot indoor clock tower climbing playground. Admission $8.

PARKS El Chorro Regional Park and Botanical Garden (www.slocountyparks.com/activities/el_chorro.htm), off Hwy. 101 at Santa

TOP 10 DAY IN SAN LUIS OBISPO

1. Dive in to the Devil's Mess for breakfast at Big Sky Café (see p. 302)
2. Take a morning self-tour of the Mission San Luis Obispo de Tolosa (see pp. 296–297)
3. Shop for fresh fruit at any SLO farmer's market (see p. 302)
4. Window-shop along Higuera St. (see p. 306)
5. Munch on a bacon cheeseburger at the Creeky Tiki on the outdoor patio (see p. 304)
6. Stroll along the pretty San Luis Creek (see p. 294)
7. Enjoy a predinner pint at the Downtown Brewing Company (see p. 305)
8. Dine on Malaysian chicken with toasted coconut at Novo (see pp. 303–304)
9. Catch a retrospective flick at the Fremont Theater downtown (see p. 306)
10. Overnight in the Cabin Still room (with waterfall shower) at the over-the-top Madonna Inn (see pp. 301–302)

Rosa St./Hwy. 1, across from Cuesta College. Located midway between San Luis Obispo and Morro Bay, the expansive El Chorro Regional Park comprises campgrounds, hiking trails, day-use barbecue facilities, the **Dairy Creek Golf Course,** softball fields, and the **San Luis Obispo Botanical Garden.** This is a favorite with outdoorsy locals.

✷ To Do

BICYCLING Environmentally conscious folks in San Luis Obispo take bicycling seriously, and there are a number of groups in town that promote bicycle safety, use of helmets, and maintenance of bike trails (e.g., the San Luis Obispo Bicycle Coalition, 805-543-5973; and the Bicycle Advisory Committee, 805-781-7590). Bike trails and bike lanes can be found throughout the city and beyond, into the undeveloped hills that surround the city, and thanks to the ubiquitous dry, warm weather, it's possible to ride nearly every day in San Luis Obispo. To find the latest information on bike routes throughout the region, go to www.mapmyride.com/find-ride/united-states/ca/san+luis+obispo. For organized bike tours, check out reputable organizations like **Central Coast Outdoors** (805-528-1080; www.centralcoastoutdoors.com) or (for longer trips) **Bicycle Adventures** (www.bicycleadventures.com/where/california).

GOLF Although the Central Coast is slightly less enamored of golfing than the communities in the extreme southern part of the state (or just to the north, in golf-centric Pebble Beach), there are still ample opportunities for avid golfers in and around San Luis Obispo.

Blacklake Golf Course (805-343-1214; www.blacklake.com), 1490 Golf Course Lane, Nipoma. A 27-hole championship-caliber course, Blacklake is punctuated with massive old-growth California oaks, stunning natural water features, and meticulously manicured greens. Green fee: $46–56.

Chalk Mountain Golf Club (805-466-8848; www.chalkmountaingolf.com), 10000 El Bordo Ave., Atascadero. This 18-hole, par 72 course is set on rolling hills amid oak groves. A pretty creek runs through it. Green fee: $36–45.

✪ **Cypress Ridge Golf Course** (805-474-7979; www.cypressridge.com), 780 Cypress Ridge Pkwy., Arroyo Grande. This highly rated Peter Jacobsen Signature course makes the most of the natural beauty of the surroundings. The challenging 18 holes wind through mature cypress and rolling hills. Green fee: $55–68.

Dairy Creek Golf Course (805-782-8060; www.slocountyparks.com/facilities/dairycreek.htm), 2990 Dairy Creek Rd., San Luis Obispo. Part of the **El Chorro Regional Park,** the par 71 Dairy Creek course offers views of rolling hills and a plethora of water hazards, making this one of the most challenging courses in the city. Green fee: $42–47.

Laguna Lake Municipal Golf Course (805-781-7309), 11175 Los Osos Valley Rd., San Luis Obispo. This city-owned nine-hole executive course is well maintained and exceptionally affordable. This is a great place to take kids, because the length of the course is manageable and the patrons aren't uptight about golfers who know little about the game. Green fee: $10.

✪ **Monarch Dunes** (805-343-9459; www.monarchdunes.com), 1606 Trilogy Pkwy., Nipomo. *Golf Magazine* voted Monarch Dunes one of the top 10 new courses in the country. Set within the planned community of the Woodlands, near San Luis Obispo, the course's links-style layout offers picturesque sand dunes, coastal views, and eucalyptus groves. Green fee: $57–78.

THEME PARKS AND ZOOS **Charles Paddock Zoo** (805-461-5080; www.charlespaddockzoo.org), Lago Ave., Atascadero. Open daily 10–5, Apr.–Oct. In Atascadero—at **Atascadero Lake Park**—this facility was begun in the 1950s by a park ranger who wanted to help wild animals recover from injuries. Today the 5-acre zoo shelters more than one hundred animals, many of which are on view, and some of which can be fed by patrons. Guests can rent paddleboats to enjoy the lake as well. Adults $5, children 3–11 $3.

✷ Green Space

GARDENS **Atascadero Sunken Gardens,** El Camino Real, Atascadero. Inspired by the Grand Basin at the 1904 St. Louis World's Fair, city founder E. G. Lewis proposed a sunken garden as a central meeting point for his community. Today walkways cut through the gardens and meet at a pretty central fountain. In the summer, this is the site of free movies and outdoor concert series (see *Greater San Luis Obispo Special Events*).

Jack House Gardens, 536 Marsh St., San Luis Obispo. Open for tours Sun. 1–4. Located in downtown SLO, the historic Victorian **Jack House** offers a glimpse into a historic garden, with one-hundred-year-old trees, Victorian roses, flower hedges, and a quaint gazebo that is a popular site for weddings. Admission $2.

Leaning Pine Arboretum (805-756-2888; www.leaningpinearboretum.calpoly.edu), on the campus of CalPoly. Open daily during daylight hours. This 5-acre garden is part of the CalPoly Horticulture and Crop Science program and features

CARRIZO PLAIN NATIONAL MONUMENT

About 60 miles east of San Luis Obispo, the 250,000-acre Carrizo Plain (805-475-2131; www.blm.gov/ca/st/en/fo/bakersfield/Programs/carrizo.html) falls at the foot of the Temblor Mountains and offers myriad opportunities for hiking, photography, camping, and wildlife viewing. This is the single largest native grassland area that remains in California. It includes Soda Lake, a shallow alkali lake, and offers the most obvious view of the San Andreas Fault, which cuts through the plain. This area is well worth visiting because of the gorgeous landscape and huge diversity of wildlife, including the highest concentration of endangered and threatened species in the state, and it is a favorite with birders in winter (sandhill cranes overwinter at Soda Lake, and roadrunners and mountain quail are in abundance) and with wildflower enthusiasts in the spring. Reach the area from CA 166, which passes the south entrance, or CA 58, which goes through the north section of the plain.

trees, shrubs, and flowers that grow readily in the Central Coast region. Collections are arranged by their native habitats and include specialty gardens from South Africa, Australia, and Chile. There are also extensive displays of succulents, palms, and dwarf conifers. Admission is free.

San Luis Obispo Botanical Garden (www.slocountyparks.com/activities/el_chorro.htm), off Hwy. 101 at Santa Rosa St./Hwy. 1, across from Cuesta College. Open daily during daylight hours. Located in the **El Chorro Regional Park,** the botanical garden displays vignettes created from plants indigenous to Mediterranean climate zones around the world. Although still growing and evolving, the garden means to become a world-class educational facility that demonstrates resource conservation through sustainable gardening. Admission is free.

✱ Lodging

San Luis Obispo

San Luis Obispo proper is awash with perfectly acceptable, moderate chain hotels, most of which are clustered outside downtown. There are also a handful of tiny bed & breakfasts. But to date there are few high-quality independent lodging options in the city. Thus, unless visitors are keen to be near CalPoly, many who are looking for options with more character choose to stay in the nearby beach communities, which offer plentiful independent lodging at a variety of price points (see *Lodging* in the "Pismo Beach, Morro Bay, and Cambria" chapter). It takes about 10 minutes to reach downtown SLO from Shell Beach, for example. There are two unique exceptions in San Luis Obispo, and both offer distinct style that may not appeal to everyone. If you don't mind a little bric-a-brac, however, these are worth considering.

PRICE KEY FOR A STANDARD ROOM:

$	$100 or less
$$	$101–150
$$$	$151–250
$$$$	$251 and up

Apple Farm Inn (800-255-2040; www.applefarm.com), 2015 Monterey St. This moderately sized inn (with one-hundred-plus rooms) offers the charm of a bed & breakfast without the lack of privacy and overly solicitous service that sometimes comes with smaller B&Bs. Each room is uniquely decorated in a cozy, kitschy country décor; most come with fireplaces and romantic canopy beds. Families traveling together will find plenty of space in the two-bedroom suites, while budget travelers will appreciate the smaller, inexpensive motel-style accommodations in the Trellis Court. Also on-site is the **Apple Farm Inn Restaurant.** $–$$

✪ ✐ ⚤ **Madonna Inn** (805-543-3000; www.madonnainn.com), 100 Madonna Rd. The Madonna Inn is known around the world as an eclectic, whimsical property in which each guest room offers its occupants the chance to live out a fantasy—whether you want to be a cowboy, a Hollywood starlet, or a moonshiner. All 110 rooms in this white and bubblegum pink complex are decorated in a different theme and feature extensive woodworking and massive stones integrated into the design of most of the accommodations. Options include the Bridal Falls room, which is encased in stone (as many rooms are) and offers a

> **INSIDER TIP:** If you can't get reservations for the Madonna Inn—or don't think you can sleep in rooms that threaten sensory overload—consider getting a taste of the over-the-top décor by dining at either of the on-site restaurants (one is open for dinner only). The walls are pink, the carpet is pink, the upholstery is pink, the ladies' restroom is bright pink: nothing is left unadorned, and nothing is done halfway!

MADONNA INN

natural waterfall shower in the bathroom; the Caveman room, which is carved out of rock as well, adorned with animal prints and featuring a rock pond; and the Madonna Suite, with lipstick pink walls and ceiling, a huge stone fireplace, pink-rose carpeting, crystal chandeliers, and bathroom sinks carved out of a massive stone slab. This family-run inn is kitschy and trippy—and thus fits in absolutely with the iconoclastic SLO vibe. $$$

PRICE KEY FOR A TYPICAL ENTRÉE:

$	$10 and under
$$	$11–20
$$$	$21–30
$$$$	$31 and up

✱ Where to Eat

DINING OUT

San Luis Obispo

Apple Farm (805-544-6100), 2015 Monterey St. Open daily for breakfast, lunch, and dinner. Northeast of downtown, this country-style restaurant northeast of downtown (which is part of the **Apple Farm Inn**) is famous for breakfast omelets, like the Mediterranean, with olives, spinach, artichoke hearts, and feta; the SLO City Limits, with avocado, mushrooms, sprouts, and jack cheese; and the Farmer's Omelet, with apple sausage, smoked bacon, fresh tomatoes, and cheddar cheese. Hot biscuits and gravy and authentic potato pancakes served with apple sauce are also great eye-openers. This friendly place serves early-bird dinners 2:30–5 on weekdays, and they guarantee to seat patrons within 15 minutes or they will take 50 percent off the bill. $$

✪ ▼ **Big Sky Café** (805-545-5401; www.bigskycafe.com), 1121 Broad St. Open daily for breakfast, lunch, and dinner. This unpretentious, bustling neighborhood restaurant is friendly and hip. The décor features a rotating exhibit of paintings by local artists, which seems perfectly fitting for a place that specializes in locally grown ingredients. Breakfast is served until 1 PM, which gives guests plenty of time to order the infamous Devil's Mess, a scramble with sautéed onions, mushrooms, spicy sausage, spinach, and chiles. If you think that dish sounds like it would require a Tums chaser, consider the healthy steel-cut oatmeal—a homey, rich bowl of goodness that is often overpriced in many restaurants but here is served with maple syrup and dried fruit for less than $6 per bowl. The Big Sky grilled tacos are extremely popular with locals

FARMER'S MARKETS IN SLO COUNTY

Throughout California, chefs and home cooks alike are embracing the idea of locavorism—in other words, eating seasonal and organic fruits and vegetables that have been grown locally. But nowhere is the spirit of eating locally embodied so completely as it is in San Luis Obispo County, which has an impressive schedule of farmer's markets. Many markets offer live evening entertainment (music, juggling, mimes, etc.), on-site barbecues, and summer concert series. Schedules and locations vary by season, so check with the San Luis Obispo County Farmers' Market Association (805-544-9570; www.slocountyfarmersmarket.org) for specifics.

for lunch and dinner, and are served with sirloin steak, shrimp, or fresh fish. There are plenty of vegetarian options on the menu, too, like garlicky hummus, baba ghanoush (a roasted eggplant puree), and black bean veggie chili. Be sure to save room for the astonishing Chinese five spice crème brûlée. $$

Buona Tavola (805-545-8000; www.btslo.com), 1037 Monterey St. Open Mon.–Fri. for lunch and dinner, Sat.–Sun. for dinner. This romantic restaurant serves up ambiance to spare: inside dining is pure northern Italy, and the outside patio could be anywhere in Tuscany. Menus rotate with the seasons, but when you can find it, don't miss the pumpkin gnocchi served with Gorgonzola sauce and hazelnuts. Be sure to save room for dessert: the homemade vanilla gelato with basil syrup is a revelation. The restaurant is on the pricey side for what is otherwise a relatively inexpensive city to dine, but the menu does offer a well-priced prix fixe choice that includes three courses for $30—or $45 for three courses and half-glass pairings of wine. $$$–$$$$

Chow (805-540-5243; www.chowslo.com), 1009 Monterey St. Open daily for lunch and dinner. Located downtown, near the Mission Plaza, Chow offers California Asian cuisine that focuses on Chinese and Vietnamese recipes, reinvented and re-created with fresh ingredients from local farms. The restaurant owners and chefs are strong believers in locavorism and adjust their menus to take advantage of seasonal produce and fruit. Look for anything that includes the yummy house-made noodles. Other menu favorites include stir-fried shrimp with bacon, sesame orange roast chicken with homemade pickles, and Chinese roast pork belly. If you like spicy food, don't miss the house-made kimchee. $$$

Firestone Grill (805-784-0474); 1001 Higuera St. Open daily for lunch and dinner. This very popular, noisy restaurant (which, as the name suggests, looks like an automotive shop from the outside) offers a huge outdoor patio for dining in warm weather and manages to fill it nearly every lunchtime. Specialties include the tri-tip sandwich—for which there is a near cult following in town—and a satisfying veggie sandwich with cheese and avocado. In addition to the traditional menu items, the Firestone offers an "underground" menu for those in the know: ask for the DA Double Down Sandwich, which is two chicken strips with spicy ranch sauce, cheese, bacon, and no bun, and waitstaff will treat you like a local. $$

Koberl at Blue (805-783-1135; www.epkoberl.com), 998 Monterey St. Open daily for dinner. This classy restaurant offers wine-country cuisine—and an impressive wine list to match, with a voluminous collection from around the world and an exhaustive list of the best of the Central Coast as well. Pair wines with classic fish dishes like crispy salmon, roasted halibut, and seared ahi as well as turf options like Colorado rack of lamb and roasted pork chops. The restaurant also offers an extensive beer selection that includes Belgian abbey-style ales, Czech pilsners, Indian pale ales, wheat beers, and Belgian fruit beers. $$

Novo Restaurant and Lounge (805-543-3986; www.novorestaurant.com), 726 Higuera St. Open daily for lunch and dinner. One of the most acclaimed restaurants in the city, Novo specializes in locavore cuisine that is impeccably fresh and sustainable, with global influences. Chef Justin Gabbert is passionate about supporting local farmers and shops three markets a week to find the best ingredients, so expect menus to change with the seasons. Regulars rave about the shrimp avocado spring rolls served with ginger soy and chile sauces, and the Korean short ribs served with jasmine rice. For dinner patrons can enjoy small, less-expensive tapas plates like lavender lamb chops, green beans with pancetta, and Brazilian prawns served in coconut milk. Larger portions of Sri Lankan butternut squash and cashew curry flavored with black mustard seeds, and Malaysian chicken with toasted coconut, are also divine. The restaurant has late hours (until midnight) Thurs.–Sat. On warm evenings, grab a table on the outdoor patio in back, which overlooks the picturesque San Luis Creek. $$$

EATING OUT

San Luis Obispo

Creeky Tiki Bar and Grill (805-544-2200; www.creekitiki.com), 778 Higuera St. Open daily for lunch and dinner. This small take-out joint backs to the San Luis Creek, and outdoor patio dining offers some of the prettiest views of the San Luis Obispo mission across the water. Look for inexpensive burgers (on surprisingly delicious thick buns), pizza, and salads. Wednesdays feature two-for-one beers (making this popular with the CalPoly crowd) and occasionally live music. $

Frank's Famous Hot Dogs (805-541-3488), 950 California Blvd. Open daily for lunch and dinner. Frank might be famous for his somewhat pricey hot dogs (and yummy corn dogs), but the real winners here are the monster burgers and mini sliders. The restaurant is near CalPoly, with plenty of outdoor seating. $$

Louisa's Place (805-541-0227; www.louisasplace.net), 964 Higuera St. Open daily for breakfast and lunch. An SLO institution for the past 40 years, this tiny diner has only a handful of tables and an old-fashioned counter, which goes well with Louisa's old-fashioned approach to home cooking. Breakfasts are legend, with homemade biscuits and gravy, fluffy hot cinnamon rolls, buckwheat pancakes, and 27 different omelets (although you can customize to create many more options). For lunch, look for hearty homemade soups and juicy hamburgers. $–$$

Margie's Diner (805-541-2940; www.margiesdiner.com), 1574 Calle Joachin. Open daily for breakfast, lunch, and dinner. Just off Hwy. 101, on the way into town, this nostalgic diner pays homage to comfort food in a casual, friendly atmosphere. Staples like meat loaf sandwiches, patty melts, and chicken fried steaks attract students, seniors, truckers, and just about everyone in between. Don't miss the huge, outrageous onion rings. Beware the large portions. $$

Woodstock's Pizza (805-541-4420; www.woodstockslo.com), 1000 Higuera St. Open daily for lunch and dinner. A favorite with CalPoly students, Woodstock's Pizza is affordable, casual, and fun. Favorite pizzas include the Classic SLO (pepperoni, mushrooms, olives, sausage, and extra cheese), the Pesto Primavera (with broccoli, pesto, artichoke hearts, and fresh tomato), and a spicy Firebird pie (with jalapeños, spicy marinara sauce, chicken, and extra cheese). Come on a Wed. night and get a pint refill for $1. $

✪ **Yogurt Creations** (805-543-2855; http://iloveyogurtcreations.com/Locations.htm), 1075 Court St. #130. Open daily 11–11. This local frozen-desserts chain (with additional stores in nearby Arroyo Grande, Santa Maria, and Atascadero) offers guests a fun, interactive experience. Start by pulling your own frozen yogurt (one flavor or a blend of a dozen—whatever you want, however you want it, and as much as you want). Top with a generous selection of syrups and fruit sauces, then finish off with candies, sprinkles, nuts, or crushed cookies. The treat is priced by the ounce (with a small but fully loaded bowl coming in at about $4). $

✷ Entertainment

CLUBS San Luis Obispo is the definition of *laid-back;* it is also predominately a college town, and the nightlife reflects these two realities. Expect a young crowd at most establishments and an upbeat, casual vibe. Most clubs—even the tiny ones—occasionally offer live music, and many feature theme nights, happy hours, and inexpensive refills on beer Tuesday–Thursday. Because the downtown is so compact, it is easy to barhop, as many of the establishments are no more than a block from each other.

🍸 **Buffalo Pub and Grill** (805-544-5515), 717 Higuera St., San Luis Obispo. The Buffalo Pub is a restaurant by day (with better-than-average pub grub, like cheesesteak sandwiches and 0.5-pound hamburgers on ciabatta bread) and a crowded bar by night. This is another of many places in downtown that is popular with the CalPoly crowd.

🍸 **Bull's Tavern** (805-543-2217), 1032 Chorro St., San Luis Obispo. Let's be honest: this is a dive bar, but the drinks are cheap, the people are friendly, and the place is an SLO institution.

🍸 **Central Coast Brewing** (805-783-BREW; www.centralcoastbrew), 1422 Monterey St., San Luis Obispo. This microbrewery offers a $5 tasting of five different artisanal beers, along with a very limited number of snacks. With an appointment, patrons can become "brewmaster for a day" (although it's necessary to return a month later to finish the job).

✪ 🍸 **Downtown Brewing Company** (805-543-1843; www.dtbrew.com), 1119 Garden St., San Luis Obispo. The popular Downtown Brewing Company offers a large selection of beers on draft, brewed on-site. Tues. is $1 pint night (9–midnight). Most evenings feature either live music or DJs. The place hosts crazy annual parties for Halloween, grad night, and New Year's Eve.

🍸 **Frog and Peach** (805-595-3764), 728 Higuera St., San Luis Obispo. Part Irish pub, part popular college bar, the Frog and Peach offers live music and dancing, as well as ample libation options.

✪ 🍸 **Mother's Tavern** (805-541-8733; www.motherstavern.com), 725 Higuera St., San Luis Obispo. MoTav is a huge

BUFFALO PUB AND GRILL

local favorite for music and dancing, and before the crowds arrive, it's a good place to enjoy one of a dozen different burgers as well.

THEATERS Christopher Cohan Performing Arts Center (805-756-2787; www.pacslo.org), 1 Grand Ave., San Luis Obispo. On the campus of CalPoly, this new state-of-the-art performing-arts center is one of the most beautiful in California, featuring a 1,300-seat concert hall (Harmon Hall—considered to be among the best concert halls acoustically in the world), a multipurpose pavilion, and a 180-seat recital hall. On-site is the Forbes Pipe Organ, a 129-pipe Fisk Opus.

Civic Ballet of San Luis Obispo (805-544-4363; www.civilballetslo.org), 672 Higuera St., San Luis Obispo. This city ballet performs in the **Christopher Cohan Performing Arts Center** and stages various public outreach performances throughout the year. Look for the annual *Nutcracker* in December.

Clark Center for the Performing Arts (805-489-9444; www.clarkcenter.org/cm/Home.html), 487 Fair Oaks Ave., Arroyo Grande. The intimate Clark Center comprises the six-hundred-seat Forbes Hall and a 120-seat Studio Theater, both of which stage performances throughout the year in this relatively new, community-funded venue.

Fremont Theater (805-541-2141), 1025 Monterey St., San Luis Obispo. Site of the San Luis Obispo International Film Festival, this eye-catching 1940s-era pink and white art deco movie theater in the heart of downtown shows the latest flicks and retro movie festivals as well. The original house still offers big-theater seating in a regal atmosphere, and in recent years three smaller theaters were added in back. Hint: It's even more striking at night, when the neon lights take center stage.

San Luis Obispo Folk Music Society (805-528-8963; www.slofolks.org), 2495 Tierra Dr., Los Osas. SLOfolks, as this acclaimed group is nicknamed, performs a wide variety of folk music from around the world, including Irish sea shanties, Appalachian folk music, and Celtic bluegrass. The group performs in venues throughout San Luis Obispo and Paso Robles, including beguiling events at the enchanting **Castoro Cellars.**

San Luis Obispo Little Theatre (805-786-2440; www.slolittletheatre.org), 888 Morro St., San Luis Obispo. This enthusiastic community theater stages nearly 400 productions in more than 20 locations around the city.

San Luis Obispo Symphony (805-528-8963; www.slosymphony.org), 1160 Marsh St., Suite 204, San Luis Obispo. Performing in the **Christopher Cohan Performing Arts Center,** the SLO Symphony offers a full calendar of events that feature many world-class touring artists. The symphony sometimes offers free tickets to dress rehearsals on designated Saturdays (check the Web site for specifics). In addition, the organization stages chamber music concerts at the Mt. Carmel Lutheran Church in San Luis Obispo.

✷ Selective Shopping

Downtown San Luis Obispo offers a number of large retail stores and a handful of smaller boutique shops, most of which are clustered along Higuera Street. Don't miss **Powell's Sweet Shoppe** (805-543-7934), 1020 Court Street, for a variety of retro candies like Valomilks, Pop Rocks, and Cherry Mash. Look as well for shopping arcades off the main drag. Antiques shops and galleries can be found on Monterey Street.

PISMO BEACH, MORRO BAY, AND CAMBRIA

With 23 miles of coastline, a 1,200-foot pier, and the chance to drive a vehicle directly on the beach (the only beach in California that allows this), famous Pismo Beach is one of the most appealing (and affordable) beachfront vacation destinations in the state. The tiny town is full of cheap eats, souvenir shops, and endless opportunities for outdoor recreation. Both Shell Beach and Avila Beach resorts to the north of Pismo offer more upscale lodging in a quieter atmosphere, with immediate access to the protected cove beaches and close proximity to restaurants and bars.

Morro Bay, to the north, is a working-class neighborhood that is still part fishing village, and it's one of the best places to find exceptionally good seafood. The birding near Morro Rock is world-class (although the smokestacks from a nearby power plant mar the view from the area beaches).

Cambria, farther north still, is a tiny jewel perched on a startlingly beautiful stretch of rugged shoreline, with several quaint lodging choices and dining options that are worthy of a much larger city. Cambria is near even tinier San Simeon, and thus is a popular overnight choice for those visiting the **Hearst Castle.**

✱ To See

HISTORICAL SITES **Avila Pier,** at the beach in Avila. The Avila Beach Pier was initially built in 1908 but was washed out by subsequent storms. It was rebuilt several times over and now is 1,685 feet long and open to fishing and strolling. Catch a free trolley on weekends from here to Shell Beach. Visitors are permitted to fish for free off Avila Pier, without a permit.

✪ **Hearst San Simeon State Historical Monument** (800-444-4445; www.hearstcastle.com), 750 Hearst Castle Rd., San Simeon. Open daily; hours vary by season. Better known as Hearst Castle, this monument to wealth and excess began in 1865, when a successful miner named George Hearst purchased 40,000 acres of land in San Simeon and Santa Rosa, overlooking magnificent views of the Pacific Ocean, as a weekend getaway for his family and friends. Eventually, his son, the famous newspaper magnate William Randolph Hearst, inherited the property—which by then had grown to 250,000 acres—and for years used it only for rugged

Courtesy of Jon Preimesberger

HEARST CASTLE

outdoor outings. In 1919, W. R. is said to have communicated to renowned architect Julia Morgan that he and his family were tired of camping on this extensive property and ". . . would like to build a little something." Hearst named the property La Cuesta Encantada—The Enchanted Hill. More than 25 years later, Morgan and Hearst had developed a magnificent estate that comprised 65 rooms and 127 acres of pools, gardens, and terraces, filled to the brim with museum-quality artwork and priceless antiquities. In its heyday, Hollywood luminaries, royalty, and presidents enjoyed Hearst's legendary hospitality in this spectacular site. Although Hearst died before the property was officially finished, the castle and grounds were opened to the public in 1958 as a state historical monument. To tour the property, it used to be necessary to purchase a ticket for a guided tour; however, recently the park began to offer the Garden Vista Tour, which allows guests to wander the grounds and property at their own pace. (The same rates apply for the self-guided tour as for the guided tours.) First-time or infrequent visitors should consider a guided option, because the grounds are vast, and hearing the guided spiel on the history of the man and his times is quite interesting. Tour 1 is recommended for first-time visitors and includes a film beforehand that gives an introduction to Hearst and his opulent way of life. Tour 2, the Casa Grande Tour, focuses on the architecture and interiors of the main house. (Note that this includes climbing four hundred steps, so be sure to wear appropriate footwear and be sure you're up for the exertion.) Tour 3 showcases the development of the estate as well as the extensive art collection. Tour 4 (offered only Apr.–Oct.) is the Garden Tour, which allows guests to explore the lush

INSIDER TIP: Hearst Castle is extremely popular, especially in the summer months. It is imperative that visitors make reservations in advance—or risk being turned away at the door.

landscaping. Tour 5 (offered in spring and fall on most Fri.) is the Evening Tour, which combines Tours 1 and 2, and offers vignettes by actors dressed in the fashion of the day playing cards, socializing, and strolling the grounds. It is also possible to arrange a special tour of the entire estate, which can take up to four hours. Individual tours for adults $24, children $12.

Courtesy of Jon Preimesberger

MORRO ROCK

Morro Rock, off the coast of Morro Bay. This iconic state historical monument is a 576-foot-high volcanic plug that is often called the Gibraltar of the Pacific. The massive rock is one of the most popular bird-watching sites in the state, thanks to the more than 250 species of birds that visit the estuary annually, including peregrine falcons, black-crowned night herons, California thrashers, and white pelicans. The rock is accessible via a bridge over the harbor. There is a short trail that circles a portion of the base of the rock, but no climbing or further exploring is allowed.

Piedras Blancas Lighthouse (805-927-6811; www.blm.gov/ca/st/en/fo/bakersfield/Programs/pbls.html), 15950 Carrillo Hwy., north of San Simeon. Open for tours (departing from the nearby Piedras Blancas Motel at 9:45) Tues., Thurs., and Sat. The striking Victorian-style lighthouse was built in 1875 on a point that is named for a white rock outcropping nearby. The original tower was 110 feet; in 1876 a light keeper's home and storage building were added. The lighthouse remained in service until 2001. Adults $10, children $5.

TIDEPOOLING AT SHELL BEACH

Port San Luis Lighthouse (805-540-5771). Open Sun. for docent-led tours. Near Avila Beach, the eye-catching San Luis Lighthouse (dating to 1889) protected the coastal waters up to 20 miles out to sea around what was a treacherous point into the harbor. The lighthouse was closed in 1974 and today is undergoing restoration. Portions of the property are open to tours, and visitors can view the exterior of the restored lighthouse, the lighthouse keeper's quarters, the historic gardens, dormitories, and workshops. Look for sea otters playing in the waters off the coast. Tours $20 (by reservation only).

MUSEUMS **Morro Bay Museum of Natural History** (805-772-2694; www.morrobaymuseum.org), State Park Rd., Morro Bay. Open daily 10:30–5. The Morrow Bay Museum of Natural History offers interactive exhibits on the native Chumash people, as well as exhibits on natural geology and local sea life. Adults $2, children 16 and under free.

PARKS ✐ **Lopez Lake Recreational Area** (805-788-2381). This 900-acre lake northeast of Arroyo Grande offers fishing and sailing on a glassy lake, along with picnicking, hiking, and camping. There are also impressive water slides on-site for kids. Admission is free.

✪ **Montaña de Oro State Park** (805-528-0513), off Pecho Rd., south of Morro Bay, San Luis Obispo. The name of this 8,000-acre park aptly translates to "Mountain of Gold," which references the springtime wildflowers, and is a favorite with local hikers and mountain bikers, thanks to an extensive network of trails. Monarch butterflies cluster here Nov.–Mar. Visitors will find rocky shorelines, sandy beaches, eucalyptus groves, equestrian trails, and more than 50 miles of hiking and biking trails. Pathways that trace the edge of the coastal bluffs offer a glimpse of **Morro Rock** in the distance. Admission is free.

Morro Bay State Park, off Hwy. 1, via the Los Osos/Baywood Park off ramp. The park surrounding Morro Bay is part of a cluster of volcanic outcroppings (i.e., *morros*) known as the Nine Sisters that runs from Morrow Bay to SLO. The park

TOP 10 DAY IN PISMO BEACH

1. Wake up with a breakfast pizza of arugula pesto, Black Forest ham, and scrambled eggs at the Honeymoon Café (see pp. 320–321)
2. Go tidepooling at Shell Beach at low tide (see p. 314)
3. Drive on the sands of Oceana Dunes (see p. 314)
4. Enjoy amazing crabcakes at the Cracked Crab (see pp. 319–320)
5. Play an afternoon round of golf at Cypress Ridge (see p. 311)
6. Sip a cocktail at the Cypress Ridge Pavilion, the "19th hole" at Cypress Ridge (see p. 311)
7. Stroll along nearby Avila Pier at sunset (see p. 307)
8. Dine on Thai ginger trout with a side of baby corn and mushrooms at Thai Talay (see p. 320)
9. Lift a late-night pint at the Boardroom Surf Pub (see p. 321)
10. Overnight in an oceanfront suite at the Dolphin Bay Inn (see p. 318)

comprises voluminous open space, hills, and a lagoon and natural bay habitat, which includes the iconic **Morro Rock.** The park also encompasses the marina across from Morro Rock, as well as an 18-hole public golf course. This park is a favorite with birders, who will find species here that exist nowhere else in North America. Hikers will want to check out the scenic Black Hill trail. Admission is free.

✷ To Do

GOLF **Avila Beach Golf Resort** (805-595-4000; www.avilabeachresort.com), 6464 Ana Bay Dr., Avila Beach. Just off Hwy. 101, between Pismo Beach and San Luis Obispo, this beautiful resort is nestled into the surrounding hills. The par 71 championship course offers tree-lined valleys, and the back nine meanders through a tidal estuary. Green fee: $50–70.

✪ **Cypress Ridge** (805-474-7979; www.cypressridge.com), Arroyo Grande. To the east of Pismo Beach, Cypress Ridge in Arroyo Grande is an Audubon National Signature Sanctuary course, designed to integrate challenging golf with environmental planning to preserve the natural surroundings and native wildlife. Green fee: $30–68.

✪ **Morro Bay Golf Course** (805-782-8060; www.centralcoastgolf.com), 201 State Park Rd., Morro Bay. Sometimes called "poor man's Pebble Beach" by locals, this hilly public course offers 18 holes with beautiful views of the ocean and well-groomed, tree-lined fairways. Green fee: $45–51.

Pismo State Beach Golf (805-481-5215), 25 W. Grand Ave., Grover Beach. North of the Pismo Beach Natural Preserve, this nine-hole course is close to the beach resorts of Pismo and Shell beaches, and offers an inexpensive experience good for older children or less serious golfers. Green fee: $11–12.

SPAS **El Colibri Spa** (805-924-3003; www.elcolibrihotel.com), 5620 Moonstone Beach Dr., Cambria. This tiny spa is part of the lovely new **El Colibri Hotel** and offers full-service treatments such as facials, body wraps, and massages. There is a small rooftop Jacuzzi, as well as steam rooms (his and hers) and a small locker room.

✪ **La Bonne Vie** (805-773-5003; www.laboneviespa.net), 2723 Shell Beach Rd., Shell Beach. Part of the fabulous **Dolphin Bay Resort,** this oceanfront spa offers treatments such as reflexology massages for the hands, feet, and head; aromatherapy combined with Swedish massage; and detoxifying cypress bark wraps. Guests at Dolphin Bay can expect discounts of as much as 20 percent off treatments.

Moonstone Day Spa (805-927-5159; www.moonstonedayspa.com), 7432 Exotic Gardens Dr., Cambria. Services at this small day spa include mud facials, aloe vera masks, body polishes, and massages. Acupuncture is also available.

Sycamore Mineral Springs Spa (805-595-7302; www.sycamoresprings.com), 1215 Avila Beach Dr. At the **Sycamore Mineral Springs Resort,** this full-service spa specializes in a signature Wine Therapy massage with grapeseed extracts for their detoxifying effect—and a glass of wine to accompany the procedure. Add on a Wild Lime Scalp Treatment for an extra $25 for total indulgence. Every treatment at the spa includes a complimentary 30-minute soak in a private mineral spring.

✷ Water Sports

The Central Coast waterfront is all about water sports, and guests will find everything from paddleboarding to kayaking to deep-sea fishing outings.

BOATING **At the Helm Boats** (805-771-9337), 845 Embarcadero, Morro Bay. Rent 18-foot vessels powered by battery to tool around the Morro Bay area. The boats are easy to maneuver and require no special skill or previous boating experience, and make for a fun afternoon on the water, even for novices.

Pismo Beach Dive Shop (805-773-2089; www.pismobeachdive.com), 470 Price St., Pismo Beach. This full-service dive and equipment-rental shop offers two kayak tours: The Port San Luis tour is designed for beginning paddlers and explores the calm waters of Avila. The Dino Cave's tour, which starts in Shell Beach and heads south to Dinosaur's Caves, is much more rigorous and meant for intermediate to advanced paddlers.

Wave Jammers (805-550-3347), Avila Beach. This outfit offers guided Jet Ski tours that take guests along the Pismo coast, to the popular Oceana Dunes region. The tour includes a wet suit and instructions.

DIVING AND SNORKELING **Pismo Beach Dive Shop** (805-773-2089; www.pismobeachdive.com), 470 Price St., Pismo Beach. In addition to selling and renting diving and snorkeling equipment, kayaks, and boards, the PBDS offers periodic dive tours, including an annual lobster-fishing trip.

FISHING There are a number of fishing options on Pismo Beach and the surrounding coastal regions; the most popular catches include rock cod, lingcod, halibut, salmon, swordfish, and sole. Pismo Beach and Avila Pier do not require a license to fish—and sportspersons are likely to haul in cod and red snapper at both locales. It's possible to rent tackle and purchase bait on the piers. For deep-sea fishing, consider an organized tour or a charter.

Patriot Sportfishing (805-595-7200; www.patriotsportfishing.com), Hartford Pier, Port San Luis. This large enterprise offers whale-watching tours, private charters, and sportfishing, the latter specializing in eight-hour rock cod fishing during open season. There are also longer trips for albacore and salmon.

Virg's Landing (805-772-1222; http://virgslanding.com), 1215 Embarcadero Dr., Morro Bay. This outfit offers charters and guided fishing trips, and rents the necessary equipment and gear. Dec.–Apr., trips depart on Sat. Apr.–July, salmon trips depart every few days. May–Nov., the charters fish for rock cod every day of the year. Virg's also offers whale-watching tours in season.

SURFING Serious surfers in the area prefer the southwest-facing Pismo Beach Pier region because of the consistent breaks and because the beach tends to be less windy than some of the more exposed beaches to the south and less rocky than most of the beaches to the north. Rip currents can be fierce in this area, so exercise caution. And as with all Southern California beaches, the locals are territorial, so exercise surf etiquette. Beginners will want to stick to "Park Avenue," 3 blocks south of the pier. Reliable surf schools include the following:

Billabong Van Curaza Surf School (805-773-0731; www.vancurazasurfschool.com), in Pismo Beach. Lessons are scheduled by appointment only and are all personally overseen by owner Van Curaza. The school also offers camps for mentally and physically challenged individuals and has hosted Operation Comfort, a surf camp designed for disabled veterans from the Iraq and Afghanistan wars.

ESB Surf School/Billabong Surf Camp (805-270-1129; www.esbsurfschool.com), in Pismo Beach. This instructional facility offers year-round private or group lessons, as well as day- and week-long camps in the summer. Surfboards and wet suits are provided, and the school caters to every ability level.

Shell Beach Surf School (805-904-9315; http://surfshellbeach.com), in Shell Beach. Owner and longtime surfer Tad Gibson offers private and group lessons for adults, as well as "tadpole" classes for kids 12 and younger.

✷ Green Space

BEACHES **Avila Beach,** off Hwy. 101 at the Avila Beach Dr. exit, Avila Beach. Avila Beach actually comprises three different beaches: The **Avila Main Beach** is the largest and most easily accessible, and is punctuated by the historic pier. This beach is the most family friendly of the three, with an expansive children's playground and good tidepooling, as well as stunning views of the ocean and the tall surrounding cliffs. **Hanford Beach** offers a boat ramp, public restrooms, fire pits, and a sandy beach where dogs are welcome. Look for sea otters and sea lions in the waters just offshore as well as sunning themselves on the rocks. **Pirates' Cove** is a rocky, clothing-optional cove accessible via a winding, steep path.

Cayucos State Beach, at the foot of Cayocos Dr. This sandy beach located in the historic beach town of Cayucos is good for swimming, snorkeling, and kayaking. At low tide there is also very good tidepooling. Note that lifeguards are on duty only in the summer.

✪ **Moonstone Beach,** off Hwy. 101 at Moonstone Beach Dr., Cambria. This magical cove gets its name from semiprecious agate and jasper stones that can be found in the sand: when wet, the tiny rounded pebbles sparkle. Offshore are large volcanic rocks that are popular with sea lions (especially near sunset, when they come in after a day of feeding). The water is crystal clear, glass green, and a little choppy. The small beach is surrounded by cliffs, and—to the north—a grassy park with picnic tables. This isn't really the place for sunbathing or swimming, but it is lovely for strolling.

Morro Strand State Beach, off Hwy. 101 at the Yerba Buena exit. This long,

> **INSIDER TIP:** Bring appropriate shoes to Moonstone Beach, because the tiny stones that constitute "sand" there are very uncomfortable to walk over with bare feet or flip flops.

MOONSTONE BEACH

sandy beach runs just north of Morro Rock. The 3-mile-long stretch of shoreline curves gently, allowing a good view of the promontory throughout the park. Small dunes rise up behind the shoreline, which provides some protection from rather windy conditions—but this remains a popular spot for folks flying kites. It is also popular with birders (because of the proximity to Morro Rock, which is a haven for seabirds) and good for beachcombing. There are 76 campsites in the park, which are available for reservation (800-444-7275) from Memorial Day through Labor Day. Campsites are extremely popular and sell out on a first-come, first-served basis.

✪ **Oceana Dunes,** off Hwy. 1, 1 mile south of the Pier Ave. beach ramp. Oceana Dunes famously is home to the **Oceana Dunes Vehicular Recreation Area,** the only place in California where drivers can roll directly onto the beach (for $5) or pull over in the dunes and camp anywhere on the sand for the night ($10). A popular activity is to ride ATVs up and down the dunes; rental agencies drive along the beach with trailers towing multiple ATVs to rent for those who don't have their own. This makes for a noisy beach experience, and thus this stretch of sand isn't recommended for those arriving without a vehicle.

Pismo State Beach, 555 Pier Ave., Oceana. This very large expanse of beach is wide, sandy, and offers tree-lined dunes. The beach has a long pier that is popular with fishermen (and those who just want to stroll out for better views of the water). The area attracts dozens of species of migratory waterfowl and is also the site of an annual monarch butterfly migration: Nov.–Mar., about 50,000 monarch butterflies—one of the largest colonies in the world—return to the area to overwinter in a grove of eucalyptus trees in the sand dunes. In season docents are available on-site 10–4. Somewhat incongruous to the plethora of natural wealth, the beach also comprises **Oceana Dunes** and the **Oceana Dunes Vehicular Recreation Area.**

✪ ✐ **Shell Beach,** off Hwy. 101 at Spyglass Dr., Pismo Beach. Although this beach, and adjacent **Silver Shoals,** just north of Pismo, are tiny, the views here are singularly beautiful, either from the high tops of the bluffs above or from the crescent shoreline. Access the beach via a steep cliff trail or a long flight of steps just north of **The Cliffs Resort.** This small beach is popular with kayakers because of the interesting sea caves and is also great for swimming and tidepooling. (Come at high tide, and the beach is narrow indeed.) This is also a popular spot for surfers.

William Randolph Hearst Memorial State Beach, off Hwy. 1, across from Hearst Castle. This protected cove offers pier fishing and ocean kayaking, along with picnic tables, barbecue grills, and full restroom facilities. The water temperatures are always on the chilly side (all but the heartiest souls wear wet suits), and the shoreline is rocky but picturesque. It isn't unusual to see sea lions and elephant seals frolicking off the coast or sunning themselves on rocks.

INSIDER TIP: Avoid the hassle of carting cumbersome beach equipment and hire an organization like Beach Butlerz (805-878-4283) to do the dirty work. For about $30, you choose your preferred beach, this company will reserve a premium spot, and at a designated time will set up a beach umbrella with small table and two lounge chairs. Guests can also rent sand toys and beach chairs.

NATURE PRESERVES **Elfin Forest Natural Preserve** (www.slostateparks.com/morro_bay/mb_elfin.asp), off Hwy. 1 at the Los Osos/Baywood Park exit. This preserve comprises a 90-acre expanse of sand dunes edged by a fantastical grove of two-hundred-year-old live oaks that have been twisted and dwarfed by the salt air and wind. The forest is located on the southeastern shore of Morro Bay in Los Osos and offers an extensive boardwalk through the dunes that protects the fragile plant life. This area is home to at least 25 species of mammals, more than 100 kinds of birds, and a dozen reptiles and amphibians. Admission is free.

Monterey Bay National Sanctuary (http://montereybay.noaa.gov), starting at the shoreline in Cambria. This extensive marine sanctuary covers 276 miles of coastline and more than 6,000 square miles of ocean, from Cambria to Marin (near San Francisco), and it is the largest of the 13 marine sanctuaries in the United States. The preserve supports a diverse marine ecosystem and is home to seabirds, fish, sea mammals, and plants in what is a uniquely productive coastal habitat. All beaches that fall within the boundaries of this sanctuary are protected, meaning absolutely no fishing is allowed offshore, and no collecting—of seashells, driftwood, or beach stones—is permitted.

Piedras Blancas Elephant Seal Rookery, on the coast off Hwy. 1, 7 miles north of San Simeon. About an hour north of Pismo Beach, this rookery is shelter to more than 15,000 northern elephant seals, *Mirounga angustirostri,* a marine mammal that comes ashore twice a year for birthing, breeding, and rest. The rookery is open for viewing year-round.

ELFIN FOREST

Courtesy of the San Luis Obispo Visitors and Convention Bureau

San Simeon State Park (805-927-2020). This park, 5 miles south of Hearst Castle, atop coastal bluffs with unobstructed views of the ocean, is a nature and archaeological preserve, accessible via a 3-mile trail with scenic overlooks. This is an especially good place to whale-watch from Jan. through Mar., when gray whales make their annual migration south to Mexico. It's also a favorite haunt for birders, who flock to the area to observe turkey vultures, mergansers, western snowy plovers, and various species of owls. Admission is free.

Sweet Springs Natural Preserve (805-239-3928), at Broderson and Ramona, Los Osos. The Audubon Society manages the 24-acre Sweet Springs preserve, which is home to several threatened or endangered species. A number of hiking trails crisscross the park, some of which wind around a salt marsh and offer views of Morro Bay and Morro Rock. There are also two freshwater ponds and Monterey cypress and eucalyptus groves. In Nov. through Mar., monarch butterflies overwinter here. Admission is free.

✱ Lodging

PRICE KEY FOR A STANDARD ROOM:

$	$100 or less
$$	$101–150
$$$	$151–250
$$$$	$251 and up

Avila Beach

Avila la Fonda Hotel (805-595-1700; www.avilalafondahotel.com), 101 San Miguel St. A comfortable, residential-feeling accommodation a few blocks from the beach, with suites and casitas that include Jacuzzi tubs, showers with multiple heads, stained-glass windows, microwaves complete with popcorn bags, and other complimentary snacks. The on-site library loans out books, DVDs, and CDs, and guests can rent out bicycles and beach gear from the front desk. $$$

Sycamore Mineral Springs Resort (800-234-5831; www.sycamoresprings.com), 1215 Avila Beach Dr. This property is a few miles from the beach and nestled in a residential neighborhood along the access road into Avila Beach. Thus, this is not a beach destination but

TOP 10 DAY IN CAMBRIA

1. Hike along Moonstone Beach in the early morning, before the fog lifts (see p. 313)
2. Sip mimosas with brunch at the Moonstone Beach Grill (see p. 318)
3. Take the Garden Tour at Hearst Castle (see pp. 307–309)
4. Drive north to see the Piedras Blancas Lighthouse (see p. 309)
5. Check out the elephant seal rookery at Piedras Blancas (see p. 315)
6. Lunch on halibut tacos at Robin's (see p. 319)
7. Stroll along the seaside boardwalk in the afternoon (see p. 313)
8. Enjoy a mud-mask facial at Moonstone Day Spa (see p. 311)
9. Dine on lobster potpie at the Sow's Ear Café (see p. 319)
10. Overnight at the FogCatcher Inn (see p. 317)

rather a spa and retreat—although the beach is never more than a five-minute drive away. Look for private hillside mineral tubs, daily yoga and Pilates classes, and guided hikes. The on-site **Sycamore Mineral Springs Spa** is one of the finest in the area. $$$

Cambria

Cambria is a destination unto itself, thanks to a spectacular shoreline. It is also an ideal place to overnight when visiting **Hearst Castle.**

El Colibri Hotel and Spa (805-924-3003; www.elcolibrihotel.com), 5620 Moonstone Beach Dr. This new, small boutique property offers fireplaces and whirlpool tubs in each guest accommodation, as well as daily breakfast and a hot tea or coffee on arrival. The Mediterranean design is serene and inviting, and the spalike bathrooms are luxurious. There is a full-service spa on the property (**El Colibri Spa**), as well as a cozy wine bar that offers selections from Central Coast vineyards. The property is close to the beach, Cambria dining, and offers quick access to nearby **Hearst Castle.** Perhaps because it is new, and yet to acquire a loyal following, rates are fantastic, considering the level of luxury. $$–$$$

✪ **FogCatcher Inn** (805-927-1400; www.fogcatherinn.com), 6400 Moonstone Beach Dr. This is one of my favorite properties in Cambria, because of its prime location: steps from the lovely **Moonstone Beach,** with easy access to the wooden boardwalk that runs along the top of the bluffs above the shoreline. It's also within walking distance to several fine restaurants. The old English-style structure has a faux thatched roof, pretty flower-lined brick paths, and a fireplace in every room. Some rooms offer premier ocean views. Accommodations come with a complimentary hot buffet breakfast. $$–$$$

Sand Pebbles Inn (805-927-5600; www.cambriainns.com), 6252 Moonstone Beach Dr. This property is across the street from **Moonstone Beach,** close to the boardwalk and fine dining. The beachy exterior is matched with naturalistic landscaping, and interiors are breezy and bright. All guest rooms are spacious, but for a splurge, check out the oceanfront balcony rooms, which offer a truly romantic perch from which to watch the sunset. Although a perfect getaway for two, the inn is also family friendly: guests can borrow board games and family movies from an extensive DVD collection. $$–$$$

Pismo Beach

There are a handful of inexpensive, slightly seedy beach motels in Pismo proper, and to be honest, I wouldn't feel right recommending most of them. The one exception follows, and it is a true bargain. (Note: Shell Beach, just a mile north, offers quieter, newer, more upscale properties.)

Kon Tiki Inn (805-773-4833; www.kontikiinn.com), 1621 Price St. This old Pismo Beach–style hotel with faux tropical kitsch is perched on a bluff above a sandy beach (accessible via a steep staircase), and most rooms offer startling direct ocean views. There is a small pool and a grassy expanse at the back of the property, and on-site fitness facilities, tennis courts, laundry facilities, and a restaurant with bar. The décor is tragically dated, but the rooms are large, clean, and offer a real bargain for oceanfront property. $–$$

Shell Beach

The Cliffs Resort (800-826-7827; www.cliffsresort.com), 2757 Shell Beach Rd. Adjacent to the steep staircase that leads to **Shell Beach,** The Cliffs is one of only three hotel properties on this quiet stretch of cliff. Although prices vary by room style, season, and view, most accommodations are reasonably affordable, rooms are comfortable, and the vistas are stunning. Service can be spotty, but given the price point for an oceanfront resort, this is the next-best bet on Shell Beach if the **Dolphin Bay Inn** is booked up (or is too expensive). The small pool is designed with a faux moat surrounding it, and the on-site restaurant, the **Marisol,** is renown for its Sun. champagne brunch. $$$

✪ 🐾 **Dolphin Bay Inn Resort and Spa** (805-773-4300; www.thedolphinbay.com), 2727 Shell Beach Rd. It would be easy to run out of superlatives to describe this family-friendly resort perched on the cliffs above **Shell Beach,** so suffice it to say that this property offers the best of both worlds: the space and amenities of a private-home vacation rental and the luxury, service, and activities of a resort. The all-suites accommodations (one- and two-bedroom and penthouse suites) have luxurious baths and fully stocked gourmet kitchens with granite countertops and stainless-steel appliances; living rooms are spacious, well appointed, and offer the latest in audiovisual equipment. All suites come with in-room washer/dryer combos and offer a large balcony or patio; most also offer panoramic ocean views. On-site is a large, heated pool; a first-rate spa (**La Bonne Vie**); and a stellar restaurant (**The Lido**). The friendly staff offer perks like welcome gifts for children, complimentary DVD library complete with popcorn and hot chocolate, and specialty furnishings like cribs and high chairs that are available to borrow. $$$$

DOLPHIN BAY INN

San Simeon

The Morgan (805-927-3878; www.hotel-morgan.com), 9135 Hearst Dr. As the name suggests, this small property was inspired by the Arts and Crafts designs of Julia Morgan, architect of nearby **Hearst Castle,** and is one of the very few lodging options in San Simeon. Rooms are sleek, impeccably designed, and comfortable, and are relatively inexpensive by Southern California standards. The hotel has a wine lounge that offers selections from nearby Paso Robles, and stays include a continental breakfast. $–$$

✱ Where to Eat

DINING OUT

Cambria

✪ **Moonstone Beach Grill** (805-927-3859; www.moonstonebeach.com), 6550 Moonstone Beach Dr. Open daily for lunch and dinner, brunch on Sun. Across from the enchanting **Moonstone Beach,** this restaurant is my favorite in the area. The large outdoor patio is a fun and picturesque place to dine (although it can get chilly once the sun sets). Do not miss the candied walnut Gorgonzola salad. The Cajun shrimp tacos (sadly, available only at lunchtime) are also something special, served with a spicy sauce in soft corn tortillas. Save room for the Royal Danish lemon cake served à la mode. $$–$$$

Robin's Restaurant (805-927-5007; www.robinsrestaurant.com), 4095 Burton Dr. Open daily for lunch and dinner. Robin's offers local produce prepared with global influences, which makes for eclectic choices like seared ahi sashimi, Singapore-style chicken sate, lamb curry burritos, beer-battered halibut tacos, and portobello lasagna with local artisanal cheeses. Every second Fri. of the month, Robin's offers a fixed-price four-course meal that celebrates a holiday, season, or cuisine. Sun. nights feature an affordable tapas menu. $$$

Sow's Ear Café (805-927-4865; www.thesowsear.com), 2248 Main St. Open daily for dinner. A local favorite, the Sow's Ear offers friendly service along with fine wining and dining. The wine list offers a bounty from Central Coast vineyards, and the menu offers a conundrum: The lobster potpie with mushrooms and shallots in a rich lobster broth, or the honey-pecan-crusted catfish in a silky white wine sauce? The sweet-tart olallieberry granita with crunchy ginger cookies, or the warm cinnamon bread pudding with brandy hard sauce? There's no wrong answer. $$

Morro Bay

Dorn's Breakers Café (805-772-4415), 801 Market Ave. Open daily for breakfast, lunch, and dinner. Across from Morro Rock, Dorn's serves fresh seafood in a casual atmosphere, which is especially appealing when the fishing boats arrive back into the harbor. Specialties include calamari steak, sole Florentine, and surprisingly tasty sardine sandwiches. Also available are oysters on the half shell, burgers, and pasta options. $$

✪ **Windows on the Water** (805-772-0677; www.windowsonthewater.net), 699 Embarcadero Dr. Open daily for dinner. Easily the finest dining establishment in Morro Bay, Windows on the Water delivers on the promise of its picturesque name with views of Morro Rock and the sailboat-studded bay: this is one of the most romantic restaurants in the region. The young chef and sommelier give careful attention to pairing local wines of the region with seasonal, locally grown food. As a result, the eclectic menus change regularly. Regardless of particular items on offer, expect fresh seafood and French-inspired California cuisine. $$$

Pismo Beach

✪ 🏅 **Cracked Crab** (805-773-2722; www.crackedcrab.com), 751 Price St. Open daily for lunch and dinner. Don't let the exterior scare you away: this place serves some of the freshest, tastiest shellfish in SoCal—including astonishing crab Louis salad and blue-crab cakes that are as good as anything out of the Chesapeake Bay. The ambiance is casual, but the impeccably fresh, sustainable cooking is worthy of upscale dining. The house specialty is the Big Bucket for Two (for just under $70): This includes a choice of three shellfish items (snow crab claws, Dungeness crab, gulf shrimp, or slipper tail lobster) plus red potatoes, corn on the cob, and sausage. Servers will dump the bucket on your butcher-paper-covered table, give you a couple of mallets and picks, and let you have at it. When available, don't miss the exquisite Cayucos-farmed abalone, served with a white wine sauce in the shell. This is a remarkable value and one of the best bets in SLO County. $$–$$$

PRICE KEY FOR A TYPICAL ENTRÉE:

$	$10 and under
$$	$11–20
$$$	$21–30
$$$$	$31 and up

CRACKED CRAB

Thai Talay (805-773-6162; www.thai talay.com), 601 Price St. Open daily for lunch and dinner. Just off Hwy. 101, a few blocks from the Pismo Beach Pier, Thai Talay offers traditional Thai appetizers like chicken and tofu sate, spicy mango shrimp, and tom yum soup. The beach location makes the most sense when exploring seafood offerings like Thai ginger trout, ka pow salmon (steamed with basil, chiles, and spices), and pla talay (deep-fried sole served with a coconut milk and red curry sauce). Not up for going out? Thai Talay will deliver to local hotels. $$–$$$

San Simeon

Manta Rey Restaurant (805-924-1032; www.mantareyrestaurant.com), 9240 Castillo Rd. Open daily for dinner. Two miles from **Hearst Castle,** in the tiny town of San Simeon, the also tiny Manta Rey specializes in fresh seafood and steaks, both of which are created with the freshest ingredients and prepared simply. The New York steak, for example, is grilled and served with the barest adornment of garlic shallot butter. The calamari plate offers simply breaded strips fried and served with mashed potatoes or pilaf. $$$

Shell Beach

🍸 **The Lido** (805-773-4300; www.the dolphinbay.com), 2727 Shell Beach Rd. Open daily for breakfast, lunch, and dinner; brunch on Sun. Part of the luxurious **Dolphin Bay Inn,** The Lido offers upscale dining in a casual atmosphere, with spectacular ocean views, either in the elegant dining room or outside on the ocean-view patio. Don't miss the almond-crusted sole, served with a buttery wine sauce. Save room for dessert: the trio of pots de crème is well worth the calories (but don't be tempted to share it just because there are three items—it's too small and too good to divide). $$$

EATING OUT

Morro Bay

Embarcadero Grill Wood BBQ (805-770-0700; www.embgrill.com), 801 Embarcadero Dr. Open Mon.–Fri. for lunch and dinner, Sat.–Sun. for breakfast (8–noon). On the harborfront, this barbecue joint offers good hamburgers and even better barbecue beef and chicken sandwiches. Views across the water are lovely, especially considering the modest prices. Upstairs from the restaurant is **Bob Zany's Comedy Club.** $–$$

✪ 🏅 **Giovanni's Fish Market** (805-772-2123), 1001 Front St. Open daily

GIOVANNI'S

9–6. Directly across from Morro Rock, this no-frills fish market has a take-out window that offers prepared fish-and-chips, fried clams, fish tacos, and—some argue—the best clam chowder in the region. Order at a takeout window, then eat at picnic tables overlooking the water—but mind your food, or the seagulls *will* carry it away. $

Pismo Beach

Honeymoon Café (805-773-5646; www.thehoneymooncafe.com), 999 Price St. Open daily for breakfast and lunch. This bright, eclectic oasis in Pismo Beach has a small outdoor dining patio and a small interior dining space, and offers items largely created using ingredients from local purveyors. Not surprisingly, the food is fresh and seasonal. The menu offers a large array of breakfast items, as well as salads, soups, burgers, and tacos. $

Palazzo Guiseppe (805-773-2873), 891 Price St. Open daily for lunch and dinner. Guiseppe's serves brick-oven fired pizzas with crispy crusts and fine-quality cheeses: don't miss the Aragosta, a pie with lobster, ricotta, roasted corn, and basil. The restaurant also offers traditional Italian entrées like veal Parmesan, lasagna, and house-made gnocchi. $$

Rock and Roll Diner (805-473-2040), 1300 Railroad St., Oceana. Open daily; hours vary by season. This adorable '50s diner a few blocks from the **Oceana Dunes State Recreational Vehicular Park** is housed in two train cars. Inside are pearly red vinyl booths, aluminum-clad tables, and plenty of nostalgia. Specialties include burgers, homemade chili, and weekly dinner specials like ground round steak and pork chops. The place can be crowded and noisy, and is especially popular with children. $$

Smokin' Mo's BBQ (805-773-6193; www.mosbbq.com), 221 Pomeroy St. Open daily for lunch and dinner. This local chain (with additional outlets in San Luis Obispo and Huntington Beach) serves hickory smoked barbecue that has been voted the best in the region by local newspapers. The secret recipes have won numerous barbecue cook-offs as well. Mo's is famous for pork ribs, served Memphis style or Carolina style (a sweeter variety), but shredded chicken and Louisiana hot links are equally as popular. Don't miss my favorite side: fried green tomatoes (available seasonally). $$

✱ Entertainment

CLUBS **Boardroom Surf Pub** (805-295-6222), 160 Hinds Ave., Pismo Beach. This dive bar near the pier is dark and moody, and just the kind of casual place to have a pitcher after a hot day at the beach.

Chablis Cruises (805-772-2128), on the Embarcadero, Morro Bay. This two-story riverboat serves a champagne brunch or summertime dinner with drinks while cruising the waters of Morro Bay. This is a relaxing evening and tends to draw a subdued crowd.

THEATERS **Great American Melodrama** (805-489-2499; www.american-melodrama.com), 1863 Pacific Blvd., Oceana. This tiny cabaret-style theater features sawdust on the floors and honky-tonk piano music, and offers classic comedies, musicals, and melodramas. Each show includes a vaudeville-style music-and-dance revue.

Murder in Mind Productions (805-489-3875; www.murderinmind.com), 2705 Spyglass Dr., Pismo Beach. This dinner theater, staged at the **Spyglass Inn Restaurant,** encourages audience participation to help solve the crime at hand. Most productions are family friendly, but be sure to check in advance.

🍸 **Pewter Plough Playhouse and Café** (805-927-3877; www.pewterploughplayhouse.org), 824 Main St., Cambria. This tiny theater presents comedies year-round. There is also an on-site piano bar and a full wine bar that offers a good selection of Central Coast wines.

✸ Selective Shopping

Although there are scattered independent boutiques in most of the beach towns on the Central Coast, true shopaholics may find little to tempt them, with the possible exception of the **Prime Outlets** mall in Pismo (805-773-4661), 333 Five Cities Dr., Pismo Beach. Shoppers will find designer labels like Calvin Klein, Polo Ralph Lauren, and Tommy Hilfiger, as well as discount shops like Crown Books, Dress Barn, and Styles for Less.

PASO ROBLES WINE COUNTRY

The rolling hills of Paso Robles are about a half hour from the Central Coast beaches. Expect much warmer inland temperatures and an even slower pace of life in this bucolic, peaceful region. Paso Robles is at the heart of the Central Coast wine region, and it is increasingly considered one of the finest winemaking areas of the world. Hot summers and limestone soil produce especially good cabernets, zinfandels, and myriad Rhône varietals. Wineries stretch from just east of Hearst Castle in San Simeon, south to Templeton, and north to San Miguel, with Paso Robles in the middle of the largest concentration of vineyards and wineries. (Note that there are also a handful of vineyards to the south, stretching between San Luis Obispo and Arroyo Grande.)

✷ To See

HISTORICAL SITES **Carnegie Historic Library,** 800 12th St., Paso Robles. This 1908 Classical Revival library is on the National Register of Historic Places. Today the building is used by the El Paso de Robles Area Historical Society, which specializes in local history and genealogy research.

Mission San Miguel Arcangel (805-467-3256), 775 Mission St., San Miguel. Seven miles north of Paso Robles, this mission is the 16th in the line of 21 California missions founded by Spanish priests. The interior is currently closed for renovation (to repair earthquake damage suffered several years ago), but guests can still visit the on-site museum and view the exterior, with its pretty redbrick campanile.

MUSEUMS ✐ **Children's Museum at the Paso Robles Volunteer Firehouse** (805-238-7432; www.pasokids.org), 623 13th St., Paso Robles. Open Thurs.–Fri. 11–4, Wed., Sat., and Sun. 10–4. This colorful, interactive museum offers great appeal for toddlers and young children, with exhibits like the giant oak tree that kids can climb on and through; the Grape Stomp (a nod to the dominance of wineries in Paso Robles), which is actually little more than a giant ball pit—but loads of fun for little kids; and the Firehouse Pizza Kitchen, which allows children to create their own faux pies. The highlight of the museum is undoubtedly Old Mac, an original 1944 fire engine on display. Children can dress up in firefighter garb and climb up behind the wheel for a photo op. Admission $7.

MEREDIAN VINEYARDS

✷ To Do

GOLF **River Oaks Golf Course** (805-226-8099; www.riveroaksgolfcourse.com), 700 Clubhouse Dr., Paso Robles. This tiny six-hole course in a residential community is fun for adults and children who are beginners on the links. Green fee: $12.

SPAS **River Oaks Hot Springs Spa** (805-238-4600; www.riveroakshotsprings.com), 800 Clubhouse Dr., Paso Robles. The Central Coast is known for natural thermal springs, which were used for their medicinal properties from the earliest history of the area by the native Chumash people. River Oaks taps into these mineral-rich waters—naturally heated to 117 degrees and ideal for soothing away aches and pains—which patrons can enjoy in private open-air hot tubs. The spa also offers therapeutic massage, facials, and herbal wraps. Note that the use of the mineral tubs is surprisingly inexpensive: less than $20 an hour for an individual, and another $8 for an additional person.

WINERIES One of the easiest—and safest—ways to experience the wine country is to take a guided tour, which allows patrons to imbibe in the many wine tasting opportunities without having to drive between the vineyards. Good choices for tours include **California Limousines** (805-440,3311), **Central Coast Trolley Company** (805-296-9633), **Stardust Cruises Limousine Service** (805-545-0018), the **Wine Wrangler** (805-238-5700), and **Wine Tours VIP** (805-239-5920), all of which can accommodate small parties and provide personalized service.

For guests planning to tour the wine region in a vehicle, first download a wine map at www.pasowine.com, or call 805-239-8463 for up-to-date information. There are more than two hundred wineries in the region, and this number is expanding every year. Following are just a smattering of my favorites.

✪ 🍸 **Adelaida** (805-239-8980; www.adelaida.com), 5805 Adelaida Rd., Paso Robles. Open daily 10–5. Up in the hills, surrounded by a walnut grove that also belongs to the owners, Adelaida has been making wines since 1981—long before the area came to be known as a premier site for vineyards. Specialties include muscat/viognier dessert wines, a very drinkable red Rhône blend (called Version), and a bold Syrah. Look for gigantic bags of walnuts for sale in the tasting room.

✪ 🏅 🍸 **Castoro Cellars** (888-DAM-FINE), 1315 N. Bethel Rd., Templeton. Open daily 10–5:30. This friendly, picturesque winery offers free tastings (three with no purchase, seven with purchase) and a small picnic area overlooking the vineyard. The affordable label offers a number of white and red wines; my husband and I are big fans of their pinot grigio. Throughout the year the winery hosts concerts, which in the summer are held outside near the beautiful vineyards.

🍸 **Dark Star Cellar Winery** (805-237-2589; www.darkstarcellars.com), 2985 Anderson Rd., Paso Robles. Open Fri.–Sun. 10:30–5. In business in Paso Robles since 1994, this small family winery specializes in red wines. Look for the award-winning Ricordati (which translates to "always remember"), a blend of cabernet sauvignon, merlot, cabernet franc, malbec, and petit verdot.

🍸 ⚥ **Eagle Castle Winery** (805-227-1428; www.eaglecastlewinery.com), 3090 Anderson Rd., Paso Robles. Open daily 10–5:30. For sheer spectacle, don't miss the Eagle Castle Winery on CA 46 (among what I think is the prettiest stretch of wineries in the area). The tasting room is built to look like a medieval castle, complete with moat outside and suits of armor inside. Also on-site is the **Crown Room,** a restaurant that specializes in food and wine pairings (open for lunch only Fri.–Sun.).

🍸 **Eberle Winery** (805-238-9607; www.eberlewinery.com), 3810 CA 46 E., Paso Robles. Open daily 10–6 in the summer, 10–5 throughout the rest of the year. The Eberle estate produces cabernet, chardonnay, and muscat grapes that are used

CASTORO CELLARS

exclusively for Eberle wines, which over the years have garnered several hundred gold medals. Look for the cabernet sauvignon and Syrahs. Cave tours are available, and the winery also offers monthly guest chef dinners and a fun bocce ball court.

Meridian (805-226-7133; www.meridianvineyards.com), 7000 E. CA 46, Paso Robles. Open daily 10–5. Drive up a stunning 0.25-mile-long driveway that runs through a massive vineyard to reach this winery, which is surrounded by lovingly tended gardens and a scenic picnic spot. Meridian wines are easily accessible and affordable, and are ready to drink at purchase.

Peachy Canyon Winery (805-239-1918; www.peachycanyon.com), 1480 N. Bethel Rd., Templeton. Open daily 11–5:30. The tasting room of this quaint winery was once the Bethel Road School House, and the grounds offer a gazebo and picnic tables overlooking the vineyard. The winery is well known for its zinfandels, as well as Petite Syrahs, merlots, and viogniers.

Sculpterra (805-302-8881; www.sculpterra.com), 5015 Linne Rd., Paso Robles. Open Fri.–Sun. 10–5 and by appointment. In addition to a tasting room and pretty picnic grounds, this winery offers an unusual sculpture garden. This is a favorite for weddings and other private events.

Summerwood Winery (805-227-1365; www.summerwoodwine.com), 2175 Arbor Rd., Paso Robles. Open daily 10–6. Lush gardens and a romantic gazebo make for inviting picnic grounds outside of the Victorian-style tasting room of Summerwood, which is staffed by knowledgeable, friendly pourers. Although this is a relative newcomer (as of 2000), the winery offers a number of outstanding blends, such as the Sentio, a melding of cabernet sauvignon, cabernet franc, and merlot.

✷ Lodging

Paso Robles

La Bellasera Hotel and Suites (805-238-2834; www.labellasera.com), 206 Alexa Ct. The Tuscan architecture and décor and the tall cypress trees surrounding the property are perfectly appropriate for a wine region. Indeed, it is possible to stand out on the private loggia of a guest suite, look out over the vineyards and hillsides (and the traffic on two major highways), and imagine yourself in the Italian countryside. Accommodations are large and stylish, and the property is convenient for wine tasting, especially the pretty

LA BELLASERA

PRICE KEY FOR A STANDARD ROOM:

$	$100 or less
$$	$101–150
$$$	$151–250
$$$$	$251 and up

strip of wineries along CA 46. On Fri. and Sat. there are complimentary wine tastings in the lobby. On-site is **Enoteca,** a fine-dining destination for locals and visitors. Note: Call ahead for explicit directions, as the road to the property is unmarked at the turnoff at Hwy. 101. $$

PRICE KEY FOR A TYPICAL ENTRÉE:

$	$10 and under
$$	$11–20
$$$	$21–30
$$$$	$31 and up

✷ Where to Eat

DINING OUT

Paso Robles

Artisan (805-237-8084; www.artisanpasorobles.com), 1401 Park St. Open for lunch Mon.–Sat., dinner Sun.–Thurs., and brunch Sun. Chef Chris Kobayashi opened this restaurant with his wife, Shandi, and his brother, Michael. The family restaurant offers wine-country cuisine that celebrates fresh produce and uses only seasonal ingredients. The Charter Oak beef burger is a favorite, made from cattle humanely raised in nearby Templeton, served on buns baked fresh at a bakery next door, and topped with tomatoes grown on a family farm in Arroyo Grande. The purveyors at Artisan have very high standards of quality, and this is reflected not only in the food but in the fine service and elegant décor. $$$

Enoteca (805-238-2834; www.labellasera.com), 206 Alexa Ct. Open daily for breakfast, lunch, and dinner. Part of **La Bellasera** resort, this small, intimate restaurant features fresh, seasonal cuisine in a relaxed atmosphere. Grab the table by the fireplace, and don't miss the coconut-crusted halibut, which is served with a mild Thai curry sauce. When available, the chocolate hazelnut terrine is a decadent, nearly unbearably rich dessert. The restaurant offers a pleasant musical duo (which sometimes becomes a trio) on Thurs. nights. $$$

EATING OUT

Paso Robles

Big Bubba's Bad BBQ (805-238-6272; www.bigbubbasbadbbq.com), 1125 24th St. Open daily for lunch and dinner. As the name suggests, this joint isn't subtle: expect huge portions, huge flavors, and huge personalities. Start with a foot-tall stack of onion rings (served with barbecue and ranch dressings) and proceed to the slow-roasted, sticky pork spare ribs. $$

House of Bagels (805-237-1818), 630A First St. Open daily for breakfast and lunch. In a strip mall near the highway, House of Bagels (part of a small local chain—there is another outpost in San Luis Obispo) is a great place to grab a quick, delicious, carb-laden breakfast before heading out on the wine trails. Egg, bacon, and cheese sandwiches on onion bagels are a favorite, and the self-serve coffee is good. $

✷ Special Events

(in Greater San Luis Obispo)

March: **San Luis Obispo International Film Festival** (805-546-3456; www.slofilmfest.org), at various locations around SLO, showcases independent filmmakers and independent and classic films. **Zinfandel Wine Festival** (805-239-8463; www.pasowine.com), midmonth, includes numerous tastings, wine-pairing dinners, and open houses throughout Paso Robles.

April: **Sculpture by the Sea** (805-927-0254; www.californiasculptorssymposium.org), in Cambria, showcases indoor and outdoor sculptures in a natural setting overlooking the Pacific Ocean.

May: **Hospice du Rhône** (805-784-9543; www.hospicedurhone.org), in Paso Robles, is a three-day event in late Apr./early May that celebrates the art of Rhône wine producing through special tastings, lectures, and demonstrations. **Paso Robles Wine Festival** (805-239-8463; www.pasowine.com), held midmonth at various locations around Paso Robles, is hosted by more than 90 area wineries with events that include winery tours, seminars, and special tastings. **Arroyo Grand Strawberry Festival,** held in downtown Arroyo Grande over Memorial Day, has live music, arts and crafts displays, and strawberry-flavored foods of every imaginable sort.

June: The **Pinot and Paella Cook-Off** (805-239-2565; www.pinotandpaella.com), in nearby Templeton, is a food and wine festival hosted by Windward Vineyards and the pinot noir producers of Paso Robles. **Country Coast Classic Bike Ride** (805-543-8235; www.countrycoastclassic.org) offers the chance to bicycle through the lovely wine country of Paso Robles.

July: **Central Coast Wine Classic** (805-544-1285; www.centralcoastwineclassic.org), a major charity wine and food event that stretches across the Central Coast region, includes dinner at the Hearst Castle, winery dinners, and wine symposia. During **Rock to Pier Run** (805-772-6281), in Morro Bay, participants walk or run along a scenic 6-mile route that rims the coastline. The **Central Coast Renaissance Festival** (800-688-1477; www.ccrenfaire.com), in San Luis Obispo, in which the El Chorro Regional Park is transformed into an English renaissance village for a weekend in midmonth, includes more than eight hundred costumed actors and musicians, and continuous live entertainment.

August: **Central Coast Shakespeare Festival** (805-546-4224; www.centralcoastshakespeare.org), running from mid-July through mid-Aug., features live performances of two Shakespeare plays, performed under the stars in an intimate outdoor amphitheater. **"Movies in the Park,"** in Atascadero Sunken Gardens every Sat. night. **Olive Festival** (805-238-4103; www.pasoolivefestival.com), in Paso Robles, is an annual event that showcases the olives and olive products of producers throughout California.

Yosemite, Sequoia, and Kings Canyon

8

SEQUOIA AND KINGS CANYON

YOSEMITE

INTRODUCTION

Hidden away like a treasure stashed out of reach of careless hands, Yosemite is nestled at the top of the Sierra Nevada range in the central part of the state. This national park and World Heritage Site is the pride of Californians and a favorite with nature lovers from around the world, who regularly make a pilgrimage to the "jewel of the Sierras." It is no exaggeration to say that the glacier-carved Yosemite Valley, with iconic geological features, majestic mountains of solid granite, and some of the tallest waterfalls in North America, make this park a must-see-before-you-die kind of place. Every year about 4 million people do just that. Although the most easily accessible sites throughout the park are overrun in the summer months—especially in the beloved Yosemite Valley, where traffic jams are common in July and August—it is possible to hike an hour or so away from the parking lots and into the backcountry to find a true wilderness experience.

To the south of Yosemite is the Kings Canyon and Sequoia National Park group. Sequoia and Kings Canyon are also located in central California and extend from the San Joaquin Valley foothills to the eastern edge of the Sierra Nevada range. Together they comprise 865,258 acres of giant sequoia forests, raging white-water river, deeply carved canyons, and the breathtaking granite formations that the High Sierra is known for. Sequoia National Park was established in 1890, thanks to the efforts of John Muir and the Sierra Club, in large part to protect some of the world's largest living things: giant sequoias (*Sequoiadendron giganteum*) are the biggest trees (by mass—California redwoods are taller) in the world and among the oldest living things. They are indigenous only to the southern Sierra Nevada range of California and are abundant in Sequoia National Park. The spectacular trees are almost mind-boggling in scale: they can grow to 250 to 300 feet tall, more than 100 feet wide in diameter, and can live as long as 2,500 to 3,000 years. Their almost furry, cinnamon-colored bark can grow to more than 2 feet thick, and this is the true secret to their survival: because of their exceptionally thick insulation, giant sequoias are not as susceptible to fires as most other trees.

Sequoia's designation as a national park didn't immediately protect the area from exploitation. By the turn of the 20th century, logging had robbed nearby unprotected groves of more than half of their old-growth sequoias. In 1891, because of the continued threat to the Big Trees, Muir proposed extending the national park perimeters to include the High Sierra country of the Kings Canyon region, north and east of Sequoia, in the hope of thwarting the encroaching lumber industry. However, it wasn't until after Muir's death that the area surrounding Sequoia earned the protection Muir had argued it deserved. In 1940 Kings Canyon was included in the national park system as an add-on to Sequoia National Park, with which it was administered until the early 1940s. Together the two parks comprised 863,741 acres. In 1943, the contiguous parks were separated by name; although today officially separate parks, in practice they are administered as a joint entity.

Sequoia lies to the south and comprises a handful of distinct regions, including Wuksachi Village, home of the Wuksachi Lodge; Mineral King, a remote, glacially carved valley; and Lodgepole, in the center of the park, which holds the lion's share of iconic sites, including the famous General Sherman Tree, Moro Rock, and Tunnel Log. Kings Canyon is divided into two distinct sections, north and east of Sequoia National Park, with Sequoia National Forest separating the two. The most visited portion is in the northwest, and here guests will find Grant Grove, which is home to the famous General Grant Tree and the aptly named Panoramic Point; and Redwood Mountain Grove, southeast of grant grove, which is the site of the Roosevelt Tree and the Hart Tree, two of the largest sequoias in the world. In the second portion of the park, northeast of Sequoia, guests will find Cedar Grove, home to Zumwalt Meadow and Grand Sentinel. Both Sequoia National Park and Kings Canyon National Park also have extensive backcountry areas, enough to provide weeks' worth of solitary hiking and camping to those looking for real outdoor adventure.

GUIDANCE There are a number of visitors centers throughout all three parks, where guests can ask questions about flora and fauna, pick up trail maps and backcountry hiking permits, and learn more about free ranger programs. An added bonus: these visitors centers usually have running water in the bathrooms, a welcome luxury when compared to the many trailhead facilities throughout the parks that generally offer only pit toilets.

Kings Canyon

Cedar Grove Visitor Center (559-565-3793), off CA 180, 0.25 mile west of Cedar Grove Village. Open in summer only.

Kings Canyon Visitor Center (559-565-4307), on CA 180, 3 miles northeast of the Kings Canyon Park entrance.

Sequoia

Foothills Visitor Center (559-565-3135), on CA 198, adjacent to Three Rivers.

Giant Forest Museum Center (559-565-4480), on CA 198, in the Giant Forest.

Lodgepole Visitor Center (559-565-4436), 2 miles north of the General Sherman Tree. Closed in the winter.

Mineral King Ranger Station (559-565-3768), on Mineral King Rd., 24 miles east of Three Rivers. Open only in summer.

Yosemite

Big Oak Flat Information Station (209-372-0200), at the Big Oak Flat Entrance. Open spring–fall.

Mariposa Grove Museum Information Desk (209-372-4386), in the upper grove of the Mariposa Grove. Open summer only.

Tuolumne Meadows Wilderness Center (209-372-0200), at shuttle stop #3. Open summer only.

Wawona Visitor Center at Hill's Studio (209-372-0200), adjacent to the Wawona Hotel. Open spring–fall.

Wilderness Center (209-372-0200), in Yosemite Village, near the Ansel Adams Gallery and the Yosemite Post Office.

MORE TELEPHONE NUMBERS

Kings Canyon and Sequoia

General park information: 559-565-3341

Camping, backpacking information: 559-565-3341

Disabled services: 559-565-3341

Road and weather conditions: 559-565-3341

Winter ski information: 559-565-4070 or 559-335-5500

Yosemite

General park information: 209-372-0200

Campground reservations: 877-444-6777

Road and weather conditions: 209-372-0200

Road service in Yosemite: 209-379-2321

Wilderness permits: 209-372-0740

EL CAPITAN

Courtesy of Jon Preimesberger

NATIONAL PARK ENTRANCE FEES A seven-day entrance pass, required when visiting each park, is $20 per vehicle or $10 per person for pedestrians and bicyclists; if you are planning to visit both Sequoia and Kings Canyon, a yearlong pass for these two parks is available for $30 per person. A yearlong pass for Yosemite is available for $40. In addition, an annual pass that is good for all national parks and monuments throughout the country is available at $80 per person (or $10 for a lifetime pass for senior citizens).

MEDICAL EMERGENCIES Call 911 for medical emergencies, as well as for emergency fire and police assistance. First-aid facilities are scattered throughout the parks; check ranger stations for more information.

GETTING THERE *By air:* The closest airports to Kings Canyon and Sequoia are **Visalia Municipal Airport** (559-733-6653; Country Road 112, Visalia), which is 40 miles west of Sequoia, and **Fresno/Yosemite International Airport** (559-621-4500; 5175 E. Clinton Way, Fresno), 50 miles west of Kings Canyon. **Sacramento International Airport** (916-929-5411; 6900 Airport Boulevard, Sacramento) is approximately two hours away.

The closest airport to Yosemite is **Fresno/Yosemite International Airport,** which is approximately two and a half hours away by car. The **San Francisco International Airport** (650-821-8211) is three hours from the Big Oak Flat Entrance on CA 120 in the northwest or four hours from the Yosemite Valley. The **Sacramento International Airport** is two hours from the Big Oak Flat Entrance.

By car: All three parks in this region are at high elevation, mountainous, and accessible only via winding, narrow roads. Exercise caution and common sense when driving to the parks along these sometimes white-knuckle roads. Remember to downshift when going downhill, to allow your engine to cool off and protect your brakes. When driving a slower vehicle along single-lane roads, be sure to pull off into the frequent turnouts to allow faster vehicles to pass. Carry tire chains in your vehicle from late October through May.

The Generals Highway (connecting CA 198 to CA 180) runs into the southwest end of Sequoia National Park and connects with CA 180 in Grant Grove, in Kings Canyon Park, to the north. The Kings Canyon Highway (CA 180) runs into the Kings Canyon National Park at Grant Grove and follows through to Road's End.

Yosemite can be accessed via four main entrances: in the south via CA 41 at the South Entrance, in the west via CA 140 at the Arch Rock Entrance, in the east via CA 12 at the Tioga Pass Entrance (open only in the summer), and in the northwest via CA 120 at the Big Oak Flats Entrance.

Call 209-372-0200 to check road conditions, for both weather-related and maintenance road closures.

By shuttle bus: From Memorial Day weekend through Labor Day, the **Sequoia Shuttle** (877-287-4453; www.sequoiashuttle.com) runs from Visalia and through Three Rivers to the Giant Forest Museum in Sequoia National Park, at which point guests can catch the free park shuttle. Round-trip fees are $15, and this includes park entrance.

DRIVING TIPS WITHIN THE NATIONAL PARKS

- Fill up before you arrive in the parks; fuel inside the parks is much more expensive. Beyond the costs, gas stations are few and far between inside the park boundaries. Note, however, that Yosemite gas stations are open year-round at Wawona (next to the Wawona Hotel) and at Crane Flat, and seasonally at Tuolumne Meadows.
- Be aware that because of high elevations, chains may be required for the mountainous roads throughout this region at any time of the year and will *definitely* be required from fall through spring.
- Entry roads are plowed in winter season to Grant Grove in Kings Canyon, Giant Forest in Sequoia, and in Yosemite to the South Entrance, to the Big Oak Flat Entrance, and Arch Rock Entrance.
- In Sequoia and Kings Canyon, the roads to Cedar Grove, Mineral King, Moro Rock, and Crystal Cave are all closed throughout the winter. In Yosemite, Tioga Road to Tuolumne Meadows is closed in winter, as is the Glacier Point Road to Glacier Point (although the road is plowed up to the Badger Pass Ski Area).

In Yosemite, **YARTS** (Yosemite Area Regional Transportation, 877-989-2787) runs to the park from a number of gateway communities, including Merced, Fresno, and Sacramento, with fares from $10 to $25, which includes the park entrance fee.

By train: **AMTRAK** arrives in Hanford and Fresno, from which point visitors can catch bus connections into Kings Canyon and Sequoia. Likewise, AMTRAK serves Merced, with motor coach services to Yosemite.

GETTING AROUND To discourage motorists from clogging narrow byways, overspilling limited parking areas, and polluting the pristine environment, the national parks provide free in-park shuttle buses. However, some automobile travel is necessary if you want to cover the expanse of the parks.

By in-park shuttle: Catch a free shuttle to the Giant Forest within Sequoia National Park during the summertime. In Yosemite, a free year-round shuttle, powered by hybrid electric-diesel engines, carries visitors along 21 stops in the valley; in the summer, three additional shuttles provide round-trip access from Wawona to the Mariposa Grove, Wawona to Yosemite Valley, and in Tuolumne Meadows from the Tioga Pass Entrance to Olmstead Point. In winter, there is also free shuttle transportation between Yosemite Valley and the Badger Pass Ski Area. Pick up route information at any visitors center, or just look for the shuttle stops scattered along the roadside.

SEQUOIA AND KINGS CANYON

As noted earlier, Sequoia and Kings Canyon were considered one park for years, and even today they are managed as a single entity. Their proximity makes it easy to move between the two parks with relative ease. Note, however, that Yosemite is farther away, which makes it difficult to move between it and either Sequoia and Kings Canyon in a single day. The drive from Yosemite Valley to Sequoia, for example, generally takes about three hours. For this reason, I've divided coverage of the region into two distinct sections, first covering the Sequoia and Kings Canyon area, and then Yosemite.

* To See

NATURAL ICONS

Kings Canyon

General Grant Tree, within the Grant Grove, 1 mile past the Kings Canyon Visitor Center on the west side of CA 180. The 0.5-mile loop trail through Grant Grove, a cathedral of trees that are two thousand to three thousand years old, begins at the parking lot and leads to the General Grant Tree, which is more than 267 feet tall and nearly 108 feet around. The General Grant is also known as the Nation's Christmas Tree and is the site of seasonal festivities (see *Greater Yosemite Area Special Events*).

✪ **Grant Grove,** off CA 180, just north of the Big Stump Entrance. In addition to the venerable General Grant Tree, this magnificent forest of giant trees is home to the rough-hewn Gamlin Cabin, an early homestead and one time ranger station, and the Fallen Monarch Tree. There is an easy self-guided trail through the forest that meanders through dozens of impressive sequoias.

Kings Canyon, running through the length of the park, along the Kings River. The spectacular namesake canyon stretches into Sequoia National Park, and at its deepest point is actually deeper than the Grand Canyon. Views and hiking are unmatched along the rim. Look for the granite formations Grant Sentinel (at 8,518 feet) and North Dome (at 8,717 feet). The best way to glimpse the canyon and these granite behemoths is via the **Zumwalt Meadow Nature Trail** in the eastern portion of the park.

Panoramic Point, accessed via a steep, winding 2-mile road from Grant Grove Village, and then a 0.25-mile hike from the parking area at the top of the road.

From this vantage point at 7,520 feet, guests get unparalleled views of the High Sierra and Hume Lake (which is in Sequoia National Park).

Sequoia

Crescent Meadow, off CA 198, 1.5 miles east of the Moro Rock parking area. This pretty grassy area is strewn with wildflowers in spring and is a good place to spot wildlife. The trail around the meadow rings the perimeter and is surrounded by tall trees.

✪ **Crystal Cave,** accessed via a marked 7-mile twisting road off Generals Hwy. This surprising area is tough to reach: after the tortuous ride up the access road, visitors must make a 15-minute hike along a steep path to the cave entrance. Be sure to buy tickets in advance at the Lodgepole or Foothills visitors centers (see *Guidance*); no tickets are available at the cave itself. But the preparation and effort to reach the site are well worth it: inside, visitors will see otherworldly sheets of stalactites (those mineral formations that drip from the roof of the cave) and bulbous lumps of stalagmites (those that grow from the floor of the cave).

INSIDER TIP: Bring a jacket and good walking shoes when visiting the Crystal Cave. Even in the flush of summer, the cave temperatures are about 50 degrees Fahrenheit. Pathways can be slippery, so hiking boots or athletic shoes work best.

SEQUOIA TREE

General Sherman Tree, in the Giant Forest, accessed from Wolverton Rd., 4 miles north of the Giant Forest Museum. This is not the tallest tree, nor is it the widest in circumference; however, the General Sherman is considered to be the largest living tree in the world because of its mass. It weighs about 2.7 million pounds—and is thought to be more than two thousand years old.

Hospital Rock, off CA 198, about 6 miles northeast of the Foothills Visitor Center. Hike a short, steep pathway from the parking and picnic area to a large boulder adorned with pictographs that date to the 19th-century native Monarche people. Nearby is a collection of grinding stones, which native women used to pound acorns into flour.

Moro Rock, off Moro Rock/Crescent Meadow Rd., in the Giant Forest area;

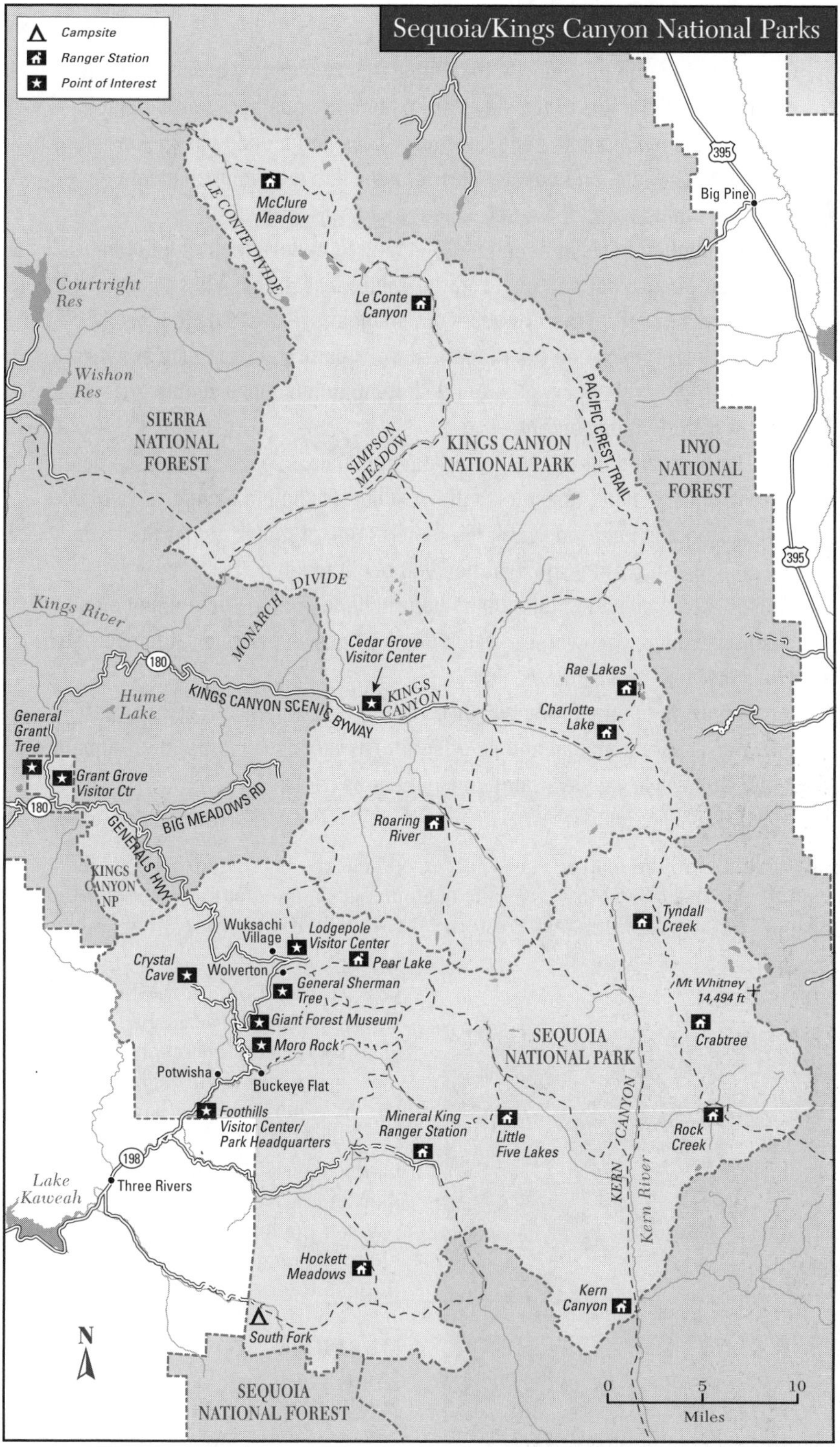

Sequoia/Kings Canyon National Parks
Campsite
Ranger Station
Point of Interest
McClure Meadow
LE CONTE DIVIDE
Le Conte Canyon
Courtright Res
Wishon Res
SIERRA NATIONAL FOREST
SIMPSON MEADOW
KINGS CANYON NATIONAL PARK
PACIFIC CREST TRAIL
INYO NATIONAL FOREST
395
Big Pine
MONARCH DIVIDE
Kings River
Cedar Grove Visitor Center
KINGS CANYON
180
KINGS CANYON SCENIC BYWAY
Hume Lake
Rae Lakes
Charlotte Lake
General Grant Tree
Grant Grove Visitor Ctr
BIG MEADOWS RD
GENERALS HWY
KINGS CANYON NP
Roaring River
Tyndall Creek
Wuksachi Village
Lodgepole Visitor Center
Pear Lake
Crystal Cave
Wolverton
General Sherman Tree
Mt Whitney 14,494 ft
Giant Forest Museum
Moro Rock
SEQUOIA NATIONAL PARK
Crabtree
Potwisha
Buckeye Flat
Foothills Visitor Center/ Park Headquarters
Mineral King Ranger Station
Little Five Lakes
KERN CANYON
Kern River
Rock Creek
198
Three Rivers
Lake Kaweah
Hockett Meadows
Kern Canyon
South Fork
N
SEQUOIA NATIONAL FOREST
0
5
10
Miles

WILDLIFE VIEWING

One of my favorite pastimes in national parks is wildlife viewing, and these three parks of the Sierra Nevadas are among the best for spotting black bears (in the mountains), mule deer (in valleys and meadows), jackrabbits, raccoons, bobcats, and coyotes. Birders will find mountain chickadees, red-breasted nuthatches, and an abundance of Steller's jays.

Although animals in national parks tend to be less frightened of humans than their counterparts in unprotected wilderness areas, it is still easier to spot them away from the crowds—which means rising early (generally before sunrise) to get on the roads and trails before anyone else comes along to frighten them away. A good spotting technique is simply to scan an area in search of movement.

Once you find them, *never* feed park animals, even the cute (and persistent) squirrels and chipmunks that will literally beg to have a taste of your picnic. And don't get too close: the general rule of thumb is that the larger the animal, the greater the distance you ought to keep. If your presence causes a wild animal to change its natural behavior (i.e., by running away, hiding its young, or—worse—exhibiting aggressive behavior), then you are too close.

Never try to take food away from a wild animal, and never, ever get between a parent animal and its offspring, especially a mother bear and its cubs. This will likely have fatal consequences.

0.25-mile trail to the feature can be accessed near the parking area 1.5 miles from the Giant Forest Museum. This magnificent granite dome formation offers a panoramic view of the Great Western Divide. (The road to Moro Rock is closed in winter.)

HOSPITAL ROCK

✪ ✐ **Tunnel Log,** off the Moro Rock/Crescent Meadow Rd. This fallen giant sequoia has been carved out so that cars can drive through it—a kitschy experience that harkens back to the gimmicks of the early days in the national parks. Come early in the morning to avoid traffic (and afford yourself the luxury of stepping out and photographing your vehicle heading through the tree).

MUSEUMS

Kings Canyon

✐ **Beetle Rock Education Center** (559-565-4251). Open summer only.

SEQUOIA MEADOW

This is a great place for kids to learn about the park or join one of the many guided programs created just for kids. In addition, this is an outpost for field seminars, teacher-education programs, and naturalist activities. Admission is free.

Sequoia

Giant Forest Museum (www.nps.gov/seki/gf/new/museum.htm), in the Giant Forest, off CA 198. This small museum is dwarfed by the sequoias that surround it; inside, exhibits explain the history and biology of the nearby grove. Although there is little to see here, it is worth a quick stop to orient oneself, especially if traveling with children. Pick up a number of interpretive trails just outside the museum. Admission is free.

✷ To Do

BICYCLING Bikes are permitted only on paved roads and in campgrounds in Sequoia and Kings Canyon. Mountain bikes may not be taken on trails or in the backcountry.

HIKING Kings Canyon and Sequoia have more than 800 miles of trails, so there is never a shortage of hiking opportunities. Below are just a few of my favorite possibilities. Note that if you plan to head into the heart of the wilderness, a backcountry hiking and camping permit is mandatory; guests can pick these up at most visitors centers and ranger stations.

TUNNEL LOG

Kings Canyon

Big Stump Trail. Find the trailhead at the picnic area near Kings Canyon's Big Stump Entrance. The 1-mile loop trail shows the remains of early logging. The highlight (or lowlight, depending on your perspective) is the

SMARTER THAN THE AVERAGE BEAR

Kings Canyon, Sequoia, and Yosemite parks are all smack in the middle of bear country, and it is imperative that visitors "bearproof" their cars before entering the area, to avoid dangerous encounters with the animals or damage to unattended vehicles. On average, one car *a day* is destroyed by bears in these parks. Never store food or beverages in your automobile, even if it is "hidden"; bears have an unbelievably strong sense of smell, and some say they can even detect food in unopened cans. Also remove all cosmetics that have scents, including lip gloss, makeup, sunscreen, moisturizing lotions, wet wipes, and bug spray. Purchase a bearproof container to store such items while hiking, or make use of bearproof food-storage lockers that are available in camping and picnic areas throughout the parks. You might think your donuts are safe locked inside your car if you park it in the middle of a busy parking area in the middle of a tourist zone: think again. Smarter-than-average park bears have learned that this is exactly where to find treats and can often be seen sniffing through such crowded lots in search of a snack.

Mark Twain Stump, which is all that is left of what was a 26-foot-wide, nearly 2,000-year-old tree that was cut down in 1891.

✪ **General Grant Tree Trail.** Pick up the trailhead at the Grant Tree parking lot and follow the interpretive signs through the very easy 0.5-mile walk through a giant sequoia grove, which culminates at the General Grant Tree, also known as the Nation's Christmas Tree, which stands at more than 267 feet tall and nearly 108 feet around.

Sunset Trail. Begin at the trailhead across the road from Grant Grove Visitor Center and proceed along 6 miles of strenuous pathway, gaining 1,400 feet in elevation. This tough day hike rewards takers with views of two ethereal waterfalls, a small lake, streams, and ubiquitous forest vistas.

Zumwalt Meadow. Catch the trailhead at the Zumwalt Meadow parking area, 1 mile before Road's End, CA 180. The 1.5-mile easy trail offers lovely views of the meadow, the canyon, and the spectacular granite features known as Grand Sentinel and North Dome.

Sequoia

✐ **Big Trees Trail.** Catch the pathway at the Giant Forest Museum, off CA 198. The relatively easy 1.5-mile trail is fully accessible to disabled visitors, and along the way it provides trailside exhibits and information panels.

✪ **Congress Trail.** This 2-mile paved path is an easy loop through the Giant Forest Grove and into Alta Plateau, the home of giant sequoias with names like General Lee and Chief Sequoyah. Pick up the trail head at the General Sherman Tree.

Crescent Meadow. Pick up the trailhead at the Crescent Meadow parking lot and picnic area, off CA 198. Follow the signs to Tharp's Log. The trail winds around the meadow and alongside giant sequoias for an easy 1.8-mile loop.

ON THE TRAIL

HORSEBACK RIDING Rental horses are available at **Cedar Grove Pack Station** (559-565-3464) and at the **Grant Grove Stables** (559-335-9292) in Kings Canyon. Hour-long, half-day, and day trips are available; reservations are highly recommended.

WINTER SPORTS Many trails are open throughout both parks for cross-country skiing and snowshoeing. Advanced snowshoers and cross-country skiers in Sequoia will enjoy the Pear Lake Trail, a steep 6-mile path beginning at Wolverton. For those with the stamina to get there, and the interest in overnighting after a vigorous day on the wintry trails, the **Pear Lake Ski Hut** (559-565-4222), three-eighths of a mile north of Pear Lake, offers accommodations for up to 10 people in season (at less than $40 per night). Advanced reservations are a must.

SWIMMING HOLE

✷ Water Sports

FISHING A valid California fishing license is required for anyone 16 and older in both Kings Canyon and Sequoia. Licenses and tackle are available at Lodgepole, Grant Grove, and Cedar Cove Markets. Trout season runs from the last Saturday in April through November 15 (catch limit five per day). The Kaweah Drainage is open year-round to fishing.

SWIMMING Rangers advise against swimming in rivers, because of swift currents and frigid waters—and of course it is foolhardy to swim anywhere near a waterfall. With that said, in hot summer months there are a number of calm swimming holes throughout the parks. Because conditions change quickly, it is best to inquire at visitors centers for specific suggestions. *Never swim in a wilderness area alone.*

✱ Lodging

Although Sequoia and Kings Canyon are not as crowded during summer months and over the holidays as is their better-known cousin, Yosemite National Park, it is still extremely important to make lodging reservations well in advance. Campers will find that Lodgepole and Dorst campgrounds in Sequoia accept reservations in the summer up to six months in advance (877-444-6777). Note that backcountry permits are required for overnight stays in all areas that are not designated as campgrounds.

PRICE KEY FOR A STANDARD ROOM:

$	$100 or less
$$	$101–150
$$$	$151–250
$$$$	$251 and up

Kings Canyon

Cedar Grove Lodge (559-335-5550; www.kcanyon.com). This tiny lodge sits on the Kings River, in the heart of Kings Canyon. Rooms are minimal, and there are communal showers and laundry facilities. On-site is a small gift shop and market, along with a snack shop. Location is prime, because guests are never more than an hour's hike from waterfalls, meadows, and both North Dome and Grand Sentinel. $$

Grant Grove Village (559-335-5500; www.sequoia-kingscanyon.com). Adjacent to the Grant Grove and walking distance to the famous **General Grant Tree,** this complex includes a lodge, rustic cabins, and canvas "tent cabins" (a favorite with children). Also on-site is a small gift shop, grocery store, post office, and a decent cafeteria. Note that of 24 cabins, only nine have private bathrooms. $–$$

John Muir Lodge (559-335-5500; www.sequoia-kingscanyon.com). In Grant Village, this tiny lodge has 36 guest accommodations, including a handful of suites. The rooms are comfortable and clean and offer access to the lodge's pretty balconies, which are equipped with lounge furniture and offer nice views. The big old stone fireplace is the ideal backdrop for a game of checkers. $$$

Sequoia

Montecito Sequoia Lodge (800-227-9900; www.montecitosequoia.com), 63410 Generals Hwy. Located in Sequoia National Forest, this lodge is only 10 miles south of Grant Grove in Kings Canyon. Visitors arrive via a

MONTECITO SEQUOIA LODGE

roadway built over a dam that contains a small lake (popular with paddleboaters). Lodging is in four lodge buildings, all rooms in which have private bathrooms, or in 14 small rustic cabins, which share bathroom facilities. $$

✪ **Wuksachi Village and Lodge** (559-253-2199; www.visitsequoia.com). This authentic timber and stone lodge at the north end of the park comprises three separate buildings for lodging and another for the dining room, which also serves as a lobby and offers a small gift shop. The complex is surrounded by a fragrant pine forest and provides guests with awe-inspiring views of Mount Silliman and Silver Peak, especially lovely at sunset and sunrise. The rooms are comfortable and spacious; suites are available for families and are well worth the extra cost for the additional space. The lodge offers campfire programs, nighttime hikes, and the grounds are fun to explore. It is almost a guarantee to see deer grazing as dusk—and it is almost as likely to spot bears. $$–$$$

✷ Where to Eat

DINING OUT

Sequoia

Wuksachi Village and Lodge Restaurant (559-565-4070). Open daily for breakfast, lunch, and dinner. Although this restaurant doesn't have much competition—it is in essence the only fine dining within the park—the cuisine is surprisingly refined and includes seasonal offerings of crispy pan-fried trout with greens, spoon-tended Kobe steak and whipped mashed potatoes, and citrus-marinated salmon with caramelized onions. The dining room is large and can be noisy, thanks to abundant families, especially in the early dining hours, but the picture windows that look out over the mountains and trees make up for the lack of ambiance. $$$

WUKSACHI LODGE

EATING OUT

Kings Canyon

Grant Grove Village Restaurant. Open daily for breakfast, lunch, and dinner. This casual diner located in the lodge registration building offers American comfort food in a family-friendly atmosphere. Kids will find plenty of standard fare like hamburgers and mac and cheese. $

Sequoia

Lodgepole Village. Open daily in the summer only. Sometimes even a prepackaged sandwich or a box of crackers and cheese is a welcome meal after hiking through the wilderness. In such instances, this small snack bar fits the bill nicely. $

PRICE KEY FOR A TYPICAL ENTRÉE:

$	$10 and under
$$	$11–20
$$$	$21–30
$$$$	$31 and up

YOSEMITE

Yosemite was set aside in 1890 as a national park by President Benjamin Harrison, after naturalists such as John Muir recognized the stunning diversity and ecological uniqueness of the region. The park is best known for Yosemite Valley, which is home to well-known sites like Half Dome, El Capitan, and Yosemite Falls. This small area is perhaps the most singularly beautiful region in the world, and it is the most heavily trafficked area of the park; in fact, nine out of 10 visitors to Yosemite see only the valley. However, there are a number of regions beyond the valley that hold an almost equal allure. Tuolumne Meadows, northeast of the valley and accessible via the scenic Tioga Road, is a subalpine meadow laced with ribbons of river and creek and distant views of perpetually snowcapped peaks. Glacier Point, a high-altitude area with panoramic vistas, is just south of Yosemite Valley, accessible only via the winding Glacier Point Road or via a *very* challenging trail. Along this mountainous route guests will pass the Badger Pass Ski Area (a fun snow-play and ski zone in the winter months). To the extreme south of the park (2 miles from the South Entrance) is Wawona, home of the Mariposa Grove, the park's large forest of giant sequoia trees. To the north of the valley, on the westernmost border of the park, is Hetch Hetchy, a region that was once described by John Muir as being as exceptionally beautiful as Yosemite Valley, replete with jutting granite mountains and ethereal waterfalls. However, before the legal protections of "national park" status were fully realized, the area fell prey to nearby politicians from San Francisco (and their supporters in Washington), who decided in the early 20th century to dam the Tuolumne River at Hetch Hetchy to harness the hydroelectric power, which in turn flooded the valley. Today at this little-visited area, the cliffs and waterfalls are still visible, above the O'Shaughnessy Dam Reservoir, and a hike here is both serene and bittersweet.

✱ To See

HISTORICAL SITES ✐ **LeConte Memorial Lodge** (209-372-4542). At shuttle stop #12. The LeConte Memorial Lodge is the first public visitors center in Yosemite and is still staffed today in the summertime (by Sierra Club volunteers). Inside is a library and a children's activity area; this is also the site of educational programs in the summertime.

Yosemite Cemetery. Across the street from the Yosemite Museum, in the Yosemite Valley, this historic cemetery dates back to the 1800s and is the final

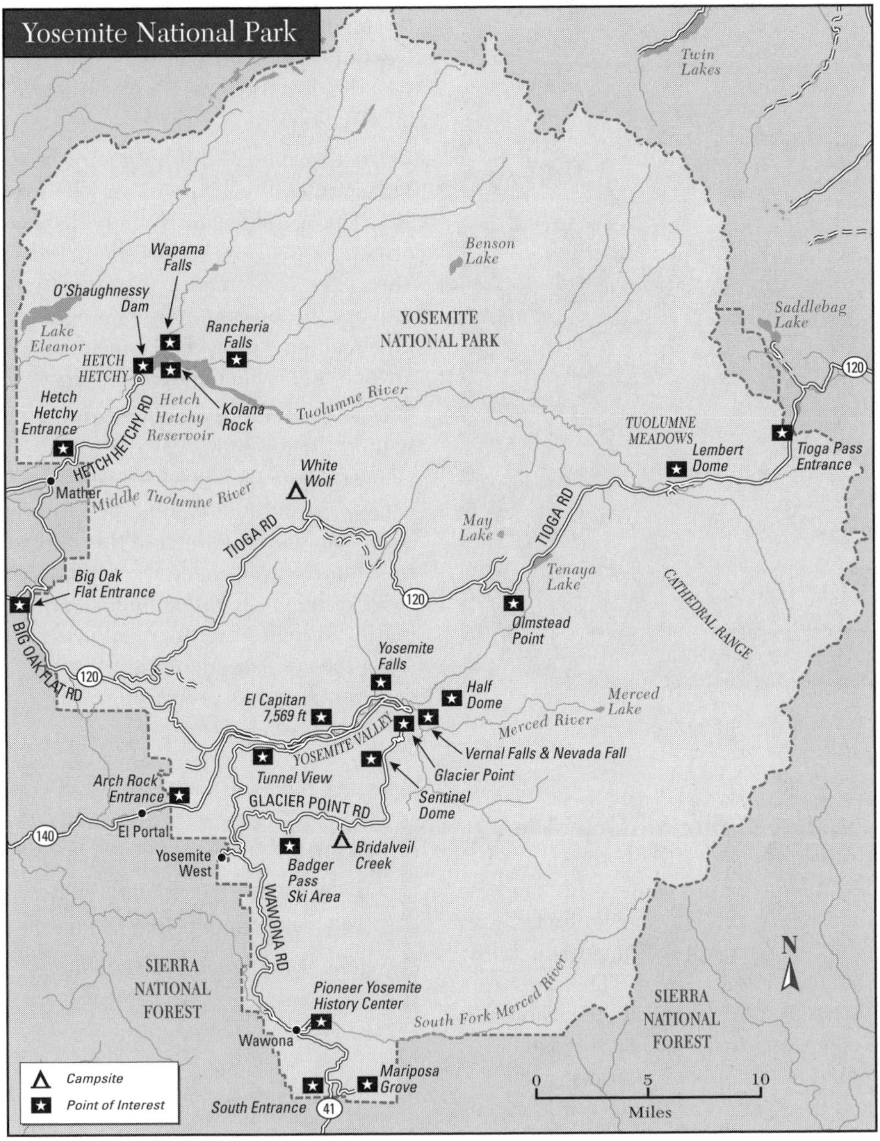

resting place for Native Americans who called the park home, as well as Yosemite Valley pioneers.

⚤ **Yosemite Chapel.** This pretty chapel, set amid the splendor of Yosemite Valley, is the oldest building in Yosemite National Park that remains in use, and it is available for private prayer and for weddings. The chapel is open 24 hours a day.

MUSEUMS Admission to the galleries and museums within Yosemite National Park is included in the national park fee. Also note that open hours and days vary by season and from year to year. Expect long hours in the heavily trafficked summer months; some galleries and museums close completely in the winter. Please check

RAFTING ON THE MERCED RIVER

the national parks Web site (www.nps.gov/yose/planyourvisit/historic.htm) for up-to-date information.

✪ **Ansel Adams Gallery,** in Yosemite Village. Open daily; hours vary by season. The Ansel Adams Gallery displays original signed worked by the noted Yosemite photographer. Also on-site is artwork by contemporary photographers, along with a good collection of art books and handcrafted jewelry.

✪ **Indian Village of Ahwahnee,** behind the Yosemite Valley Visitor Center. Open daily. Guests can explore an outdoor exhibit of Native American camps (which in this part of the country were made from bark and twigs rather than animal hides). During the summer there are cultural presentations on-site, demonstrating crafts such as basket weaving and carving obsidian.

Nature Center at Happy Isles, near shuttle stop #16, in Yosemite Valley. A large nature center with hands-on exhibits, this is a magnet for children, who will find many programs designed just for them. There are nearby trails (short and easily accessible for youngsters) that focus on the habitats found in Yosemite: fen, forest, river, and talus. There is also an outdoor geological exhibit on Yosemite rock falls.

INSIDER TIP: The Ansel Adams Gallery offers free photography walks year-round. Stop by the gallery to sign up beforehand.

Pioneer Yosemite History Center, off CA 41, north of the South Entrance. Adjacent to the **Wawona Hotel** and accessible via a pretty covered bridge, this small area has preserved pioneer cabins and other historic buildings, many of which are open (sporadically) for touring. The highlight is a wild horse-drawn stage ride through the historic area and through the nearby covered wooden bridge.

Tuolumne Meadows Visitor Center, off Tioga Rd., just west of the Tuolumne River. Open summers only. This visitors center offers exhibits on ecology, Yosemite wildlife, wildflowers, and geology. Also on-site is an exhibit that explains naturalist John Muir's perspective on the importance of Yosemite.

WAWONA COVERED BRIDGE

Yosemite Museum. Adjacent to the Yosemite Valley Visitor Center. Guests will find the Indian Cultural Exhibit at the Yosemite Museum, which educates visitors about the Miwok and Paiute peoples from 1850 to modern times.

Yosemite Valley Exhibit Hall, in the Yosemite Valley Visitor Center. A small exhibit space explores the geology of the Yosemite Valley, as well as the flora and fauna that call it home.

NATURAL ICONS The whole of Yosemite is iconic: the valley is startlingly beautiful, with dramatic granite cliffs rising up from the verdant floor and ribbonlike waterfalls cascading down—tumultuous during the spring snowmelts, enchanting in the deep freeze of winter, and ethereal in the less-wet summer and fall. It simply isn't possible to enumerate every must-see natural site in a park filled with incomparable wonders, but the list that follows comprises the best known and most visited—and surely a trip to Yosemite is incomplete without seeing them.

✪ **El Capitan.** This sheer, massive granite cliff stretches 2,593 feet from the base to the summit, and it is one of the first things to greet visitors to the Yosemite Valley. It is wildly popular with hard-core rock climbers, who can be seen scaling the monolith from spring through fall. Because of its smooth, flat face, the surface reflects stunning colors at sunrise and sunset.

Glacier Point. About 30 miles south of Yosemite Valley, Glacier Point can be reached by a winding mountain road (open only from late May through early Nov). From Glacier Rd. turnoff, the drive takes about an hour, even with pristine road conditions. The high elevation offers some of the most panoramic views of the valley and a nearly eye-level glimpse of Half Dome. Note that from Dec. through early Apr., the same road in is plowed partway, up to **Badger Pass Ski Area,** a popular ski resort and snow-play zone.

✪ **Half Dome.** Rising nearly 5,000 feet, this granite rock formation is visible throughout Yosemite Valley. The feature is particularly striking because a glacier rubbed off the lower portion of the otherwise round formation. Despite its name, about 80 percent of the rock remains, leaving the distinctive hooked dome that is one of the most photographed sites in the world. Hard-core hikers trek to the top via a half-day climb to the rock and then scramble up the rock itself via cable lines that are left in place year-round.

INSIDER TIP: To avoid rope burns and blisters, bring gloves if you plan to scale Half Dome. If you happen to forget them, there are often discarded pairs at the point of departure.

Happy Isles. At the eastern edge of Yosemite Valley, this pretty area is accessible via footbridges, which will take visitors over marshland and alongside the Merced River, which roars through in spring and trickles along in late summer. If traveling with children, be sure to check out the **Nature Center at Happy Isles.**

Hetch Hetchy, northeast of Yosemite Valley. In the early 1900s, Hetch Hetchy Valley (which was described at the time as being as beautiful as Yosemite Valley and is just to the northwest—well within park boundaries) was the center of a battle between conservationists and politicians. The growing city of San Francisco needed additional water sources and hydroelectric power, and turned to the

HALF DOME FROM GLACIER POINT

O'SHAUGHNESSY DAM AT HETCH HETCHY

Tuolumne River, running through Hetch Hetchy. Preservationists, led by Yosemite champion John Muir, waged a bitter fight to save the valley. Despite these efforts, the U.S. congress authorized the construction of the O'Shaughnessy Dam, which resulted in the flooding (many would say destruction) of the Hetch Hetchy Valley. Today the Hetch Hetchy Reservoir that resulted from the damming of the river is privately owned and off-limits to boaters and swimmers, but hikers can still catch a glimpse of two stunning waterfalls: Tueeulala Falls is visible about 2 miles from the trailhead that begins just beyond the dam; Wapama Falls is another 0.5 mile beyond.

✪ **Mariposa Grove.** Located in the southern end of the park, Mariposa Grove is the park's most expansive forest of giant sequoia trees (there are more than five hundred mature sequoias), the massive size of which can only be appreciated in person. Highlights include the Grizzly Giant, one of the world's largest trees. Trails run throughout the grove (see *Hiking*), and this is one of the best places to see bears in the park, especially in the early morning and at dusk. (Note that vehicles longer than 22 feet are not allowed on the Mariposa Grove Rd. 9–4 daily.)

✪ **Tuolumne Meadows.** The Tuolumne Meadows region of the park is much less visited than Yosemite Valley and is a bit farther flung. Access the area via the Tioga Rd. (CA 120) from late May through early Nov. This wildflower-strewn subalpine area has jaw-dropping views of the surrounding granite cliffs, tiny lakes, and miles of easy flat hiking trails (see *Hiking*).

INSIDER TIP: When visiting Yosemite in the spring, do not miss the 39-mile stretch of scenic roadway from Crane Flat to Tuolumne Meadows; this is one of the most beautiful drives in California.

✪ **Yosemite Falls.** This combination falls—comprising the Upper Yosemite Fall and the Lower Yosemite Fall—tops out at 2,425 feet, which makes this the highest falls in North America. In the center of the Yosemite Valley, Yosemite Falls is fed

TUOLUMNE MEADOWS

almost entirely by snowmelt, so its character changes dramatically with the seasons. After spring thaw, the waters roar down the falls and through the valley, creating pools and streams in their wake. By late summer or fall, they can dry up entirely—although the area is always stunning and well worth a visit.

✷ To Do

BICYCLING There are more than 12 miles of paved bicycle paths throughout Yosemite Valley, and these are ideal for bypassing the clotted roadways. Bike rentals are available at Curry Village (209-372-4386). Off-road biking is not permitted in the park, and helmets are required for anyone under 18.

GOLF Wawona Golf Course (209-375-6572). Across from the Wawona Hotel, this course was the first in the Sierra Nevada. Golfers at every level will appreciate the tranquil fairways, which are lined with evergreens; the challenging holes; and the occasional deer grazing the greens. Green fee: $36–42.

HIKING Yosemite National Park offers trails and sights enough to occupy a visitor for years; it simply isn't possible to list all trails, but a handful of favorites follow. Check at any ranger station for trail maps, path conditions, and additional ideas for day hikes. Note that if you plan to head into the heart of the wilderness, a backcountry hiking and camping permit is mandatory; guests can pick these up at most visitors centers and ranger stations.

YOSEMITE MOONBOWS

If you are lucky enough to be in Yosemite Valley during a full moon, especially in the spring (when water levels are up), take an evening hike to Yosemite Falls in search of a moonbow. This romantically named phenomenon is a rainbow that is produced when moonlight reflects off the mist that rises from the waterfall—and it is an unforgettable experience (as is viewing the valley by moonlight).

✪ **Bridalveil Fall.** Catch the trailhead at the Bridalveil Parking Area. Bridalveil Fall is so named because it falls in delicate ribbons that sway with the winds. Look for markers to the trailhead about 1.5 miles after exiting the Wawona Tunnel as you travel eastward into Yosemite Valley via CA 140. There is ample off-road parking near the falls, as well as a large parking lot. Walk a few feet from the trailhead that begins just off CA 140, and you'll hit a fork in the path. Head right and climb up about 0.5 mile toward the falls. As with other falls in the park, the flow is seasonal—although this fall usually never dries up. At the top, there is a small overlook that provides a good view. (During the spring, when water gushes through the falls, you're bound to get soaked from this vantage point.)

✪ **Lower Yosemite Fall.** Find the trailhead at the Lower Yosemite Fall shuttle stop #6. As noted earlier, Yosemite Falls are actually a series of connecting falls. The Lower Fall is accessible to just about everyone, thanks to a wide, paved pathway just north of Yosemite Lodge. Follow the trail up a slight incline, cross the bridge to the east, and you'll see the falls to your left. It's an easy 0.3-mile walk to the base of the falls, and my family and I have done this in the worst of the summer heat, as well as in rain and snow, with no difficulty. If you want to extend your hike, continue over the bridge and catch the unpaved path that runs beside the cliff. This extended section of trail is much less trafficked than the extremely popular paved portion. After about 0.2 mile you'll hit a dirt horse path. Follow it to the south, through pines and over a series of pretty little bridges. You'll soon come to a clearing with a stone bench and an idyllic view of the falls.

YOSEMITE FALLS IN WINTER

Mariposa Grove. This slightly vigorous 2-mile out-and-back trail through the Mariposa Grove of giant sequoias can offer a secluded, peaceful hike—*if* you arrive early, before the crowds. This pathway is the most accessible trail in the park through the Big Trees. Pick up the trailhead on Wawona Rd., about 2 miles east of the South Entrance to the park. Follow the winding trail through the forest to reach the Grizzly Giant, the largest sequoia in the park, believed to be at least three thousand years old. Walk about 60 feet beyond, and you'll come across the California Tunnel Tree, which was carved up in 1895 to allow stagecoaches to pass through.

INSIDER TIP: Resist the temptation to crawl over the boulders at the base of Yosemite Falls, even when the water flow is low, in late summer and fall. This is enormously dangerous, and several people have lost their lives in this foolhardy endeavor.

Mirror Lake. The name is deceptive—there isn't always water in Mirror Lake these days (although when there is, this area offers a lovely reflected view of Half Dome). What you will find instead is a level, mostly paved, 2-mile round-trip trail that is easily accessible, even for strollers. Catch the trail from the Mirror Lake shuttle stop #17. In May, the early part of the trail offers a glorious view of blooming dogwoods. After about a mile you'll step out of the forest to see sandbars and enormous boulders in the lake bed. Hike back via the bridle path loop and look for Native American grinding stones along the way.

✪ **Mist Trail.** This steep, challenging, 7-mile round-trip hike winds past two beautiful waterfalls that are otherwise not visible from Yosemite Valley: Vernal Falls and Nevada Falls. Catch the trailhead at Happy Isles (shuttle #16). Note that the trail is also one of the starting points to reach the summit of Half Dome, so the narrow, winding pathway can be very crowded, especially early in the morning when folks hoping to make the daylong trek to the summit of Half Dome head out. Also note that the pathway can be quite slippery near the falls.

HIKE ALONG MIRROR LAKE

Courtesy Jon Preimesberger

Tuolumne Meadows and Soda Springs. Catch the trailhead from Lembert Dome Parking Area in Tuolumne Meadows, off Tioga Rd. An easy 1.5-mile round-trip on mostly flat pathway winds through the lovely meadow, past tiny Soda Springs. It is possible to connect to the **Lembert Dome Trail** from here as well, which is a more strenuous 4 miles round-trip.

✪ **Valley Floor.** Catch the trailhead at the Lower Yosemite Fall shuttle stop #6. This 13-mile loop trail winds its way around the Yosemite Valley floor, affording hikers with incomparable views of Yosemite Falls, El Capitan, the Merced River, and Half Dome. Along the way expect to see deer and occasionally bear. This is one of my favorite hikes in the park; it is moderately difficult because of the length of the walk, but because the terrain is flat, it is approachable for hikers of just about any skill level. Don't try this in the summertime, however, when the lack of shade along most of the pathway will be oppressive in the July and Aug. heat.

Wapama Falls. In Hetch Hetchy, catch the trailhead just over the O'Shaughnessy Dam. The trail hugs the cliffs and circles the Hetch Hetchy Reservoir for an easy, flat, 5-mile round-trip. Note that swimming and boating are prohibited in the reservoir.

HORSEBACK RIDING Stables in Yosemite Valley, Tuolumne Meadows, and Wawona offer guided trail rides for all levels, from two-hour introductions to all-day explorations. Call 209-372-8348.

SPAS **Tenaya Lodge Spa** (559-683-6555; www.tenayalodge.com), 1122 CA 41, Fish Camp. Located in the **Tenaya Lodge,** just 2 miles south of the South Entrance to Yosemite, this spa offers massage and body treatments, facials, and services such as hand-brightener therapy and eye and lip revitalizers. Hikers will appreciate the 90-minute Sports Relief massage; my personal favorite is the Focused Tension Mud Treatment, which begins with a 30-minute massage for the back and neck, and finishes with a detoxifying mud pack.

WINTER SPORTS Trails in Yosemite are open in winter for cross-country skiing and snowshoeing. Visitors can rent shoeshoes and skis at the **Badger Pass Cross-Country Center and Ski School.** Note that sledding is not allowed in the park.

BECOME A JUNIOR RANGER

Young children shouldn't miss the chance to become Junior Rangers. Purchase an inexpensive activity booklet, available at most ranger stations; kids (starting at reading age) complete a certain number of paper-and-pencil activities designed to teach them about environmentalism and park stewardship, participate in a ranger-led program (like a guided hike or a campfire talk), and fill a trash bag full of litter (sadly, not a difficult thing to do in crowded Yosemite Village). After tackling the assigned tasks, the newly educated pint-sized environmentalists return to a ranger station to receive their official Junior Ranger badge and to get sworn in. Yosemite rangers really seem to enjoy the opportunity to conduct impromptu induction ceremonies, which culminate in letting the child wear the ranger's hat and pose for a photo.

Ice Skating

✪ ✐ **Curry Village Ice Rink** (209-372-8319), in Curry Village, Yosemite Valley. This seasonal ice rink (open from mid-Nov. through early Mar.) is one of the most romantic on the planet. Glide along the groomed ice while gazing at Half Dome, often dusted with snow at this time of year, and amid sugar-frosted evergreens. Especially enchanting by moonlight, the rink is open for evening sessions. On-site is a warming hut with snack machines and a nearby cozy fire pit. Adults $8, children $6. Skate rentals $3.

Skiing

✐ **Badger Pass Ski Area** (801-559-4884), off Glacier Point Rd. Open winter only. Twenty miles from Yosemite Valley, this ski resort offers downhill skiing, snowboarding, and specially groomed slopes for tubing (perfect for young children). There are also more than 90 miles of trails for snowshoeing and cross-country skiing (including 25 miles of groomed trails) at this popular winter resort. Folks without experience on the trails can check out the **Badger Pass Cross-Country Center and Ski School,** which offers lessons for all levels, as well as ski tours and overnight excursions to the Yosemite backcountry. The center also offers ski rentals and some overnight snow-camping equipment.

✷ Water Sports

BOATING One of my favorite Yosemite pastimes in the summer is a river raft down the Merced River, which cuts through the heart of Yosemite Valley. The gentle current makes for an easy ride, and relaxed paddling will open up some of the most breathtaking vistas in the park. The river is open to rafting from Stoneman Bridge, near Curry Village, to Sentinel Beach, a few miles downstream. The entire river is closed to all boats whenever the river gauge at Sentinel Bridge is beyond 6.5 feet. From late May through the end of July, rent rafts for four to six people at the **Curry Village Recreation Center** (209-372-4386) for approximately $20 per person. Cost of the rental includes a ticket for the bus at the end of the line (marked by can't-miss-'em buoys in the river that indicate where you are to pull out your raft, at which point Curry Village personnel will see it back to the rental center). Note that children of any age must weigh at least 50 pounds to qualify for the raft rental; the Yosemite concessionaire is unbending about this rule. Each rafter must wear a life vest and attend a short demonstration before heading out onto the river.

"GO CLIMB A ROCK"

Rock climbers from around the world flock to Yosemite to scale the smooth granite walls and massive domes. The **Yosemite Mountaineering School** (209-372-8344; www.yosemitepark.com) offers rock-climbing classes for all levels, as well as guide services and equipment rentals. The school specializes in a Go Climb a Rock class that introduces beginners of all ages to the sport of rock climbing. In addition, the school offers guided hikes, overnight backpacking tours, and seasonal cross-country skiing tours.

You can also bring your own inflatable rafts; the rental office at Curry Village has an air hose available to the public. If you float your own boat downstream, you can still catch a ride back on the Curry Village bus at the end, but you must deflate the boat before boarding and store it beneath the vehicle. Bus tickets are about $2 each.

FISHING Lakes in Yosemite are open for fishing year-round, and rivers and streams from late April through mid-November (although restrictions apply on the Merced River from Happy Isles to the Forest Bridge in El Portal). Trout season is from late spring through November 15 (except Frog Creek near Lake Eleanor, which doesn't open until June 15)—but note that fishing here is catch and release only for rainbow trout. The two-fish-per-day limit is strictly enforced, and only artificial lures and flies with barbless hooks may be used. A valid California fishing license is required for everyone 16 and older. If you forget your rod and reel or any other angling supplies, you can find what you need at the well-stocked **Yosemite Village Sport Shop** (209-372-0200) in Yosemite Valley.

SWIMMING There are a handful of swimming holes along the Merced River that are appropriate for cooling off during the summer months (July, August, and possibly September, if temperatures allow). Be aware that no one should enter the water when the currents are fast and the water level is high; also note that the river is fed from snowmelt, which means the water temps are always frigid. My favorite swimming spot is just west of **Swinging Bridge;** bathers will find a rocky beach on the north side of the river, picnic area to the south (with pit toilets), a section of deep water for wading, and startling views of Yosemite Falls and Half Dome.

INSIDER TIP: To make the chill of the Merced bearable for children, bring along wet suits. Also, the river bottom is rocky, so water shoes are a good idea for all ages.

SWIMMING HOLE NEAR SWINGING BRIDGE

✷ Lodging

Yosemite is enormously popular during the summer months. If you plan to stay within the park boundaries—which I highly recommend, because the drive into the large park otherwise is just too time-consuming—it is *imperative* that you make reservations well in advance; reservations are taken 366 days ahead. The Ahwahnee and Yosemite Lodge at the Falls book up immediately, and most other accommodations book up at least six months in advance for visits between the months of June and August.

PRICE KEY FOR A STANDARD ROOM:

$	$100 or less
$$	$101–150
$$$	$151–250
$$$$	$251 and up

✪ **Ahwahnee** (801-559-4884). Named with the Native American word used to identify Yosemite Valley, this elegant Arts and Crafts lodge is nestled in the Yosemite Valley, within easy reach of Yosemite Falls—many upper rooms have magnificent views of the falls and the nearby dramatic granite cliffs. For decades the Ahwahnee has attracted the rich and famous, including presidents and royalty. Although the historic rooms are small and somewhat modestly decorated, the grand interior spaces are festooned with Native American artwork, enormous fireplaces, and hand-stenciled cathedral ceilings. There is a grand piano in the lobby—reputed to be a favorite with Ansel Adams when he lived in Yosemite (he was a respected musician as well as a photographer)—a fine-dining room (see *Dining Out*), and a handful of lovely shops. In the summer months guests can use the tennis courts and pool. Perhaps the best amenity in the summertime is the air-conditioning: this is the only lodging in the park that offers it. In cooler months, guests can enjoy complimentary cookies and tea in the magnificent grand hall, where wintertime fires are stoked day and night. $$$$.

CAMPING IN YOSEMITE

Guests looking for an authentic wilderness experience in Yosemite have the option of a number of campgrounds scattered throughout the park; a portion of them are left open for walk-ins on a first-come, first-served basis (be sure to arrive early in the day to secure such sites). The other sites can be reserved five months in advance (209-372-0200). The Yosemite Valley offers several campgrounds—all somewhat noisy and smoky at night, and always crowded. More peaceful options are available in Wawona and Tuolumne Meadows. Another fun option is the High Sierra Camps, a series of five sets of canvas cabins that fall along a loop trail in the backcountry. Rental of these dormitory-style cabins includes hot meals, and each is about a day's walk from the next—which allows for a real outdoor adventure without the necessity of packing in all the gear for camping. These are such highly coveted accommodations that they are allocated by lottery system. (Meals and lodging start at about $140 per person.)

THE AHWAHNEE

🐾 ✐ **Curry Village** (801-559-4884). This complex, in the Yosemite Valley, near Happy Isles and close to the trailhead to Mirror Lake, offers economical lodging in a number of modest (quite rustic) accommodations, including motel rooms, very basic cabins with private baths, and canvas cabins. Within the village are public showers, gift and provision shops, a tour and activity desk, and a swimming pool. $–$$

✐ **Housekeeping Camp** (801-559-4884). Location is everything at Housekeeping Camp: the complex is smack in the middle of Yosemite Valley, with views of Half Dome and Yosemite Falls. The lodging option here is a cross between a tent and a cabin: three concrete walls, a concrete floor, a canvas roof, and one canvas wall. Each structure offers a double bed and two bunk beds (linens are not included), and are equipped with electricity. Many of the structures are sited directly on the banks of the picturesque Merced River. Additional amenities include public restrooms and coin-operated showers, laundry facilities, and a camp store. Open spring to fall. $–$$

✐ **Tenaya Lodge** (866-387-9909; www.tenayalodge.com), 1122 CA 41, Fish Camp. Just 2 miles outside the South Entrance of Yosemite National Park, Tenaya Lodge sits on 35 acres bordering the lush Sierra National Forest. This full-service resort offers luxury and amenities that aren't typical for national park lodging. In addition to spacious indoor and outdoor pools; numerous on-site dining opportunities, including the upscale **Embers,** the less stuffy **Sierra Restaurant** (which offers a hearty daily breakfast buffet),

INSIDER TIP: Beware of falling rocks throughout Yosemite, especially in the winter and spring, and especially in Curry Village, which has been the site of some dramatic and dangerous rockfall in recent years.

and the casual **Jackalope's Bar and Grill;** and a full-service spa (see *Spas*), guests can enjoy a rock-climbing wall, archery, guided hikes, and trail rides. The timber-and-stone architecture of the public spaces is grand and inviting, with a massive fireplace and oversized leather armchairs in a welcoming lobby. Guest rooms are large and comfortable, and there are a variety of suites available for families. Although the concierge is understaffed and always busy, the service is otherwise quite helpful. $$$–$$$$

Tuolumne Meadows Lodge (801-559-4884), off Tioga Rd. Open only in the summer months, this complex offers canvas cabins, public shower and restroom facilities, and small gift and provisions shops. The Tuolumne River is adjacent, and the Yosemite Mountaineering School and Mountain Shop are on the premises. $

Y ⚤ **Wawona Hotel** (801-559-4884), off CA 41, north of the South Entrance. Open mid-Mar. through early Jan. Near the Mariposa Grove, the Wawona is a bit far flung from the popular Yosemite Valley, and for this reason it is often the easiest accommodation in the park to book at the last minute. The 19th-century beauty offers a dozen whitewashed buildings scattered among serene, sequoia-studded grounds. Tiny Victorian rooms are furnished in period style and have high ceilings, antique iron beds, and almost no closet space. Many rooms share a bath. Most accommodations include access to a common outside porch area equipped with rocking chairs. Expect the trip to Yosemite Valley attractions to take about an hour by car. There is an always-frigid pool at the front of the hotel, and the **Yosemite Pioneer Center** is accessible by foot, over the river via a covered bridge. In the evenings there is piano music and singing in the guest lounge. In addition, there is a fabulous golf course on property (see *Golf*). Don't miss the Sat. evening barbecue on the grounds. $$–$$$

✐ **Yosemite Lodge at the Falls** (801-559-4884). By far the best value in the valley, given the nearly perfect location in the Yosemite Valley (and as the name implies, within easy walking distance of Yosemite Falls), the Yosemite Lodge at the Falls offers large, comfortable accommodations and plenty of hotel amenities—on-site dining, a large gift and sundry store, an outdoor

WAWONA HOTEL

INSIDER TIP: When overnighting at Yosemite Lodge at the Falls, never leave food outside on the patio or balcony. Although park officials work through the night to keep bears away from Yosemite Valley lodging, snacks are not safe from another Yosemite mammal—raccoons, which travel in packs and will clean out any food left accessible in a matter of minutes, even if it seems to be securely locked away in a cooler. (They can and will open ice chests.)

amphitheater that is the site of nightly education programs in the summer, and a large pool (open seasonally). The guest rooms themselves are a little stark—no air-conditioning, no television, no phones—although this suits me fine. Just remember to pack a good book or a couple of board games. Rooms offer either a balcony or a patio. Some rooms have incomparable views of the cliffs and valley—and some look out over a busy bus stop and crowded parking lot. There is no way to secure particular rooms in advance, but if you arrive early enough (check-in time is 5 PM), it doesn't hurt to request a particular vista. $$–$$$

PRICE KEY FOR A TYPICAL ENTRÉE:

$	$10 and under
$$	$11–20
$$$	$21–30
$$$$	$31 and up

✷ Where to Eat

DINING OUT ✪ 🍸 **Ahwahnee Dining Room** (801-559-4884). Open daily for breakfast, lunch, and dinner. Guests who lodge elsewhere can still enjoy the spectacular surroundings and impeccable service at the pricey **Ahwahnee** in this very popular lodge dining room. Diners relax in a 34-foot-tall log dining hall to the accompaniment of live piano music. Exceptionally prepared meals of osso buco, venison chops, and Maine lobster tail are served in first-class style, with fine linens, china, and silver. My favorite way to start a day in Yosemite Valley is with a completely civilized breakfast of raisin brioche French toast served with warm maple syrup and a thick slice of ham. On Sun. the Ahwahnee offers a decadent Grand Brunch, featuring divine eggs Benedict, healthy yogurt and fruit parfaits, and an extensive seafood bar. Reservations are absolutely necessary for every meal of the day. Note that casual dress for breakfast and lunch is fine, but management requests dress pants and collared shirts for men and dress pants or dresses for women for dinner. $$$$

🍸 **Mountain Room Restaurant** (801-559-4884). Open daily for dinner. In the **Yosemite Lodge at the Falls,** this fine-dining establishment has stunning views of the falls in a relaxed and casual atmosphere, thanks to floor-to-ceiling windows. Steak and fish are specialties. Don't miss the Mountain Mud Cake for dessert, a concoction of coffee ice cream, cookie-crumb crust, and decadent amounts of chocolate sauce. The restaurant offers a full bar and an extensive wine collection. $$$

🍸 **Wawona Hotel Dining Room** (801-559-4884). Open daily for breakfast, lunch, and dinner. The quiet Wawona Hotel, near Mariposa Grove, has a small, rustic Victorian dining room, with an appealing patio for warmer months. (Although beware the overly warm months: there is no air-conditioning in the restaurant, and the old windows barely crack open, so it can be stifling here in July and Aug.) Try the bacon-wrapped grilled trout or the flat-iron steak with herbed mashed potatoes. Guests can take cocktails in the quaint sitting room, just off the tiny hotel lobby. On Sat. nights, don't miss the Wawona Lawn Barbeque, held under the stars on the pretty grassy expanse in front of the hotel. $$$

EATING OUT **Degnan's Deli** (801-559-4884). Open daily for lunch. In Yosemite Village, this small deli serves sandwiches, salads, and ice cream. Expect crowds and slow service in the summertime. $

✪ 🎗 ✐ **Degnan's Loft** (801-559-4884), upstairs from Degnan's Deli in Yosemite Village. Open daily for dinner in the summer. Degnan's serves up surprisingly good pizza and draft beer. This is a favorite for families, because the atmosphere is casual and the prices are reasonable. Hiking boots and trail attire are perfectly acceptable. $$

✐ **Katie's Country Kitchen** (559-683-8418), 40470 CA 41, Oakhurst. Open daily for breakfast, lunch, and dinner. Oakhurst is the last outpost before the South Entrance of Yosemite, and Katie's Country Kitchen makes for a convenient stop before hitting the park. The small, friendly diner serves breakfast all day. Guests will also find good hamburgers and salads, fast service, and a casual atmosphere. The chatty owner and servers treat passing tourists like neighbors. $–$$

Todd's Cookhouse Barbeque (559-642-4900; www.toddsbbq.com), CA 41, Oakhurst. Open daily for lunch and dinner. Conveniently located on the way in to the South Entrance, Todd's offers up hearty, Southern-style meals that will fortify any mountain man or woman ready to take on Yosemite. Favorites include the chopped brisket sandwich, the St. Louis ribs, and the house chili. Pick up smoked chicken wings to go for less than $5 per pound. $–$$

KATIE'S COUNTRY KITCHEN

✪ **Whoa-Nellie Deli** (www.whoanelliedeli.com), 22 Vista Point Rd., in Lee Vining, at the Tioga Gas Mart at the US 395 and Tioga Rd. intersection, east of Yosemite. Open daily in the summer for lunch and dinner. This astonishing "restaurant" is housed inside the quickie-mart of a gas station—but don't underestimate it because of the locale. Inside you'll find a small rustic café that serves shockingly good food, like herb-crusted pork tenderloin with wild berry reduction, rich buffalo short ribs served over fettuccine dressed with wild mushroom sauce, and addictive lobster taquitos. There are a handful of tables inside and pleasant communal picnic tables outside. This is *the* place to be in the evenings, when there is usually live music, and sometimes wine tasting and other special events. $$–$$$

✷ Entertainment

THEATERS For up-to-date information on show times and offerings in Yosemite, check the National Park Service Web site at www.yosemitepark.com/Activities.aspx.

✪ **Yosemite Valley Visitor Center Theater.** Who knew it was possible to enjoy live theater inside a national park? This small venue in Yosemite Village, which in the past has featured programs such as *Ranger Ned's Big Adventure* and riveting one-man shows based on the writings of naturalist John Muir, is an evening treat, especially for

TOP 10 DAY IN YOSEMITE VALLEY

1. Watch the sunrise over Half Dome (see p. 348)
2. Breakfast on cheese blintzes and applewood bacon at the Ahwahnee Dining Room Grand Brunch (see p. 359)
3. Raft the Merced River (see p. 354)
4. Picnic for lunch on the river with supplies purchased at the Village Store (see p. 361)
5. Take a frigid plunge in the swimming hole just west of Swinging Bridge (see p. 355)
6. Hike along the Mist Trail in the afternoon (see p. 352)
7. Shop for books at the Ansel Adams Gallery (see p. 361)
8. Dine on pepperoni pizza and a pitcher at Degnan's Loft (see p. 360)
9. Watch actor Lee Stetson's one-man play on John Muir at the Yosemite Valley Visitor Center Theater (see pp. 360–361)
10. Overnight in a canvas cabin at Housekeeping Camp (see p. 357)

guests overnighting in the Yosemite Valley. Tickets are available from the Valley Visitor Center at a modest cost, and because in-park lodging doesn't provide televisions, this is usually the best nighttime show in town. Throughout the day, guests can also view a 23-minute film titled *The Spirit of Yosemite,* which is an entertaining introduction to the cultural history of the park as well as the natural beauty of the area.

✷ Selective Shopping

There are a handful of gift and sundry shops throughout the park that sell trinkets, T-shirts, mugs, and the like. To find a slightly wider variety of souvenirs, check out the **Ahwahnee Gift Shop** in the **Ahwahnee** hotel, which sells Native American dolls, pottery, fine jewelry, and lovely carved wood and stone vessels. In **Yosemite Lodge at the Falls,** there is a large gift shop that offers apparel and hiking gear, along with the aforementioned Yosemite trinkets. But the best bet for serious shoppers is in Yosemite Village, where guests will find the **Village Store** (a huge souvenir and grocery shop); the **Village Sport Shop,** *the* place to find unusual camping provisions and hiking gear; the **Ansel Adams Gallery,** my all-time favorite place to purchase books on Yosemite, as well as photographic prints and handcrafted jewelry; and the **Yosemite Museum Shop,** next to the Indian

ART CLASSES IN YOSEMITE

The Yosemite Art and Education Center (http://yosemiteart.blogspot.com) in Yosemite Village offers art classes (for adults and children) from early spring through fall, both indoors and out (weather permitting). Instructors are visiting artists and in the past have offered classes in myriad genres, from Japanese ink painting to block printing to watercolor journaling. The center is also a good place to pick up art supplies. Classes are free, although donations are welcomed.

YOSEMITE VALLEY

Cultural Museum, which offers Native American arts and crafts, books, and silver jewelry.

✷ Special Events

(throughout Sequoia, Kings Canyon, and Yosemite)

February: **Yosemite Nordic Holidays** (209-372-8444), a 10-mile cross-country ski race held at Badger Pass Ski Area.

March: **Yosemite Springfest** (209-372-8430), a carnival at the Badger Pass Ski Area on the last Sun. of the ski season, includes ski races, costume contests, and obstacle courses. **Ahwahnee Heritage Holidays** is a chance to step back into the roaring '20s with music and cultural performances at the Ahwahnee Hotel.

August: **Tuolumne Meadows Poetry Festival** (www.nps.gov/yose/planyourvisit/programs.htm), held in the Parsons Memorial Lodge in Tuolumne Meadows over a midmonth weekend, features poetry readings and music.

November: **Vintner's Holidays,** through Dec., is a gala dinner at the Ahwanee Hotel sponsored by dozens of respected wineries from throughout California and featuring their wines.

December: **Bracebridge Dinner,** held over eight nights in Dec., including Christmas Eve, is when the Ahwahnee dining room is decorated to resemble an old English hall, depicting the abode of fictional character Squire Bracebridge, from a short story by Washington Irving. Music, dancing, elaborate costumes, and even more elaborate meals ensue. This is highly popular, so be sure to make reservations at least a year in advance. **Yuletide Celebration at the Nation's Christmas Tree** (559-875-4575), aka the General Grant Tree in Kings Canyon National Park, is held the second Sun. of the month, with caroling and presentation of a wreath.

INDEX

Page references in italics refer to photographs.

E

I

M

N

P